James B. Angell Esq.
with the cordial regards
of the Author

...ooklyn N.Y.
...an 1st 1865

B. C. Cutler

New York. A.D.F. Randolph. 770 Broadway.

MEMOIRS

OF THE

REV. BENJAMIN C. CUTLER, D.D.

MEMOIRS

OF

REV. BENJAMIN C. CUTLER, D. D.

LATE RECTOR

OF

ST. ANN'S CHURCH, BROOKLYN, N. Y.

BY

REV. HORATIO GRAY, A. M.

"THE RIGHTEOUS SHALL BE IN EVERLASTING REMEMBRANCE."

NEW YORK:
ANSON D. F. RANDOLPH,
No. 770 BROADWAY.
1865.

EDWARD O. JENKINS,

STEREOTYPER & PRINTER,

No. 20 North William Street.

TO

THE PARISH OF ST. ANN'S,

BROOKLYN, N. Y.,

THIS MEMORIAL

OF A

DEPARTED PASTOR, WHOSE BEST YEARS WERE SPENT IN THEIR SERVICE, IS RESPECTFULLY

Dedicated

BY

THE AUTHOR,

WHO WOULD REVERENTLY LAY UPON HIS GRAVE THIS TRIBUTE OF ESTEEM AND LOVE.

"*HE BEING DEAD, YET SPEAKETH.*"

"*Peace to the just man's memory; let it grow*
Greener with years, and blossom through the flight
Of ages; let the mimic canvas show
His calm, benevolent features; let the light
Stream on his deeds of love, that shunned the sight
Of all but heaven, and in the book of fame,
The glorious record of his virtues write,
And hold it up to men, and bid them claim
A palm like his, and catch from him the hallowed flame."

PREFACE.

RELIGIOUS memoirs have been so multiplied, in the present day, that it may seem to some presumption to lay before the public another work of similar character; and if there are any who expect varied incident and stirring scenes, with much of human eulogy, let them lay down this work at once. But, if any desire to see how a saint struggled, fought, and won the heavenly prize; how a servant of God, by assiduous culture, grew in grace, almost to the stature of a perfect man in Christ Jesus, and became eminent for personal holiness; how a soldier of the cross loved to bring in recruits to the army of the Lord, and add to the trophies of the Great Captain of our salvation; how, "with all his armor on," he laid down to die, while angel hosts were shouting, "victory!"—let such peruse this volume, adore and magnify the grace of God, so wondrously displayed in the life and labors of his righteous servant.

His death was indeed a great loss to the Church of Christ on earth, but of such infinite gain to him, that, weeping over his bier, she can truly say:

"Go to thy grave; no, take thy seat above;
Be thy pure spirit present with the Lord!
Where thou, for faith and hope hast perfect love,
And open vision for the written word."

BROOKLYN, N. Y., *December* 1, 1864. H. G.

CONTENTS.

CHAPTER I.

CHILDHOOD AND YOUTH.

1798–1818.

THE memory of few men in the Church of God is embalmed with so much love—so many tears, and yet with so much thanksgiving, as is that of the subject of this memoir. Earnest wishes have been expressed by those who knew him long and well, that his life and character might be portrayed, and, through the press, made accessible to others. A record of his life may, also, prove profitable to those to whom he was not personally known. His life here on earth was, indeed, a *fertilizing moral stream*, blessing every thing in its course! Let us go back, then, and trace its current; notice its wanderings; observe its depths; watch its enriching expanse, as it flows along the fields of Zion, reflecting the sweet flowers it nourishes, yet never resting while other fields are to be watered, other fruits and flowers to be quickened into life and heavenly beauty. Let us carefully note its greater volume and richer hues, as it rolls onward toward Eternity, till it is lost from our sight over the heavenly borders, and disappears from human vision only to be absorbed in that river of Eternal Life which flows for ever at the Saviour's feet, around his Throne above.

BENJAMIN CLARKE CUTLER, son of Benjamin C. and Sarah Cutler, was born at Jamaica Plains, in Roxbury, near Boston, Massachusetts, February 6, 1798. Of his antecedents and his family history, of his own childhood and youth, we have the following brief record in a few pages of autobiography, which he wrote out in the year 1834:

"My grandfather was John Cutler, of Boston, who was born in 1723 and died in 1805, aged eighty-two years. He was a member of Trinity Church, in that city. My grandmother was Mary Clarke Cutler, the sister of Benjamin Clarke, Esq., a wealthy bachelor, for whom my father was named. This uncle adopted my father, educated him, and sent him to Europe; but, as my father afterward married against his uncle's wishes, he left him only a portion of his estate.

"My father, Benjamin Clarke Cutler, was born in 1756 and died in 1810. He was High Sheriff of the county of Norfolk, in Massachusetts, and though a decided politician in high party times, yet, by the courteousness of his manners, he held his office under Governors of opposite parties. My mother, Sarah Cutler, was born in Georgetown, South Carolina, in 1761. Her maiden name was Mitchell; she was a niece of General Francis Marion, of Revolutionary memory, and she named her youngest son for that distinguished man. My great grandfather, on the maternal side, was Gabriel Marion, of South Carolina. His father, who was born in France, was among the earliest emigrants who sought a shelter in Carolina from the persecuting spirit which desolated the homes of the Huguenots after the revocation of the Edict of Nantes. My parents were married in the year 1793. They had five children—three daughters and two sons: 1, Maria Eliza; 2, Julia Rush; 3, Benjamin Clarke; 4, Louisa Charlotte; 5, Francis Marion. The first married J. W. Francis, M. D., of New York; the second, Samuel Ward, Esq., of New York; the fourth, Matthew H. McAllister, Esq., of Savannah; the fifth, Miss Caroline Martin, of Avon, New York.

"My parents resided in Boston, Massachusetts, but just before my birth they removed to Jamaica Plains, five miles from Boston, where, on the 6th of February, 1798, I was born. I have often heard my mother say that I came into the world with great haste—without waiting for any ceremony; and that the nurse predicted that I had much to do in it. How this prediction will hold good I know not. Bodily activity and restlessness of mind have, certainly, been very prominent in me. I was baptized, in infancy, by my uncle, Rev. Samuel Parker, D. D. (who was afterward Bishop of Massachusetts), in Trinity Church, Boston. I remained at home until I was seven years old, when I was sent away to school, on account of my mother's ill health. My mother early and diligently taught her children the great truths of religion, and enforced the observance of the Sabbath. My first religious thoughts were in very early childhood. I heard a sermon on the Prodigal Son, and it made a deep impression on my mind. I got my mother to teach me the chapter, by heart, before I could read. In 1805–6 I went to school at Cohasset and at Medway, Massachusetts; but in 1807 was sent to Milton Academy. Here I studied Latin and Greek. I disliked the idea of ever going to college, and wanted very much to be a merchant.

"My father died in 1810, aged fifty-five years, and I was adopted by my great uncle, Benjamin Clarke, Esq., of Boston. He died in a year, and my Uncle and Aunt Dunn, of Boston, then took me, and I resided with them until the year 1818. My father's death made me serious, and led me to seek a Heavenly Father. It, however, threw a gloom over this world, which has never been removed. It led me to think of the family thus left orphaned with me, and I felt my responsibilities, and this made me manly. I pursued my English studies in Boston for two or three years, when I entered the counting-house of Mr. James Andrews, 37 Long Wharf, Boston, where I stayed three years. Here I saw much of business, and in the evenings much of fashionable society.

"When I was about sixteen years of age, I was advised by my godmother, Mrs. Martha Babcock, to receive confirmation, which I did from the hands of Bishop Griswold, of the Eastern Diocese, in Trinity Church, Boston, in 1814. For this rite I was poorly prepared, but ever after it I felt some checks of conscience. In the year 1816 I became a communicant in Trinity Church, Boston. Soon after this I was led to take a more serious view of religious matters and gave up all fashionable amusements—mingled much with pious people, and became a Sunday-school teacher. I felt constrained to give up the world. This produced a great struggle. I was ridiculed, but God's grace was sufficient, and I was made to rejoice in my portion."

We turn aside from the autobiography at this point, to allow our readers the privilege of perusing an extract from a letter to the youthful Christian from his cousin, who, after the death of Mr. Cutler's father, wrote many letters to him full of kind counsel and affectionate interest in his spiritual welfare:

"NEW YORK, *September* 17, 1815.

"DEAR CLARKE—If I have been in the slightest degree the humble instrument of exciting one aspiration of heavenly love in the heart of one I so dearly value, it will shed a ray of comfort over my life, and illumine a prospect which appears quite gloomy. I had almost given over the hope of any happiness below, and had begun to look on the world as but one trying scene of misery. But thanks to my Almighty Father, his grace has enabled me to bear the exquisite affliction he has laid upon me, and his goodness still cheers my path. In you, and in your affectionate, pious correspondence, he has raised up a source of comfort to me. If my experience (trifling and imperfect as it is) of the vanity of worldly things, has been of the remotest service, I shall thank my God, in humble gratitude, that I have not lived entirely in vain. Your last letters excited feelings of pure and exquisite delight in my breast. Go on, my excellent cousin; go on, conquering and to conquer; go on and bear the victorious banner of the Cross to the very gates of death and hell, and still press forward to the prize of our high calling in Christ Jesus. Do not let any groundless scruples deter you from doing what your Saviour has commanded you to do. If we were to wait until we were perfect, where would be the necessity of at all approaching this holy ordinance? He bids us taste the sweets of His heavenly banquet. Do not, then, allow the fear of falling from your duty deter you from engaging in it. Believe me, the heart which has once felt the glow of heavenly love, though it may be affected by human frailty, will never totally forsake the path of duty. To be eminently virtuous you must be singular! Let not then the dread of seeming better than your fellows prevent you from discharging your duty. Our duty must inflexibly be observed, whatever a carping, censorious world may say. Our blessed Lord did not escape its revilings, and can we expect to go through life without partaking of his sufferings, if we wish to partake hereafter of His glory? How wondrous the goodness of that Lord! He bestows the will and the power to please him, and he rewards us for using the talents he has given us. Consult, dear Clarke, with your pious friend, and I hope, when next I hear from you, to know that you have consummated the dedication of yourself to the service of God. Need I say that I shall be happy to see you? Come as soon as possible. I have much to say, which I cannot express on paper.

. . . .

Adieu, dear Clarke! you have my prayers and best wishes; and believe me, your ever affectionate

THOS. C. MITCHELL."

But the subject of this memoir, though encouraged by some friends of congenial taste and temper, often met with reproach and ridicule from others. We have every reason to believe that the period of his conversion to Christ was not as distinctly marked as in the case of many others.

The Spirit of God deals not precisely alike with every heart. He opens some hearts with a gentle touch. It has been justly remarked, " When the lofty palm-tree of Zeilan puts forth its flower, the sheath bursts with a report that shakes the forest; but, thousands of other flowers of equal value open in the morning, and the very dew-drops hear no sound ; even so, many souls blossom in mercy, and the world hears neither whirlwind nor tempest."

In the case of our friend, his heart, like the morning flower, was gently but surely opened to receive those beams which were to illumine and vivify his whole being.

The Sun of Righteousness dawned gradually upon his soul, and kindled his youthful desires into heavenly aspirations after a spiritual life—even "a life hid with Christ." He was secretly led and taught by the Holy Spirit of God, and after long deliberation and searching self-examination, he openly professed Christ before men. From that hour his purpose was fixed, and nailing the attractions of the world (which were great and powerful to him) to the Cross of a Divine Redeemer, he determined to spend and be spent in his Master's service.

To appreciate fully the stand he took at this time, let us look at the state of society around him. The Rev. Dr. Tyng, an early friend and cotemporary of his, thus truly writes :

"At the period embraced in Dr. Cutler's youth, the higher classes of society in Boston were peculiarly averse to that which we should call evangelical religion. The cold spirit of intellectual pride and the secularizing influence of wealth and luxury had banished the Gospel almost equally from the ministrations of the pulpit, and from the habits and acknowledgments of private and social life. The bold rejections of Socinianism had cast off, among many of the leading Congregational Churches, all that was peculiar and vital in the principles of the gospel, and the practical deadening influence which this scheme of infidelity exercised, had spread far beyond the limits of the congregations in which its reign was adopted and acknowledged." *

Under such influences did this disciple of Jesus grow up; nor could he ever blind his eyes to their real tendency. He, with a few others, often repaired to Christ Church, at the north end of the city, where the Rev. Mr. Eaton with great

* See "The Son of Consolation," page 26.

fidelity preached the Gospel of Christ. Here he was cheered onward in his religious course, and became a manifest blessing to others. He endeavored to lead other young friends to the feet of the Saviour, to whom he had devoted himself. In one case in particular he was repelled; but that same young man, whom he besought with loving entreaty to turn to the Lord, afterward devoted himself to the ministry of the gospel, and was influential in persuading Mr. Cutler, at a later date, to follow his example. We refer to the Rev. B. C. C. Parker, who was for many years an Episcopal missionary to seamen in the city of New York.

"I was persuaded," he says, in his autobiography, "in 1816, by the Rev. Asa Eaton and Rev. B. C. C. Parker, my cousin, to study for the ministry of the Protestant Episcopal Church, to which my parents and grandparents on both sides belonged—and commenced my studies in the winter of 1816-17."

His thoughts and inclinations had long been turned toward another pursuit, in which he was actively engaged, so that his determination to enter the ministry cost him a severe struggle. Of it, his younger sister says: "I think the greatest struggle my brother passed through, was when he first thought of entering the ministry. My mother had recently become a widow, and he, as her eldest son, was expected to sustain her and restore all she had lost by his father's death. Some of his friends said, 'As a layman you can work for God; it is your duty to remain in business, and assist your mother.' He struggled hard through this terrible conflict; perhaps it assisted in breaking up his constitution, which at this time lost its vigor. His wish was to devote himself exclusively to God, and the ministry alone gave him the opportunity of calling men to Christ. He loved his mother devotedly, but he knew God was 'the father of the fatherless, and the husband of the widow,' and he felt called by God to his work. There was much to contend with; his active habits had unfitted him for study; but he fought his way manfully through every difficulty. All things were made plain. God took care of his mother, opened vistas of brightness, and showered down blessings on her, till she could almost exclaim, 'It is enough.'"

Mr. Cutler had faith enough to believe this would be the case, and looking upon dying sinners around him, his sole endeavor was to bring men to a knowledge of that Saviour who came on earth "to seek and to save that which was lost." To this end he desired to consecrate his life.

The Episcopal Church in Massachusetts, at this time, was in a very low state—small in numbers, and still weaker in spiritual life. The want of zealous men in the ministry was pressingly felt, and Mr. Cutler's clerical friends earnestly besought him to commence a course of preparation for this work. His own convictions of duty, combined with their entreaties, at length prevailed. He seemed to hear the divine call from his Lord and Master, "Follow me!" and finally left the walks of commercial life, with all their brilliant prospects, and cheerfully consecrated himself to the work of preaching the Gospel of Christ.

In speaking of this period, he says: "My religion, while I was fitting for college, was a perpetual source of joy and peace; I felt like a new-born babe, desiring only the sincere milk of the Word." Thus is it ever with the young disciple of Jesus who holds back no part of the price, but gladly relinquishes the world for the service of God. The sacrifice may be great, but the reward is "an hundred-fold." And when, as in this case, the disciple is fully committed to his chosen and loved work of preaching the unsearchable riches of Christ, he cannot rest till others around him are brought to love and serve that Saviour to whom he has devoted himself.

The strivings of the natural heart, however, manifested themselves in this as well as in every other similar case.

"When I felt called to the ministry," he says, it was a trial to my faith. I was fond of business—I disliked study from my childhood—I had no encouragement to expect that I would ever make any thing; but *love to immortal souls prevailed!*"

A steady and unquenchable flame of love for the souls of others burned in him, and he longed to tell to others "the good things the Lord had done for him."

In correspondence with his friends "the one thing needful" was ever uppermost in his mind, and he failed not to give advice, encouragement, or consolation on the all-important subject of religion to every one who came within the sphere of his influence. Even at this early age he evinced a remarkable fervor of spirit and great spirituality of mind.

To a dear friend (absent in Montreal) he thus writes:

. . . . "Oh, how weak and feeble are our best efforts to serve and please God! We are indeed vile and sinful, but we have a Saviour; what could we do, how could we exist, without that blessed, that only hope? Deprive a Christian of this hope, you deprive him of his very breath. Can there be any thing more exhilarating to the drooping Christian, almost ready to sink under the pressure of trials, than a consciousness of having a Mediator at the Throne, and a Saviour who is both willing and able to save, to the uttermost, those that come unto him? Oh, let us to his bosom fly; there alone will be peace and joy in believing; there alone that unalloyed bliss which never ceases, never cloys, but remains one continual, never-ending day of rest. . . . My dear friend, at all times, and at all seasons, the fountain is ready at which you may drink. About ten days ago, after pretty hard study, I was thinking what enjoyment could most pleasantly fill an hour at the close of the day. My mind first suggested this friend, and then that, and while I was deliberating, I seemed to hear a voice saying, 'Instead of vainly seeking for happiness from the streams, why not ask your Heavenly Father to afford it, in communion with him?' I knelt down and asked, and what was the consequence? I received! Oh, can I ever quit this safe refuge, and this indulgent Parent's feet, to covet earth's alluring toys?"

In the summer of 1817 he resided, a portion of the time, at the homestead, in Jamaica Plains. From thence he writes to the same friend, and we thus learn how ardently he longed for more extended means of grace:

"I am sometimes at a loss," he writes, "to say which affords me the greatest happiness, or rather pleasure, the country or Boston; the beauties of the former, fresh from their Creator's hand, afford a constant theme for gratitude to the feeling heart, and a full conviction of the being of Omnipotence to the doubting heart accompanies the investigation of the smallest shrub; his eyes wanders over the whole face of nature, admiring, at once, the object and its Creator; the stillness, so propitious to reflection and so foreign to the din of a populous town, almost induces him to decide at once; but then unless he can have that constant 'line upon line' from lips touched, like the Prophet Ezekiel's, by 'a coal from the altar,' his gratitude will diminish, his thoughts become grovelling, and his feelings cold and dead; then, of course, there would be a want of something which can only be obtained by using those means of grace God has appointed. Without peace of mind the most splendid palace would become a dungeon, and the beauties of creation cease to charm. You remember the lines you quoted to me from Cowper:

'Give what thou canst, without thee we are poor,
And with thee, rich—take what thou wilt away;'

so that I think, though the country displays the most elevated objects of the bounty of an Almighty hand, yet, the key that unlocks the feelings of gratitude is chiefly found 'where two or three are met together.' I do not undervalue private prayer, but when (with a little exertion) I can hear spiritual preaching—above all, *join in spiritual praying*—should I neglect these and feed on the 'husks' of modern preaching? Without a doubt, I should return again to the 'beggarly elements of the world.' Therefore, at present, the country must be given up by me for the city; where I must trust that the same arm which protected Shadrach, Meshach and Abednego in the furnace will proportion my strength to my day. . . .

"My health improves; for six weeks past I have shut up my books and taken exercise on horseback. I have lost much study, but the Lord knows best; I am his servant, and he knows best when and where to lead me. I have given myself to him; will he not keep what is committed to him? . . . B. C. C. P. goes on very well, and will make a scholar and a minister, I hope!" . . . . .

He traced the hand of God in the smallest affairs of his daily life, and loved to recognize the dealings of his Heavenly Father in every thing that befell him, and while diligently cultivating Christian graces for himself, he was not unmindful of others, but often, very often, spoke " the word in season to the weary soul." Thus, to a friend (S. P. B.) oppressed with fears, and evidently tried in outward circumstances, as well as inwardly in spirit, he declares:

. . . . . . "Take comfort in this thought, it is not as Satan would have it. Satan would not permit you to have a single trial or conflict! He would have all go smoothly, and feed you with food pleasant to the taste, but bitter in the end. Be thankful that you have a watchful Parent, who will provide for you and who will not let Satan have dominion over you. Do you sigh for fuller manifestations of Christ's love for you? Alas, you know not what you ask! Christ walks with his followers nowhere but in the furnace. Be content with all God orders here, and look with faith to a 'brighter reality' to come; then, there will be no weariness in his service; no more fighting or fainting; every affection sanctified, and we shall be filled with all the fullness of God. Thus it shall be, but it is not so yet. The contest goes on here, and we often desire to flee and capitulate, but the Captain of our salvation renews our strength and animates our courage. Dear fellow-sinner, let us gird up the loins of our mind and fight on, confiding fully and steadfastly in our Leader; he will arm us and shield us, and bring us off conquerors at last. When wounded, he will heal us; when cast down, he will lift us up. He will do all this for us. Then, let us renewedly dedicate ourselves to his service and follow on to know the Lord. Oh! can you, when once in sight of Canaan (peace of mind), turn back to the Egypt of your doubts and fears? Cheer up, dear fellow-pilgrim! fight a little longer, and the victory will be yours. Keep out of the length of Satan's chain and he can only frighten you. Don't let him entice you to put your foot upon one inch of his field of *unbelief;* for, if you do, you will surely be unmercifully bruised. Whenever you happen to meet him unexpectedly, it will always be with a lie in his mouth; but hold fast the beginning of your confidence, and, in due time, you shall reap, if you faint not. May we both so pass the waves of this troublesome world as to meet, the other side of Jordan, in the heavenly Canaan. Depend upon it, the Ark won't move one inch, until we are all safe over. Yours, B. C. C."

In this last epistle we see his own soul beaming forth in every line. We know not which to admire most—his patient tenderness, his striking faithfulness, or the remarkable clearness of conception with which he thus depicts the experience of every child of God.

No one who ever heard him speak of the things of God, in after years, can fail to recognize in this letter his own peculiar style of expression—clear, pointed and forcible. He was only nineteen years of age when he penned these lines, but the Spirit of God seems to have early taught him in the school of Christ, and his blessed influences were imparted in no small degree or scanty measure to this earnest soldier of the Cross. The captious critic may deem it out of place for one so young to advise others, even in confidential correspondence, and apply to him the words of the ancient king of Israel, "Let not him that girdeth on his harness boast himself as he that putteth it off!" but he knew "in whom he trusted," and with the eye of faith fixed on his Great Master, then, as in after years, he pressed forward toward the heavenly prize, and like "Valiant-for-Truth" in the Pilgrim's Progress, he boldly urged onward every fellow-traveller in the heavenly road, and particularly every tried and tempted believer. We can almost hear him singing by the way:

"From strength to strength go on,
Wrestle and fight and pray:
Tread all the powers of darkness down,
And win the well-fought day."

CHAPTER II.

COLLEGE LIFE.

1818–1820.

IN September, 1818, the youthful Cutler entered Brown University, in Providence, R. I. The religious advantages connected with this institution were, no doubt, the chief inducements which led him thither. But he could also enjoy the ministrations of the faithful rector of St. John's Church, in that city, and would also be in close proximity to Bristol, where Bishop Griswold resided, and from whose home and parish emanated so many happy influences. And the apostolic example, judicious precepts, and watchful care of this godly man, were, as he hoped they would be, of great advantage to him, at this critical period in his religious history.

In this new position, he took hold of his studies with zeal and earnestness, ever keeping before him the particular object upon which he had set his heart. His life, as seen by others, was irreproachable. His manners were attractive, his deportment excellent, and in all his intercourse with others he cultivated the things "which are pure, lovely, and of good report."

His natural refinement and frank sociability won for him many appreciative friends; and when all these elements of character had been touched and sanctified by the Holy Spirit, diffusing over his whole being a glow of heavenly love and earnest interest in the religious welfare of others, he became a great means of usefulness to all his associates, and they "took knowledge of him that he had been with Jesus."

Nor was he unmindful of friends at a distance, as his correspondence will show; and, permitted as we are to make full extracts from his letters, we gladly avail ourselves of the privilege to exhibit to others the interior life of the man—careful, at the same time, not to infringe upon the sacredness of private confidence, or needlessly wound the susceptibilities of survivors, who still cherish his memory with grateful reverence and hallowed love.

Under date of September 5, 1818, he writes to a dear friend in this strain:

"I returned last evening from the tour to Providence. I am now a member of Brown University, after having passed a satisfactory examination. Our class will consist of about forty, most of them of my own age, but I can hardly inform you what prospect there is of a serious class, which I most earnestly desire. The companion of my journey was our mutually dear R. J. P., and a most delightful day we had in riding to P., interspersed with conversation of a spiritual nature. We remained at P. two days, where we were joined by our beloved Mr. Eaton and B. C. C. P., with whom we returned to Boston yesterday. We breakfasted and dined without interruption, drank tea at my dear mother's, and returned to town I hope grateful to God for every privilege."

Having returned to the University toward the close of the month, to commence recitations with his class, he writes in his journal thus:

"This day commences my actual connection with Brown University, commensurate with which, shall be my prayers for its prosperity and the individual salvation of each and every person connected with it. I am, and shall be, surrounded by many temptations by which I shall fall, if God's Holy Spirit shall not support and comfort me. I faintly trust in him; I can, I am sure, say, 'Lord, if thou canst do any thing, save thy servant; lead him not into temptation, but deliver him from evil.' I fear much a decline in spiritual life; I pray against it. I trust I shall be supported. O God! go on with thy work which, I trust, is begun in my heart; if not begun, begin, O God! and convince me of 'sin, righteousness, and a judgment to come.' Amen."

Mr. Cutler was pleased with his new situation. His health was fast improving, his spirits were good; and, as he declared to his friends, he had no reason to regret, but to rejoice, that he had followed what appeared to be the path of duty.

His mother, two of his sisters, and a younger brother, formed a delightful home circle for him, making the city of Providence a temporary place of abode during his collegiate course. Some of the members of the household, though occasionally spending the winter months at the South, with the relatives of his mother, were always glad to return and enjoy the companionship of a son and a brother so dear to them.

His daily studies, and continued exercise (which was so necessary to his very existence), occupied nearly every moment of his time; yet he did not neglect the instruction of his brother, or give up correspondence with his friends.

On Sunday, September 27, he rose an hour before sunrise, and after attending prayers in the chapel, walked out to Pawtucket, (four miles north of Providence) and officiated as a lay-reader in the Episcopal Church there, and in other ways assisted the rector.

This he often did, and when not engaged at St. John's Church in Providence, he rejoiced to go out to this place and participate in the ministrations of the sanctuary.

Blest as he was with health and temporal enjoyments, he was anxious to grow in grace and to make constant improvement in his spiritual state, fearful lest the things of time might render dim and imperfect his view of Eternity.

His journals show his particular attention to this point, and his desire to be kept from ambition; to do his duty to

God, and profitably to spend his time, seeking that reward which comes from God alone.

We find the following in his diary, which will show how he improved every means of grace, and how much of his time was spent when he was not occupied with his studies:

"*Oct.* 3, 1818.—I resolve to devote one hour each day to reading the Scriptures; and if I can command but one, I will devote it to that purpose. My God, strengthen me to keep this resolution, and bless thy Word to my soul! I will rise at 5 o'clock A. M., and retire from my study at half past 9 P. M. I acknowledge with gratitude the blessings I have this day received; may my heart be fully sensible of them! I have found in my own class four Christian brethren, engaged in the same cause with me, and one in the class above. We met, providentially, yesterday, and in a few moments embraced each other in the arms of Christian fellowship, and united in prayer. It was a sweet meeting, the union of souls and spirits. I do believe our blessed Master smiled upon us! I shall never forget the pleasure and joy it afforded me. To-day we all met in this room for devotional purposes. O Lord, bless these meetings! may they be channels of thy grace to our souls, for Christ's sake! O my Heavenly Father! fit and prepare my mind for the solemn duties of the Sabbath, for Christ's sake; and if this night thou call me hence, may Jesus wash me in his blood. I have no hope but in Jesus! I cast my polluted body at his feet, believing that he is God over all, blessed for ever, able and willing to save all who come to him by faith. Amen.

"I feel more happy in my present situation, than in any I have ever been in before."

"*Oct.* 4.—I passed this evening at a conference meeting in Mr. Crocker's parish. If I had not so wicked a heart I might have been much edified and instructed. I have discovered to-night a besetting sin. Lord help me to subdue it, and bring it down! humble, O Lord, my proud heart, and support me by thy strength! May I so spend thy Sabbaths on earth that I may learn how to spend an eternal one with Thee!

"Rev. Mr. Taft of Pawtucket called, after church; also, two classmates, Farnum and Crocker. Had a faithful conversation with my dear brother, and united with him in prayer. The day imperfectly spent, has, however, not been wholly unprofitable. But oh, this wicked heart loves any thing better than God, I fear. Purify it, O Lord, and incline it to love thee!"

"*Oct.* 14.—Received a letter from dear Edson to-night, and, after reading it, considered how much greater my progress in holiness ought to be."

"*Oct.* 30.—Attended Mr. Crocker's this evening, and had a comfortable and refreshing season. He is an impressive preacher. His subject was, 'the Rock in the Wilderness,' which he beautifully compared to Christ."

"*Nov.* 1.—Arose at 6 o'clock, attended the college prayer-meeting at sunrise; after breakfast went out to Olneyville and opened a Sunday-school, with Howe and Fuller. After the instruction was over we had prayers, and I read a sermon to the people who had assembled for the purpose; after that I returned to town, and went to St. John's Church and received the Holy Sacrament. In the afternoon heard an excellent sermon from Rev. Mr. Crocker. Called on Gov. Jones, and had a religious conversation with him."

"*Nov.* 5.—Went this day to Bristol and dined with our most excellent Bishop; returned in the evening much benefited. Received a call to-day from the 'Providence Female Tract Society' to take charge of a missionary school, in a destitute part of this State, for eight weeks. I hope in this, as in every thing, I may never be left to myself to decide, but that God will lead me in the right way."

"*Nov.* 16.—Spent the evening with Alexander Jones, Esq.,

a spiritually-minded man. Rev. Mr. Crocker and others were present."

As the year 1818 drew to a close, Mr. Cutler set apart a special day for fasting and prayer, and dedicated himself afresh to the service of God. He drew up a paper, which he sealed with his own seal and affixed his name in full. He styled it, "An Instrument of Solemn Surrender of Myself, Soul and Body, to God!"

"In the presence of God Almighty, Father, Son and Holy Ghost, three persons, but one God; and in presence of the blessed inhabitants of heaven—those holy angels who surround the Throne and witnessed my redemption—I, Benjamin Clarke Cutler, of Boston, now at Providence, December 13, 1818, in the twenty-first year of my age, in firm health and sound mind—feeling that I received all I possess from God, having publicly professed the faith, and knowing I am surrounded by so many temptations, and that I ought to fight resolutely against them—do hereby solemnly (with death, judgment and eternity in view) give, covenant, and make over myself, soul and body, all my faculties, all my influence in this world, all the worldly goods with which I may be endowed, into the hands of my Creator, Preserver and constant Benefactor, to be his for ever, and at his disposal. This solemn covenant is made in consequence of certain promises which God Almighty has made to me, as a sinner; that his strength shall be perfected in my weakness; that 'his grace shall be sufficient for me,' and many other like precious promises!

"Under a conviction of my awful transgressions and backslidings; feeling that I am covered with sin, which makes me odious to God, and that I should have been undone without a Saviour; not daring to hope for pardon or acceptance but through his blood, and knowing what a detestable fountain of horrible pollution is within me, from which streams are constantly flowing and defiling my very prayers; naked and undisguised before a heart-searching God, who knows me better than I know myself, I now set my seal and place my name to this, taking God's blessed Word for his instrument; never intending to revoke or change this decision, but meaning it to be a solemn and everlasting bond and obligation. Witness, ye holy angels! I am God's servant; witness, thou, Prince of Hell! I am thy enemy, thy implacable enemy, from this time forth for evermore.

"BENJAMIN CLARKE CUTLER."

We find Mr. Cutler, during his winter vacation, spending a part of his time in Boston, and enjoying the society and counsels of his friend, the Rev. Mr. Eaton, the rector of Christ Church in that city. He was enabled to visit many friends and relatives here, and also in the vicinity. He passed a day or two with the Rev. Mr. Smith, of Marblehead, and "made a profitable visit;" then he went to Salem, where he enjoyed meeting the Rev. Mr. Carlisle, and thence to Newton.

Of course his duties to society often brought him in contact with others who took no interest in religion, and like Gallio they cared for "none of these things;" but to all, he was the same kind and faithful friend.

His self-scrutiny (while mingling with others) was remarkable, and he often feared that, in prosperity, he should forget God. He shrank not, therefore, from any cross his Heavenly Father saw fit to lay upon him. He counted the cost when he first engaged in the Lord's service, and knowing that the path to the kingdom of heaven was ever a straight and narrow one, he ceased not to ask himself,

"Are there no foes for me to face,
Must I not stem the flood?
Is this vile world a friend to grace,
To help me on to God?"

He declared, "I have got much to suffer here below; this proud heart has yet to take much medicine. These imperious passions have yet to feel the yoke and the chain, and days of darkness, doubtless, will cure my love of earthly brightness." The following record in his diary in January, 1819, shows to us his own searchings of heart at this period: "Satan is always trying to overcome me; this casement of my soul is formed of materials which compose the most luxuriant soil for Satan to plant his evil thoughts in, and for them to thrive in; all things around me, in the world, conspire to lead me astray, and so corrupt am I, that even my Christian friends are often the cause of my falling. By nature, I love the world and prosperous circumstances; but in these, I need the grace of God more than in adversity. I read in the lives of all his saints, the many trials, crosses, disappointments, they were permitted to benefit by, and I cannot suppose that I am so much better than they were, as to make them unnecessary for me. This must be the ordinary road for me to go to heaven by—the road of affliction, of trials, of wearing crosses. I do not doubt that God is able to carry me to heaven without a cross; but would this be the way that his children have gone before me? would not my path be almost a new one? Certainly. Well, then, I must expect those medicines which are to heal my sin-sick soul, to keep me fervent in spirit, constant in prayer; and near to God! Such as sickness and pain, loss of property, persecution, loss of dear friends, separation from all earthly objects of delight, and the sight of human misery around me—this I must expect as a private Christian! But, as a minister of the crucified Jesus, I must expect even more. I must be tried and tempted in many ways, that I may succor those who are tempted also; and purified, to be an example to the flock over which the Holy Ghost may make me an overseer. Who is sufficient for these things? Not I; for I am a boasting Peter, all profession; and if left one moment, all denial.

But Jesus knows my frame and remembers I am but dust, and he will not lay on me more than I can bear. 'Fear not, thou worm Jacob,' etc. Lord Jesus, give me *faith!* 'tis all I need.

> 'Oh, for a strong and lasting faith
> That mountains can remove.'"

On the 25th of February, 1819, Mr. Cutler is again diligently engaged in his studies at the University. Very little occurred during the earlier part of this year to interrupt the ordinary routine of college study. That nothing occurred to ruffle his peace of mind, or to teach him by experience the frailty of human nature, it would not be consistent with truth to affirm. On the 20th of March, he writes in his journal: "A slight occurrence took place this week, arising from my pride, which for an hour took full possession of me, and I have been spiritually cold ever since. I had expressed my disapprobation, in a respectful manner, to my tutor, of his manner of speaking to the class, and I felt afterward that it was pride, which ought to be humbled, and I suffered for it mentally. I learned two things from this: one, never to take up any thing which belongs alone to the class; and another, to bear whatever is laid upon me as an individual in silence, and to be subject, 'for conscience' sake.'"

While Mr. Cutler was in Boston, during his vacation, he was often at the bedside of his beloved aunt, Mrs. Dunn, who had been a sufferer for many years, and was then drawing near the gate of death. On the 8th of June he received the intelligence of her death, and this to him was a heavy affliction. For nine years previous he had been "with her in trouble and distress of the most afflictive nature;" and he had, with wonder, beheld her patience when the rod of affliction was laid upon her; and now that she was gone, he mourned that so bright an example of unshaken faith was removed from his observation, yet he rejoiced that the weary were "at rest."

He attended the funeral with his friend, Gov. Jones, of Rhode Island; and when, with the large circle of relatives, he stood at the family vault, as they laid away her precious remains, most solemn reflections filled his mind. In that same receptacle for the dead were the bodies of his father, his uncles, Mr. Dunn and Mr. Clarke, and of other relatives; and his thoughts were busy, he tells us, with his whole past life.

He returned on Monday to his studies, and was engaged also in his usual labors on the Sabbath, through all the term. In the month of August he was compelled for a while to relinquish his books, and we find nothing of importance recorded in his journal.

On resuming his place at college in the Fall, he framed a series of resolutions for the guidance of his future conduct, which, as far as man can judge, he seems to have faithfully kept:

"Resolution I.—I will devote more time to special prayer, will cultivate nearer intercourse with God, and read the Scriptures with more attention, and will read one chapter in the Greek Testament every day.

"Resolution II.—I will avoid the society of the light and trifling, and will try to have my conversation seasoned with salt. I will converse with some one unconverted student every week.

"Resolution III.—I will correspond oftener with my religious friends.

"Resolution IV.—I will converse more with my fellow Christians around me.

"Resolution V.—I will be more humble, both in appearance and reality.

"Resolution VI.—By the grace of God, I will strive to keep perfectly these resolutions, having broken many before. Lord Jesus have mercy on me!"

While thus faithful with himself, Mr. Cutler was ever solicitous for the spiritual welfare of others. In October he was privileged to hear the Rev. Mr. Meade, of Virginia, preach on the Christian's assurance of future happiness. He was filled with admiration and delight, and says: "Mr. M. told us many believers were careful in observing outward attendance upon all the means of grace, yet were not happy until the Spirit of God witnessed with their spirits that they were the children of God. I thought of my friend, who appears to be just in the case described. How I long for the time when her heart will rejoice and her joy not be taken from her." At this time he penned a letter to this friend, who was in spiritual darkness, from which we make the following extract:

"There is such a thing, my dear friend, as assurance of acceptance. The holy apostle possessed it when he said, 'I have fought a good fight,' etc. Christians in all ages have possessed it; martyrs, in an eminent degree have possessed it—some of the most humble followers of the dear Redeemer. Yes! some poor worms of the dust, whom you and I know, have received the Spirit of adoption! Oh! my beloved friend, why can you not cry, 'Abba! Father?' Why can you not break down the wall of unbelief which hides you from your Saviour's face? Hear what God says: 'Wilt thou not from this time cry unto me, My Father, thou art the guide of my youth?' How can you resist such sweet calls? How can you starve, while angels' food is before you? Do you say, This is too great a privilege for me to receive the spirit of adoption; it is too great a gift? But can any gift be so great as the gift of his only Son, which he has already given? Oh, no! lay aside, then, all your doubts; claim the promises—take them in your hand—carry them to your Father in heaven—show them to him—plead them before him, and he will not turn his face from you! Only believe! Then will you know, indeed, 'how good the Lord is'—then will you be able to cry, 'For me to live is Christ! to die is gain;' and when you come to die, you will say, with a pious woman, who summed up all at the moment of death, in saying, 'I am all joy!'"

With such hearty counsel and earnest entreaty did he

persuade others to rejoice in the Lord. He had no exalted view of his own attainments, but walked in all humility before God. The edifice of his faith was built upon the rock Christ Jesus, and not upon the shifting sands of varying frames and feelings in the religious life. The day after the letter alluded to was written, the following record is made in his journal:

"I feel myself an undone sinner, condemned for past transgressions, unable to keep myself from the commission of sins in the future. I feel that I must be lost and ruined for ever through eternity, unless some atonement is made for my sin, and some source opened, from which I may obtain grace to help me in time of temptation. But I read in my Bible that Christ Jesus came to save sinners; that he has settled the account for my sins; that he is able and willing to take my filthy rags away, and clothe me in the white garments of salvation, and is able and willing to keep me from defiling them. He says, 'Come unto me all ye that are weary and heavy laden;' and when I see these words, and read of so many sinners coming to Him to be saved, and after they have come, having so much joy and peace—why, how can I help going too? I feel my load of guilt; I want to lay it down; I am tired of it, and he tells me to bring it to him. O Lord Jesus, I believe! help thou mine unbelief!

"With my Divine Redeemer's aid I would struggle through this life to arrive at the lowest place in heaven. I am indeed sinful—a worm, and no man, but Jesus is my rock, and I shall never sink."

Mr. Cutler writes: "*Oct.* 5.—This morning heard of the death of Thomas C. Mitchell, at Charleston, S. C. I have been intimate with this dear friend and cousin from childhood. He gave me the first religious impressions I ever received, and now he is taken and I am left. O Lord, I beseech thee to sanctify this bereavement to my good!

Heard also of the marriage of two friends in Boston to-day. This evening my dear sisters, Mrs. Ward and Louisa, arrived. The emotions of sorrow, joy and surprise which I have felt to-day, combine to tell me this is a chequered life."

"*Oct.* 27.—Walked down with Goodwin to see Rev. Mr. Crocker. Mr. C. was not so encouraging toward him as I expected. I think he errs on the safe extreme. But there are some lambs whom the shepherds of Israel should take in their arms and CARRY into the fold—those who have been gradually enlightened. G., in my opinion, is a Christian."

"*Oct.* 30.—Vanity has been my besetting sin this week. I cannot enumerate one single sin *conquered!* I cannot look back on one victory. Alas! this is living like a soldier on half-pay; or more like a soldier in full pay and on duty, who skulks around the tents, instead of fighting the enemy."

"*Nov.* 7. *Sunday.*—I went to the altar to-day with my friend Goodwin, where he was baptized. Afterward, partook with him of the symbols of the body and blood of our Lord. I hope and pray God will make him a 'burning and shining light.' As to myself, I am vile and sinful; I have nothing to say for abusing God's grace, but that Jesus died for me. . . . Satan has buffeted me sorely to-day. I have had to look up and say, Lord Jesus, drive Satan from me! . . . I walked home to-day with the Misses G.; intelligent, refined and pious ladies. I am quite intimate with the family, and find it a pleasant and profitable acquaintance."

The college friend referred to above, the Rev. Mr. Goodwin, has survived Mr. Cutler, and thus gives his testimony to the value of his friendship:

"PROVIDENCE, R. I., *February* 4, 1864.

"REVEREND AND DEAR BROTHER— . . . I am glad to say a few words respecting one who was very dear to me, and to whom I feel myself to be under the highest obligations. Dr. Cutler and

I became acquainted after entering Brown University, in 1818. He was then in the full exercise of all his powers—of his exceedingly amiable and attractive qualities. He had come from Boston, had been reared in society of the best kind, had gentlemanly manners, and was in the ardency of his first love for Christ, and for the spiritual welfare of all who came within the sphere of his influence. I had myself just come from Phillip's Academy, Andover, and I distinctly remember the surprise I felt at seeing the cheerfulness, good humor and almost gayety of one who professed to be a man of seriousness and piety. For some reason, which I did not then understand, but which I afterward found to be a resemblance to some friend of his, he soon became quite interested in me, and treated me with the kindest attention. In the latter part of our first term, I commenced my first school in a town not far from Providence, and on reaching the school-house from my father's residence, I found a letter on the desk from my friend Cutler, recommending me to begin my school with prayer, and urging the daily performance of the same duty. I was then eighteen years old, some two or three years younger than himself; but in maturity and manliness he was very far in advance of me.

"During the next year, after many friendly and serious conversations, he took me to Dr. Crocker, of St. John's Church, with a view to my baptism; and subsequently, when I was baptized, he himself was one of my sponsors on that solemn occasion.

"Soon after, when I had another school in Rhode Island, and had been there but a few days, he found a more desirable situation for me in Scituate, Mass., and even engaged another man to take my place, that I might go where I should be near a very worthy and pious clergyman, and called upon every fourth Sunday to read the Church service. After returning to college the next spring, he resigned the superintendence of the Sunday-school in St. John's and procured my election to the same place. But, while I shared largely in his affectionate and self-sacrificing regard, I must mention that he was the kind friend and faithful spiritual counsellor of all with whom he could gain an influence. In mentioning to a class-mate the other day that you wished for some account of Dr. Cutler's college life, he replied, 'I could give a bright record of that period;' and then told me that he felt himself indebted to him, for the serious impressions that not long afterward issued in his decided conversion to God. His heart was set upon doing good at all times, to all persons and under all circumstances, and he was wonderfully adapted to such benevolent work; for he had the respect of all, and knew how to approach each one in a kind and conciliating manner, and to leave him deeply convinced that he had in this friend one who purely and honestly desired his good.

"While he was popular and of great influence in college, he also had a large acquaintance and was highly useful outside of this limited circle. He was a favorite wherever he went. His mother and sisters residing in Providence, he mingled considerably in society, and that, too, of the choicest kind; and he shone as brightly among the intelligent and refined, as in the humble dwellings of the poor, the sick, and the afflicted. In the social religious meetings that were extensively held in Providence at that time, he was where he delighted to be, and where his presence was most welcome to those who attended. Here his ardent piety, his universal benevolence, his ready eloquence and affectionate bearing shone eminently conspicuous. Many who are now no more, have acknowledged their obligation to God for the blessing they have received through his instrumentality, and many still live, who speak of him and of his usefulness with ardor and delight. . . .

"Yours, etc., D. L. B. GOODWIN."

Thus we see how ready Mr. Cutler was to bring others to Jesus, even as Andrew brought Simon Peter to his Lord; or, like a second Barnabas, gladly taking by the hand any Saul whom others might for a moment distrust, and declaring to them how the Lord had spoken to his soul, and that he was indeed a true follower of Christ.

Our readers will not weary of the detailed experience of such a man; but it is proper to state that his journals were often written for the benefit of an absent friend, to whom he was tenderly attached, and are often addressed, as we see, to another party. This is evident from the next extract:

"MY DEAR H.—I am a poor, feeble soldier of Christ; my Captain fights all my battles, and if I conquer, he must fight them still; yea, and he will fight them. You will see by this journal how low I live; yet I have had peace—much more than I deserve. I am seldom, if ever, distressed. I find comfort, I hope, in Jesus my Master. My frame of mind does not vary much; I seldom am very high—still less frequently very low; seldom long without some solemn sense of the Divine Presence; my secret devotion is often performed in the open air before sunrise—retirement is sweeter to me than it was. I am sick, but Jesus can cure me; I am bruised, but Jesus can heal me; I am naked, but Jesus can clothe me; I am blind, but Jesus can lead me; I am ignorant, but Jesus can teach me; I am weak, but Jesus can strengthen me; I am poor, but Jesus can make me rich; I am in prison, but Jesus can open my prison door; I am condemned as a sinner, but Jesus can reprieve and deliver me."

About the 20th of this month (November) Mr. Cutler visited Bristol, R. I., where he enjoyed the hospitality of Bishop Griswold, and found three or four candidates for Orders studying with him. Mr. Cutler's impressions of that good man are thus recorded: "He is a true saint. Both in his public and private life he is purely apostolic; the most perfect humility and meekness you can conceive of, are constantly visible in all his deportment."

The pattern of holiness he was thus privileged to see stimulated him, and we see by his recorded experience that he was indeed hungering and thirsting after righteousness!

"*Dec.* 5. *Sunday.*"—He writes: "Now may thy presence go with me, O God! Control my thoughts; help me to guard my eyes and my tongue. Oh! I pray thee, let my soul bathe this day in the ocean of pure pleasure, which is thy presence. Thou knowest, O my Father! how I long for it. Oh, give me a morsel of bread to keep my soul from starving, for Christ's sake! I am a babe—a very babe in Christ."

Dec. 7.—Received a good letter from my dear friend, B. C. C. P. It caused me to be grateful; for it breathed more piety than any I have ever received before from him."

Dec. 11.—I went down to the wharf, as I saw a vessel

come in, and just as I arrived there, I saw my dear mother and sister Eliza in an open boat, which had come to shore from a packet just in from New York. They were out in a most severe, cold storm. How grateful I ought to be to God for thus sparing them to me. They were hurried along by the storm fifteen miles an hour. Oh the perils of the deep! but the child of God has nothing to fear; his Heavenly Father holds the sea in the hollow of his hand."

"*Dec.* 19.—Went to the altar with Miss W—d, who was baptized. It was very solemn. Miss W—d is an adopted daughter of a rich and fashionable woman, and I may add, a sweet and benevolent woman, who is a relation of my Sister Julia. For several months I have conversed with her and with the family on vital religion. God has changed her heart, I think, and I trust will keep her unto the end. He has done all, and his is all the glory!"

"*Dec.* 26.—Have had a day of darkness; but in the evening realized the presence of the Saviour; was favored with a smile, which was refreshing; for when Jesus hides his face, all, all is distress within. Nothing gives me comfort, but when he smiles; it is 'like marrow to my bones.' O Lord Jesus, may I embrace thee fully, as my Prophet, Priest and King!"

On the opening of the new year (1820), Mr. Cutler spent his vacation with the Rev. Mr. Eaton, at Boston, which he noted as a visit of peculiar interest and profit.

To others he appeared to have grown in grace, but on his return to college he laments his own coldness in these words: "I fear I shall be only 'a hewer of wood and a drawer of water' for the children of God. Pride is so conspicuous in my life! God is so little in my thoughts! His love constraineth me so feebly! O God, break this flinty heart! may I be humbled at the feet of Jesus, and lie there until he takes me home!"

"*Jan.* 22.—This week I have possessed a peace of mind

worth thousands of gold and silver! Yet how unworthy I am of God's mercy!"

"*Feb.* 6.—My sins stare me in the face. My base ingratitude, my vile thoughts, my idolatry of self—all, all, rise up before me. Can God pardon me, and yet be just? I am covered with sin—tears rush into my eyes; but in a moment they are absorbed by my wicked heart. If I could bathe my Saviour's feet, I might conclude that I have some feeling; if my tears were my meat and drink—but no, this proud, hard heart refuses to be broken! My God,

'Oh! make this heart rejoice or ache—
Decide this doubt for me;
And if it is not broken, break!
And heal it, if it be.'

O blessed Jesus! thou knowest all things, thou knowest that I love thee. Leave not, then, thy poor, tempest-tossed child to go starving all his days! Thou hast promised not to leave him comfortless. Remember thy promise! Oh, look upon his emptiness and poverty, and fill and clothe him with thyself! Thou knowest he would not give up his hope in thee for all the world!"

CHAPTER III.

COLLEGE LIFE—CONTINUED.

1820–1822.

IN the year 1820, while Mr. Cutler was in his junior year in college, there was a remarkable revival of religion throughout the whole State of Rhode Island. In Providence and in Bristol, the two great centres of influence, the Holy Spirit was poured out in abundant measure, and as in the Apostles' times, "many were added unto the Lord."

The Rev. Dr. Tyng (who was at this period studying with Bishop Griswold) thus speaks of it: "The churches in Providence grew and flourished under this Divine blessing. The Rev. Dr. Crocker, the beloved rector of the Episcopal church there, entered into the blessings of the occasion with his whole heart. . . . . In Bristol it commenced suddenly, with no preparation by human agency. Every meeting for prayer or religious teaching was crowded. The people for months seemed wholly given to the one work of prayer, and praise, and hearing of the word. Religious meetings were held by various congregations on every day in the week, and often several times in one day. The business of the world seemed almost suspended for this one purpose and employment of life. Many hundreds were in the course of this Divine interposition added to the various churches in Bristol. Some were thus gathered in the most remarkable instances of conversion. The power of the Holy

Ghost was wonderfully displayed, arousing, renewing, refreshing multitudes for Christ."*

This must have been a blessed season, indeed, for both Mr. Tyng at Bristol and Mr. Cutler at Providence, and they doubtless were privileged to enjoy a foretaste of that great delight with which afterward they saw sinners brought into the kingdom of God and saints edified, under their own respective ministries, in the various fields of labor to which God called them.

In Mr. Cutler's journal of March, 1820, we find a record of this season : " The Lord is visiting us now with his Holy Spirit in this place. More than one hundred persons have been converted in this town within two months. Thirteen persons were baptized to-day, and forty more are ready for this rite. This embraces persons of all ages. In Warren and Bristol great religious interest is felt. What will grow out of it I cannot say. May great numbers be added to the Church of Christ of such only as shall be saved! Though so much is doing around me, my love does not burn so brightly as it ought, and I am altogether a short-comer. My prayers are poor, and my practice worse ; my thoughts are often wandering on forbidden ground, and there is no health in me."

" *March* 6, 1820.—The revival in this town increase ; upwards of one hundred and fifty persons have been converted. God be praised! Our prayer-meeting in college was very solemn this evening. Bishop Griswold has sent for me to go down to him at Bristol. There is a great revival of religion in his church, and he is ill.

We may remark, in passing, that at such seasons of religious excitement the great enemy of souls always sows his tares among the wheat, and if he cannot destroy, will try to impede the work of genuine conversion, and he often blasts the influence of those who are prominent in furthering a

* See " Son of Consolation," p. 37.

work of grace of this kind, by inflating them with a sort of spiritual pride, which is most pernicious in its effects! Mr. Cutler seems to have been watchful on this point, with "godly jealousy."

"*March* 11."—He says: "I have just returned from B., having passed a very pleasant week at the house of Bishop G., and have seen the effects of the Spirit of God in the conversion of many souls. I have attended religious meetings every evening, and have conversed with inquiring souls, and with those who are confirmed in the faith, and have publicly exhorted sinners to come to Christ; but yet I have seen much of the exceeding sinfulness of my own heart, enough to destroy any thing like self-complacency. How careful I should be to keep the precept, 'esteem others better than thyself!' I have compared myself with others, rather than with Christ. I have hungered more for the meat that perisheth, for the praise of men, rather than that of God. So much pride and selfishness! Oh, if I had not a Saviour, what could I do? Blessed Jesus, purge me from my sins and prepare me to worship thee in heaven!"

"*March* 19.—I went to church with my heart full of praise, for the outpouring of God's Spirit in this place.

'The Lord has heard our feeble prayer
And sent his Spirit down;
The stubborn hearts around us melt,
His power and goodness own.'

I have heard the true doctrines of the gospel preached in a most arousing and searching manner; our beloved pastor (Mr. Crocker) gave all 'their meat in due season, and rightly divided the word of truth.' May God bless it to my soul, and the souls of my friends!"

"*April* 4.—The revival in this town and in Bristol cheers my heart; a few of my fellow-students are serious and inquiring the way to be saved. Oh that the revival would enter our college!"

"*April* 14.—A happy day; the revival has commenced in college; received letters from my beloved H.; also letters from dear R. J. P. and S. C. D."

"*April* 15.—The revival continues in college; a most glorious work; sinners tremble and saints rejoice."

"*April* 16.—The Lord reigns! let the earth be glad! Bless the Lord, O my soul! for he has heard the prayers of his children, and his Holy Spirit has been poured out upon this college. Scoffers are weeping and sorrowing for their sins. O God, do thy own work! convince, convert, and sanctify thy creatures!"

"*April* 17.—A day of happiness; five of my class-mates have a hope in Christ, and ten in the other classes. Morning and night I have been trying to do something for immortal souls."

"*April* 22.—Three more persons have been brought into the marvellous light and liberty of the sons of God—making the number twenty. I went out to Pawtucket, last evening, with some of the new converts to try to awaken a spirit of inquiry there."

"*April* 23.—I rejoice that I have been permitted to live in this time and at this place. I seem to have been translated into a new world."

Thus the work went on, till more than *thirty* students in college were brought to a saving knowledge of the Lord Jesus Christ. The account of this season of deep religious interest we close with an extract from a letter of Mr. Cutler's to Miss S. P. B., a friend in Boston:

"You have, doubtless, heard what a glorious work the Lord is carrying on in this town. Hundreds of stubborn sinners are bowing down to the mild sceptre of the Prince of Peace. More than three hundred persons have been hopefully converted. Religious meetings are held every night, and the work is general with young, middle-aged and old; with rich and poor, learned and unlearned, sceptics and moralists, and with persons of all denominations (Socinian excepted). Our church members have prayer-meetings, many of our congregation are serious, and about fifteen have been brought to Christ. Mr. Crocker is very faithful in his preaching, and particularly so in examining candidates for the Communion; he has not admitted any of the new converts yet, wishing them to wait, I presume, till the excitement is a little abated, that they may be able to determine, whether they are really born again, or whether their feelings only are engaged.

"I have long wished and prayed for such a glorious sight, that my own heart, also, might be more deeply impressed and my love inflamed. I wish you were here, your heart would rejoice; but you must pray that God would grant the same Divine blessing upon Boston. . . . . Yours, in Christ, B. C. C."

The impressions received by Mr. Cutler during this precious season were never erased from his memory, and his own earnest labors of Christian love are still recounted by many on earth, and, doubtless, reviewed with unceasing gratitude by very many, whom he has now met again, among the great multitude of ransomed sinners, who have entered in, "through the gates," into the heavenly city above!

Mr. Cutler spent his summer vacation of this year in travelling, as his health had become impaired, and we close the record for the year with a portion of a letter which he addressed to a friend in Massachusetts. It is dated

"New York, *September* 25, 1820.

"You will be surprised to find that I am in New York. I have spent this vacation in traveling with my cousin, Miss Waring; she intends to return to Charleston, S. C., soon. I find my health much improved by my journey—coming by the way of Boston, Albany and the North River to this place. I am now with my sister, Mrs. Ward, four miles from the city, on the banks of the East River; she has a fine flock of sweet little lambs, which afford me much amusement. I expect, however, to leave this place, with my sister Louisa, for Providence, to-morrow. I am tired of seeing new things; my eyes sicken with the blaze of worldly splendor, and my ears are tired of worldly and unmeaning conversation. I long to return to my retirement, *unenvying and unenvied.*

'Let me be little and unknown,
Loved and prized by God alone.'

I have, however, derived much comfort from the society of my sister, Mrs. Ward, from Miss W., and one or two other Christians. But the unsettled manner of life to which travelling subjects one, is uncongenial to the growth of real piety. Still, I am more alive to religious things than when I last saw you. I have felt more comfort and delight in Christian conversation, and have felt more disposed to serious reflection and self-examination.

"God grant this may not be 'as the morning cloud and as the early dew,' but that I may have his grace to advance in holiness as I grow in age."

Early in the year 1821 Mr. Cutler made another visit to New York, spending a part of his time with Mr. and Mrs. Bethune. He notes it in his diary that he had not been in company once during his stay, and he found it a season of great religious enjoyment. He writes to R. J. P., a friend in Boston:

"I have enjoyed, since I have been in New York, every spiritual comfort possible. Gospel preaching and ordinances; gospel society; and, though I have been wholly undeserving, gospel *peace*. And what a privilege have I enjoyed in sitting by the bedside of that dear saint, Phœbe Ward; she is now preparing for her rest in heaven. I went up to see her, at Jamaica, and spent the Sabbath there. She is just such a Christian as I want to be. She is perfectly resigned, and told me she would not change places with any being in the world. My happiest hours have been spent at her bedside."

On the same day (January 14, 1821,) Mr. Cutler writes to another friend, S. P. B., in this strain; and though the letter is full of sober truth, we see the playful humor of the writer toward the close:

"'Tis true, the world won't own you, and, I am sure, you are too fond of *praying* for Satan to own you. Where, then, do you belong? To the kingdom of Christ! Who, then, dares to call you poor, or wretched, or forsaken? when God is your Father, Christ your Saviour, and the treasures of heaven your riches! I know of no stronger evidence that a man is born again, than that his constant desire is to be holier than he is; if you are conscious of having this, you have good reason to embrace a hope, which will be to your soul an anchor both sure and steadfast. But,now to temporals. Where are you, my dear ——, and where do you expect to be? I shall be here till February 17. . . . . . I am surrounded by dissenters—don't you tremble for me? I see Dr. Mason, and hear Dr. Romeyn frequently, and passed an evening with the former. I am in a delightful, pious, and praying family."

Mr. Cutler returned to his studies with much improved health, and prosecuted them with his usual diligence; yet an interest in the religious welfare of others was ever uppermost in his mind. His prayers for the eternal salvation of his relatives and friends were unceasing. May 8, 1821, he enters this record upon his journal: "This day will ever be memorable. My dear Sister Eliza has professed this day to have obtained a hope in Christ, and is rejoicing in Christ Jesus. She is triumphing in her Saviour. God be praised for evermore!"

A few days later (in writing to a member of the family, with which he was afterward connected by marriage), he says: "You have heard, I presume, of the conversion of my dear Sister Eliza. She is now a spiritual, zealous Christian."

Thus, one by one, was God gradually bringing into the fold of his church on earth the different members of Mr. Cutler's family. His prayers entered the ears of the Lord God of Sabaoth, and a gracious answer seemed to be given: "Be it unto thee even as thou wilt." In due time, all, save one, were professed disciples of the Lord, and forty years of intercessory prayer for him will yet be answered by a prayer-hearing God. Though the petitioner has gone to his rest, a covenant-keeping God, we doubt not, has heard every petition, and will graciously reveal himself in his own chosen time. In the efficacy of prayer, Mr. Cutler put a strong faith, and he has left the following on record: "The prayers of Mrs. Isabella Graham, for my mother and her children—to these I owe much; and to the Saviour of sinners and his Spirit, I owe infinitely more."

His beloved mother, in writing to him at the close of this year, from New York, says: "Dear E. is as good as ever; and her principles, 'through grace,' stand as firm as the rock of Gibraltar."

Our readers must not imagine that the experience of Mr. Cutler was in any sense different from that of every faithful child of God.

Days of darkness and days of brightness both worked together, for his religious welfare and advancement.

"*June* 2, 1821."—He writes: "How little does my life resemble the holy, self-denying life of the humble Christian; yet I have a hope in Christ that is better than millions of worlds. I feel that I am a sinner—a vile and helpless sinner. I have no confidence in my own strength."

"*June* 18.—After the restraints which religion imposes on the Sabbath, the mind seems to fly like a bird from a cage. Oh! why is this? Because my mind is occupied constantly in worldly pursuits, and because of the natural alienation of the mind from God. When, oh when! shall I be conformed to the will of Christ?"

"*June* 28.—What a poor, feeble, rebellious creature I am. If my heart has ever been sanctified, how incomplete is the work! How far I am from what I ought to be; from what I promised to be; from what I desire to be!"

"*Aug.* 12.—A profitable day. I have heard the gospel preached with sweetness and power, by Rev. Mr. Henshaw, of Baltimore."

"*Oct.* 11.—Returned to college, and began my routine of duties. May I be faithful in the discharge of them."

"*Oct.* 12.—Followed to the grave my dear friend, Miss A. E. Goddard. God grant this event may be sanctified to me."

"*Oct.* 29.—How holy I should be; but, alas! my heart is so wicked; my temptations so great, that I often fall. Lord, heal my backslidings."

"*Nov.* 1.—If I would be a Christian, I must be so indeed, and must cease to esteem the praise of man. Lord, help me to rise above the vanities of time!"

"*Dec.* 23.—I have performed service to-day at Pawtucket, and trust my labors in that church will be blessed to its members."

It was a special trait in Mr. Cutler's character that he took delight in giving encouragement to others. His sensitive spirit sympathized with those who lay along the path of life, prostrate with utter despair, and it seemed to be his province to lift them up and send them on their way rejoicing. Instances of this kind mark almost every year of his life. Even at this early date, the germ of this spirit began to be developed.

After a college exhibition some severe criticisms appeared, and Mr. Cutler replied in this way:

"*To the Editor of the Rhode Island American:*

"DEAR SIR—I was much pleased with the remarks of 'A Lover of Early Genius,' upon the college exhibition, December 27. His reproof of the non-resident professors was delicate and appropriate, and his criticism upon the taste and style of the speakers was liberal and judicious. The objection against publicly crowning the precocity of genius must commend itself to every lover of literature. But the same scruples which influence him in withholding pointed praise, should have operated upon him in restraining pointed reproof; for, if it is true that the minds of some young men are so bold, ardent, and enterprising that early applause would too much elate them, it is just as true that the minds of some are so extremely sensitive that early and severe censure will paralyze and ruin them.

"For if the dews of Helicon, falling too early and abundant, injure the unripe fruit; so the frosts of Academus, when hurried by the cold wintry winds, wither and blight it.

"Your correspondent, and you, sir, and all who honor the exhibition with their presence, should consider, before you enter the college walls, that you are not about to be shown the accumulated wealth of aged and industrious intellect; the calm, dignified eloquence of mature oratory, or the dazzling effulgence of meridian talent; but that a few young men, whom but four years ago, science called from the plow, or the voice of the Saviour drew from the market-place, are here unwillingly presented to you to exhibit the fruits of their ephemeral labor.

"Instead of courting your praise, and desiring to walk in the zodiac among the stars, they shrink intuitively from the withering ken of the critic, and ask you only to tell them if continued industry and persevering application, will ever make them your compeers in honor and usefulness. But I wish not to silence the friendly severity of criticism, nor to deter you and others from attending the exhibitions. No! your presence and opinion are absolutely necessary to elicit the reluctant powers of the mind, and, as has been justly observed, to hold up a mirror which shall faithfully discover to the youth the awkwardness of untutored genius. Go, then, as the constituted guardians of science and literature; not only with critical sagacity, but with parental solicitude; encourage the timid and irresolute; check the ambitious and the forward; and hold out to those who never can distinguish themselves in literature, the hope of their becoming important and useful, if not honored, members of society. B. C. C."

During the winter of 1821–22, Mr. Cutler was deprived of the society of his mother and sisters. The tie which connected them with their friends at Savannah was very strong, and they were always welcomed at the South by a very numerous circle of loving kindred.

To her sons Mrs. Cutler thus writes, in January, 1822:

"While you are enveloped in snow, and freezing with cold, we find it pleasant some days to throw a window open, and see the oranges hanging on the trees, and the roses in bloom in the open air. Yet, notwithstanding these enjoyments, I can say, with the poet,

'Where'er I rove, whatever realms to see,
My heart untravelled fondly turns to thee.'

Yes, in the midst of all, I look forward with pleasure to the time when I shall return to my two darling sons."

Mr. Cutler makes special note in his journal of his twenty-fourth birthday; and on that day his mother addressed to him a letter, which deserves to be put on record, as a testimony to his filial obedience:

"SAVANNAH, *February* 6, 1822.

"This auspicious morn brings to me the pleasing recollection that twenty-four anniversaries have elapsed, since the precious privilege was given me of calling you my son. A gift I hold so dear that no bounds can reach my gratitude; nor can language express the tenderness your mother feels for you. Let me, then, invoke a blessing upon you, my son, for all the obedience, affection, and tenderness you have shown your mother in these revolving years; in which time my memory can scarce record, even in the period of childhood, an act of opposition to my will! May the Lord bless you, my son! for this life of filial obedience to me, in that 'bright inheritance' he has prepared for you in a better world; may all your labors in the Lord reap a rich harvest until your soul shall be satisfied; may the Lord comfort you in all the way he shall lead you through this wilderness, and refresh you, when thou art weary, with 'the dew of his grace,' that thy strength fail not. May your health be precious in his sight; may you be fed by his bounty, and your 'basket and store' be blessed, that it fail not; and last, though not least, in your estimation, may your daily offerings at the Throne of grace, for all whom you love, be heard, blessed, and answered to you. . . . .

Your ever affectionate mother,

SARAH CUTLER."

On the 8th of May Mr. Cutler passed his senior examination, with great credit to himself and to the satisfaction of his instructors. A short vacation followed, at the end of which, he received tidings of the safe arrival of his mother and sister in New York. Early in June, on their reaching Providence, he greeted them with joy and gratitude, after an absence of eight months. The 12th of this month he set apart as a day of special thanksgiving and praise.

About this time his brother entered upon business life and left the city.

The 3d of July Mr. Cutler set apart as a day of special prayer for the conversion of the members of his family; and on the 4th, his other sisters, Julia and Louisa, joined the home circle at Providence.

The 10th of July was the day of final examination in the University, and on the following day he says: "The parts for Commencement were given out, and justice was done me in awarding me an oration."

To this period Mr. Cutler thus alludes in 1834, when he drew up a brief autobiography: "I was four years at Brown University, making the first and the last recitation with my class. I received at Commencement what I believe was the third part, which I shared with four or five others who, as I had, received English orations. A part of the officers were desirous of giving me the second part (as I learned from good authority), but it was given to another, who, for talent, deserved it. It was decided rightly; I was perfectly satisfied. Nobody disputed my right to the part I obtained—a higher one would have drawn upon me envy and satire, at least.

"During these four years I studied steadily, never overtasking my mind (as my body was still feeble), and taking constant exercise.

"I stood as high as the highest in classical literature, in rhetoric and composition. In Enfield's Philosophy, I was never deficient; in Moral Philosophy, I took much interest; and in Paley and Butler, on the Evidences of Christianity, I studied well. In Algebra and Metaphysics, I was nothing. This was owing in part to a poor preparation for college, and a native dislike to abstraction."

A classmate of Mr. Cutler's has told us that, "as a scholar, he excelled in most of his studies; particularly in all that pertained to literature and composition, but for mathematics he had no taste." His case is not unlike that of the celebrated Dr. Beattie, of whom it was said: "The only science in which he made no proficiency was mathematics. In this, he performed the requisite tasks, but was eager to return to subjects of taste and general literature."

Mr. Cutler's college essays bear marks of more than ordinary scholarship. One of them, on "Posthumous Respect," is of great interest, and could he have looked forward with a prophet's eye, through the vista of future years, to his own departure from earth, he could not have used language more true or more pertinent than that with which, he concludes the essay to which reference is made. The final paragraph reads thus : "When near his dissolution, the Christian does not look back into the world ; he does not anticipate the feelings or the actions of the world at his death, but he 'treads it beneath his feet;' he cares not whether his death is unknown to his fellow-creatures, or whether he is canonized by them as a saint. His eye is fixed on heaven ; his ear is already tuned for its melody, and he longs to associate with its inhabitants ; till at last his happy spirit, borne on the wings of angels, takes its flight and enters Paradise amid the hallelujahs of the blessed !"

In later life, Mr. Cutler, in looking back over this portion of his history, left the following on record, and we do not feel at liberty to withhold it : "In college I might have ranked much higher as a scholar had I staid away from extra religious meetings. But I adopted a rule here, that every thing must give way to religion, and the heart must first be attended to. I took special care to attend to religion, and sacrificed reputation to it. I went to conference meetings in my own church, spoke and prayed ; visited a few pious ladies often, and kept up a friendship with them. Thought I was doing good. Life appeared too short to study all the time.

"On this subject I have only to say, that I think it very doubtful whether young men studying for the ministry *(while in college)* ought to speak in public religious meetings, even for devotional and practical purposes.

"Perhaps I ought to have taken the course which those good men, Buchanan and Martyn, recommend in college—silent, retired, studious piety."

Though Mr. Cutler entered college with a good measure

of health, he was often subject to a weakness of the lungs and extreme languor, and he often complained of a nervous irritability, which was at times almost beyond control. This difficulty he struggled with, through life. Nature seemed ever in combat with disease, and the only wonder is that he accomplished so much.

His conduct in college was exemplary, and both respect and obedience he invariably gave to those in authority. During a rebellion in college he stood almost alone in loyalty, but he says he was "enabled to bear the finger of scorn."

Mr. Cutler graduated in September, 1822. His oration at Commencement, on "The Old Age of a Scholar," having elicited high approval.

Immediately after, he repaired to Quincy, Mass., where he had already began his labors as a missionary, a few weeks previous. His dearest friends gathered together at Providence, in order to be present at the Commencement exercises; and while Mr. Cutler was at Quincy, during the vacation, he received the following letter from his mother:

"My Dear and Precious Son—To God only is the praise due for giving me such a son—so good, so dutiful, so affectionate, in all your deportment toward me. . . . My heart runs over with gratitude for the precious boon that God has given me in my children; in the midst of poverty they would be exhaustless riches to me! Yet my Heavenly Father has also given me a competence in addition to these rich treasures. Surely, I ought to be the most grateful of all his creatures. I have been asking this morning, at his hands, humility—that I may give my God the glory, as he is the 'bounteous Giver,' without the alloy of self-gratulation and pride; for, as Newton says, this 'dead fly will insinuate itself in all our offerings, all our duties, and taint the best of them with its odious savor;' to which I can testify from too great, too dear experience.

"Your letter came to hand last night, and was truly a refreshment to my spirits. I am delighted with the account of your situation, prospects of usefulness, etc., etc. I wish I were with you, quietly settled at the parsonage, as I am tired of the bustle of life, and long for peaceful retirement once more, to 'ride at anchor' in my old age. Had it not been for the prospect of Louisa's marriage this fall, and my wish to be present when you take your degree, I should have been quietly settled at Quincy by this time. . . . I have made arrangements with a friend to bring our dear H——t on from Montreal. . . . Love to dear Francis, and keep 'Benjamin's portion,' for yourself. Your ever affectionate Mother."

Two weeks later Mr. Cutler received his diploma from the University, and then hastened back (with his friends) to Quincy. But his interest in the institution with which he had been so happily connected, continued through life, and he rejoiced, as opportunity offered, to be present at many succeeding Commencements. An unusual number of his class became clergymen—not less than fifteen; and among his classmates we find Prof. Caswell and Prof. Farnum, Hon. Messrs. Burgess, Davis, Kinnicutt, and other men of note.

It is a remarkable fact that so many Episcopal clergymen (including two bishops of the Church) have graduated from "Brown University," and thus attested by their own example to the wisdom of Mr. Cutler's choice, as regards a place of collegiate instruction.

A faithful portrait of Mr. Cutler, at this period of his life, has been kindly given us by one of these clergymen, the Rev. Dr. Muenscher, of the Diocese of Ohio, which will not fail to attract every reader.

"Mt. Vernon, O., *January* 19, 1864.

"Rev. and Dear Bro.— . . . My acquaintance with Dr. Cutler commenced in early life. I entered Brown University in the fall of 1817, and he entered in 1818. At that time we were the only members of the Episcopal Church connected with the college, and looking forward to the ministry in that Church. I soon found that his views, in regard to the Church and its doctrines, accorded with my own, and I formed a strong attachment for him, which I never ceased to cherish during his life, though Divine Providence afterward assigned us to different and distant fields of labor. He was a universal favorite among the undergraduates, and greatly beloved by all the professors of religion in the college, irrespective of denomination.

"In the extensive revival of religion which took place in the college while we were connected with it, he was among the most active and efficient in administering counsel, instruction, and encouragement to the young men whose thoughts had been turned to the subject of their soul's salvation.

"His whole soul was engaged in the work, and Eternity alone will disclose the extent of his usefulness during that precious season of refreshing from the presence of the Lord. My own opinion is that there was not a single professor of religion connected with the college, whose religious influence was as great as his.

"This was owing partly to the elevated tone and living character of the piety which he uniformly maintained, and partly to the warmth and sincerity of his affection, and his easy and winning address.

"I had the pleasure of meeting him frequently at the table of his excellent mother, and had numerous opportunities of witnessing his uniformly affectionate bearing toward her, and toward his estimable sisters. His social qualities were such as to render him, at all times, an agreeable companion; and his unaffected humility at once captivated your heart and inspired your confidence. There was no disguise, no ostentation, no pretension in Dr. Cutler. He was perfectly transparent, and you had only to see him frequently to know him as well as you knew yourself.

"In the year 1856 I happened to be in New York, providentially, and spent several months in his family, rendering him such assistance as I could, in the preparation of his volume of sermons for the press; and during this period I found him ever the same kind-hearted friend, agreeable companion, and devoted Christian, that I had known him to be in early life, constantly engaged in his work, unwearied in his zeal, 'an Israelite, indeed, in whom there is no guile.'

"I shall look forward to the publication of your Memoir with great pleasure, and have no doubt it will be perused with satisfaction and profit by his many personal friends and the Christian public generally.

"Very truly your friend and brother in Christ,

"To the Rev. H. Gray. Joseph Muenscher."

CHAPTER IV.

LIFE IN QUINCY, MASS.

1822–1829.

IN the retired town of Quincy, Mass., near the centre of the village, in 1822, stood an old church, whose simple construction and antique style of architecture told the beholder of ancient days. Its venerable appearance seemed to claim for it a reverent recognition, for it had weathered the storms of nearly a hundred years, and remained a precious relic of the zeal and piety of its founders. Within the gate there stood one lone poplar tree, like a hoary-headed sentinel, guarding the dust of many sleeping saints who lay in their graves around. A few old, but graceful elms waved their branches over the hallowed place, while here and there the monuments erected over the dead, declared to all who lingered to read their inscriptions, the names and virtues of those who had in succession ministered at the altar within those time-honored walls! These had in their turn been gathered to their fathers, "in the confidence of a certain faith," and in the communion of the church they so dearly prized.

Miller, Winslow, and the faithful Cleverly (a lay reader), had all gone to their rest at the close of the last century. Since the year 1800, three or four other clergymen had officiated here, but they had been transferred to distant portions of the Master's vineyard; and now, the congregation, destitute of the regular ministrations of the sanctuary, were like "sheep without a shepherd!" Some hearts began to fail lest a much longer period should elapse before another watchman would lift up his voice in this part of God's Zion.

Here, and under these auspices, Mr. Cutler commenced his ministerial labors. The venerable "Society for Propagating the Gospel in Foreign Parts," for more than half a century, had contributed annually sixty pounds sterling to the support of the minister of this church; but this benefaction had ceased at the time of the American Revolution. A house and glebe for the use of the minister was yet in the possession of the parish, a goodly portion of the original expense having been borne by various members of the Apthorp family, to whose timely aid, both in early and later days, the Church here has been much indebted. But this church was never independent of assistance till about the time Mr. Cutler began to officiate here, when, though the congregation had dwindled to a small remnant of people, new zeal was infused into every heart. In May, 1822, during a vacation in his senior year in college, Mr. Cutler first visited the parish, and in July of the same year he went there to reside. The family circle at Jamaica Plains had long before been broken up, and his mother removed from Providence to Quincy, and superintended the domestic affairs at the parsonage. Here his affectionate sisters, some of whom had formed other ties, and were then living at a distance, often came, and this became a central point where the various members of the family circle could enjoy intercourse with each other and often receive the greetings of their only surviving parent.

In the autumn of this year, Mr. Cutler took deacon's orders (under a special license). The *Gospel Advocate*, a Church periodical printed in Boston, thus records the fact:

"On Thursday, September 14 (1822), at Christ Church, Quincy, the Rt. Rev. Bishop Griswold admitted to the holy order of deacons Mr. B. C. Cutler, of Boston, a graduate of Brown University. Morning prayer by the Rev. Dr. Gardiner,of Boston, and the sermon by the Bishop, from the 2 Corinthians iv. 7 : 'We have this treasure in earthen vessels, that the excellency of the power may be of God and not of us.'

"The Holy Communion was then administered by Bishop Griswold, assisted by the Rev. Dr. Gardiner. The candidate was presented by the Rev. Jasper Adams, President of Charleston College. The services on this occasion were very interesting and impressive. Many of the clergy and a great number of the laity were present; among others, the venerable John Adams, late President of the United States. This ordination is an event of peculiar interest to the Church at large, and particularly to the society at Quincy. For many years that parish, having been destitute of a rector, has been in a low and depressed state, though they have sometimes been supplied with lay-readers, and have occasionally had the services of clergymen. We trust that the gentleman now admitted to orders will long continue with them, and prove to them a faithful watchman upon the walls of Zion. May the great Head of the Church vouchsafe his blessing upon them. It may not be amiss to state that the venerable Ex-President John Adams has given to this society the privilege of taking from his quarry a sufficient quantity of stone to erect a church, whenever they are disposed to avail themselves of the gift."

The Bishop of the Diocese, thus rightly estimating the uncommon worth of Mr. Cutler, placed him in charge of this unpromising but important post, where he read printed sermons, performed pastoral duties, and at the same time pursued his theological studies. He studied Hebrew with Rev. Dr. Jarvis, of Boston, and the New Testament in the original Greek, with critical commentaries. He also read works on Divinity and Church History, and profane history at large. He gave particular attention to the Evidences of Christianity and to polemical theology, especially that which related to the Trinitarian controversy, then very bitter in that region.

Six weeks after his admission to the diaconate, his happiness and his interests became completely identified with those of another individual, for whom he had formed a very early attachment.

On the 30th of October, 1822, the Rev. Mr. Cutler was united in marriage to Miss Harriet Bancroft, daughter of Mr. James Bancroft, of Boston, and sister of Charles Bancroft, Esq., of Montreal. The ceremony was performed by the Rev. Dr. Eaton in Christ Church, Boston—the sanctuary of so many sacred associations to them both. The ardent longings of his heart, which had been gathering strength during several previous years of endeared friendship, were now gratified, and his wishes consummated, in having a companion of substantial qualities of mind and heart.

By her consistent piety, gentleness of spirit and evenness of temper, she was fitted pre-eminently to be a real helpmeet for him, and verified for him, in all subsequent years, the truth of the wise man's saying, "A prudent wife is from the Lord." It could truly be said, "She opened her mouth with wisdom, and in her tongue was the law of kindness." This is not the time or place to descant at length upon her virtues, as this most estimable lady still survives to mourn his loss.

Immediately after his marriage Mr. Cutler returned to Quincy, and on the same evening united in marriage his Sister Louisa and W. H. McAllister, Esq. (a son of Judge McAllister, of Savannah).

Thus were the bonds of family affection still further increased and strengthened. The Rev. Mr. Cutler promptly engaged himself in the daily routine of duty in parish life, and, with redoubled energy, set himself to the task (under God's blessing) of reviving this ancient parish of Quincy.

Collecting the scattered embers, he endeavored to kindle a flame of sacred love in the hearts of many who had grown cold and indifferent in religious matters, and strove earnestly to awaken others still "dead in trespasses and sins," to a new life in Christ Jesus. He constantly sought the blessing and quickening agency of the Holy Spirit upon all his work, and realizing that though a Paul might plant and an Apollos water, in the spiritual husbandry of the Church, unless God gave the increase, it would be in vain.

Thus he diligently toiled and prayed, and with expectant hope looked for the Divine blessing. Nor was he disappointed in this hope. He lifted up the Lord Jesus before his people as the only Saviour for perishing sinners, and many believed and turned unto the Lord. He was permitted to see many fruits of his toil in the ingathering of souls into the fold of Christ, and God graciously gave him such seals to his ministry as proved that the Holy Spirit was indeed working with him, and awakening many, who, as in the Apostles' time, had not "so much as heard whether there was any Holy Ghost" to realize the fact, in their own experience, that the Gospel of Christ was "the power of God unto salvation to every one that believeth." Families from neighboring towns gathered around these ministrations, and believers "walking in the fear of the Lord, and in the comfort of the Holy Ghost, were multiplied."

In all the details of pastoral life Mr. Cutler was remarkably faithful. He counselled those that were ignorant and out of the way, he cheered the sick and bound up the wounds of the broken in heart, with tender hand. He ceased not to teach and preach Jesus Christ in every house.

Nor were the young ever forgotten; with delicate tact he sought for the favorable moment to speak a word for his Master, and by letter, if not in person, he would ever remind them of the things that belonged to their eternal peace.

The following note will give us a glimpse of his faithfulness in this respect:

"THE PARSONAGE, 17*th March*, 1823.

"MY DEAR SICK FRIEND—Our excellent Bishop requested me to send you this packet, and to say that Emily's book was not yet done. The Bishop intends returning to Bristol on Friday next, and if you have any thing to send, our chaise is going to Boston to-morrow, and our man shall carry any thing to the Bishop. I cannot possibly neglect this opportunity of expressing to you, my dear friend, how thankful I am that God has spared your life and is restoring you to health, to the enjoyment of life, and to usefulness. . . . . I have no doubt the reflections which have visited you since your confinement have chastened your expectations of earthly bliss, and gently drawn out your mind toward the 'Father of mercies' as the true source of every good and perfect gift. Go to him, Helen, as the fountain of wisdom, holiness, and strength, and by much prayer, give back to him a body and soul which he has so skillfully and so mercifully made, and so wisely and bountifully endowed for his own glory and the good of his children.

"Remember him who redeemed you with his own blood—redeemed you, a captive to Satan and to death; who purchased you at such a price! Think of him interceding for you with God, and extending his arms daily, and saying, 'Come unto me and take my yoke upon you, which is easy, and my burden, which is light!' . . . . . Let me remind you of the gentle chastisement lately sent you, speaking in a still small voice, 'Daughter, give me thy heart!' give it not to strangers, to enemies, to base deceivers; 'give it to *Me*, who from eternity has loved you and who died that you might live!' When you have reflected on these things, my dear friend, God grant that you may be disposed to repeat and to sing those sweetly evangelical words:

'Jesus, lover of my soul,
Let me to thy bosom fly.'

And forget not an humble servant of your Saviour, who watches over the *lambs* of the flock of Christ.

"To Miss H. M." B. C. CUTLER."

Such were the missives from his pen, and the overflowings

of his heart filled with love to Jesus, which were gladly received by friends here and elsewhere.

That he knew well how to counsel those of riper years, appears in the following extract of a letter, dated January 14, 1824, and addressed to Miss B——, (a relative):

"H. and I have formed a complete picture of you in the mansion-house of M., with no cares and no sorrows, but those which appertain to your own soul, and the souls of others. I suppose you have a class in Sunday-school, and strive to build up, by prayer and bright example, the church to which you belong, and enjoy its ordinances. By enjoying, I do not mean to be in raptures, and in the ecstacies of devotion, but in an humble, emptied, self-abasing and Christ-exalting frame. You will truly enjoy the ordinances of God's house, if you are permitted to go, feeling as if you were the very least Christian there; and even not meet to be called a Christian, if you creep into God's house, hardly daring to go, and yet, Esther like, fearing to stay away! Oh! if God has spoiled all your fine thoughts about yourself, and all your great expectation of being an exalted Christian, and of outshining the cold Christians around you, so that you can sit at the feet of any disciple of Christ, then you should bless him, even if it were with words of anguish. The sick need a physician, and can have one, but the well will never apply. . . . . . In my little church are pious people, who do not 'restrain prayer before God.' I have made several calls to-day, and had prayer in each house. I have great hopes that the gospel will be experienced in its power among us. My people are taught to seek for 'a change of heart,' and acceptance with Christ. Pray for me, and you shall not be forgotten by

"Your affectionate brother, B. C. C."

His fervent breathing after the influences of the blessed Spirit upon his work, was not unnoticed by a prayer-hearing God, and in May of the same year, we find him writing to one of the Ward family (in New York), with which his Sister Julia was connected by marriage:

"I am earnestly desirous of being a channel through which the Holy Ghost may pour forth his blessed influences upon my little flock. Thanks be to God he has not left me without a witness, that he has used so worthless a vessel for this purpose of mercy.

"One young man has experienced religion in the most delightful and unquestionable manner, and one young woman, about twenty years of age. Twelve adults have been baptized, with more or less evidence of genuine piety. Fifty infants have been baptized, and twenty-eight persons admitted to the Holy Sacrament. My aim has been to humble the sinner; then, to exalt the Saviour, and then to promote holiness.

"Ministers are God's clouds; some are made to rain upon fruitful fields, and others to rain upon wildernesses, deserts, and the ocean itself.

"But is one cloud better than another? Certainly not. God has placed me over fields white for the harvest, and some have been gathered to the praise of his holy name! He shall have all the glory, and I will take all the shame of my short-comings, back-slidings, and infirmities. The Lord bless you prays!

"Your unworthy brother,

B. C. CUTLER."

"P. S.—Our church is full, and we are too poor to enlarge it; but the Lord will provide ways and means."

Even while these words were penned, the hearts of the people were moved to make the necessary enlargement, and, before the close of the year, a wing was added to the church building, in order to provide seats for the increased number of worshippers. Thus, the Lord's hand was not straitened, even in temporal things, and the hour of their extremity proved to be God's opportunity.

About this time, affliction *again* entered Mr. Cutler's family circle, in the death of Mrs. Samuel Ward, of New York. To his youngest sister (Mrs. McAllister), then at Savannah, he thus writes:

QUINCY, *December* 14, 1824.

"I wrote you, my beloved sister, soon after I arrived in New York, and I have written to you many times since, in spirit and intention.

"Keenly as we all have felt this dreadful stroke, you must have felt it still more so. Having last seen our dear, departed Julia; having looked upon her, and leaned upon her as a mother, and above all, being at such a distance from all of us, who, alone, can be expected to weep with you, you must have been overwhelmed. Oh, it was, and is, a heavy and solemn affliction!

"Not till I returned home and sat down to reflect, did I really estimate my loss, and really consider the object of this chastisement. . . . . My great desire has been, and still is, that this may be sanctified to my good. I think it has been. I think I feel more solemn, in view of my certain change. I think I desire to live more devoted to Christ, and more dead to the world. My castles of earthly comfort are dissolved, and I see an eternal world, as the proper object of my attention and concern.

"May this lead us to a *closer walk* with God; to seek his favor and our own salvation.

"Afflictions are blessed things when they lead us to God. But the same sun which melts wax, hardens clay! Let us endeavor, by the grace of Christ, to improve to our spiritual profit this present season.

"God is by it knocking at the door of our hearts, and saying, 'Be wise and consider your latter end.' My prayers are for you, my darling, that both you and your husband may yet become children of God. May he grant it for his mercy's sake!

"I went to the grave of our dear Julia. It was behind St. Thomas' Church, New York. I went into her room, and saw her picture; but ah! I saw not what will never be seen again in this world. My dear L., the city of New York has now no charms for me. What made it interesting is gone. She died a Christian, and a penitent Christian too.

"Your most affectionate brother, B. C. C."

On the 16th of March, 1825, the Rev. Mr. Cutler was admitted to the holy order of Priests in St. Ann's Church, Lowell, Mass., by the Rt. Rev. Bishop Griswold.

The Rev. Theodore Edson (minister of that parish, and in charge of the new church consecrated on that very day), was admitted, at the same time and place, to the same sacred function. The candidates were presented by the Rev. Dr. Jarvis, and a highly appropriate sermon was preached by the Bishop. The Rev. Dr. Gardiner assisted in the services.

Of all the group who stood at and within that chancel, on that day, none remain on earth save the Rev. Dr. Edson, who still abides the faithful and zealous rector of the same church around which clustered his earliest affections.

The shadows of the evening-time of life fall upon his path as he ministers at the same altar, while all the others have ascended to the perfect service of the upper sanctuary, with its perennial and unhindered praise.

The Rev. Mr. Cutler was now admitted to full rank as a standard-bearer in the church militant, and at a peculiar time. Worldliness and spiritual coldness had come like a blight upon the churches around him, and a subtle, but proud, rationalistic spirit was eating out of the Church the core of true piety. At such a crisis he clung in simple faith to the doctrines of the Cross, and elevated the standard of a Divine Saviour. His piety belonged not to a superficial or a fastidious generation, and with vigor he girded on the spiritual armor and

"High the gospel banner bore."

Surrounded by a skeptical atmosphere, he resisted all its temptations and lived in an element of his own, kept pure and healthy by the life-giving fountain above. Thus enabled to bring forth the pearls of gospel truth, he proclaimed to all, "Buy the truth, and sell it not!"

He delivered the message of his Master with great force and simplicity, as some of the old parish at Quincy can still testify. He was often privileged in private life to lead others out of their spiritual darkness, and bring them into the clear sunlight of the Saviour's presence. If any of our readers are out of the way from the path of righteousness, longing to walk therein, but stumbling at the free grace of God in Christ Jesus, let them read the following letter from Mr. Cutler's pen, addressed to a near relative, dated—

"QUINCY, *August* 12, 1825.

. . . . "You cannot be satisfied until you think God thinks well of you. If you only thought that in the sight of God you appeared well, then you could be happy. The law is beating and bruising you. Fly to Christ! wash by faith in the fountain of his blood; desire to be clothed from head to foot in *borrowed raiment*—the raiment of your Redeemer, and thus come before God. Look out of yourself. The great secret of religion is 'looking unto Jesus,' and following Jesus. Let the Christian have no separate character to establish, but making common cause with Christ and his people, give all diligence to be found in him. Let him be the hardest worker in the world, yet, after all, he must inevitably be a *bankrupt;* he must fail, break all to pieces, and lie at the mere mercy of that creditor, to whom he owes ten thousand talents. Now comes the freeness and fullness of the love of Christ. Just at the extremity, Jesus passes by! and, beholding the despair of the case, all his bowels of compassion move, and he exclaims, 'Be of good cheer, thy sins are forgiven thee;' 'rise and follow me.' Never will the poor wretch forget the compassion of the Saviour; never will he wish to rob him of the glory and joy of saving a lost sheep. And there is more joy in the presence of the angels of God over one sinner that repenteth, than over ninety-and-nine which need no repentance.

"Such views as these, dear ——, are sunshine to the soul! They are simple, and so much the better. . . . . . I often wish you were here, and wonder whether you would be able to sit under such foolish preaching as mine; whether you would not steal off on Sunday morning to Brother S., who lives two miles off, and who is a true Puritan—whom, nevertheless, I love much. I have sent you the 'Lady of the Manor,' a new book highly recommended, and also a bundle of Andover tracts, which need no recommendation. The last you will do me the favor to distribute, and may the Lord bless them to the salvation of many. Adieu.

"Your affectionate B. C. Cutler."

In the year 1826 the church at Quincy had prospered to such a degree that it was found necessary to make another enlargement of the building, and accordingly another wing was added, to correspond with the former addition made two years previous. Of the state of things in and out of his church, we find a record in a letter to a friend, dated July 17, 1826:

"I came here in 1822. Of eighteen hundred inhabitants, it was supposed not five persons were Trinitarian. It was frequently said there was not one person in my church who was not a Unitarian. There were seven communicants, and perhaps twenty families. Religion was at a low ebb, indeed. It was considered a cold region even by those who would not themselves be called warm with the love of Christ. Lectures and evening meetings were bitterly opposed; and every thing like vital religion, was counted one degree above insanity! But God has blessed us beyond our most sanguine expectations! The congregation has become larger and larger, until we have had to enlarge the building twice. My salary has gradually increased. We have purchased an organ. We have a parish library of the most approved religious books, among which are two sets of Scott's Family Bible, which are always out. We have a Sunday-school of fifty scholars and ten teachers, and a Bible-class, well attended. All opposition has ceased against evening lectures, and we have them regularly in the church. We have a female prayer-meeting, and two missionary societies.

"I carried into Boston, recently, forty dollars for the American Education Society, from the sewing circle of our church. We have not been left without a witness that God is gracious, and we have now sixty or seventy communicants! The Lord be praised for all!

"I write this to the praise of evangelical truth, which I have tried to preach, and of gospel grace, for which I have not ceased to pray. Prudence and patience, God has enabled me to exercise, although not congenial to my nature. But God forbid that I should lead you to think that I am any thing more than 'the voice of one crying in the wilderness!' Tell my dear Brother Charles not to be too much engrossed in business. Busy men are sometimes stopped short for ever, and from the counting-house summoned at once to the presence of God.

"Yours, with Christian affection, B. C. C."

In November of this year we find Mr. Cutler absent in New York, for a short time. He was on his way to Philadelphia, as a delegate to the General Convention of the Protestant Episcopal Church. From the dwelling of the then well-known Mr. Bethune, "whose praise was in all the churches," he pens a few lines to his beloved companion:

New York, *November* 3, 1826.

. . . . "By the goodness of God, I am seated at a table which has fed many a prophet and many a poor wayfaring man; where I see holiness and hospitality, and many things which impress deeply upon my mind the truth of these words: 'It is better to trust in the Lord, than to put any confidence in man!' . . .

"Yesterday I saw Dr. Milnor, and Mr. Meade, of Virginia, and dined with Rev. Manton Eastburn; visited the Repository of the Bible Society, and took my seat at a meeting of the Directors in the afternoon. . . . . In the Convention for choice of a Bishop in Pennsylvania there was a drawn battle between the two parties. Mr. Meade, of Virginia, has twenty-seven votes out of fifty-three. This is good news to me. But parties and battles, etc., etc., I shudder at. *Peace*, peace! the blessed Saviour left with us. . . .

"Your —— ——, B. C. C."

In the spring of 1827 Mr. Cutler went (at the Bishop's request) on a missionary tour to Maine, and spent a month in the town of Saco (fifteen miles west of Portland). While it was beneficial to his health, it was not without profit to his own soul, and proved a great spiritual benefit to those around him. He has said himself: "I shall never forget one season of prayer that I had, while very solitary in this place! It was not a mere frame; it was as if my mind had been awakened to see and receive in all their fullness the promises of the gospel; that God was my guardian, my shield, and my exceeding great reward! I enjoyed a peace of mind which is remembered with gratitude; and this is the inference I draw from it: That the servants of God may go out upon solitary services of his, trusting to 'him for consolation! yea, for a peace which passeth understanding!'"

In a note to Mrs. Cutler (dated Saco, May 3, 1827), he speaks of seeing some fruits of his labors there:

"Here," he writes, "are the right materials to build up a church with—all orthodox and evangelical persons; the young men want none but a pious and faithful minister—'*none else need apply;*' they are not all Christians, but all know what the truth is. . . . How cheering is it that our pulpits are so faithfully supplied as you say mine has been, and that our people love to have it so. . . . At sunrise I took a long walk down the banks of the Saco, rejoicing with

Nature in the appearance of the sun. It is clouding up again to-night. But why complain? What matters it if the rain pelt against our windows—our hearts must not be troubled! God can make sunshine there! Heaven bless you!

"Prays —— ——, B. C. C."

The seed sown in this portion of God's vineyard was not in vain. Mr. Cutler was probably unconscious of the extent of the good he accomplished; but in the wondrous providence of God, the clergyman who succeeded him in this place—afterward the revered Bishop of the Diocese of New York—stood over his earthly remains, thirty-five years later, in the city of Brooklyn, N. Y., and testified in the most affectionate manner to the value of Mr. Cutler's labors during this short period, and to his admiration of their influence.

"His name was in every body's mouth, and everywhere the warmest and most grateful references were made to his public teaching and to the wonderful, kindly, animating, engaging influence which he carried about with him in his private intercourse. In a few weeks he seemed to have done the work of months, or of years. In a place where our church had been wholly unknown, he had taken the somewhat ample, but disorganized materials, and cemented them together; he had breathed the breath of life into them, and given them a character in their own eyes, and in the eyes of the community; he had set their feet in the true path; he had turned their faces in the right direction and given them high aims and high hopes."*

After his return from the eastward, Mr. Cutler pursued the even tenor of his way in the rounds of parish duty. During the summer the happiness of the family circle at the parsonage was increased by the arrival of his sister and her family from Savannah, and at one time during the season, their fond mother greeted her children—all who were then living—under the roof of her eldest son.

* See "Son of Consolation," p. 113.

His social spirit evidently delighted in these gatherings of cherished relatives, and his only regret was that he did not turn these visits to the spiritual profit of all. Yet, while in his humility he took a low estimate of the value of his own example and intercourse, there is abundant testimony to his faithfulness in every relation of life. The sister, to whom allusion is made above, will not soon forget how kind and faithful he was, when she was at a distance from her early home. It was only a year or two before this visit was made to Quincy that he wrote her the following letter :

"MY DEAREST LOUISA— . . . . Savannah, after all, may be your spiritual birthplace, my dear L., and you may yet have reason to bless God to all eternity for carrying you there. We are led, indeed, as the blind, 'by a way that we know not.' Oh, what treasures may not the Lord be reserving for our dear family—treasures of grace, treasures which neither moth nor rust can corrupt! If I could only see you and my dear brother brought into the fold, into the ark, then I should rejoice indeed! Yes, melt up your life in a crucible, and see whether one grain of pure gold survives the fire! You have, doubtless, like us all, been living in vanity; have forgotten him who made you, him who redeemed you, him who offers to sanctify you; and God Almighty grant that you may now be coming to your senses; that you may now be preparing to go to Jesus. And what now is your duty, dear L.? Your duty is to go to Jesus Christ in secret prayer! Pray, 'Lord Jesus, take from me my wicked, abominable heart, and give me "a new one." Here, dear Saviour, I give myself, a sinner, to thee! I give thee myself, soul and body; my time, talents, influence—all! I desire to fly from the wrath to come, and cling to thy Cross. There would I nail my follies, my sins, my hopes of false glory and pleasure. Henceforth I would be a holy vessel, sanctified and meet for my Master's use. Oh, my dear Saviour! wash me in thy blood; wash away all my sins; clothe me in thy righteousness; breathe upon me, and infuse into me thy meek and lowly spirit!' . . . . This, dear L., is the simple river of Jordan. Go, then, and wash in it seven times; yea, seventy times seven, and thou shalt be clean. I say this with as much confidence as Elisha said it to Naaman. Thou hast no proud reasonings, as the Syrian had; but let not any worldly thing keep thee away. 'A burned child dreads the fire;' do you dread the world, and escape from it, as Lot out of Sodom, and flee to Christ. You will have the poor prayers of dear H. and myself. She sends you and your husband much love; not more than your brother sends. Oh, how shall I pray, that I may embrace you next summer as a sister indeed!

"Yours, most affectionately, B. C. C."

But let us look at Mr. Cutler in his relation to his flock. On Christmas Day, 1827, being the centennial anniversary of the church at Quincy, he preached an appropriate sermon, giving a valuable historical sketch of the parish, and exhorted his people to stand fast in the faith of the gospel. On the border of another century of parochial existence, he entreated them to be faithful to the memories of the past; not to rely too much upon their "admirable forms," and too little upon the adorable Head of the Church and the Holy Spirit. "The purity of the Church," said he, "depends upon the power of Christ and the continual influences of the Holy Spirit; forms, without prayers fervent and constant, and doctrines, without practice careful and consistent, will bring reproach rather than defence. The *gospel*, under which you have been 'born again,' brought into a holy and happy walk before God; which has borne, as upon eagle's wings, the souls of the faithful through much tribulation safe into the kingdom of heaven; which has sustained its believers amidst the 'violence of fire,' and strengthened the martyrs who have shed their blood in its defence; which has been torn, in defiance of earth and hell, from the unhallowed embrace of error and corruption, and set once more upon the golden candlestick—the Church, this gospel, determine, by God's grace, to keep in this church. Without it, the church will crumble to the dust; and with it, flourish in immortal youth!

"As Episcopalians, our duties are peculiar. We have received, through many dangers, the oracles of God and the scriptural liturgy of this church. The lives and the wealth of many, gone to their long home, have been devoted to the preservation and perpetuity of this church. It has descended from generation to generation as an inheritance to us, enclosing, as its precious charge, the pure Gospel of Christ, breathing it in all its forms and offices ; displaying it in all its creeds and articles, and defending it in all its counsels and ministrations. The forms of our church are not necessary to acceptable prayer, nor necessary for 'saints made perfect in heaven ;' but they seem to be important for saints imperfect on earth, and well calculated to preserve the spirit of devotion amidst all the fluctuations of feeling and sentiment in the church and in the world."

[Mr. Cutler here sounded the key-note of that interest in missions, which, in an ever-ascending scale of harmony and force, characterized his whole ministerial course.]

"The friends of religion have spared no expense in furnishing this church with the means of grace ; let us be ready to furnish others with the same liberality ; let destitute churches in this State and in the Western forests never plead in vain ; and even should the cry come to our ears from perishing millions over the waters, let us remember that the cries of this very church were heard for fifty years continually across the Atlantic, and that three thousand miles of ocean afforded no excuse for withholding aid ; 'freely ye have received, freely give.'"

This sermon proved to be one of great interest ; was immediately printed at the request of the people, and had a wide-spread circulation.

At the close of this century sermon, the following anthem was sung. It was composed for the occasion by a parishioner, who (to use Dr. Cutler's own language) "was a powerful auxiliary in raising up the church from the sleep and dust of ages :"

"Awake, my harp, 'tis holy ground !
But let thy notes be deep and low ;
For those, who raised these altars round,
Sleep in their robes of death below.

"This day an hundred years have run
  Since those whose earth beneath us lies;
To Thee, Eternal Three in One,
  Here first bid hallowed anthems rise.

"Their tuneful tongues have turned to dust;
  Their crumbling stone itself decays;
But hark! the spirits of the just
  Surround thy throne perfecting praise.

"'Tis holy tide—the shepherds, led
  By Bethlehem's star, pursued their way,
And found the manger and the shed,
  Wherein the sleeping Jesus lay.

"Come, Holy Spirit, and excite
  Our hearts of clay to love and fear;
And lead us, by the day-star's light,
  To seek our Lord and Saviour here. L. M. S."

In January, 1828, Mr. Cutler made an address at a missionary meeting at St. Paul's, Boston, which will not be forgotten by those who heard it.

Let it be remembered that at this time the Protestant Episcopal Church had not awoke to a sense of its high privileges, weighty responsibility, and obvious duty in sending the gospel to the Heathen.

The Church Missionary Society in England had been doing a noble work for years; with disinterested zeal and catholic spirit they endeavored to give an impulse to the cause of missions on this side of the Atlantic, and in 1817, authorized their Secretary (the Rev. Josiah Pratt) to write to Bishop Griswold, and offer the sum of two hundred pounds "to encourage the contributions of the friends of the church," in case an American Episcopal Missionary Society should be formed.

Most interesting correspondence between the Church Missionary Society and the venerable Bishop White and Bishop Griswold is still on record. In 1820 the General Convention met, and at this session "The Protestant Episcopal

Missionary Society in the United States for Foreign and Domestic Missions" was formed. Very little, however, since that date had been accomplished, and Mr. Cutler's ardent spirit was oppressed by such apparent sloth and negligence. He longed for the extension of the Redeemer's kingdom throughout the world, and for the free and full proclamation of the blessed gospel everywhere. It was at the meeting referred to above, that Mr. Cutler gave vent to his feelings. His friends tell us it was a memorable scene, and every heart present was stirred up. By his eloquence and force, he produced a total change in the tone and temper of the meeting. Glowing remarks followed, and a large sum was contributed for missionary purposes.

After some introductory remarks, " Mr. President," said he, " we are no longer allowed to think that we may sleep through a long religious profession and die in peace! Whatever has been done in times past can be no criterion now. The Lord has, as far as we can see, poured out his spirit upon the churches; the power of the world has been thrown off, and the different tribes of the household of faith are arming for the good fight—nay, more, are fighting!

" And soon the curse shall be pronounced. Curse ye Meroz; curse ye bitterly, the inhabitants thereof; because they came not to the help of the Lord against the mighty. This curse may be written upon our walls—may consume our churches! Why are we the last in Christ's dominion to the work of the Lord? We who have got the true church! the Divine government! the holy priesthood! the peculiar people! May it not be because our pulpits do not their duty? because the ministers of the church do not preach to the people the necessity of this fruit of their faith? We, my brethren, are not to sleep in this work! We have, once a year, a missionary harangue, which is but a decent compliance with the spirit of the times; but do we preach, and pray, and converse about perishing souls in heathen lands?

Do we read to our people the reports which our missionary sentinels are continually sending out from every side? Do we spread before our people, in faithful lines, the actual suffering of hundreds of millions of the human family? I speak from observation! I speak from experience, from conviction, from sorrow and shame! We do not! And why we do not, I am utterly at a loss to say! Why we have not set in motion that holy spirit among our people; why we have not moved that mass of wealth; why we have not roused up that heavenly zeal, that consecrates houses and lands, wife and children to the work of the Lord, I am utterly unable to say! Has the command, 'Go, preach the gospel to every creature,' been blotted out of the Bible? No! Have we done all that our means will allow! have we furnished our men and our money for this most holy war! Oh, no! I tell it, and I blush for the church of my fathers! Not one dollar; not one man has embarked on the bosom of our waters for a heathen land! I speak of the church in this single State, and speak of the church as a body! Individuals in our communion have thought and felt! The example of our neighbors, their awakening appeals, have reached the walls of our houses, if not of our churches, and prayers have been offered and vows made; but, alas! when an Episcopalian has cut off from his hard earnings a generous portion for a suffering and sinking world, to whom has he carried it? To another household! and what is the language of such a transaction? 'Here is my gift.' 'We have no altar for such an offering. We have no men among us who are willing to go out among the Heathen! We have no mission in operation.'

"'How is this?' replies the receiver. 'You who have the Divine succession; who have the true church! you who have the incomparable liturgy; who have the scriptural articles!'

"Mr. President, for fifty years, the Society for Propagating the Gospel in Foreign Parts, sent missionaries to our shores; for fifty years they annually levied contributions upon Episcopalians in England, to plant the church in this land. One of their missions I have been sent, under God, to revive, and upon this church alone, they bestowed in all thirteen thousand dollars. They had missions also in Newfoundland, New York, Delaware, and even in Georgia. What has the church done in return? British Episcopalians have done more; they have offered us two hundred pounds to begin a mission, and have actually sent more than five hundred pounds over to this country to push the church into our Western forests; to send the Ark of the Covenant, with our tribes, which are wandering toward the setting sun.

"And here we are still! And here we shall live and die, unless we make some vigorous efforts, some fervent prayers, some noble offerings upon this holy altar.

"It is a new year! Let it be an honorable new year to our church! Let it be said, the year 1828 was the birthday of Episcopal benevolence. It requires no prophet's eye to see the signs of the times. The church has begun to awake. Missions are inevitable! We shall have missionaries and stations and pulpits and presses, all in operation for this glorious work. But how long, O Lord! how long must we wait?

"I well remember that ten years ago the sounds which I have uttered this night were uttered to others. I well remember the blast which the trumpet blew into the dull ears of neighboring Christians. I heard them reproach themselves. I saw their sloth published from their own housetops. They confessed and forsook their sins, and rising slowly, but with unanimity and determination, they have redeemed the time. [Referring to the American Board of Commissioners for Foreign Missions.—Ed.] Mr. President, this same spirit, the Lord seems bestowing upon us. It will surely prevail! God grant your eyes may see what your heart has long desired! that all here may see it, and often be permitted to assemble and rejoice together!"

But Mr. Cutler did not rest here. In his own parish he established a missionary prayer-meeting, which was held on the first Monday evening of every month. During that year he enjoyed two very interesting visits from Mr. Bronson, a missionary to Ohio, and Mr. Robertson, a missionary to Greece. These visits resulted in much good; and a meeting at the parsonage, just before the departure of Mr. Robertson, was very solemn and affecting.

In a letter to his wife, then at Montreal on a visit, Mr. Cutler writes, under date of September 22, of this year:

> "One of Bishop Chase's right-hand men from Ohio, the Rev. Mr. Bronson, has been in Boston, and I induced him to spend a Sunday with me at Quincy, and such a house-warming as he gave our church, it would have done your heart good to have witnessed. He preached the gospel with true unction, and I have not heard our blessed Saviour preached before in such a manner for years. It was simple, sincere, soul-felt gospel truth. His text was, "They shall cry unto the Lord because of the oppressors, and he shall send them a Saviour, and a great one, and he shall deliver them."—Isa. xix. 20. The sermon was full of soul, as the man himself was, and yet it was the farthest possible from oratory of any kind. . . . He stirred us up, and did it so sweetly, that all were charmed. In the evening he collected a handsome sum for his mission."

The extension of the Redeemer's kingdom was a subject very near to Mr. Cutler's heart.

"I rejoice," he says, "when I reflect on the missionaries of the Cross attacking the kingdom of Satan on all sides; see them buffeting the shores of Greenland, sweltering on the burning arid sands of Africa, piercing through the shades of American forests, climbing the walls of God's ancient city, and enjoying their triumphs in Western Europe!"

But Mr. Cutler did not forget that "charity begins at home." We see he did not, like too many others, let it end there.

The seed of the Divine Word he planted in many towns in the vicinity of Quincy, as opportunity offered. The *Gospel Advocate* has on its records an interesting report concerning the Church at Bridgewater, Mass., which he read before the Massachusetts Episcopal Missionary Society. The Episcopalians of Hanover, Dedham, Worcester and others, could testify to his zeal in their behalf. He was truly among the number of those of whom the prophet has said, "Blessed are ye that sow beside all waters!" His friends observed his spirit, and at one time he received from some unknown individuals sixty dollars, to constitute him a member of the American Bible Society and also a member of the Missionary Society of the Protestant Episcopal Church.

In the town of Quincy Mr. Cutler labored for the good of others, even outside of his parish. Once every week he was found at the alms-house feeding the hungry, and alleviating in every way the distress of the stricken children of poverty, and gladly preaching the glad tidings of the gospel to many a weary and downcast sinner, and strengthening the faith of those who believed.

Those of our readers who have read the tract, *The Poor Cripple*, written by Mrs. Frances Parker, will get an excellent view of Mr. Cutler's labors of love in this old alms-house.

Mrs. Parker accompanied her friend and relative, the rector of Quincy, in one of his weekly visits to this place, and was led by this interview to portray the riches of Divine grace, so marvellously displayed in one of the inmates.

But let us hear Mr. Cutler's account in a note to his wife:

"I went last week to see Nat Field. He had gone to bed; the room dark and desolate. You know how deformed even his face is; he had been neglected, and his beard was long and black; yet, when he saw me, the first words were, like a gushing fountain. 'Oh, Mr. Cutler!' said he, 'I am very happy! I enjoy myself very much!' 'You are not alone,' I said. 'Oh! no, sir. God is with me! I am ready to die or to live, according to his will.' After conversing and praying with him, I rode home, well satisfied that God fills the desires of the heart, and he alone. . . . . My dear H., happy will it be for us if we take a seat by Nat Field, in the kingdom of heaven."

Mr. Cutler loved to labor among the poor, and there was not a single plan put in operation for the moral or spiritual good of men around him, in which he did not unite heart and soul. And when he could not *do* much, he gave the kind word, and manifested that hearty interest in the welfare of others, which bound many a heart to him with cords of love never to be broken.

His motto seemed to be, "*Homo sum, et nihil humani est a me alienum puto*," and in his daily rounds of duty, he wore it as a signet upon his right hand.

With such a spirit he, both directly and indirectly, accomplished much good.

One of the most *telling* incidents in the whole history of his parochial life in Quincy, related by an early friend and parishioner (L. M. Sargent, Esq.), we give below:

"Dr. Cutler was a most amiable Christian gentleman. He certainly possessed the happiest talent for converting sinners from their evil ways, rather by the employment of that moral suasion which has been accounted so effectual in the matter of temperance, than by holding the terrors of the law over the heads of his hearers.

"This good man and valued friend has gone to his reward, and I may speak of him without reserve. The expression of his countenance was remarkable for its benignity; and his enunciation was so clear and distinct, that every word told upon the ears of his congregation, with little effort to the speaker.

"Riding, one day, in the direction of the stone quarries, in Quincy, I saw my friend returning, as I conjectured, from his parochial visits to some of his poor parishioners. As we drew nearer to each other, I perceived he had something in his hand, which I soon discovered to be a pair of chickens. 'Good morning, my friend,' said I, 'what do you ask for your chickens?' 'You are not rich enough to purchase them,' he replied. He then proceeded to tell me their brief history. As he was passing the humble dwelling of a poor woman, whose husband had been very intemperate, she called after him, and holding up these chickens, begged him to accept them. 'I told her,' said he, 'she could not afford to give away such a fine pair of chickens.' 'Mr. Cutler,' said she, with a sad expression, 'you will hurt my feelings if you do not take them. I have fatted and picked them on purpose for you. It is the only return I am able to offer for the very great service you have lately done me and my little children.' 'I am not aware,' said Mr. Cutler, 'of having done you any service of late.' 'Sir,' said the poor woman, 'you have reformed my husband.' 'There must be some mistake,' said Mr. Cutler; 'I knew your husband was intemperate; but I have never said a word to him on the subject.' 'I know you never have,' said she; 'if you had, his pride is such that it might have made matters worse. It is now more than two months since he left off. It has happened, oddly enough, that often, when you have stepped in to say a few kind words to us, he has been taking his dram, or taking down his jug, or putting it back again. About two months ago, just after you went out, he went to the door, and, to my astonishment, poured nearly a pint of rum out of his jug on to the ground, and said: "Debby, rinse out that jug with hot water. I have done! I can't stand that man's looks any longer. If Mr. Cutler would look savage, I shouldn't mind it; but he looks so sad, and so benevolent all the while, when he sees me taking a dram, that I know what he means, just as well as if he preached it in a sermon, and I take it very kindly of him that he didn't give me a long talk." I know you will take the chickens, Mr. Cutler,' said the poor woman."

Mr. Sargent says (in a note to us, in 1864): "I can see him now, as I saw him on that fine June morning; the benevolence of his Christian heart brightening every feature, and amusingly blended with an expression of exultation over the prize which he held in his hand. He was a most amiable and faithful disciple, and his character is well exhibited in John xiii. 23."

Mr. Cutler often journeyed for his health; but unless he could return soon to his accustomed labors in the vineyard of his Master, he became restless and uneasy. Toward the close of the year 1828, he makes a record in his journal, thus:

"Of one thing I am convinced by this late journey, that 'to have nothing to do' is by no means desirable. Very much pleasure, my fancy pictured, would be afforded me; some I certainly have found, but not of the kind I supposed; such as I might find in abundance at home. Henceforth and for ever let pleasure be forgotten! It is a phantom of the mind! Let me seek the kingdom of God and his righteousness."

The year 1829 opened with fair prospects for Mr. Cutler and his flock. Before it closed, a dark cloud had overspread their horizon. On the 9th of February, Mr. Cutler makes a full record in his journal:

"For some years past, it has been my custom to spend my birthday (February 6) in retirement and reflection. It happened this year on Friday, and I could not spare that day from my sermon. I now sit down to reflect upon the past year. May the Spirit of God bring all things to my remembrance. Health! What reason have I to bless God that he has given me such good health as I now have. Twelve years ago (in 1817), when preparing for college, I was supposed to be in a decline, and I was so weak I was unable to read family prayers aloud. But then I felt that if God had any thing for me to do, he could make me as strong as Samson. He has found something for me to do, and has enabled me to go through it with ease. I can preach twice on the Sabbath without injury, and feed my Sunday-school beside. God be praised! He is my God, and I will praise him; he is the God of my fathers, and I will bless him; he filleth my mouth with good things, making me young and lusty as an eagle! Now I can trust in his covenant mercy, that at the last I shall have all my desire and all my hope—which is a useful life, if possible a peaceful one; to see the church in which I am placed rising from the dust, and putting on the Saviour's righteousness, zeal and love; to know that the comfortable Gospel of Christ is truly preached, truly received and truly followed in our church; and to see it alive to the wants of the world, and active in supplying them. Good Friday was a memorable day last year. There was much solemnity and many tears at the supper of the Lord. Easter was also spent with comfort. The preaching was well received.

"Religion has been evidently gaining ground in the parish this year, and we have some good fruits, although we see clearly that the enemy has been sowing tares. The Bible-class has been kept up with spirit, and has been of as much use to the teacher as to the scholars. I feel grateful to God and to my dear young friends; particularly do I esteem it a great favor that my dear and valued communicant, Miss M—n, has taken a seat at my board, together with her own pupils. Amid many discouragements, a few such things as these have been cordials."

In another diary, Mr. Cutler frequently speaks of discouragements, but "Heaven," he says, "doubtless intended them for my good, and I have thought that to make a young minister flourish in his parish, there must be two or three powerful opposers—a few supercilious scorners, one or two Deists, and a few tale-bearers, backbiters, etc.! But blessed is he who overcomes evil with good!"

He speaks of it as one of his trials, that he was seven years in an Unitarian atmosphere. "God be praised that I did not sink under it. Flattery I had little of; opposition I bore, not without complaint; it seemed as if I was such a poor, dwarfish plant, that I could exist in a climate as spiritually cold as Greenland!"

But there was also a bright side to the picture. One Sabbath evening he sits down and writes in this strain to his wife (then absent):

"I have now finished the duties of the day. I could not help feeling happy after church this afternoon. To have the confidence and affection of my people is to me a greater luxury than an ocean of wealth!

"But what are the smiles of Christian friends compared with the smiles of Jesus and of God? One sweet smile which faith could discern on the Saviour's dear face, would make up for months and years of toil! Oh! am I destined to know and love this dear, precious Saviour? are the treasures of his grace, the depths of his love, the extent of his compassion, to be revealed to me? I am indeed unworthy of them, but they would be my glory.

"Pray for me, not that I may be great, nor rich, nor learned, nor *strong*, but that Christ may reveal himself to me in all his suitableness to the sinner's wants. I know but little of him now; but he can come to me; he can touch my lips with a live coal from off his altar."

We may safely ask our readers to produce an instance of more genuine humility and fervent love toward our adorable Saviour, than is here combined and laid in one offering, at his sacred feet. It reminds us of the spirit of a Fenelon or Madame Guion, or, to speak more correctly, of the breathings of soul with which the saintly Henry Martyn made fragrant even the deserts of Asia!

With the interior life of faith, Mr. Cutler combined untiring activity in the Lord's service, and this produced the beautiful harmony of his character.

To show how he was appreciated by others at this period, we are permitted to lay before our readers the following letter from an eminent minister of Christ, who was of another branch of the Church of God. It is placed out of its chronological order, but it can be no violation of good taste to produce it here:

"BRAINTREE, MASS., *February* 23, 1863.

"MY DEAR AFFLICTED FRIEND—I need not tell you that my heart was pained when my eye fell on the notice of your now sainted husband's death in the public papers. You are aware how dear he was to me, as doubtless to thousands more, for who could know him ever so slightly and not love him? . . . One of the choicest plants in God's earthly garden has been removed to that higher sphere of growth and fruitfulness, for which the great Gardener had been so long preparing it by most happy culture.

"I loved your husband not so much for his personal beauty and elegance, nor his genial and fraternal disposition, nor his all-pervading *spirituality* of mind (I fear) as for the ceaseless *activities* of his soul in the great work God had given him to do. He was absorbed in the love of Christ, in the love of souls, in the love of the saints, in the love of the Redeemer's kingdom, and all his energies were heartily devoted to whatever service promised a revenue of glory to his Saviour!

"The mind *will* run over the scenes of the past; and I cannot check its movements when it brings back the days, and months, and years, hallowed now by sweet remembrances of pleasures found in the social intercourse and devotional exercises of the period blessed to Quincy by his prayers and labors. Not only was Quincy blessed, but Braintree and other towns, by the noble and catholic spirit that animated his whole course. . . . He has reached the home of his most fervent aspirations—the blessed world he has thought of so much, pointed out to others so clearly, and prepared for so constantly.

"Will it not be delightful to meet him there, where he will no more say, 'I am sick;' where his heart will be no more depressed by surrounding wickedness, nor by the lukewarmness of his Christian brethren; where all sin and imperfection shall have passed away?

"My heart most deeply sympathizes with you, with the bereaved Church of Christ, and with a *world* no longer enjoying the prayers and labors of one of the holiest, loveliest men God has ever made for the benefit of the human family. . . .

"Most truly and affectionately yours, R. S. STORRS."

This letter requires no comment from us—a model as it is of Christian sympathy and love. The journals of Mr. Cutler are full of allusions to this dear friend, who lived so near him during all his rectorship at Quincy.

But Mr. Cutler was not destined to remain in this place. The current of his life was to be turned in another direction. Having done the will of God, he was now to suffer it; his faith was to be tested in other ways, and God was about to prove to him the truth of the promise, "I will lead them in paths that they have not known; I will make darkness light before them, and crooked things straight. These things will I do unto them, and not forsake them."

In June, 1829, after a period of unusual labor, Mr. Cutler was laid low by a severe and alarming illness. For three weeks he was in a critical condition, and life was almost despaired of; but by the 1st of July he had so far recovered as to be removed to the city of New York, at the earnest entreaty of his family relatives, and friends.

Of course, all public duties were suspended for a long time, and, on the brink of the grave, as he seemed to be, he gave up all hope of resuming ministerial labors in Quincy. His people would not listen to any thing like resigning his charge, and lived in hope that he would yet again return and break to them "the bread of life;" and it was not till nearly two years after this time, that this hope died away, and their beloved pastor, from a far distant State sent them a farewell letter, and formally resigned his rectorship. This letter will appear in the next chapter; meanwhile, let us read his own account:

"While in Quincy, I had various invitations to other

churches, but I was opposed to removal, and remained at my post until declining health and a hectic fever, in June, 1829, drove me from that part of the country. I left Quincy, July 1, 1829, wrapped in blankets, in a close carriage, with a physician, my wife and sister; and as I rode away from the place

> 'I looked at sun, and sky, and plain,
> As what I ne'er might see again.'"

But "God's ways are not as our ways," and Mr. Cutler stood again, in a few years, in the pulpit of a new church, built upon the same spot; and yet again, as our merciful Father would have it, thirty years later, in 1860, with uncovered head, and a heart almost overwhelmed with gratitude, he passed beneath the porch and along the aisle, with an imposing array of revered brethren in the Lord, gathered there to consecrate another new Gothic church (of stone), which should be a lasting memorial to future generations. How wonderfully, how graciously God had led him! and as he then looked upon the countenances of many there, he could say of his spiritual children, as Jacob said to Joseph, "I had not thought to see thy face again, and lo! God hath showed me thy seed" unto the third generation.

Mr. Cutler further says, in 1834: "I should never have left Quincy, had my health continued. I should say to young men who are happily settled in their first parishes, let them be your last. [This opinion, however, was modified and changed with increasing age and experience.—ED.] My labors in the parish were much blessed, for which thanks be to God! I found in it eight or nine communicants, and left in it ninety! The church building was enlarged twice, and before I left, a subscription was opened to build a new church, which was accomplished by my successor, Rev. W. T. Potter. A most beautiful church was consecrated November 27, 1832."

The tie which connected Mr. Cutler officially with his first parish, was, indeed, abruptly broken by the hand of God; but the living links of affection by which he was bound to the hearts of so many of God's children, were never sundered while life lasted. His correspondence with one family, at least, continued for a quarter of a century, and the names of Marston, Apthorp, and Sargent were ever hallowed in his memory with no small measure of esteem and regard.

On the walls of Christ Church, Quincy, there now rests an elaborate mural monument in memory of the Rev. Dr. Miller, which has been erected by one of his lineal descendants. Time's effacing fingers may crumble this marble into dust, or the building itself may disappear, but the name of *Cutler*, like that of the *first* rector, can never fade away from the remembrance of those who knew and loved him here, engraved, as it is, on the tablets of their hearts. His deeds of Christian love will be strung among the jewels of memory, lasting long in their preciousness, and his name will be handed down from generation to generation.

CHAPTER V.

JOURNEY TO SAVANNAH — TEMPORARY RESIDENCE AT SACO, ME. — A YEAR AT LEESBURG, VA.

1829–1831.

A MODERN writer has said, "We never feel Christ to be a reality until we feel him to be a *necessity*. Therefore God makes us feel that necessity. He tries us here, and he tries us there. . . . He afflicts us in ways which we have not anticipated. He sends upon us the chastisements which he knows we shall feel most sensitively. He pursues us when we would fain flee from his hand; and, if need be, he shakes to pieces the whole frame-work of our plans for life, by which we have been struggling to build together the service of God and the service of self, till at last, he makes us feel that Christ is all that is left to us."

In the year 1829, and during much of the two following years, Mr. Cutler's history could attest the truth of such an experience. Like Jacob, he was tempted to say, "all these things are against me," but God was only preparing the way for his servant's greater happiness and greater usefulness. After patience had had her perfect work, as we shall see, his Heavenly Father opened the way before him, and "set his feet in a large room."

At this particular period, however, every thing seemed dark to the eye of sense. Weary and worn, and in declining health, with no present or prospective pecuniary support, he was enabled, with the eye of faith, to look up to a merciful God for the supply of every want; to cast every burden at the feet of a compassionate Saviour, and to trust where he could not trace such providential dealings.

The prevailing sentiment of his heart was—

"The night is dark, and I am far from home,
Lead thou me on;
Keep thou my feet; I do not ask to see
The distant scene; one step 's enough for me."

Mr. Cutler slowly recovered from his severe illness, and during his convalescence was at the house of his brother-in-law, Samuel Ward, Esq., in New York.

He considered his sickness "as a fatherly correction," and thought the Saviour was thereby saying to him, "I have somewhat against thee;" "repent and do thy first works."

In August, 1829, he took a trip to Saratoga, thence to Avon, N. Y., and going as far as Rochester and Niagara before his return.

His health being still impaired, and change of scene being the chief remedy prescribed by his medical adviser, we find him, during September, visiting Philadelphia, Baltimore and Washington.

By this journey, and the visits connected with it, he was much refreshed, both in body and mind. Especially did he enjoy intercourse with, and the preaching of many brethren, some of whom were old friends, and others of whom, were shining like stars in our ecclesiastical firmament, casting light upon the pathway of multitudes of souls.

He availed himself of the privilege of hearing the Rev. G. T. Bedell, D.D., then rector of St. Andrew's Church, Philadelphia. His reflections on the occasion are thus noted in his diary: "The preacher was in his element—the pulpit; he has very popular and useful talents; he makes you think and feel deeply!"

Again he turned his feet to the same sanctuary where he received the Holy Communion (in company with his wife, his cousins, S. W. and Mrs. H.), at the hands of this servant of God of blessed memory. The circumstances are peculiarly affecting, as for four months he had been detained from the Lord's table by sickness. The effect of the sermon on this day, he says, "was to convince men that the Cross of Christ was the great power of God to salvation; that man must look there in order to be moved. The excellence of Mr. B. appears to consist in his holding up a Saviour, and in his impressive delivery."

Mr. Cutler also enjoyed the ministrations of his early friend, the Rev. B. B. Smith, D. D., who was at this time the rector of a flourishing parish in that city. He speaks particularly of him at a later date. While in P. . . . he often went to see West's celebrated picture of "Christ Healing the Sick," which he thought "inimitable;" he further says of it, "it is a great privilege, and very profitable to the reflecting Christian, to see this picture." What would I have said had I seen the Saviour's majestic, yet meek and sorrow-chastened face on earth? That, let me say now in prayer."

On the 26th of September we find Mr. Cutler at Baltimore. After hearing a sermon from the Rev. Mr. Higbee, (a talented preacher who was officiating at St. Paul's Church,) on the text, "There is to be a resurrection both of the just and of the unjust," he complains of his own weakness of body and imperfection of worship, and says, "I am a babe; but in the resurrection I hope to have a body, powerful and incorruptible, in which I shall be able to worship God without distraction of thought, and to serve him without weariness. Oh! may this be a good hope—I need a complete and an almighty Saviour."

After visiting Washington, Mr. Cutler returned to Baltimore, to the hospitable abode of the Rev. J. P. K. Henshaw, D. D.

He called to see Mrs. Wyatt, the daughter of his predecessor, the Rev. Mr. Winslow, in Christ Church, Quincy. He also paid a visit to Carrollton, where the venerable Charles Carroll still lived. Being the sole survivor of the signers of the Declaration of Independence, Mr. Cutler eagerly embraced the opportunity of seeing him, and Mr. Carroll was equally pleased to converse with Mr. Cutler about Quincy, as the home of the Adamses, and especially of his worthy compatriot, the Hon. John Adams, Ex-President of the United States. The conversation naturally turned upon Jefferson, Franklin, and other noted men of the past age of the Republic, and this social interview, marked with the high-toned courtesy of Mr. Carroll, and usual frank cordiality of Mr. Cutler, was long remembered.

Early in October, Mr. Cutler turned his face homeward to the city of New York, enjoying another "spring by the way," as he rested a few days in the city of Brotherly Love, in precious interviews with his friend, the Rev. B. B. Smith, D. D., afterward the Bishop of Kentucky.

Saturday evening, October 10, 1829, he writes in his diary:

"I have spent this day with my friend and brother, Mr. Smith. He is always the Christian; he always approves himself as the minister of Christ. We united in prayer before leaving his house.

"*Oct.* 14.—Heard my friend, the Rev. Mr. Smith, preach on Sunday, and to-day attended his lecture, and was much edified. I had a good day on Friday last with Mr. Smith. He is a very excellent and delightful Christian, and one at whose feet I should always like to sit."

On Sunday, October 18, he listened to "a most useful and impressive sermon" from the Rev. S. H. Tyng, D. D., and the next day returned to New York.

In speaking of his own state of mind during the previous season, he says: "Death before me did not fill me with dread, neither did it fill me with joy. I was calm, and looking to Christ; I was (physically) very nervous, the least thing would upset me; the lively exercise of triumphant faith I certainly had not; the truth no doubt is, that if I am a Christian I am a very ordinary one; not that holy, self-denying, spiritualized believer, lover and follower of a crucified Master I ought to be. O God, give me more soul in thy service! O Lord, if right, give me more strength of body!"

Against this weakness of body Mr. Cutler strove earnestly, and many were the petitions he offered at the Throne of grace that it might be removed. But the only answer, vouchsafed, seemed to be: "My grace is sufficient for thee, for my strength is made perfect in weakness!"

The few lines which commence this chapter of his history are specially pertinent to his individual case. Let us read his own words, and then follow along the stream of his life, with its various windings, for two or three years, and see if this is not strictly true.

"Whoso is wise, and will observe these things, even they shall understand the loving kindness of the Lord!"

On the 24th of October, 1829, Mr. Cutler is seated in his chamber in New York, and makes this record, which reveals his whole condition:

"By the Lord's patient goodness I am brought to this period of life (thirty-one years and eight months), half the life of man; and my life has been one of mercy. Although, by the providence of God, I am at this moment without a dollar in my pocket, and without the means of making one, yet his mercy and goodness have placed me in such circumstances that I am cheerful and contented. God has promised that 'no good thing will he withhold from them that fear him!' God has commanded, 'Say ye to the righteous, It shall be well with him;' well in prosperity, well in adversity, well in life, and in death—at the judgment and in eternity. 'All things are *well* ordered and sure!'

He was then at the house of his brother-in-law, Samuel Ward, Esq. He soon accepted a pressing invitation from his beloved sister, Mrs. McAllister, to pass the coming winter at Savannah, Ga.; and late in November, in company with her and her children, Mr. and Mrs. Cutler sailed from New York in the ship Florian, Capt. Harrison, for that port.

When off Cape Hatteras they were not exempt from the usual experience of travellers on the sea, and a terrific gale, which lasted seventy-two hours, threatened to engulf them in the roaring waves. The whole party (including four children and three servants) expected every moment to be called into eternity. Again, just as the vessel had made Savannah Light, another fearful blow was experienced; and, though the passengers begged Capt. Harrison to hasten on to the city, with the foresight of a wise and cautious seaman, he put out to sea again, and another night of anxiety was passed. The event proved their commander right; for, as they passed up the bay in the morning, wrecks of vessels which had passed them were pointed out. Thus, after a trying passage of eleven days, Mr. Cutler reached his destined port.

"I felt in this voyage," he says, "the power of prayer, and I said, while entering the desired haven (Savannah), 'I shall walk softly before God all the days of my life.' The Sunday after, I preached in Christ Church, Savannah, from these words: 'What shall I render unto the Lord for all his benefits toward me?' How forcibly, during the storm, did these words possess my mind: 'The waves of the sea are mighty and rage horribly; but yet the Lord, who dwelleth on high, is mightier!'"

Mr. Cutler had now reached a delightful home, where the kindness and attention of all the McAllister family were unceasing. He found very agreeable society in his clerical brethren of that city—the Rev. Mr. Mott (who had been a classmate of his in Brown University, ten years previous to this date) and the Rev. Mr. Neufville, of Christ Church.

The Christmas season, which is enjoyed with such peculiar pleasure at the South, brought Mr. Cutler in contact with a host of relatives and friends. Merriment and good cheer abounded; and it was especially grateful to his heart to meet so many kindred in the flesh. But even this did not satisfy the yearnings of his soul after a higher fellowship. Unless he could hold intercourse with those who were bound together by ties of *Christian* love, he was disappointed. He thus speaks for himself: "I dined with a near relative, in company with all my relatives in this place; and though I think the season one calculated to inspire joyful feelings, and it is proper to cultivate social intercourse, yet it is next to impossible to meet people of the world on any ground of rejoicing which is not entirely temporal and trifling.

> "'Joy is a fruit that will not grow
> On Nature's barren soil;
> All we can boast, till Christ we know,
> Is vanity and toil.'"

The year with which this record closes had been an eventful one to Mr. Cutler, and to his family circle. He had been brought down to the gates of death, but raised up again. His brother, Mr. Francis Marion Cutler, had settled himself at Avon, Livingston County, N. Y., where he married Miss Caroline Martin, of that place. And his eldest sister, Eliza, who, since the decease of Mrs. Ward, had acted a mother's part to her motherless children, had accepted an offer of marriage from the celebrated Dr. John W. Francis, of New York, a man who had no superior in the medical profession. The affectionate sister and faithful daughter had now become the devoted companion of him whose name, both philanthropy and medical science love to cherish and honor.

From all these friends, as well as from his mother, whose advancing years made the parting, more than ever, a trial, Mr. Cutler was separated. But his best beloved friend, the partner of every joy and every sorrow, was at his side; and he was under the roof of a sister, whose spirit, so congenial with his own, shed many a ray of light and comfort along his path.

For all this he was grateful, indeed. He, in turn, was also able to administer the balm of healing comfort and consolation in Mr. McAllister's household, when sickness invaded it.

God was soon to lead them all "in a path they knew not;" and most truly, as far as regards the subject of this memoir, did our Heavenly Father "make darkness light before him," "and crooked things straight," in the path in which he led him.

In January, 1830, we find Mr. Cutler at the residence of Thomas S. Clay, Esq. (at Richmond, twenty miles from Savannah). Here he enjoyed an interview with a dear Christian friend, Miss Anne Clay, whom even to mention is to awaken in many, many hearts, both at the North and at the South, memories which will never die. So generous a heart, and so exalted a Christian, is rarely seen in any religious circle, and Mr. Cutler well knew how to appreciate it. His "kind host, Mr. Clay," urged a prolonged stay, but Mr. Cutler felt obliged to hasten back to Savannah. During February, he was quite ill again, and he thought himself fast sinking into the grave. To use his own language: "The same serious frame of mind continued, with more irritability of the nerves, and with a desire to preach to the last—to serve God and man with my latest breath. I, however, recovered, and thanks to God, kind friends have bountifully supplied all our needs. It is humiliating not to be able to make the fruits of one's labor supply all his temporal wants; but it is delightful to live by faith, and to trace the hand of God interposing in our behalf, and supplying, one by one, all our needs."

The month of March was spent at Charleston, S. C., with his cousin, Mrs. Charlotte Mitchell, where every kindness was lavished upon him with an unsparing hand.

Mr. Cutler was enabled to preach occasionally, during the winter, in the cities of Savannah and Charleston; and whenever at the plantations of any of his friends, he always took occasion to preach to the negroes, who assembled with delight to hear him. He began to think seriously of a return to continued public duty; but he could not readily decide whether he ought to return to his former parish, or to take the position of a missionary in "the Eastern Diocese," which, before he left the South, was offered to him. Bishop Griswold had, in strong terms, alluded to the dearth of ministers in his address to the Convention of that Diocese in 1829, and Mr. Cutler, for the first time, read the address while at the South, and it made a deep impression upon his mind. The Rev. Mr. Cutler had been Secretary of the Convention for several years previous, and his canonical relations were still with that diocese.

His determination was soon made, and the auspicious season having now arrived, he decided to return to the North. He had enjoyed exercise in the saddle all the winter, and now he determined (with the advice of Dr. Francis and many other friends) to travel to New York all the way on horseback.

Leaving his wife to return by sea with a party of friends, a month later, he set out upon his journey.

Our readers will not fail to be interested in the following account of it, which we find on an old and torn sheet of paper, written out in his own hand:

"*Savannah, Ga., April* 13, 1830.—I rose quite weak, having taken but little food for a day or two, and felt hardly able to sit upon my horse; but having appointed the time for my fellow-traveller(Mr. Ripley) to be ready, I could not shrink. But I almost wonder at myself for having the courage to leave my dearest friend and every comfort, and set out upon a journey of one thousand miles on horseback, when many persons might have thought my chamber the fittest place for me, and the most skillful physician declared to me it was a bold undertaking. But I have courage—I have undertaken it; it is the only thing I know of, which promises to restore my health. The Lord has appeared kindly to favor it, so far, and to him I commit the result. I am not very solicitous about the result, although I felt anxious to use the means. I know that my health is very seriously undermined, and my complaints are considered consumptive. I am glad I know this, for I would not be deceived; but I also know that if the Lord has any work for me to do yet on earth, he will make me strong enough to do it. Nothing is impossible with Him. I shall constantly pray for a blessing on the means I am now using, and thank him for every addition to my health. And why? Is this world so delightful a place to me? I know that if my life is spared, labor and sorrow, sin and suffering, will be my lot. I shall labor for Jesus Christ, and I shall sorrow to see but little fruit of my labors. I fear, from my corrupt heart, that I shall sin, and I know that I shall afterward suffer for it, in my heart and conscience at least. On the other hand, I hope, through the infinite mercy of God in Jesus Christ, that death, except the bodily pain, would be no death to me. I have long ago died to the *world*; I loathe myself for what of sin still remains in me, and I pray that through Christ I may gain the victory over Satan. I hope for me to die would be gain; but I follow an instinct of nature when I wish to get well.

"This day (April 13) I left Savannah in company with Mr. Ripley, who was in a gig, I being on horseback. We rode off from my dear wife and friends at 8 A. M., and after proceeding slowly for twelve miles, we alighted, unharnessed our horses, and sat down in the shade ; but Mr. R.'s horse being an unruly animal, we were soon obliged to go on. Four miles farther we found a tavern, kept by 'Keibler.' Here I was so much overcome by my ride that I begged to stop, and we remained till morning."

"*April* 14.—Started at 6 A. M. Rode (through woods beautifully variegated with flowers and animated with birds) twelve miles to breakfast at 'Grovenstein's ;' rode four miles to 'Mrs. Blake's,' and rested during the heat of the day. 3½ P. M., set out and rode thirteen miles to 'White's.' Kindly treated here, and I closed the evening with prayer in the family."

"*April* 15.—Started at 6 A. M. and rode to 'Reeves' to breakfast ; eleven miles farther to Jacksonboro' and rested ; and rode nine miles farther to 'Mrs. Brunell's' to sleep. Here I acted as chaplain, and tried to improve a family affliction."

"*April* 16.—Just as I was departing, Rev. Mr. Neufville rode up with Dr. Reid. With them we travelled that day. Here my horse was sick and lame. The Lord was better to me than my fears.

"On Saturday, 2 o'clock, April 17, we arrived at Augusta, Ga., one hundred and twenty miles from Savannah. All well ; my health improved."

"*Augusta, Ga., Sunday, April* 18.—Brother Neufville preached an excellent sermon before the Convention in the morning, and I preached in the afternoon on 'the moral death and resurrection of the sinner.' I am staying with Rev. Hugh Smith, rector of St. Paul's, here. Mr. S. took Brother N. and me to see a dying Christian, formerly an officer in the United States Army. He seemed truly to have 'a reasonable, religious, and holy hope.' It was a valuable opportunity. I desire to take the sight home and lay it to heart. He is just about my age, has in some degree my complaints, but far more faith and love. He said it was 'not play' that he was then called to. The agonies of death! O Saviour, let not any pains from thee afflict my dying hour! If my body is full of pain, may my soul be full of pleasure!

"This man was a high-spirited Carolinian, who, to use his own words, 'would as soon have fought a duel as eaten his breakfast.' But now he is humble as a little child. He said his happiness was 'inexpressible.' His gratitude to Mr. S., his spiritual father, is touching, and Mr. Smith's comfort in him it is delightful to witness. May he have very many such seals of his ministry as crowns of his rejoicing. May it be my business to get ready for such a state. O my soul! what would be thy workings? What thy hopes?"

"*Columbia, S. C., April* 24—200 *miles from Savannah.*—Arrived here to-day with my companions, Mr. Ripley and the Hon. D. Buel. We were about three days from Augusta to this place. . . . . My soul! how hast thou been kept this week? How far am I from what I ought to be? I want more the grace of self-denial. I want to take up my cross daily and follow Christ. Oh! let me meditate upon his cross and passion. Could he endure the agony and bloody sweat for me, and shall I shrink from little acts of self-denial!"

"*Salisbury, N. C., Saturday, May* 1.—I have travelled this week from Columbia, S. C., one hundred and fifty miles, without accident, thanks to a kind Providence. The country through which I passed was rough but picturesque. And what has been the state of my mind? How have I walked with God? I have been led into levity of manner this week, and have bitterly regretted it. Oh! that in all things and all times I might approve myself the minister of Christ! Let me preserve that simple, sincere, and cheerful manner, which will do good and no harm!"

Prince Edward County, Va., May 9,—*near Hamp-*

den Sidney College.—We arrived here at sunset last evening, and put up to spend the Sabbath. One hundred and eighty miles have I travelled this week. Journeyed for nearly a month, and have not been delayed by rain one hour. This is a subject of gratitude."

From this place Mr. Cutler passed on to Alexandria, Va., thence to Winchester, Va., then to Philadelphia. The next note of his journey is made in that city.

"*June* 5.—It is nearly a month since I wrote in this journal. Sunday, May 16, I preached at Alexandria; had a very delightful Sabbath amidst true Virginia hospitality. Here I parted with my companions (Buel and Ripley), and altered my course. I now travelled with a Christian friend, Dr. Keith; with him I did, indeed, take sweet counsel. I attended the Virginia Convention held at Winchester, and had a delightful season. I admire the character of Virginia Episcopalians.

"The next Sunday I spent here; heard Brother B. B. Smith and Mr. Hawkes preach.

"Found a dear sick lamb of my fold here (Miss Emily Marston, of Quincy), and am ministering unto her. My soul was strengthened and refreshed at the above named Convention, and I have felt far more life ever since."

"*New York, June* 12.—I arrived in this city on the 10th, and found my beloved wife here, well; and my dear mother, Sister Eliza, and my brothers-in-law. I have been engrossed in cares and perplexities, and have not enjoyed so much tranquillity of mind as I could desire. When shall I learn to cast my cares upon Him who careth for me?"

Soon after the above date, Mr. Cutler went to Massachusetts, and even as far as Saco, Me., travelling on horseback, as before. Bishop Griswold, anxious to secure his services, wrote to him from Salem, June 21:

"REV. AND DEAR SIR—When I had the pleasure of seeing you in Boston I said a little, and had opportunity of saying but a little, to you, on the subject of your officiating in some of our churches; and now I cannot write much, but your zeal for the Church will, I trust, supply that in which I am deficient. . . . . I have again heard from Saco, where the Church is thought to be in a very critical and dangerous state from the want of a minister. . . . . I wish you would ascertain what Mr. H. intends to do. If he does not intend to go to Saco, I wish very much you might visit that place, were it only for a few weeks, to encourage them with the hope, that in a short time, through the Lord's blessing, they will be supplied. . . . . In such case, on your way thither, we shall hope for a visit from you and Mrs. Cutler here. With my kindest regards for you both, I remain your very affectionate friend,

ALEXANDER V. GRISWOLD."

Mr. Cutler entered upon missionary duty at Saco, early in July, and Mrs. Cutler joined him there. Their mother, then at Newport with children and grandchildren, including Mrs. McAllister's family from the South, urged her son and his wife to join them there and enjoy a season of entire rest. But however feeble in body Mr. Cutler was, the activity of his mind and his extreme conscientiousness would not allow him to take such repose.

Until the middle of September Mr. Cutler labored faithfully and constantly at Trinity Church, Saco, rejoicing to proclaim the unsearchable riches of Christ.

A few extracts from his journal will indicate to us in what manner of spirit he was.

"*Saco, Me., July* 17, 1830.—I came here and remain, in fear and trembling, as my health is so poor. Oh! may the Master, whom I serve, through his Son, be the strength of my heart, and my portion for ever."

"*July* 24.—Received a letter from Quincy, and feel grateful for the affection of the people."

"*July* 26.—Wrote to Bishop Meade, of Virginia, in answer to a letter from him to come to his diocese, which I desire to do; also, wrote to a friend (E. M.), very ill."

The letter last referred to has been happily preserved, and is treasured up with much care by the family of this young friend. We are sorely tempted to transcribe it for the benefit of our readers, for it is a remarkable exhibition of pastoral tenderness and love, but the limits of this chapter will hardly allow. All the members of the Marston family were dear to Mr. Cutler's heart, but this one, to whom the letter was addressed, has long since passed away, and he hath now met her in glory, where pain and suffering never enter, and where the tears are wiped away "from off all faces."

To the same disciple of Christ, who was in much dejection of soul, Mr. Cutler, with his usual discrimination, wrote a few weeks later:

> . . . "You could not, dear afflicted child, have considered well what you said, when you declared yourself not a Christian. You may not be a great Christian, a matured Christian, or a happy Christian; you may not be such a Christian as St. Paul or St. John, but may you not be such a Christian as the Thief on the Cross, or as one of the three thousand converted on the day of Pentecost. You may not be as resigned and triumphant as Mrs. Graham, or Mrs. Huntington; but to be like them, must you not have exactly their minds, exactly their trials, their knowledge and their grace, and, I may add, their bodily diseases. In every one of these respects you are made to differ from them, and also in some respects from every other Christian that ever lived. . . . . . But if it were true that you were mistaken, that you are no Christian, is that a reason why you should not be one this very day? You know the Lord Jesus; at least, you know that he forgave the Thief instantly. You know that he has said, 'Come unto me all ye that are weary and heavy-laden, and I will refresh you.' You can but perish, if you now go to the Saviour by prayer. Resolve, then, 'I will go in unto the King, which is not according to law; and if I perish, I perish.' The Lord be with you, dear E., prays your pastor."

But, returning to Mr. Cutler's journal:

"*Aug.* 7."—He writes: "I have had mournful experience of the weakness of human resolution, but I am enabled to go to God with some degree of confidence. He may be viewed as pitying one of his children, who has yielded to sudden infirmity of natural temper, and when he cries out in shame and sorrow to God for mercy, perhaps he may feel for him, and say, "Son, be not dismayed; go and sin no more."

"*Aug.* 14.—I have reason to hope that, through the mercy of God, I shall have some seals of my ministry, as crowns of my rejoicing, through Jesus Christ."

"*Aug.* 28.—I have this week decided on a new field of labor in Virginia. New trials, new temptations, await me; but I desire to trust in God. Whether I am at the South or at the North, in a city or a village, sin is to be fought, and my principal happiness is in God. It is therefore of little moment where I preach the gospel, but of great moment that I preach it faithfully."

"*Sept.* 4.—On Wednesday I went to Portland, and saw the Hon. Simon Greenleaf and his family; had formed the highest opinion of him as a true Christian and Churchman. Conversed freely and at length, and was not disappointed. What a valuable man to the world is a man of high and holy principles, large capacity of mind, and great energy! Oh! could my eyes have seen the human nature conjoined with divinity, in the man Christ Jesus!

"'A veil of interposing night
His radiant face conceals.'"

Mr. Cutler's labors at Saco were blessed to the good of the Church and of the community in that place, and many hearts were bound to him in cords of love, as was the case at Thessalonica, in St. Paul's time, even though his abode there was short.

And, in looking at the future, he felt assured God would be with him. "I am like a passenger in a good vessel," he writes, "with an able and experienced commander. How can any thing go wrong where God directs? and have I not asked him to direct? I perceive abundant reason to be abased before God for my sins; yet I see abundant reason to trust and to rejoice in him."

The mother of Mr. Cutler, as the autumn was near, wrote to him and his wife to come to Newport, and then accompany her with his sister's family to Savannah. She knew of his contemplated return to Virginia, and that as winter drew on, it was important for him to be in a southern climate. The idea of her son's removal to such a distance was painful; but she at last acquiesced in his decision and saw the wisdom of his plan, although a parent's heart could not refrain from uttering the language of the patriarch Jacob: "'If I be bereaved of my children, I am bereaved.' Eliza in New York, Francis at Avon, you in Virginia, and Louisa in Savannah; and I am to lead a meteor-like life by wandering from one star to another; but your plan will probably promote your own health better than any other."

Before Mr. Cutler finally left Saco he wrote the following letter to one of his family, and we can thus see how correctly he appreciated his own condition:

"SACO, ME., *August* 27, 1830.

"DEAR SISTER— . . . . I thank you for the caution you sent me. I endeavor to be careful of myself, and consider the wound in my health just beginning to heal. A little imprudence might be fatal to life. But with all this, preach I should; watch for souls I must; for such have been the habits of my mind and body for some years past, that if I was totally unoccupied without responsibility, and without the joy of encouragement in labor, I might sink down into a morbid state of feeling, and body and mind might go to wreck. 'Make haste slowly,' is my motto. I have had trials, dear S——, since I saw you, but I can say

'I love thy chastenings, O my God!
They fix my hopes on thy abode;
Where, in thy presence fully blest,
Thy stricken saints for ever rest.'

Harriet and I would delight to pay another visit to Montreal, but our faces are providentially turned to the South. Perhaps next summer we may reach your city; but let us both look mainly at 'a city which hath foundations.' There may we all meet, prays

"Your friend and brother, B. C. C."

Mr. Cutler left Saco, September 14, in order to spend a week in Lowell, Mass. During his visit here he went over to Andover to attend the annual exercises of the Theological Seminary there. He made the following notes about this time in his journal:

"May a blessing attend that seminary where it follows Christ. The great controversy in which it is now engaged, has, no doubt, an effect upon the spirit of its pupils and of its professors; and, of consequence, dross is mingled, as it must ever be, with the fine gold.

"One of the epigrammatical sayings of my excellent Bishop is this: 'To be *willing* to perish, is to be opposed to God's will; for God is not willing that any should perish.' May I think as prayerfully and patiently about Divine truth as he has done!"

Before leaving Lowell Mr. Cutler received a letter from one of his Quincy parishioners (J. M., Esq.), begging him to return to his old parish; or, at any rate, to visit them once more. His reply shows that he was not only a kind counsellor to the sick and sorrowing, but also a judicious adviser in the pecuniary difficulties of a parish:

"LOWELL, *September* 30, 1830.

"MY DEAR SIR—Yours of the 6th came safely to hand, and conveyed mournful accounts from your family. I almost dread to hear from you again; and yet, why should I? Is death an event, an evil, to which dear Emily alone is subjected. Have we not all to pass that fiery ordeal of our faith? and would she not have met it at some distant period, if not now? and is it at all probable that she would have been more willing? I am inclined to the belief, that, invariably, as we advance in life, we are afraid of death! . . .

"It was not without an effort that I concluded to deprive myself of the pleasure and satisfaction of visiting Quincy; and it requires a greater effort, now that I am so near, to refrain from turning my horse that way. But *prudence* has pointed out my course; and of late I am getting into the habit of following more closely its admonitions, having smarted oftentimes for my disobedience to that heavenly guide. . . . . . It is an important, as well as delightful thought, that however distant our friends may be to *us*, they cannot be distant from God. 'Whither can we go from his presence?' And if we cannot speak to them and comfort them, we can speak to One, any moment, who can speak to them the next. I would fain speak to dear E—— a word of consolation; but, while heart and flesh are failing, who can strengthen the mind but God?

. . . .

"Why should you wish to detain her in a world of sin and suffering, when from her bodily diseases she must 'ever groan, being burdened,' and to withhold her from those joys of Paradise which, I am persuaded, she will taste the very day of her departure from earth? . . . .

"It seems hardly proper to pass from a subject so serious to one of a secular nature; but I must follow, in reply, the course of your last favor. . . . . . I am clearly of the opinion that one of the most important duties Christ Church has to perform, is to set about settling all their affairs. And I am also decided in the opinion that vigorous measures to collect back taxes should be now made, even at the risk of giving some offence; and upon this principle, that no man is more likely to be alienated than one who owes you money and does not mean to pay, unless compelled. Better bring matters at once to issue and take the consequences.

"Most affectionately theirs and yours, B. C. Cutler."

"P. S.—Give my best love to every member of your family; to your sisters, and to my dear sisters in the faith of our Lord. Heaven bless you, from the warmest place in my heart. B. C. C."

We find Mr. Cutler soon pursuing his journey to Providence, R. I., on horseback, as usual, and while musing by the way, he sighs that "sickness was about to exile him from a land which all other lands outvies."

He preaches for Dr. Crocker at P., and then, after meeting his wife, turns from his proposed path and accompanies her to Newport, where many of his own family are gathered together.

He then pursues his solitary journey, on horseback, to New York (after returning to Providence).

"*New York, Oct.* 10, 1830."—He writes: "Blessed, hallowed hours that I spent at Saco! Dear friends that I left there! dear brethren! dear church! God grant that my visit to Virginia may be attended by as good effects upon my own soul! May Leesburg be to me a place of great spiritual consolation and strength. Let me go there, with a single and a simple aim to promote the glory of God. With Christ in my heart; with Christ on my lips, and with Christ in my life, may an abundant entrance be ministered to me into that part of Christ's vineyard!"

"*Tuesday, Oct.* 19.—Occupied in putting my beloved mother on board of a ship for Savannah. May a kind Lord protect her!"

"*Wednesday, Oct.* 20.—I left New York, on horseback, for Virginia. Travelled alone, feeling desolate."

"*Friday, Oct.* 22.—I reached Philadelphia; stayed at Mr. Randall's."

"*Frederick Town, Md., Saturday evening, Oct.* 30.—At the house of Rev. Thomas Jackson. Arrived last Thursday, having travelled one hundred and forty-five miles in three and a half days. Riding alone, I hoped to have meditated and communed much with God, like David Brainerd. But, alas! alas! my piety is not a deep and overflowing fountain; it is more like a brook, swelled at times by sudden showers, from heaven, but often shallow. God grant it may not be worse than this."

"*Leesburg, Va., Nov.* 2, 1830.—I arrived at this place last evening, and on entering the town set up my 'Ebenezer.' Hitherto the Lord hath helped me. As I rode here yesterday, I called often upon God for a blessing on this people and on myself. I was received with great kindness by the people.

"'In the Christian warfare, to maintain the conflict is to gain the victory!' The promise is made to him that endureth unto the end. Let me thank God and take courage.

He hath not yet given me up, a prey to my adversaries or to my own heart."

The Rev. Mr. Cutler here took charge of two missionary stations (in addition to St. James' Parish, Leesburg) in Loudon County. These places, Aldie and Middleburg, were several miles from Leesburg, and from each other, and the journeyings required in this circuit afforded much opportunity for riding on horseback, which was essential to Mr. Cutler's health.

He found it "difficult to be happy and contented" while separated from his wife, but early in December his beloved companion cheered him with her presence, after an absence of six weeks.

An excellent view of his situation here, is afforded by a letter addressed to Mrs. McAllister, on the last day of the year:

"LEESBURG, LOUDON CO., VA., *December* 31, 1830.

"MY BELOVED SISTER—Your sweet letter to H. and myself we received a fortnight since. It was full of interest to us. . . . Every thing that relates to you or yours, or to your neighbors and friends, will find a welcome with us, for we remember Savannah with great pleasure. The proper return for your letter would be a graphic description of our condition, and expressions conveying assurances of the affection we bear you. My dear H. joined me three weeks since. I went down to Alexandria to meet her. The change of scene from New York to Leesburg is great, and it undoubtedly requires true Christian philosophy to be contented—I mean for H.; for myself, it matters less where I am, than how I live toward God. For such a poor, miserable laborer as I am, it is an honor to be anywhere in the vineyard. When I was so ill, last year, I often thought if God would only restore me to health and return me to usefulness, the *place* where I should labor would be of small moment. I am engaged here only till May, when I shall be free to choose a place of labor. But perhaps by that time, the charms of Loudon having gradually unfolded themselves, I may be captivated and engaged. It depends upon our Heavenly Father. If he points out this as the place where he will meet me and bless me, all the world could not supply the loss of his blessing! So far my health has decidedly improved, the two months I have been here, although the weather has been uncommonly damp and cold. Out of sixty days, about thirty have been rainy. Twice, the mercury has been down to ten degrees above zero.

"We are on what may be called the summit level of our Atlantic coast, on a central ridge between north and south, and within two miles of mountains, and we have consequently all varieties of climate—from the blasts of the North to the breezes of the South, every thing by turns, and nothing long. I ride every day; and it is well for me that I have a warm heart and a lively imagination, or else I should be eaten up with *ènnui*. Imagine a man, but half well, wrapping himself up (like John the Baptist), not in camel's hair, it is true, but in a coarse, camlet cloak, buttoned close at the neck and girded fast round the waist, concluding with overshoes. Imagine such a man, turning his face toward a leafless forest, a cloudy sky, a cold northeast wind, and moving over ground saturated with water, preparing to bring home mud enough to do justice to a *ditcher*, and you will see just the figure of your affectionate, and I may add, happy brother. For, with increasing health, a dear friend, affectionate parishioners, and the smiles of heaven, I may well laugh at the wintry elements.

"I have given you the outside picture, which is dreary enough; but the inside one has little else than comfort. We live a mile out of the village, in the family of my senior warden, Mr. S., who is a wealthy Virginia planter, living in the midst of very extensive possessions of rich land, and abounding in the real luxuries of life, with five hundred or one thousand acres of wood adjoining his garden. His house resembles a baronial castle on a small scale, with wings, lodges, etc. The lady is a most amiable, intelligent, and pious woman. The gentleman, a fine-looking old man, more than six feet tall, with a venerable, hoary head, perfectly upright in stature, and always well dressed. Religion here finds a most respectful reception. The parlor and the kitchen, I believe, the fear of God pervades.

"In the poor blacks I have felt much interest, and allow no opportunity to pass without trying to say something for their good—at least for their comfort. Poor things! the least we can do for them is to try and get them free IN THE NEXT WORLD.

"O that God, who can make men eloquent, would give me a heart and a mouth to speak to these poor souls, and to treat them with that Christian kindness and consideration that a man should, who knows that he has a Master in heaven. (Col. iv. 1.) . . . . But now of your own spiritual state. Ah! my dearest sister, what a risk are you running while you remain undetermined. Alas! that I feel so little of what I ought about your everlasting safety, and that of your dear husband and children. True it is, that daily, at times, when you are busy, or asleep, or thoughtless about your soul, I am lifting up a short, poor and low, but sincere prayer; 'O God! save their immortal souls, for Jesus' sake.' Pray, dear sister, that God will convince you of your guilt and danger, and lead you to His Son, whose blood cleanseth from all sin; and may we who are now united by mortal ties, be joined in those of divine grace and eternal glory. "Your own, B. C. C."

A more single-hearted minister of Christ than this our friend, who was now laboring for Christ, far removed from those successful activities and extended agencies which stimulate the laborer in other portions of the Lord's vineyard, could not be found; following as he did the Master's footprints in the daily round of duty, transfiguring his circumscribed and lowly life into a living testimony to the truth of Christ's gospel. He was glad to have God arrange for him his present and his future, without any undue solicitude on his part.

"Only my life can I lay down,
Only my heart, Lord, to thy throne
I bring; and pray,
A child of thine, I may go forth
And spread glad tidings through the earth,
And teach sad hearts to know thy worth;
Lord, here am I!"

The record in his journal, as he stood on the threshold of another opening year (1831), the close of which found him in quite a different sphere of labor, is affecting indeed.

"If I am only in the Lord, what have I to fear?

"Suppose I am *poor;* God hath said, 'Blessed are the poor'—rich in faith.

"Suppose I am *sick* and weak; the sick often have the happiest views of God. One whom Jesus loved was sick.

"Suppose I am deprived of my *dearest friend;* 'Blessed are they that mourn;' and I should not mourn as those who have no hope!

"Suppose I myself should die; 'Blessed are the dead who die in the Lord.'

"Suppose I have no offspring; I may have 'a name better than that of sons and daughters.'

"Suppose I should ever live in obscurity and die unknown to fame; 'The memory of the just shall be blessed.'

"Suppose I have had adversity through all the first part of my life; 'God blessed the latter end of Job more than his beginning.'

"Let me not covet this world's goods. 'I brought nothing into this world, and I can carry nothing out.'

"Let others obtain *conspicuous* stations. Somebody must live and labor in obscure ones; and if I do, for Christ's sake, Christ will find time and place to make me conspicuous in a better world, where honor is not connected with toil to one's-self and envy from others.

"'Say ye to the righteous, It shall be well with him.'

"What an insurance have I effected by going to the Bible! Now I am safe; now my affairs are well ordered!"

In February, 1831, Mr. Cutler received a very urgent letter from the Vestry of Christ Church, Quincy, Mass., desiring his return to them, if consistent with his health. The Rev. W. T. Potter had been officiating there, with much acceptance; but the tie which bound Mr. Cutler to them as their rector, was not sundered, and the Committee appointed to write him, expressed the hope "that neither time nor distance would ever separate them from the love which had so long existed between them!"

To this letter Mr. Cutler replied: "It is uncertain whether I can live as far north as Quincy. . . . I resign, not because your affection and kindness has abated (for your communication shows it has not), nor because my love for you has diminished; but I resign because the hand of God has been upon me, in a severe and protracted illness, and seems evidently to have placed me in a less laborious and more retired situation. . . . You are, and ever will be, dear to my heart; and our Heavenly Father knows that nothing but a fear of closing quickly my mortal career, restrained me from returning to you the last summer. Your communication I shall preserve as a memorial of your regard, which will ever be valued by me; and it will be a consolation should the Lord in his providence suffer me to languish in ministerial uselessness."

Having thus sent his resignation of the parish to the vestry, Mr. Cutler on the same day wrote a farewell letter to the parishioners at Quincy, expressing his fervent love for them, and his deep and continued interest in their spiritual welfare. It is too long to place on record here.* What effect such a farewell, from such a pastor, had upon the people of his late charge, one can readily imagine. After its reception, the Committee of the Vestry wrote again to Rev. Mr. Cutler:

. . . "A communication from one who holds so great a place in our affections, who has devoted eight years of the best of his life for our best good, who, with unshaken zeal and unwearied effort in the cause of his Master, has always preached to us evangelical truth, could but awaken in us the most lively interest. It would have imparted to us the greatest satisfaction could you have been able to return and once more mingle with us in the joys which arise from social intercourse as Christians, and again be able to participate with us in the delightful exercises of Christian worship; but it appears to be the will of Him who orders all things for our good that it should be otherwise. . . . May the sweet smiles of Heaven rest upon you; may you be unshaken in preaching the doctrines of the Cross, and steadfast in the faith, ever imitating the blessed example of Him who went about doing good.

EBEN'R CHAMBERLAIN,
CHAS. HARDWICK, JR.,
GEORGE HARDWICK,
Committee.

Thus ended Mr. Cutler's pastoral connection with the parish at Quincy. It had been, and has since been, called

* See Appendix A.

a hard field of labor; but under his ministrations, with the Divine blessing, it had been made to bud and blossom and to bring forth abundant fruit.

Under date of April 15, 1831, we find the following note in his diary: "I accepted the invitation of this church (Leesburg) to stay six months more with them. May the Lord bless my feeble attempts to serve them. Oh may I know myself—my real state before God! Fletcher says, 'a good-natured man without grace maketh a fairer show than grace with an evil temper.' Oh, I fear no one would ever think of calling me a holy man! I have just light enough in religion to perceive that I am yet dark; just warmth enough to feel that I am *cold*; and just strength enough to know that I am weak. . . . Religion at best in me bringeth forth her *thirty* fold! Oh, the sixty! the *hundred* fold! hast thou no ambition, O my soul?"

This scrutiny stands in pleasing contrast with a sentiment of another, which we find in his journal:

"*May* 10.—Visited a poor black female disciple of our Lord Jesus Christ, and was struck with one of her expressions: 'Sometimes she grew so cold, that she was obliged to *hunt after* her religion and try to make it better!'"

The Diocesan Convention of Virginia, which met at Norfolk in May of this year, afforded Mr. Cutler great delight. Such a spirit of true brotherly love he had rarely seen, and it proved a refreshment to his soul. He was in the midst of a circle of clerical brethren "after his own heart;" and could it be otherwise, when such men as Dr. Bedell, of Philadelphia, Dr. Henshaw, of Baltimore, and Dr. Brooke, of Georgetown, were all gathered to greet the patriarchal Bishop Moore and the devoted Jackson, of Alexandria? The services connected with this Convention were like "a feast of fat things" and "marrow to the bones" of the dear missionary at Leesburg. The Rev. William Jackson, speaking of this season, in a letter to a friend, wrote, "The last day of the feast has been a Pentecost, indeed. Brother Cutler says, since he had eyes to see he never beheld so glorious a day; and Dr. Bedell says, he never will, if possible, miss another Virginia Convention."

After Mr. Cutler's return to Leesburg, he found death had invaded his circle of clerical friends. If "death loves a shining mark," the insatiate archer, in this case, proved the adage true, when the Rev. Sutherland Douglass was called away. A very touching allusion to this gifted spirit, our readers will find in the Memoirs of Rev. William Jackson (by his widow). As Mrs. J. truly says: "When his sun went down, ere yet it had reached mid-day, a pure and beautiful light passed from the Church on earth." Mr. and Mrs. Cutler laid this affliction much to heart; and Mr. Cutler wrote to Mrs. Douglass, his words proving like "oil and wine" poured into the wounds of her bleeding heart:

"LEESBURG, VA., *June* 25, 1831.

"DEAR MRS. DOUGLASS—Mrs. Cutler and I would much prefer to sit down beside you and to weep in silence over your loss, than to interrupt your sorrow by the poor consolation of a letter. But this is the only way left us of expressing to you our sorrow and our sympathy. . . . . How difficult it is to love God with all our hearts, when we have dear earthly friends. It is not wonderful that he takes them away, but wonderful that he ever permitted them to occupy so much of our affections. Take those holy women of your own days, who have been saints, for your pattern—Mrs. Graham, who, through much tribulation, entered the kingdom of heaven; Mrs. Huntington, whose holy soul is still breathing its chastened sentiments into many an expanding mind. But why am I imposing any effort, or proposing any work, to one whose tears have just began to flow? You have just lost one who was all that a human being could be to you. Yes! and we have all lost him. The church and the world have lost him. Dear, dear brother, thou hast left us to labor and struggle still longer in a world of sin, whilst thou hast, early in the day, gained the victory and won the crown! Thou wast a holy man of God, a faithful and fearless minister of Jesus Christ, an affectionate and steady friend. . . . . The Lord have mercy on you, dear Mrs. D.; may he support, and soothe, and sanctify your broken heart! and enable you to say, 'The Lord gave, and the Lord hath taken away, and blessed be the name of the Lord!' . . . . That our gracious Saviour, who was himself a man of sorrows, may ever be with you, is the prayer of one of your husband's most affectionate friends,

B. C. CUTLER."

As a consoler of the afflicted, Mr. Cutler had few equals; and his faithfulness, in all the relations of pastoral life, had won for him a name in all the churches.

After a long and weary ride, one day, he found on his table a call from the Vestry of Grace Church, Providence, R. I., to become their rector.

He replied he would preach for them during the coming August, and then decide what plan to pursue. In his diary, he says: "I look upon a change of situation not as I once did. I know too well the lot of man in this life. I know, too, that temporal things have just as much happiness for me in them as God sees fit, and no more; therefore I say,

'Live where I will, without Thee I shall sigh,
And with Thee sing, wherever I may die.'

Ever since the Lord raised me from a pining sickness, and delivered me from the howling ocean (in 1829), I have been, and I ever desire to be, willing to go or stay where he directs."

In the latter part of July Mr. Cutler went to Alexandria, where a deep and solemn interest pervaded the churches, and the Holy Spirit was poured out abundantly in refreshing showers upon the people. It was just at the close of the session of the Theological Seminary near that city. All the exercises were mingled together in happy concert, and more than thirty clergymen had participated in the various meetings. The series of special services closed at St. Paul's Church, Alexandria (of which the Rev. William Jackson was rector), when (though a confirmation had just been held, and forty-five persons had ratified their baptismal vows) forty persons gathered around the chancel to consecrate themselves in this rite to the Lord.

What a scene it was! It lived long in the memories of those who were present on that memorable occasion! The Rev. Mr. Cutler, after his return home, drew a picture of the scene in a letter to Mrs. Jackson, hoping an artist's pencil would, in reality, portray the sketch, the outline of which, his pen had formed.*

Mr. Cutler was warmly attached to his Virginia friends, and he found "some things delightful in the Episcopal Church there."

But "the institution of slavery made his situation unpleasant." "This was an evil," he says, "I could not mitigate, nor well endure." This, together with the illness of his wife, no doubt influenced him to accept a call elsewhere.

At midsummer, Mrs. Cutler was prostrated by a severe attack of bilious fever and as soon as it was practicable was removed to the house of her brother, Capt. James Bancroft, in Philadelphia. From thence, Mr. and Mrs. Cutler both went to Newport, R. I., at which place they arrived on the 11th of August.

Here were gathered together his mother, his sisters, and ten nephews and nieces; Mr. Ward and Dr. Francis making occasional visits, as their duties in New York would allow.

The Rev. Mr. Cutler went up to Providence and preached at Grace Church, but felt constrained to decline the call to that important parish. "I pray God will send them" he says, "a man strong in body and strong in spirit, and bless him and them." The loving Cutler would have been, indeed, one worthy to lead the way where, in the long line of witnesses to the truth of the gospel, stood afterward the holy John A. Clark, the faithful Bishop Henshaw, and in

See Appendix B.

these days, the eloquent Bishop Clark! But the finger of God's providence seemed to him to point out another path of duty.

In September Mr. Cutler went to Boston, and to Quincy, where he was received with open arms. Thus he comments on his trip: "Not soon, not ever, shall I forget my visit to Quincy. Dear, affectionate people, hungering for the bread of life; may the Master bless your present pastor, to be indeed your shepherd."

"*Monday*.—I went to Salem, and saw Bishop Griswold. This venerable man is still a monument of simplicity and fidelity."

We soon find Mr. Cutler in New York, ready to start again for Virginia. His friends urged him to remain, in view of a call to some situation in that city. But he simply asks of God, "What wilt thou have me to do?" His own language will best express his state of mind:

"*New York, Oct.* 11, 1831.—O my Father, let not my pride lead me; my desire is to please and serve thee, in the gospel of thy Son. I commit all my ways to thee. If thou sayest go north, I will cheerfully go north; if thou sayest go south, I go south; if thou sayest stay here, I stay here in the city or in the suburbs, in village or country. I am willing to-morrow to go, only go with me, blessed Saviour! I am expected next Sunday at Leesburg. It is said, If you go before Sunday, you lose all chance of advancement. But my idea is, that no present duty is to be omitted for the sake of some future advantage. It appears to be my duty to go; it is not necessary nor desirable, in a spiritual point of view, that I should have that particular call! Oh! what an honor to live and labor in the cause of Christ. Let me be faithful over a few things—omit no duty. There will be time and place for honor and distinction; no man can leave houses, etc., but he shall receive an hundred fold!"

Mr. and Mrs. Cutler returned to Leesburg on the 21st of October, and he was again in the midst of parish labors, though a few weeks more would complete the year of his engagement with this people. What would be the next turn of the wheel of providential events, it was impossible to foresee. But, remembering the remark of Cecil: "Duties are ours, events are God's," he went forward in the path of duty, leaving all results with God.

> "What Thou shalt to-day provide,
> Let me as a child receive;
> What to-morrow may betide,
> Calmly to Thy wisdom leave."

Scarcely a fortnight elapsed, ere letters came from various friends in New York, all pointing to a probable call from that city; and on the 8th of November he received a letter from Bishop Onderdonk, the first sentence of which was, "It gives me much pleasure to inform you that, at a meeting of the Executive Committee of the Board of Managers of the New York Protestant Episcopal City Mission Society, you were, on my nomination, chosen the missionary of said society," etc., etc.

Such men as Drs. Milnor, Wainwright, and Eastburn, Mr. Richmond and Mr. Duffie, were members of this Board.

Dr. McIlvaine (then rector of St. Ann's, Brooklyn,) was desirous of having Mr. Cutler as rector of a proposed new church (an offshoot of St. Ann's) in Brooklyn, and wrote, under date of November 3, 1831: "Dr. Wainwright told me to-day that Bishop Onderdonk had nominated you for first City Missionary, with a salary of one thousand dollars; of course you will be elected. It is considered a great step on the part of the Bishop. All are rejoiced at it. I would urge you to accept the appointment. Thus, you can be laboring here, and our church going up meanwhile and be ready for you as soon as you are ready for it." But God had another plan in view for his servant, not yet unrolled to mortal vision.

His family friends urged every motive upon Mr. Cutler to induce him to accept.

His sister, Mrs. Francis, whose affection was measured not by words only, but in deeds, besought him earnestly to come, knowing, in case of anxiety about his health, her husband, one of the most eminent practitioners in the city, would cheerfully afford his aid and counsel.

Mr. Ward, his brother-in-law, placed every facility in Mr. Cutler's way, and offered him the hospitalities of his home for the winter.

But how was Mr. Cutler affected by all this? After due deliberation he accepted his appointment, the promised year at Leesburg having now expired. His diary tells us the sentiments of his heart:

"*Nov.* 12, 1831.—My wife and I greatly prefer living in that part of the country where we were born, and, as the wants of the church are as great there as here, and we have been called to a station of great usefulness, we feel at liberty to go. It is, however, with great reluctance that I quit the people of this parish (Leesburg). The communicants of this parish are as pious and devoted people as I have ever met in the Church. The Lord continue to bless them."

The Mission Church in New York (situated in Vandewater Street) was consecrated by the name of the "Holy Evangelists," on the 19th of November. Thereupon the Bishop wrote Mr. Cutler to come without delay, and on every side he heard an entreating voice, saying: "Come, for all things are now ready!" and on the 1st of December, 1831, Mr. Cutler departed from Leesburg, where he had eight or ten seals to his ministry, leaving the sweet savor of his life and teaching, alike in the mansions of the rich and the hovels of the poor. Over this very ground, now desolated by the ruthless hand of war, the writer of this volume was permitted to travel, in 1861. Under the roof of a mutual friend, Dr. Clagett, whom Mr. Cutler never ceased to respect and esteem, the days of Mr. Cutler's ministry here were happily recounted. Everywhere throughout the parish, childhood had been taught to lisp his name with reverence, and old age, with gratitude, hallowed the remembrance of his deeds.

CHAPTER VI.

CITY MISSIONARY IN NEW YORK.

1831–1833.

> " Thou shalt be rich in orphan's love,
> The poor shall bless thy name ;
> Where wilt thou find reward more sweet,
> More satisfying fame ?"

IF the great mass of mankind are to be regenerated and saved, more men like the subject of this memoir must, and doubtless will, be sent into the dark places of the earth, to bless their fellow men. Their lives and labors are like so many healing streams, refreshing multitudes around them, in their onward course to the city of our God.

Blessed be God that Mr. Cutler did not shrink from any cross that his Divine Master imposed ; but ever obeyed his gracious voice through life, following closely, so that he could touch the hem of his garment, and placing his feet in the footprints of his Lord as he led the way, even as the traveller among the snowy Alps follows in the path of his guide, over rugged mountains and dark ravines, implicitly trusting to him for safe guidance and a glorious prospect at the end of the journey. Our sainted friend has reached the end of this life's pilgrimage, but he still lives !—lives in the hearts of many a widow and fatherless child on earth, as well as in the immediate vision of him, to do whose will here was his meat and his drink.

In December, 1831, Mr. Cutler commenced his labors as city missionary in New York, taking the charge of the new Mission Church, in Vandewater Street, in that city.

On the 10th of the month at the house of Samuel Ward,

Jr., he made this entry in his journal: "To-morrow I expect to enter on my new field of labor! O Lord Jesus Christ, stand by thy servant! He hopes to preach thee. Give me a proper sense of my responsibilities. Enable me to feel for perishing sinners; and O, multiply the bread for the hungry! May the people receive with meekness the engrafted word which is able to save their souls!"

Thus did he set out, seeking a fresh anointing of the Spirit of God; looking for strength to be imparted by his Divine Master alone. Without any reserve, he had come into another diocese, and with that frankness which was so eminently characteristic of him, he had stated his true position to his Diocesan. How many difficulties would be obviated, and how much suspicion and distrust averted, were the same candor and courtesy, which were so conspicuous in this case, to attend the removal of every clergyman from one part of the vineyard to another. The extracts from the correspondence here, reflect credit on both parties:

"NEW YORK, *November* 3, 1831.

"REV. AND DEAR SIR—Allow me, my dear sir, to express my sincere hope that you will meet our wishes, by entering on the interesting and important duties of a mission to the poor, in a city presenting so loud a call for such services, and opening so wide a field for their useful prosecution; and also to assure you that it will afford me much pleasure to have you as one of the presbyters in this city and diocese.

"These feelings are the result of the personal acquaintance which I have had the pleasure of forming with you, and the full conviction that, however we may differ as to some consequences flowing from church principles, and the degree and mode in which it is proper to sustain and defend them, you are as sincerely attached as any man to the institutions of the church; a lover of order and harmony in its councils and policy, and one who had always infinitely rather honor her appointments, as instruments of spiritual good and ministerial success, than the exhibition of any gifts of your own, or modes of private device.

"Hoping to hear favorably, I remain your affectionate brother,

"To the REV. MR. CUTLER. BENJ. T. ONDERDONK."

REPLY.

"LEESBURG, VA., *November* 10, 1831.

"RT. REV. AND DEAR SIR—This is a noble enterprise, and if my services can be of use to the society, in the capacity of a missionary to the poor, I do not feel willing to withhold them, although I perceive that the undertaking is an arduous one. . . . . You are aware, I perceive, my dear sir, by your letter, that I have been trained up in a portion of the Church which may differ, in some respects, from that over which you preside, and you probably conclude that I have been conscientious in my union with the above Church. But it will be a very unfit return for the Christian courtesy with which you have considered the subject, to take advantage of the opportunity now offered, to bring such differences in opposition to your government.

"To the flock over which I am placed I wish to devote my undivided attention, and I desire and pray to live in peace and charity with all men. To the church, to which we happily belong, I am in reason, conscience, and feeling, strongly attached; and I believe her particular institutions eminently calculated to promote the glory of God and the salvation of men. The manner in which you speak of my coming into your diocese is most grateful to my feelings, and I hope, if permitted to labor as one of your presbyters, I shall be so happy as to justify your expectations.

"I remain your faithful servant, B. C. CUTLER.

"To the RT. REV. B. T. ONDERDONK, D. D."

Though called to the arduous duties of a city mission, Mr. Cutler paid increased attention to those private duties of religion which the slothful and self-indulgent Christian is so apt to neglect. February 6, 1832, was the thirty-fourth anniversary of his birthday, and he improved it by special prayer and self-examination, asking the blessing of God upon his meditations, and thanking Him "for the preservation of life, the patience exercised, the deliverances vouchsafed, the restoration to more of the joys of his salvation than formerly, for a wide field of usefulness, and a measure of health."

How many servants of God find their experience precisely similar with that recorded in Mr. Cutler's journal, on the subject of self-examination. "Of all duties, I find this the most difficult. If Satan attempts to drive me from any duty, it is this; although I have now practiced it for fifteen years, I can hardly promise myself that the next regular period for this duty will not be pre-occupied—company comes in, fatigue and languor prevail, or some pressing and important duty, more external, is at hand. Search me, O God! and know my heart; try me, and know my thoughts."

Mr. Cutler did not forget the personal or the relative duties of religion in whatever sphere of labor he was placed. Hearing of the illness of his beloved parent, who was sojourning at the South about this time, he wrote in haste to his sister, under whose care and protection their venerated mother then was:

"I wish I was at hand to pray with my dear mother; but in times of deep distress human aid seems almost a mockery. God is our readiest and best help! The pains of disease and the pangs of dissolution, no man, not the holiest,(not the Son of God,) was or is, exempt from. But the consolations of Christ have ever been sufficient to blunt the edge of pain, and to counteract the terrors of, death. St. Stephen, although mangled by the brutal ferocity of his persecuting countrymen, no doubt, was raised above his bodily sufferings by beholding the glory and joy which in a few moments was to be his. Succeeding martyrs have sung in dungeons and in death! It is the great hope which the true Christian has, that *he* shall have dying grace in a dying hour. The Lord Jesus Christ, who knows, and who once said, 'Without me, ye can do nothing,' will not forsake his trembling, but believing, worms! He knows whereof we are made; he remembers that we are but dust. He who bled and died for us will be a present help to all who put their trust in him!"

The affection of a son, blended with the wise counsels of a faithful pastor, shed many a beam of comfort along the pathway of this aged servant of the Most High, as she descended the hill of life, and even after she had passed the allotted term of three-score years and ten.

We find the following record in Mr. Cutler's journal:

"16 *Bond Street, New York, March* 31, 1832.—For several weeks past I have been busily engaged in the work of the mission. I have rejoiced in perceiving that my labors have been blest. It is the Lord's work, and his be all the glory. Though I have too much self-indulgence to record, yet I have had much peace in believing. Prayer and the word of God have both been more satisfying to me, and my desire to do good and to become holy has been distinct. I have not enjoyed so much in religion for many years as I have, since I have been engaged in this city mission. There is a benign and holy spirit at work in this mission; and, although I am a little constrained in my movements, yet the consciousness of doing good quite overbalances the inconvenience. Oh, let me be more holy, more useful, more devoted!"

The same day Mr. Cutler met with the following lines in the *Episcopal Recorder*, which he copied, under this date, into his journal, with the expressed desire that they might animate *him*. Little could he foresee what he was to pass through, ere another season closed, but the spirit of these verses was always with him, nerving him at every post of duty and danger! Very often, in after years, did he repeat them from memory; and only a short time before his earthly warfare was actually ended, he requested a dear relative to read them to him. We therefore think them worthy of a place here:

CHRISTIAN WARFARE.

"Soldier, GO! but not to claim
Mouldering spoils of earth-born treasure;
Not to build a vaunting name,
Not to dwell in tents of pleasure;
Dream not that the way is smooth,
Hope not that the thorns are roses;
Turn no wishful eye of youth
Where the sunny beam reposes;

Thou hast sterner work to do,
  Hosts to cut thy passage through;
Close behind thee gulfs are burning,
  Forward! there is no returning.

"Soldier, REST! but not for thee
  Spreads the world her downy pillow;
On the rock thy couch must be,
  While around thee chafes the billow.
Thine must be a watchful sleep,
  Wearier than another's waking;
Such a charge as thou dost keep
  Brooks no moment of forsaking.
Sleep, as on the battle-field,
  Girded—grasping sword and shield;
Foes thou canst not name or number
  Steal upon thy broken slumber.

"Soldier, RISE! the war is done.
  Lo! the hosts of hell are flying.
'T was thy Lord the battle won,
  Jesus vanquished them by dying.
Pass the stream—before thee lies
  All the conquered land of glory;
Hark! what songs of rapture rise—
  These proclaim the victor's story.
Soldier, lay thy weapons down,
  Quit the sword and take the crown;
Triumph! all thy foes are banished,
  Death is slain, and earth is vanished."

During the time Mr. Cutler had charge of the mission he made quarterly reports to the Board of Managers. These reports, some of which were printed, were extremely interesting, and show how unceasingly he labored; but we can only give one extract, from that of June, 1832, which will show how diligently he toiled for souls, and how judiciously his charities were bestowed:

"The case of a poor woman, who was buried from the Mission Church, April 11, is an interesting one. Her name was A—— T—— T——. She was the wife of a United

States soldier stationed in Florida. I found her in a garret at No. 106 Madison Street. She had three small children, one an infant only twelve days old.

"It was a day in midwinter; she was sitting up and working for a tailor, in extreme poverty, and with evident symptoms of consumption; but, what was worse than this, with no apparent sense of religion or tenderness of conscience.

"I purchased for her a blanket and a pair of shoes.

"I soon called again; exhorted, prayed, and gave some alms. She evidently began to decline in health; the weather was very severe, and her deprivations were great. Finding her not much interested in religious conversation, after attending to her wants I generally offered prayer.

"When I next called she was sinking fast, and received miserable attention. Her bed and clothing were squalid, and no proper nourishment was found her. I advised her to give up her children to the Commissioners of the Poor, to which she consented. The two younger ones I baptized in her presence.

"Believing there was one ray of hope, that by private nursing she might live through the spring, to take leave of her children and to see her husband, I had her removed to the house of a pious English woman, 71 Cliff Street, who consented to take her to board. Here she lingered four weeks; pious ladies visited her; she became more and more tractable, and at length, after faithful examination, I concluded she had been converted to God, and I then gave her the Sacrament. She lived two weeks after this—always patient; and on the 10th of April, she gently fell asleep in Jesus without a struggle.

"As I had drawn largely on my charity fund I at first concluded to let her be buried in the Potter's Field, but considering *her spiritual relation to our great Redeemer*, I determined, for his sake, to give her a Christian burial.

"We all followed the corpse to the grave in St. John's

Burying-ground, trusting that 'the soul of our deceased sister' was in heaven.

"Here, then, is one of the fruits of a city mission. A poor, sick and perishing sinner converted, by God's blessing, into a believing, though suffering and dying, saint; her offspring baptized and secured during their tender age; her soul led to feed upon Christ; her last hours peaceful and happy, and blessings invoked by many upon the city mission.

"Our regular clergy might have been more faithful, but none except a city missionary could have given the time which was bestowed upon this woman."

So multiplied were the labors of Mr. Cutler in this position that he found little time for correspondence, and, in general, he adhered to his resolution (formed on his removal from Virginia to New York), to give up his correspondents at the South.

But known throughout all the churches as a true "son of consolation," many of the suffering children of God hesitated not to seek his sympathy. To one such, at Alexandria, Va., he wrote:

"MY DEAR MADAM—Your letter and your troubles have left such an impression on my mind that I cannot forbear writing you a few lines. It has pleased God to adopt you into the family of his suffering believers. You have tasted of the *cup* he put into the hands of his Son, and which has never been out of mortal hands since. But the bitterness of the draught has been greatly lessened. It is now but a health-giving cup. Would you, my dear madam, wish to alter one single circumstance in your past trying life? Would you not choose affliction with the people of God, rather than to enjoy the pleasures of sin for a season?

"I am greatly mistaken if you have not weighed in a true balance the pleasures of sin and the vanity of earthly possessions, and if you have not set a price upon the favor of man which shows its worthlessness. Dearly has your aching heart purchased the experience you now have of the world, and expensive the experiment which has been made by your Heavenly Father to wean you from it. He does not willingly afflict, and yet he has afflicted you. Like as a father pitieth his own children, even so is the Lord merciful to them that fear him. What must a human father have felt in witnessing all your trials, exertions and sacrifices! What if he could have seen all your tears, heard all your sighs, and known every wound from which your heart has bled.

"God saw, and heard, and knew all and suffered all; yea, even while he could have prevented all, pitied all, but permitted all. Why was this? It was, I trust, that he might purify you unto himself. He put you into the school of affliction for the very purpose that you put a dear child into a school of intellectual discipline. How cruel the indulgence that would gratify the waywardness and levity of the juvenile mind until it was too late to improve it, until it found itself amidst the duties of matured life, calling for concentrated and cultivated powers, when there was nothing but imbecility to respond to that call!

"Bless God, my dear fellow-sufferer and fellow-scholar, that you have been thus distinguished by his parental love, and anticipate the time when the lessons you have learned with so much pain shall be put in practice to your eternal praise!

"With affectionate regards to our Christian friends in Alexandria, I remain, dear madam, your faithful friend,

"B. C. CUTLER."

But sorrow and trial were about to draw still nearer to the faithful missionary, who could thus appreciate and point out to others (as far as human ken can do) the designs of an All-wise God.

This epistle was, indeed, a fitting prelude to those exhortations which, by word of mouth, he was about to give in many a house immediately around him.

Just as the fervid heats of summer came, the angel of Death, with the wan face of pestilence, appeared and stood over the devoted city!

This was the first time that fearful scourge, the cholera, had visited our shores; the panic throughout the city of New York and the adjacent counties was great and widespread. The crowded city became deserted, and those who remained shrank away in seclusion from contact with their fellow-men. Mr. Cutler, just before this date, had taken rooms in Walker Street, in order to be nearer his immediate field of labor. As missionary to the poor, he was now much exposed to the worst ravages of the pestilence; but he was enabled, with his fellow-laborers in the mission, to perform its regular duties. In season and out of season he labored "in perils oft," and for several weeks he lived on the borders of the eternal world, expecting his own summons "morning, noon, and night." The distress and solemnity of the scenes he witnessed "no language could describe." His diary at this period gives us further details:

"76 *Walker Street, New York, June* 18, 1832.—The cholera is in Quebec and Montreal. This city is beginning to be alarmed; Christians are waking up. My soul, how stands the case with thee? May the Holy Ghost inspire me with wisdom; and as I examine my heart before God this morning, may I rightly judge myself that I be not judged."

"*July* 21.—I am now in the midst of the pestilence. The cholera, the universal plague, arrived in this city four weeks ago. It has caused the death of over nine hundred persons. This day the report of the Board of Health was three hundred new cases and one hundred and thirty deaths. I have been in it and exposed to it every day; visited many ill with it, and followed some to the grave who had died with it. I have great need to live prepared for death; and, if I am not mistaken, I have been enabled, through grace, to feel that death would be gain to me. Still I view it as a great and solemn change—one at which nature shudders; but grace can *calm* nature, and God can support the dying Christian so that he may triumph over death, and exclaim, 'O death, where is thy sting? O grave, where is thy victory? Thanks be to God, who giveth us the victory through our Lord Jesus Christ.' Christians appear to rise up to the exigency of the time; they are frequent in prayer, and charitable with their means. Oh that their prayers and their alms might come up as a memorial before God and stay the plague! Sinners appear stupid and insensible, as they generally are. Thousands and tens of thousands have fled from the city; thousands more may be seen intoxicated with ardent spirits. O Lord, have mercy now upon their souls, for thy Son's sake!

"I have not been well to-day, and am not able to do what I would for the poor. My mind to-night is calm, but solemn, and much inclined to rest above all earthly consolation, and to commune most with the truths of the new revelation which Jesus Christ, the Son of God, came to make. His precious promise is, 'I am the resurrection, and the life; he that believeth in me, though he were dead, yet shall he live; and whosoever liveth, and believeth in me, shall never die.' This is my staff. B. C. CUTLER."

In after years, Dr. Cutler spoke with deep interest of this season. So silent and lonely were the great thoroughfares of the city, that even a solitary traveller on Broadway was a novel sight, and as he was on horseback he often saw faces peering out of an upper window, attracted by the strange sight. So great was the consternation among residents of neighboring places, that intercourse with the citizens of New York was restricted to the supply of the very necessaries of life.

At Newport, R. I., the inhabitants would not allow steamboats to land their passengers, and no communication with the infected city was allowed, except by the way of Providence, and even this avenue would have been closed up, if the plague had not soon abated.

Mr. Cutler's mother, then at Newport, wrote to him to "flee while it was yet day!" In the strongest language she implored him to leave the city, where the destroying pestilence was carrying off its victims, by hundreds, to the grave. "My most precious son, oh come out from thence! I entreat you; linger not within its walls, as Lot would have done, but for the friendly angels that drew him perforce from it!

Oh that such kind messengers may be sent (though invisible) to persuade you to escape, while you may, to our 'little Zoar,' as I trust the mercy of our God will make it to us, as a refuge from the storm that is now threshing down its multitudes around us!"

But a parent's entreaties could not turn him aside from what he conceived to be the path of duty. He would not desert his colors, as a soldier and a standard-bearer of the Lord, but obeying the orders of his Great Captain, "Go, preach my gospel," he unfalteringly went forward, even though Death threatened him at every step.

> "No matter where, if duty called, he went
> Amid contagion, poverty and death;
> Bent o'er the sufferer, as his hours were spent,
> Nor feared the blast of pestilential breath."

He stood often between the living and the dead, whispering words of comfort, and proclaiming pardon and peace to many a dying sinner. The constraining love of Christ kept him at his post; and his Divine Master preserved him, as "the anointed of the Lord," from the "pestilence which walked in darkness and the destruction which wasted at noonday." And not till this sickness had spent itself, and the horrible scourge was abated, did he leave the place to recruit his wasted energies and refresh his exhausted frame.

At the time of this visitation from the hand of God, Mr. Cutler's heart was cheered by the presence and companionship of his friend, the Rev. William Jackson, at St. Stephen's Church, in that city—a man of equal fidelity with Mr. Cutler, who would not be deterred from entering upon the charge of the important church to which he had been called. He gladly welcomed this brother into the circle where "the fellowship of kindred minds" had endeared such laborers in the Lord's vineyard as Dr. Milnor, and Dr.

McIlvaine, Mr. Cutler, and Mr. Eastburn, very much to each other.

In the autumn of this year, Mr. Cutler, in making his customary report, alluded to the severe scourge with which the Almighty had visited the city, and gratefully acknowledged the hand of God in preserving him and his fellow-laborers in the mission.

"Not one," says he, "of the active missionary members of the church has died; and but two of the communicants, both of whom were strangers in the city, but I trust not in *that 'city which hath foundations*, whose builder and maker is God.'"

Mr. Cutler preached the annual sermon in behalf of the New York Protestant Episcopal City Mission Society about this time, which proved to be a discourse of deep interest, and it was immediately printed. The text was Mark xvi. 20, "And they went forth, and preached everywhere, the Lord working with them." With his usual earnestness and pointedness of appeal, Mr. Cutler urged the managers to provide another missionary church, "with its missionary, its Sunday-schools and daily schools, its library, its prayers, and its alms!"

Though Mr. Cutler performed all the duties of the mission with great faithfulness and regularity, he never contented himself with a bare outline of duty, or trammelled himself by a strict routine of professional service. With an open heart and a ready hand he cast his bread upon the waters, not knowing which would prosper, either this or that.

Wherever a soul could be saved, or a fellow-being raised up from the mire of a degraded and down-trodden humanity, there he was found ever at hand, to assist in the work of mercy. He searched out the forsaken and the wretched, even in the hospitals of the city where he dwelt, proving the poet's words true:

"Nor, till invoked,
Can restless goodness wait; your active search
Leaves no cold wintry corner unexplored—
Like silent-working heaven, surprising oft
The lonely heart with unexpected good."

The case of a poor woman in Forsyth Street interested our city missionary to an unusual degree. Her pain was excruciating, as she was "dying, piecemeal," of cancer. After many faithful visits on the part of the missionary, she came to the knowledge of the Lord Jesus as her Saviour, and Mr. Cutler rejoiced that he had "not labored in vain." He thus makes mention of her reception of the Holy Communion:

"In no condition can a human being appear so wretched as in severe sickness, in the most oppressive weather, and almost neglected. From this condition our poor sufferer was taken; and when I gave her the Sacrament, there was a cleanliness of person, a composure of expression, and a fixedness of devotion which invited your assistance and attention, instead of making such attention the greatest act of self-denial.

"I have now in my mind a perfect picture of her, while I presented the consecrated elements. She was raised up in the bed, by a chair against her back. The teachers had disposed the plain articles of her dress with more than common care. Her face was almost unearthly pale, a clean white cap covering her smooth, dark hair. Her cold hands were stretched out and clasped in the attitude of devotion; and every thing about her discovered kindness and care. Three of the teachers, and the mother of a fourth, were kneeling in front of the bed; and although the only objects in the room which spoke of the riches of this world, were the silver vessels which held the consecrated elements, and which reflected the light of a single candle, yet there was a spiritual importance and an eternal reality about the hopes and the feelings, at that time experienced, which no earthly splendor could have dissipated or diminished."

A few days later, and the spirit took its flight to a better world,

"From the silence that falls upon sin and pain,
To the deathless joys of the angels' strain."

The heart of Mr. Cutler rejoiced indeed, when, in October, so many clerical friends were gathered together in New York, at the General Convention of the Protestant Episcopal Church. Gladly he availed himself of the services of his early friends, Dr. Edson, of Massachusetts, and Dr. Smith, of Kentucky; the latter of whom was advanced to the episcopate (together with Drs. Hopkins, Doane and McIlvaine) before the month closed. Drs. Hopkins, Whitehouse, Stone and Jackson, and many others, were also glad to help on the good work of the City Mission.

A most interesting meeting, in behalf of the mission to Greece, was held at this time in the Church of the Ascension, of which the Rev. Mr. Eastburn, the beloved friend of Mr. Cutler, was rector. One of the missionaries about to sail for that mission was present, and the meeting was addressed by Bishop Meade and by Rev. Messrs. Smith, Richmond, Van Pelt, Eastburn and Cutler. The collection on this occasion amounted to nearly one thousand dollars.

Thus was Mr. Cutler obeying the Scripture injunction: "In the morning sow thy seed, and in the evening withhold not thine hand." One or two instances in his own field of labor may with propriety be cited.

Finding a very poor man who was distressed to pay his rent, Mr. Cutler paid it; and as the man was quite ill, he continued often to visit him. He was stupid and unconcerned about his soul, and remarkably callous. He said more than once, "My heart is cold; I want to feel warm *here*," putting his hand upon his breast. Mr. Cutler inquired, "Do you take opium?" "None," was the reply. "Have you ever imbibed infidel notions?" "No." Mr. Cutler then went through the Apostles' Creed, step by step, and found out at last that the man had been a Universalist. He pointed out to him several passages of Scripture on eternal punishment. He prayed with him and for him, and requested him to put up certain petitions after him, aloud.

Mr. Cutler's journal runs thus: "My attempt to convert this man was not abandoned. I told him the story of the fall of man, the coming and death of the Son of God, and the way in which a sinner might be saved, and urged him to cast himself upon the Saviour."

"*Nov.* 10, 1832.—Called and found him feeble; inquired particularly into his wants and those of the family, and put them in the way of supply. Then I inquired whether there had been any change in his feelings since I last saw him. 'Yes.' 'What change?' said I. 'I can now keep my mind upon God, and pray to him.' 'Do you feel that warmth in your heart you desired?' 'Yes; since yesterday. I feel so easy and happy; but I want more strength—strength in my heart.' I repeated a hymn, offered prayer, and conversed with him about death. I hope and trust this is a conversion to God; if so, it is the second one in the mission this week, and will greatly encourage me."

"*Nov.* 12.—My poor patiént died to-day. I hope he is happy. Just as I left him, dying, I was called to another sick-bed. Oh, while I am preparing one and another sinner to meet his God, O God! prepare *me*, for Christ's sake!"

Another interesting case was that of a poor woman with ten children. The father had died of cholera, and most all the articles of furniture were destroyed, by public authority, to prevent contagion. Mr. Cutler had the family removed to clean and comfortable quarters. Four of the children he placed in the Sunday-school, and two smaller ones in the daily infant school. He procured a place for one of the daughters in a family; and a situation in a store for the eldest son. The mother herself he admitted to the Communion at the Mission Church. Grateful, indeed, was the poor woman to God and to her earthly benefactors.

Mr. Cutler made his next report at the close of this year, and the mission was in a state of unexampled prosperity in every department. The pulpit labors had been blessed. Three Bible-classes for adults had been formed under favorable auspices ; one of which was under the care of a candidate for holy orders. The main Sunday-school consisted of twenty-four teachers and one hundred and eight scholars ; and the daily infant school registered the names of four hundred little children. A new organ had also been purchased, through the exertions of the missionary and a few friends.

Mr. Cutler took especial interest in the daily school, thereby gaining admittance to many families, and enabling him to supply the temporal and spiritual wants of multitudes who lived in the vicinity of the mission.

Early in January, 1833, the anniversary was celebrated, and exercises of an unusually interesting character were enjoyed by all. Besides the missionary, the distinguished Hon. W. A. Duer, LL. D., and Peter A. Jay, Esq., made addresses.

Indeed, in advancing the interests of the City Mission, both clerical and lay assistance was often sought, and a cheerful response was always given.

The Rev. Drs. Milnor, Eastburn, Jackson and Turner, as earnest friends of the mission and its missionary, and the Rev. Drs. Schroeder, Anthon and Wainwright, were chief among the many who rejoiced, as occasion offered, to lend their personal sanction and aid to this noble enterprise.

It was while engaged in this mission that Mr. Cutler put in the form of a tract " A Narrative of the Shipwreck of the Brig Empress, of New York, March 16, 1824, by Capt. F. Washington." It was published, with notes, by the missionary, who then, as in all his future ministry, took so deep an interest in the welfare of those who "go down to the sea in ships" and "do business in the great waters." The spiritual welfare of seamen, of every grade, ever lay near the heart of this devoted man of God.

None but a mind comprehensive like his, and varied in its tastes, could have touched the welfare of so many classes of men; and only a patient, wise and loving spirit would have so readily entered into the details of every case of ignorance, error, guilt or sorrow, which on every hand presented itself. Thus snatching a few hours, at times, from pressing duties, he read the memoir of his friend the Rev. Sutherland Douglass, and before the first month of the new year had passed, he pens a few lines to Mrs. Douglass in this language:

"The memoir of your departed husband is faithful and true; larger extracts from his journal would have enriched the sketch; but as it is, I consider it a beautiful miniature of a saint, now made perfect in heaven. Dear sister! why wast thou so soon and so sorely wounded? and how sweetly has thy spirit seemed to bend beneath the blast! Heaven heal the wound which Heaven has made.

"Your interest in the Man of Sorrows was happily secured before the tempest rose, so you had a covert all ready to which you repaired. . . .

"Your sympathizing brother, B. C. CUTLER."

On Sunday, the 10th of February, 1833, Mr. Cutler preached, as usual, at the Mission Church in the morning, and visited his Sunday-school. The new mission in North Street claimed his attention in the afternoon. The evening he spent with his mother and family.

On Monday, he made several calls among the poor, and devoted the evening to a mission family, closing the day with reading and prayer with them.

On Tuesday morning, he retired to his own room, "to hold communion with his own heart."

He writes in his journal:

"76 *Walker Street, February* 12, 1833.—I have stolen a few hours this day to retire from the business of my mission and perform the duty of self-examination. Just as I finished writing the above, I received a Committee from the Vestry of St. Ann's Church, Brooklyn, conveying a call to me to the rectorship of that church. I have spread it before the Lord! May he direct me! He made me, he called me, I trust, to the ministry of his Son! He has owned me in doing some little good! When sick, he has healed me! when hungry, he has fed me! when forgotten and considered as dead, he has brought me up again! The Lord has blest my labors, and now he has given me a call to a station of honor and profit, and whether I accept it or not, I shall bless him!"

The correspondence on this subject was as follows:

"BROOKLYN, *February* 11, 1833.

"SIR—I have been instructed to inform you that at a meeting of the Vestry of St. Ann's Church, in this place, held this evening, you were duly elected Rector of said church, to succeed the Right Rev. Dr. McIlvaine, upon his resignation, on the 1st of May next, with the salary of sixteen hundred dollars per annum, the use of the parsonage-house and grounds, and other privileges connected with the rectory. And by a resolution of the Board, Mr. Peet and myself were appointed a Committee to present to you this call, and to request your acceptance of the same.

"I am, with great respect, your obedient servant,

"F. C. TUCKER,

"*Secretary of the Vestry of St. Ann's.*

"To Rev. Mr. CUTLER, New York."

REPLY.

"NEW YORK, *February* 18, 1833.

"DEAR SIR—I have taken into serious consideration the call which I received on Tuesday last, from the Vestry of St. Ann's Church.

"After seeking direction from God, and asking the advice of some of the best friends of our church in this city, I have concluded to accept the same.

"May Almighty God, the source of all *life*, and *light*, and *love*, give us, as pastor and people, an abundant blessing, for his dear Son our Lord Jesus Christ's sake.

"I remain, with due respect and consideration, yours, etc.,

"B. C. CUTLER."

As in ancient times, the servant was found at his humble post of service when the Master said "Come up higher." David was feeding the sheep when he was summoned to be king over Israel; Elisha was plowing with the oxen when called to the prophetic office; Nehemiah was bearing the cup when he was deemed worthy to be advanced to signal distinction.

And Mr. Cutler was truly at the post of duty when God called him to another sphere of labor. Who can fail to see that God had been training his servant, through all the previous chapters of his history, for the noble life-work upon which he was about to enter? The life-plan for his dear servant, conceived by God in his paternal love, was now partially unfolded. The chart of the Divine purposes had not, indeed, been laid down beforehand to mortal eye; but it had been the privilege of this disciple to live very near to his Master, and, with implicit trust, he rejoiced that God had determined all things for him, and was leading him on, shaping his life for him, day by day, and year by year. This assurance gave him inward peace, amid all the vicissitudes through which he had passed. Each event, change, and experience was but a turn in the wheel of God's providence, which he felt would, when rightly viewed, add to the lustre of God's glory, even though, at times, to his confused and finite vision, there appeared only a great cloud, and an amber brightness round about it, like to that which Ezekiel, the priest of the Lord, beheld by the river Chebar.

"Ah! God is other than we think;
His ways are far above,
Far above reason's height, and reached
Only by childlike love."

Mr. Cutler thus ever recognized the hand of Divine Providence, and realized at this time that God had indeed "led him forth by the right way, that he might go to a city of habitation!" The notes in his journal tell us of what spirit he was in with regard to this subject:

"*April* 2, 1833.—With the advice of the best friends of the church, I have accepted the call to Brooklyn. It has been with much prayer. May it be heard and answered. I have had many severe regrets at leaving this mission. If I can trace the hand of the Lord in it, it is his intention to humble me; to make me more charitable to ministers who move from their stations, and to give me experience of the practical evils arising from too frequent removals. But in this world we are called continually to *act*. The wisest and holiest of my friends recommended the course I have taken.

"I have refused promotion before, because it seemed my duty to stay where I was; but I think it as proper to accept with gratitude temporal blessings when God gives them, as to submit with patience when he takes them away.

"In two great events of my life I have followed the advice of pious friends, contrary to my own opinion.

"In the first case, I am satisfied now they were right. In this last case, it remains yet to be proved. If God should not make my union with the people of St. Ann's profitable to them and to me, if he should not bring me off conqueror over any difficulties that may arise, I shall never listen to friends again."

At the close of his labors at the City Mission, Mr. Cutler made a deeply interesting report to the Board of Managers.

He took a general survey of this field of labor, and prefaced his statement with the question, "Have we gained any ground on the territory of human misery and woe?

"We have heard the salutes of friendly ordnance and the sound of unfriendly reports. The smoke of both, however, has blown off from the field, and we may now survey at leisure our actual acquisitions.

"The operation of the City Mission had been different from what was expected. The idea of those who originated the plan, was that it should be a mission to the habitations of the poor, which is a simple, practicable, and noble plan; unencumbered with difficulties of any kind, and abounding in blessings to its objects. But this idea was soon connected with another, no less simple and noble; not quite so practicable, but far more useful. It was that of a Free Church, which was the planting of a tree, which, by God's blessing, might bear fruit, year after year, instead of carrying the same fruit to the hungry, from trees more distant, and which yield a less certain supply.

"The society has certainly established a new church in this city, and without permanent injury to any other church. The doors of this church have been opened hundreds of times, and thousands have joined in the worship of God and listened to the Gospel of our Lord Jesus Christ, we cannot but hope, to the good of their immortal souls. The rite of baptism has been administered to sixty-one infants and eleven adults; thirty-six persons have, for the first time, partaken of the Holy Communion. The history of a Free Church, however, is not readily known.

"Such a church attracts hundreds from the fact that it is *free*, and who can tell how many are drawn thither who never think of approaching a church where pews are held as private property; and these very persons, of all others in the community, in a most critical state of mind, just wavering between religion and irreligion.

"Some instances we may here cite:

"1. One man, alarmed at the ravages of the late pestilence in the silence and desertion of the city, like the Prodigal Son, turned his thoughts toward his Father's house, 'where there was bread enough and to spare, while he was perishing with hunger.' He had heard of this Free Church; came here to worship, and exclaimed, 'This is what I want!' This man is now, with a large family, numbered amongst its constant worshippers and laborers.

"2. Another man, a mechanic, whose constant occupation had ensnared him and caused him to absent himself from the sanctuary, was urged by his family to permit them at least to join some church. He consented just as this church was opened, and they came here. By God's blessing they were converted, at length; they prevailed on him to attend, and now that whole family, parents and children, have been received by baptism and the Lord's Supper into the ark of Christ's Church, and appear to be 'steadfast in faith, joyful through hope, and rooted in charity.'

"3. A promising young man came to this city as a clerk, a year or two since, who had no inducement to attend any particular church. He resolved to attend, in rotation, all the churches in the neighborhood of his dwelling, but this proved to be impracticable and unsatisfactory. He came to this church about a year since, has attended regularly on its services, and is now, we trust, a worshipper in spirit and in truth. We point out these cases as specimens of three classes of people to whom this church is profitable, and to whom other churches would be of little service.

"Hundreds of young men who enter the city for business, come and go; the history of whose coming and of whose attendance on these means of grace is, and will be, unknown.

"This mission has a daily school for the children of the poor, and several hundred families have thus become acquainted with the Church and its blessings. The pastor of this church has been truly a missionary to the poor, visiting constantly the poorest part of the population.

"The work which is now given out weekly from our house of industry to respectable females among the laboring classes, almost every piece of which is accompanied with a short

Tract, cannot fail of securing the interest of the poor in this church, and in time lead, perhaps, to permanent religious good. Have we not then effected some good which is not contemplated by other Episcopal Churches?

"The results of the mission may have varied in detail from what it was expected would be accomplished, but its influence for good has doubtless been great. It is not surprising that when this river of God burst from the flinty rock, it should move in a course which those, through whose instrumentality it gushed out, had not intended; especially, since it has become a wider stream than they expected, and promises to course with them through the entire length of the wilderness. To God be all the glory if any good has been effected, and to him, let us look for all that yet may follow."

The value of Mr. Cutler's services at this mission were far above any estimate he placed upon them. Here he labored a year and a half. He was the first missionary, and he had the satisfaction of seeing this infant institution grow in favor with God and man. Here he distributed one thousand or twelve hundred dollars among the poor, and saw about sixty persons added to the Communion.

The quarterly sermon for this season, by Rev. Mr. S., was a most faithful discourse, but Mr. Cutler, in his humility of mind, was almost pained "by the praise, which was without measure, given to him," as the missionary.

"I have also had some very severe things said against me," he says, in his journal, "since I have been in the mission. So I must go through evil report and good report. *It has always been so from my childhood*, and will be so, without doubt, till my death. Let it wean me from the praise of men."

Mr. Cutler found much of his time had been consumed in the temporal matters of the mission. He had little or no time to write sermons, or to study, which he so much desired. When, under peculiar circumstances, therefore, he was called to St. Ann's, without any effort or desire of his own, he felt it his duty and his privilege to accept it, especially as his health was now restored.

When the time came for actual separation from his people, and from multitudes of others among the poor, to whom he had been both father and friend, the tie was found to be exceedingly strong. He could say, with Job, "I was a father to the poor, and the cause which I knew not I searched out." "I delivered the poor that cried, and the fatherless, and him that had none to help him."

Through all the ravages of pestilence, too, he stood by them, and it could not be without many tears and longings of heart that the tie was broken which had so closely bound together pastor and people in this interesting field of labor. Many a one could say of him, He was a real friend to me, and warned me privately of the dangers which beset my path, or, he aided me in time of need ; I owe what I am to him. And many a widow, with choking utterance, could, and did tell her children, "There is your friend and mine. He visited me in my affliction and found you, my son, an employer, and you, my daughter, a happy home."

A good man once said of such, "I would rather such persons should stand at my grave, than to have erected over it the most beautiful sculptured monument of Parian or Italian marble. The heart's broken utterance of reflections of past kindness, and the tears of grateful memory shed upon the grave, are more valuable, in my estimation, than the most costly cenotaph ever reared!" The offerings of such hearts were at this time laid at Mr. Cutler's feet, even in life, an earnest and pledge of that remarkable outpouring of sorrow which, from countless multitudes of grateful hearts, bedewed his new-made grave, many years later, and hallowed his memory with an undying fragrance.

Mr. Cutler often spoke of his life as a city missionary as "the happiest period" of his history. The memories which it left were abiding, and never lost their interest with him, while his short but active ministry for Christ here, was an eminent blessing to the souls committed to his charge. It was here he ministered to those who have been styled "God's heroes;" "the heroes of poverty and of the work-shop; of silent, patient endurance, having learned, through much tribulation, that waiting and suffering is their destined work; the heroes of long-suffering, forbearance and charity, or, of victory over pain, of the unostentatious self-denials of the household; the lowly toiling men and women, climbing mounts of sacrifice, under heavy crosses, without a human hand held out in sympathy; the noble army of martyrs who have found and followed the Master's footprints, in the daily round of humble duties; priests by a heavenly consecration, offering the sacrifices of praise, in garret and cellar; men and women, far from stimulating delights of successful activities; co-workers with Christ, sowing, in hope, the seed whose increase they should never reap." To such he ever loved to minister, wherever they were in the densely thronged city, and point them in faith to that Saviour, who, as they passed up from their dark homes below, through the gates of the morning, into the city without a temple, would greet them with his welcome, and place the crown upon their lowly brows.

In this field, as well as in that where his service was so long rendered, Mr. Cutler went forth often weeping, "bearing precious seed," and in the great harvest-day of souls, he "will doubtless come again with rejoicing, bringing his sheaves with him," not a few of which he gathered for his Lord, as he humbly toiled at the City Mission in New York.

CHAPTER VII.

RECTOR OF ST. ANN'S CHURCH, BROOKLYN, N. Y.

1833–1836.

"Come, as a teacher sent from God,
Charged his whole counsel to declare;
Lift o'er our ranks the Prophet's rod,
While we uphold thy hands with prayer.

"Come, as a messenger of peace,
Filled with the Spirit, fired with love;
Live, to behold our large increase,
And die, to meet us all above!"

ST. ANN'S, Brooklyn, is one of the oldest churches in that city. Its history runs back to a period long anterior to the American Revolution. Owing to the destruction of records during the war, the early history is obscure. In 1785 a small church edifice on Fulton Street was purchased for the use of the congregation, and not long after this date, the society was incorporated by an act of the Legislature, under the title of "The Episcopal Church of Brooklyn." Among the earnest and liberal supporters of the church were Joshua Sands, Esq., and John Cornell, Esq. It might be deemed invidious to make distinctions, but none will deny that these two individuals were the chief benefactors of this ancient parish.

The wife of the former, Mrs. Ann Sands, was foremost in every good work. She devoted her energies, time, and large pecuniary resources to this church, and ere long it was called, out of regard to her unwearied benevolence, "St. Ann's Church." It was "a day of small things" with the church, but this constant friend lived to see its un-

ST ANN'S CHURCH, BROOKLYN.

bounded prosperity, and often called on her venerable cotemporaries to thank God for the blessings he had vouchsafed, and could exclaim with unusual emphasis, "Behold, what hath God wrought!"

In 1795 the church was re-organized and incorporated anew under the title of St. Ann's Church. It has been known by this name up to the present day. For forty years it stood alone, the only Episcopal Church in Brooklyn. From it, sprang nearly all the other churches of her communion, and they may look back with profound reverence, and point to her as the venerable mother of them all.

In 1805 a new stone edifice was erected on the corner of Sands and Washington Streets; but this being injured by the explosion of a powder mill a few years later, and pronounced unsafe, another building was erected in 1824. The Rev. Henry U. Onderdonk, D. D., was then rector of the church.

A long line of faithful witnesses to the truth had ministered to this society: Rev. Messrs. Sayre, Wright, Rattoone, Hull, Nesbitt, Ireland, Feltus, Henshaw and Smith.

Two years more passed, and again St. Ann's lost her pastor, Dr. Onderdonk having been elected Assistant Bishop of the Diocese of Pennsylvania. The same year (1827) his place was supplied by the election of the Rev. Dr. McIlvaine to the rectorship.

In 1832 this able and eloquent man became the Bishop of the Diocese of Ohio. Again was the shepherd of this flock removed to become the chief shepherd in another portion of the field, and St. Ann's was without a rector. Many changes had passed over the church. The loss of their last rector, with his great natural gifts and commanding powers, was deeply felt. The people, lamenting the successive changes in the rectorship in so short a period of time, longed to have a pastor who would continue to feed this flock during a long term of years. On the part of some, unceasing prayers were offered that God would send them "a man after his own heart."

God had prepared for them just such a man. A fearless, faithful preacher; a devoted, loving pastor—one who, by long experience and discipline, had been fitted for the work before him; a man of practical wisdom and sagacity, and unusual knowledge of the human heart in its every phase; one in whom moral courage, ardent zeal, and fervent love, strove for the mastery; and one whose elements of character were so combined as to unite a large congregation in their appreciation of all the essentials of religious truth, whatever minor differences might exist.

No ordinary man could effectively fill such a station; and it was not easy to find one of suitable qualities of mind and heart, who, as a lover of evangelical truth and apostolic order, would satisfy the desires of such a people. The hand of Divine Providence seemed to point to the Rev. B. C. Cutler, A. M. (then city missionary in New York). He was accordingly called to St. Ann's on the 11th of February, 1833; instituted into the rectorship on the 21st of April; and on the 5th of May he opened his ministry, preaching from Zech. iv. 6: "Not by might, nor by power, but by my Spirit, saith the Lord."

The ministry thus commenced, in sole reliance on the blessing of the Holy Spirit, continued the joy of the people of St. Ann's for thirty years, blessing other fields in its course, gathering richer hues reflected from the Cross of Christ, which was faithfully held up to others, increasing in its all-pervading influence, till death set the seal, and the beloved Dr. Cutler was called to a higher ministry than that of earth.

Three months after Mr. Cutler became the rector of St. Ann's, he writes: "I have been well received, and have not been without hope that I have done good. The church, which some foretold would be, in a measure, deserted, has been and is now full. It is now about being closed for painting, and I can have leisure for retirement, meditation and prayer. I desire to mature plans for more vigorous and systematic pastoral labor. I have no object on earth but the good of the Church of God and the salvation of my own particular people. My soul! how is that? I have entered upon a state of prosperity. Seven-and-twenty years of education, discipline and affliction I have passed through. 'It is of the Lord's mercies that I am not consumed.' The Lord enable me, in this new situation, so to labor, so to pray, and so to study, that I may receive the Holy Ghost from on high. I have every thing to thank him for, and every thing to make me humble. I desire to serve him faithfully in the gospel of his Son; and I am willing to serve him painfully, laboriously, and prayerfully."

How prophetic was the closing sentence of this record. We who knew him best, as we look upward and behold his triumph, and, in imagination, gaze upon the radiant crown upon his brow, can with truth say, as we cast a glance backward:

"Not without patient care,
Sore suffering, day-long toil,
And many a wrestling night of prayer,
Didst thou divide the spoil."

Under date of November 11, 1833, another record is made in his journal:

"Six months at Brooklyn. Have had some fruits of my labors. Six persons have become hopefully pious. Two new Sunday-schools have been formed; a mission church opened; a Bible-class established. Thirty-four persons were yesterday confirmed. The last two months, however, have been months of trial. This is a difficult people. They have been instructed by two men before me of great talents, who are now bishops; proud of this, they want every thing, both in and out of the pulpit.

"I have been in 'the depths' crying out to God. In the valley of humiliation, there is hard travelling for human nature; but, if my health is not injured, I hope to derive lasting benefit from my present trials, which are well adapted to cure me of vanity, and pride, and indolence. My hope is, that Christ will help me in my arduous duties. He has said to his ministers, 'Lo! I am with you always, even unto the end of the world;' and one of his ministers has declared, 'I can do all things through Christ, who strengtheneth me.' Lord Jesus, hear my cry, and come and help me!

"If this is prosperity, I shall be well content in adversity. Yet I would not complain of this parish. It is a very noble parish! I commit myself and it to God, determined to lay myself out for awhile longer in doing its duties, remembering that, for the least attainment, great grace is needed, yea, and promised! The Lord be with me! Be this my direction: prudence, patience, perseverance, and, above all, prayer! May God help me to serve this people faithfully, and never give me cause to remove again."

The parish had indeed prospered; but it must not be supposed that even the most faithful man will be exempt from trials in a world where so much human infirmity always remains. The records of Mr. Cutler's journal may require some explanation. Some of the people had requested him to abstain from *ex tempore* efforts in the delivery of his lectures. It seemed to be an infringement of his ministerial rights, and his sensitive spirit was wounded. We do not care to publish all the details of what he regarded as a "sore trial," but, to use his own language, "it was hard work to rise above this trial." He feared it would "interrupt the affections of his heart for the parish;" and yet, he asks, "why should I wish their affections? Let them bestow them on God! He fully acquitted the parties involved of any intentional disrespect, and desired that the trial, permitted by God, might have its perfect work.

With the appointment of Mr. Cutler, the various benevolent operations connected with St. Ann's received a new impetus; and with a rector who judiciously sustained and encouraged every enterprise so nobly begun by his predecessor, new life was infused into every department.

Neither Sunday-school work, nor missionary work, nor charitable societies were allowed to languish; but with fostering hand he diligently cultivated and cherished the seeds of every good work springing up around him, toiling and waiting till they should bud and blossom, as fruitful plants in the garden of the Lord.

His former parish at Quincy still held a place in his affections; and when Capt. E. S. wrote to him from the scene of his early labors, he made the following reply:

"BROOKLYN, *November* 12, 1833.

"MY DEAR SIR—I have had two silver cups made in New York. The price of the one which was made to your order is twenty dollars. The other, I now, through you, present to the Wardens and Vestry of Christ Church, Quincy, as a token of my continued regard. I would add the *hope*, that every member of that congregation may, by the Holy Spirit, be brought in love to the Saviour to drink from that Cup, and the *prayer*, that all who drink therefrom may live for ever. With love to all Christian friends,

"Yours, etc. B. C. CUTLER."

At the parsonage in Brooklyn, the household was increased by the addition of Mr. Cutler's venerable mother, and of a relative from Montreal.

Early in the year 1834 Mr. Cutler prepared a short autobiography up to that date; important portions of which have already appeared in this volume. We give the remainder of it a place here, to show with what spirit, desires and aims he commenced his labors in Brooklyn. The ancient motto, "know thyself," was indeed never forgotten by him, and few men ever lived who were equally impartial in scrutinizing their own heart and life.

The record is thus made:

"*Brooklyn, L. I., Parsonage, Feb.* 10, 1834.—I have often set apart my birthday as a day of meditation and prayer. This year I determined to do so; but the pressure of other duties prevented retirement on that day, which was the 6th of this month, and I have embraced the first opportunity. May the Lord, the searcher of hearts, be with me! On the 6th of this month I reached the thirty-sixth year of my life. I have lived more than half the life of man. In many respects it has been eventful; a brief record of it may serve to make me cleave more closely to the Lord." [Here follows what has been already given, and therefore omitted in this place.—ED.]

The record of his "religious life," up to this date, he thus closes:

"I think I am more humble than I ever was, and feel more as if I were less than the least of all saints. What is the history of—My praying to God?
My reading the Holy Scriptures?
My self-examination?
My conversation?
My preaching?

"1. *Prayer to God.* The character of my prayers for many years is but poor. They have been short, and productive of little immediate comfort. I have been regular in them; never omitting them. I think I have had answers to them, and have continued to pray as if I had. I have been for years in the daily habit of ejaculatory prayer, and I retire three times a day for prayer, but my noon prayer is very short. I have, for many years, felt concerned to think that those prayers which have afforded me most enjoyment, at the time, have been social. I feel that I have not that intimate union with God in sacred prayer which enriches the soul. In church, I do not think I have that sense of God's presence which I once had; neither do I think I have that tenderness of conscience which I once had. I fear I want watchfulness joined to prayer. I feel more confidence in the result of prayer than I ever did, and more freely and more confidently commit *all* my ways to God. But enjoyment of the light of God's countenance, and the trembling anxiety not to sin, are wanting in me, I fear. At family prayers I always sing, read twenty verses in the New Testament, and make a short prayer.

"2. *Self-examination.*—This duty I faithfully performed when I first became a member of the church. I used to spend two hours every Saturday night in this duty.

"In college, I could recall at night almost every word I had uttered during the day. I have practiced this duty all my religious life; of late I have been more resolute in it. I have kept a diary for years. My rule has long been, and now is, to spend two hours a week in this work—Saturday or Sunday evening.

"3. *Reading the Scriptures.*—I have read these daily. I generally read a chapter in the Old Testament in the morning, and a chapter in the New Testament with my family. My reading I commence with a short prayer for the Holy Spirit, and I keep on my table the work of some spiritually-minded author, to peruse after the Bible is read—Baxter or Newton, or Leigh Richmond, or Martyn, or Edwards, or Mrs. Rowe. I have not the faculty of applying Scripture to my own situation, as I suppose many Christians have. But the general views which it gives of God, of Christ, of the Church, of the Divine government do me good, I think. But I fear I read the Bible without gathering the instruction I might from it. Oh that my mind were more calm, more spiritual! The Bible appears to me as a great ocean, and I seem only to have seen a part of its surface, and to have picked up a few pearls upon the shore. This is the result of sixteen years steady reading, and much study. Oh, the depth of the riches, both of the wisdom and knowledge, of God! How unsearchable are his judgments, and his ways past finding out."

"4. *My Conversation.*—When I first became a communicant, my conversation was almost exclusively spiritual—'how sweet is memory still!' When I went to college, my conversation began to be more literary, as I had a relish for the beauties of the classics. Still it was in a measure spiritual. In my first parish I had some sweet seasons of spiritual conversation. During my travels (two years) in different parts of the country, my conversation, as far as I can remember, was in a degree spiritual. In the New York City Mission (eighteen months) more spiritual than ever. In St. Ann's, conversation has been of a cheerful character. The duties of a large parish have burdened my mind, and an *over-pressure* has produced *over freedom*—a natural consequence. I have to deplore the fact, that my conversation at home has not partaken more largely of religion. It is utterly a fault. God forgive me, for Christ's sake! What would my companions say of my conversation? They might say, He strives to be agreeable, and aims to please; but ought he not to *strive* to make conversation with his family, and in every circle, profitable? *Strive* he ought, for the natural heart and mind are averse to spiritual things. How would I converse if left for weeks without any restraint? I fear, 1st, cheerfully; 2d, theologically; 3d, spiritually.

"5. *My Preaching.*—It has often been intimated to me that I am not a powerful or an impressive preacher, but an experimental one, and in some degree interesting. I should be content, if it could be said, His preaching is *always* instructive, generally interesting, and often impressive. My preaching is too much addressed to the understanding. It should be more directed to the conscience and to the heart. I have not kept near enough to the Cross. I have too many sermons *about* religion. Of old, the watchword was, 'to the law and to the testimony;' now, it should be, 'to Christ and to the Cross.' I determine not to know any thing among my people, 'save Jesus Christ and him crucified.'

"I have had fruit after my labors, and my communicants have generally been drawn to Christ by love. Thanks be to God for any fruit!"

As the mariner often consults his compass and observes carefully every variation of the needle, so did Mr. Cutler, as a Christian voyager over "life's solemn main," with extreme solicitude watch the direction of his heart and inmost thoughts. Lest he should make shipwreck of his faith, he was often sounding the depths where his soul was, and while realizing that God was working within him to will and to do, he felt that he himself must work " with fear and trembling."

Another year passed since he came to Brooklyn, and in his parish he could mark sure and steady progress. He thus writes to a former parishioner :

TO J. M., ESQ., OF BOSTON.

"*April* 9, 1834.

MY DEAR SIR—Your esteemed favor by Mr. Stone, I received from his hands. He spent the Sabbath here, and embarked on Wednesday for Europe. . . . . Since I wrote you, things appear very differently from what they formerly did, in this parish. I have had many formal and substantial proofs of the respect and growing attachment of this people. Gentlemen of the vestry have called at my house to assure me that the parish was in a most harmonious condition. They talk of building a new parsonage the coming year. For a fine house I care little; for the *respect of my parishioners* I care much. . . . I had seven persons added to the Communion in February, and seven more are now ready.

"We have about four hundred children in our two Sunday-schools; one hundred and fifty persons in the Bible-class. Our monthly missionary meeting has been well attended. . . .

"Our household is well. To all your dear group give our best love. Let us look and live above the world. If God has given us salvation, he has given us more than all the world. Let us study to serve and please God, and to prepare for that hour when heart and flesh shall fail us. Then may God be the strength of our heart, and our portion for ever.

"Ever yours, B. C. CUTLER."

The journal of Mr. Cutler will give the most accurate view of the routine of his life in the family circle and in the parish :

"*April* 24, 1834.—I received the intelligence of the death of my brother-in-law, Charles Bancroft, Esq., of Montreal. This is a heavy stroke for my family, and I pray that it may be sanctified. An afflicted family survive to mourn his loss. They have our prayers. I desire to be faithful to the friends I have remaining—my brothers-in-law, at least—by example, if I may not be permitted to speak plainly. Oh, may I stand with my loins girt about, and my lamp trimmed and burning, as one that waits for his Lord, lest coming suddenly, he find me sleeping !"

"*May* 5.—Oh ; what a privilege it is to preach the unsearchable riches of Christ to a perishing world ! I bless God a thousand times for permitting me to preach !"

"*May* 19.—I attended a missionary meeting on Tuesday, in company with some of the best ministers of our church. The prospect is delightful for the success of missions in our church. I have never witnessed such a spirit before. O Lord ! send the Holy Ghost into my soul, that I may open my mouth with all boldness, to make known the mystery of the gospel, for which I am an ambassador in the bonds of infirmity !"

"*June* 30.—My soul is more alive than it has been ; but I have to mourn over the conquests of my spiritual enemies, which have often covered me with shame. Oh, that I might have grace from on high, to live just as I ought to live—a holy and spiritual life ! I must rise earlier in the morning ; I must visit my people more, and strive to make my conversation profitable. Yesterday I exchanged pulpits with Rev. Mr. Shelton, of Newtown."

"*July* 14.—'Faint, yet pursuing,' is my motto now. When will Christ be made to me the chief among ten thousand ?"

"*July* 21.—Went to Rockaway, to find relief from the heat. Rockaway is too fashionable a place for me. The world is too powerful in its influence, and I desire never to have any relaxation from which God is excluded. How am I living? I think I am living a life of faith, not expecting my happiness here, but hereafter, and seeing him who is invisible. I do not think that I am making provision for the flesh, or courting the praises of men."

In the summer of 1834 cholera prevailed, to some extent, in the city of Brooklyn, and many souls among Mr. Cutler's people were summoned from time into eternity. Mr. Cutler was at Newport, passing the summer vacation there, and from thence he wrote to a dear friend and parishioner.

TO MRS. P., OF BROOKLYN.

"MY DEAR MADAM—Though I am trying to forget my cares, I cannot forget my friends. Amidst every thing pleasant, and many things to charm me, I bear on my mind, with affectionate remembrance, my flock. They occupy my mind in my happiest and best moments. In a few days I intend to commence my journey homeward, which will be hastened, in proportion, as I perceive by the papers the increase of that scourge of heaven, the cholera. . . . Mrs. C. and I were quite sick before reaching this place, and I did not recover for two days after my arrival. Of the sea, I can say, as good Bishop Hall of old said, 'The sea brooked not me, nor I the sea, an unquiet element made only for wonder and use, not for pleasure.'

"In this retreat every thing is delightful. This morning I spent alone, rambling over the most glorious battlements of ocean scenery I ever saw. It is a place called Paradise, an immense pile of rocks, affording a view of the whole southern end of this fine island, and of a noble amphitheatre of sea and sky. Around are highly cultivated fields and farms, and near by, entirely sequestered, are groves of forest trees, affording a perfect shade, broken only to give a view of the neighboring ocean. The morning has been peerless; a cool, bracing air from the northwest, a bright sun and a clear sky, relieved only by a few silvery clouds. I confess I have not for years been so elevated by natural scenery. . . .

"Believe me the obliged and affectionate friend of you and yours,

B. C. CUTLER."

He hastened back to his people, and soon had the pleasure of welcoming his predecessor back to St. Ann's. No one of his flock was more pleased with this visit than the pastor himself. Let us look at his diary, and read his notes at this time :

" *Oct.* 6, 1834.—St. Ann's Church has enjoyed the presence and assistance of its former pastor and eminent friend, the Bishop of Ohio. What a glorious preacher of the gospel! glorious in the best sense. I earnestly desire that what he said may be blest. What a favor to hear him preach! I have, indeed, been blest. I had a meeting of the communicants on Saturday night. In my address, I animadverted upon the decay of spiritual affections in the parish.

" O God, I commit this parish to thee! Thou must order and overrule, or all will be confusion. If thou shalt bless, we shall be blessed ; and if thou shalt smile, all will be sunshine!

" O God, I am nothing! keep me ever under thy eye! I am resolved ever to live to thee, and to take prayer to God, through Christ, as my great catholicon—a medicine for every disease, a defence against every enemy."

" *Oct.* 13.—The visit of the Bishop of Ohio gave me great searchings of heart ; not that I envied his noble greatness, but that I felt so keenly my own deficiencies! How can I teach the people after him? How will they listen to me? I have to fly hourly to Christ, in my poor way, for aid. How is my soul? It is lean, distracted with cares, which are of no avail. Let me take up my cross.

" How could my friends have counselled me to accept this station, after such a man as Bishop McIlvaine? My situation has been trying, indeed. God knows it all! Oh, what a heart I have! Oh, that I could rise above all earthly cares and earthly fears! Lord, stretch forth thy right hand and help me!"

"*Nov.* 3.—I desire that this short and vain life should be spent in prayer, and in building up a spiritual temple. My reading of the Scriptures has been very edifying for some time past. I feel more and more disposed to follow the example of the Apostles—'Daily, in the temple, and from house to house, they ceased not to teach and preach Jesus Christ.'"

"*Dec.* 29.—Yesterday I preached twice, and had, in some measure, the presence of God. Yet I mourn my leanness. All my righteousness is as filthy rags. My preaching is powerless, compared with what it ought to be. Some of my people praised my sermon, but I felt its want of holiness. Glory to God for such a gospel sermon as Bishop Smith preached yesterday! Oh that the stream of sweet and solemn truth from the river above might flow through our sanctuaries below!

"The extra labors and extra rejoicing of Christmas season have exhausted all my spirits; but I feel more than ever determined to be devoted to God. Cleanse, Lord, my heart. Last week I received many tokens of kindness from my parishioners. Oh that I might repay them by increased holiness, wisdom, and love!"

The following letter will show that wisdom and love, and humility, too, adorned his life in his pastoral intercourse:

TO MRS. P., ON THE DEATH OF A CHILD.

"*December* 19, 1834.

"DEAR MADAM—Your note gave me pain, and yet pleasure. While it informed me that you had *lost* much, it plainly discovered that you had *found more.* Affliction stands little in need of human comforters, when there are such feelings in the hearts of the immediate sufferers. I said, involuntarily, 'They can preach better than I.' 'I will go and sit with them, and be a listener.' . . . . How sweet to possess such a faith at any time, but, most of all, when nature is inclined to rebel. For the loss which Mr. P. and you have sustained, I sincerely grieve, and for the affliction which your daughters have been called to bear. . . . . This dispensation says, 'All flesh is grass;' that no age is secure. Oh, happy if all would become as little children, 'for theirs is the kingdom of heaven!' Happy are those who have made a short voyage across the sea of life, and have been wafted by zephyrs into a calm and quiet haven! while we are tossed upon mountain waves, troubled on every side, and have the certainty of shipwreck to the *body*, at least.

"Without the consciousness of a single sin; without entertaining, for one moment, the fear of death; without the slightest idea of a justly provoked God; and without running the risk of eternal ruin for a single hour; to pass this 'vale of tears,' with all these exceptions, and to be transferred from the arms and the smiles of an earthly, to the arms and the smiles of a Heavenly Father, is a favor which could hardly have been expected to attend any of the posterity of our fallen race. Such reflections, I trust, will mitigate your grief. If you could see the little cherub now, smiling, safe with the thousands of Christ's little ones, you could not, you would not, call him back again to sin, to suffer, and again to *die!*

"Respectfully and affectionately, your friend and pastor,

"B. C. C."

The year 1835 opened with encouraging prospects in every department of his work at St. Ann's. He enters upon its untried duties with this record of his heart's desire: "Let me not leave one stone unturned, for the salvation of this people! I hope God will bless me in saving my own soul, and the souls of those who hear me."

"*Jan.* 19, 1835.—I feel a strong desire to be holy and prepared for heaven; but *hell is paved with good intentions!* God is blessing the word preached in this place. Oh may I live to see thy saints in full prosperity!"

"*Jan.* 26.—Bishop Smith is now with me, a holy man, and a holy atmosphere he breathes out around him. But my own peace is destroyed often by bodily infirmities and temptation. Oh, weak and worthless disciple that I am! 'who shall deliver me from this body of death?'

"My interest in the Scriptures increases. Oh may the Bible soon be my garden, my palace, my home, heaven my journey's end, immortal souls my hire and my riches, and a clear account at the day of judgment my great concern!

Woe is me, that I am constrained to dwell in the tents of Mesech and among the dwellings of Kedar! I see, and feel, and deplore defilement in my heart, in the Church, and in the world.

> 'Who, who would live alway, away from his God;
> Away from yon heaven, that blissful abode!'"

Mr. Cutler ever regarded his Sunday-schools with affectionate interest and deep solicitude, knowing that the good seed of the Divine Word must be sown in early youth if it is to bear much fruit unto eternal life. On the 9th of February of this year, the public examination of these schools was held, and the pastor made an interesting address, noting the wonderful and blessed change which had taken place in the development of so much interest in, and attention to, this department of Christian labor. With heart and hand fully engaged in building up the kingdom of Christ, Mr. Cutler was never satisfied with what had been done, but was ever "pressing forward," lamenting he could accomplish no more.

"*March* 23, 1835."—He writes: "I want a soul, enlarged, to take in a wide extent of duty for myself, and to point out a wide circle for others. O Lord! give me, I pray, large ness of heart! I propose to myself no object but the service of Christ, and I trust God will own and bless my labor."

"*March* 30.—Last week was one of labor in my study. My heart and my parish are becoming more engaged in the great realities. Oh, we are but half awake!

> 'My drowsy powers, why sleep ye so?
> Awake, my sluggish soul!
> Nothing has half thy work to do,
> Yet nothing 's half so dull.'"

"*April* 6.—My day yesterday was only tolerable. Oh, what miserable coldness in the pulpit! When shall I awake to the great and God-like work of saving souls? I do not feel as if I ever preached a sermon in my life. Oh, for unction! Oh, for solemnity! Oh, for courage! By the grace of God, I am resolved to lay out my whole soul in preaching the gospel! But, then, without the power of God, all will be as sounding brass and a tinkling cymbal."

"*April* 24.—'Passion Week' has proved a good season to my soul. Christ never appeared so precious. My Rev. Brother Edson came and spent the week with me. We had a most delightful season."

"*April* 27.—Last week was full of work, and I had much to regret in my own spirit. O sin! sin! how thou dost defile my soul and rob me of my peace! Oh, for a closer walk with God!"

In May, 1835, the Rev. Mr. Cutler was appointed, as a special agent for the Domestic and Foreign Missionary Society, to attend the Convention of the Diocese of Virginia. An important change took place this year in the missionary operations of the Protestant Episcopal Church, when the Domestic and Foreign Boards held their triennial meeting, and a new constitution was adopted. This was simultaneous with the meeting of the General Convention, held this year at Philadelphia. Earlier than this, however, the Missionary Society, desirous of exciting a deeper interest in the cause throughout the whole church, appointed Mr. Cutler to represent the society in Virginia, and Dr. Milnor to do the same in Massachusetts. Mr. Cutler had always been the steadfast friend of missions, deeming it a primary duty of the church to carry on the missionary work. He felt it a privilege, too, to contribute of his time, his energies, and his resources, to such a cause. In this, his people held up his hands and cheered him with a ready response. Missionary intelligence was ever given to the people, and the missionary spirit fostered and increased in old St. Ann's. The rector became this year a life member of the Missionary Board, and a member of the Foreign Committee.

Whatever embarrassments surrounded the work, or whatever difficulties he met with, Mr. Cutler never relaxed his exertions or ceased to encourage others. He constantly looked at what has been termed "the marching orders" of the Church of Christ; and, while upon his banner was always inscribed "Go forward," he was willing to leave all results to his Divine Leader.

He was ever ready to present the subject to the churches, and on this occasion he wrote home from Lynchburg, Va.:

"The Bishop and Convention received me kindly. Resolutions were passed respecting my visit. I preached on missions, and Bishop M. made an affectionate notice of me and my cause in his concluding address. The result was beneficial to the society; six hundred dollars was raised on the spot. The interest awakened in the breasts of the clergy who were assembled, will operate upon all their parishes when they return. The Lord bless his own work!"

He returned home by the way of Staunton, visiting the three great natural curiosities of Virginia—the Peaks of Otter, the Natural Bridge, and Weir's Cave. To a dear and valued parishioner, whose kindnesses to him were often (to use his own language) "like a cup of cold water to a thirsty disciple of Christ," he wrote a long and glowing account of these scenes. The magnificent views from the lofty peaks of Otter filled his very soul with grand emotions; and, thrilled with delight, he knelt down, exclaiming, "Great and marvellous are thy works, Lord God Almighty!" He sent to this friend a flower plucked from the very summit (and faded when sent), saying: "You see by it how hard it is for those who once tasted of the dews so near to heaven to flourish on the earth again! An apostle says 'it is impossible!'" Of the main object of his journey, he thus wrote to the same friend:

"Of my reception by the Bishop and clergy of this ancient and chivalrous State, who were assembled at L. to spend a week in holy duties, surrounded, too, by many of their respective flocks, who have followed the shepherds to this 'high place of the field,' I have hardly time to speak. Suffice it to say, I had 'a feast upon that holy mountain,' a feast of fat things. I felt from the services a sweet stimulus to duty and a 'holy luxury.' The object of my special agency was accomplished, by the blessing of God, and I left the place after I had set up 'a stone of help.'"

Mr. Cutler reached home from this journey on the 5th of June.

Among the early records of his journal, after his return, are the following; and they show how, while engaged in Christ's work, he did indeed "cleave unto him:"

"*July* 6, 1835.—I must be conformed to the image of Christ. Without special devotion to Christ, I am a withered branch. Christ is our life—the life of our souls; the life of our graces, our duties, our ordinances. O Christ! if I am deceived in supposing myself thine, open my eyes to see, before it be too late!"

"*Aug.* 2.—Since I have been here, I have had but little freedom in the pulpit. I have been sorely tried, but it has been for my good. 'But these sheep, what have they done?' My ministry would have been more vigorous had I *felt* as I desired; but who am I? what are my thoughts? Let me take up my cross! This is a cross I have always had, and always shall have, and it will always be painful, but then comes the crown! When that is once on my head, I shall not regret or repine at the past. These are my portion now: silence, prayer, labor, and indifference to the opinion of men. O Lord, enable me to attend to them!"

"*Aug.* 30.—I have little to record about my life and walk with God, only that my mind is continually reverting to him; that I make ejaculatory prayer a constant practice, and that I strive to do the work of an evangelist. But oh, how far from that holy, untiring, undaunted soldier and ambassador of Christ which I ought to be, which I profess to be, and which I promised to be!

"'Hast thou a lamb in all thy flock
I would disdain to feed?
Hast thou a foe before whose face
I fear thy cause to plead?'

Let this be my appeal to Christ."

In September, 1835, the General Convention of the Protestant Episcopal Church met in Philadelphia. Two missionary bishops for the West were elected. Four votes in the House of Bishops were given for Mr. Cutler, but the majority were for Dr. Kemper. The rector of St. Ann's was thankful to be counted worthy of this high office by some of his brethren, yet rejoiced in the adverse decision; for he felt no desire to leave his people at this period, and he saw the hand of God in it all, pointing him to a less extensive, but not less comprehensive and laborious field of labor where he was. His journal reads thus:

"*Sept.* 21.—I feel a settled desire to live near to God. I know that on earth I have no abiding city, but seek one to come. Yet I wish to keep in an *active, working* frame of mind, and I purpose to devote all my days to the service of God and the good of man. The rest I leave to God, looking only for a permanent pillow on which to *rest* in the grave, and a perfectly peaceful residence in the tomb."

"*Sept.* 28.—Attended a large meeting at St. George's Church, New York, as a farewell to the missionaries about to sail for Greece. Bishop Kemper preached from the text, 'Go ye into all the world and preach the gospel to every creature.' For this, and every thing respecting the church, God's holy name be praised!"

On the 6th of October, 1835, the Rev. Mr. Cutler received the degree of Doctor of Divinity from Columbia College, New York. In a note on this fact, he says:

"As I take every thing from the Lord, I suppose he has inclined the hearts of that corporation to confer it.

Through evil report and through good report, O Lord! conduct me safely.

> 'Each blessing to my soul more dear,
> Because conferred by thee.' "

Religious and literary societies often loved to couple the name of Dr. Cutler with their cause, and felt privileged to have him as a participant in their aims and plans. What did this humble man of God say of himself?

"*Nov.* 9, 1835.—If I know myself at all, I love God and Christ. I have no esteem for myself and the world. I desire to be conformed to the will of God. The fear of man bringeth a snare; the love of ease steals from soul-time and spiritual comfort. Oh, I would take unto me the whole armor of God, that I may be able to stand!"

"*Nov.* 30.—I feel a strong desire, and a determination, by God's help, to preach the Word boldly. There are great temptations to preach it timidly. With me the great temptation is to avoid breaking up my friendship with many amiable people, who will yet cleave to the world. But I pray God to give me boldness. My sources of happiness are getting more and more circumscribed, and I am looking more to Christ as the great and refreshing object. Nothing on earth gives me happiness, and I perceive little enjoyed by others. It must be Christ, the desire of all nations, who can refresh a penitent sinner's soul. Come, thou fount of every blessing!"

Dr. Cutler, wherever he went, always gathered about him many cordial friends. Among his clerical friends in Brooklyn and New York, none were more dear to him than the Rev. Dr. Eastburn and the Rev. William Jackson. The latter, then rector of St. Stephen's, New York, sailed for England early in 1836, and the temporary absence of this friend he much lamented. Every thing that love and friendship could do, however, was freely bestowed in the way of furthering all the prospective plans of Mr. Jackson, and Dr. Cutler accompanied him to the ship, "bidding him 'God speed!'"

In the midst of active duties, in March of this year, Dr. Cutler received a fall, but providentially escaped without serious injury. Thus prevented from going out of doors for days, he was obliged to send a note (instead of a visit in person) to one of his parishioners, who was ill:

TO MRS. P.

"*March* 9, 1836.

"MY DEAR AND RESPECTED FRIEND—However severe your indisposition, I know you will say, It is the Lord, let him do what seemeth to him good. It is said there is a nobleness in the very expression of a Musulman, which would distinguish him from a large group of (to him) unbelievers, and why? His whole character is formed on the single and grand idea that God does every thing. There can, therefore, be no mistake in the past; there can be no error committed in the future—*all* is fixed in adamantine laws. Baptize and graduate this idea by the revealed word of God, and let it be the basis of the Christian character. The pious Dr. Payson said, 'I was run away with, in a stage coach, and was I alarmed? No! I knew that my God and Saviour had the reins.' *What* shall harm you, if ye be followers of God, as dear children? This is certainly a sure and safe sentiment. Nothing shall harm me; nothing shall overtake me; nothing shall happen to me, but by permission of God. My valued friend, whose warm heart meets with as warm a one in your pastor's bosom, ponder on the word of God, and give yourself to prayer. Then will you be able to rejoice in every thing, in every earthly condition, and even to triumph where most mortals are left to tremble.

"Gratefully and affectionately yours, B. C. CUTLER."

Later in the year, when absent at Newport, Dr. Cutler wrote to another parishioner, who was suffering a long and protracted illness:

TO MISS M. C—L.

"MY DEAR AFFLICTED FRIEND—Your case is peculiar, and yet others have been called to similar trials, and for a similar purpose.

"This is precisely the way by which your soul could most easily and safely be prepared for an inheritance incorruptible, and that fadeth not away. 'Shall not the Judge of all the earth do right?' Can he err who has displayed so much wisdom in the world of creation. Behold how he bringeth light out of darkness, and fruits and flowers out of the dry roots and barren fields. Oh, my dear, and as an afflicted, *doubly* dear friend, all will yet be *right*. Light shall be brought of your darkness, and fruits and flowers shall yet spring up in your pathway; for that path is the path of the just, which shall 'shine more and more,' unto the perfect day. Pray without ceasing, and forget not

"Your friend and pastor, B. C. CUTLER."

This devoted parishioner was raised up from the borders of the grave, and for years after, welcomed her faithful pastor beneath her roof, who never failed to point out to her, amid the comforts of an earthly home, the more enduring joys of an heavenly one while she—profiting by his instructions, is still abounding in every good word and work.

Dr. Cutler often said, in life, Christians were too anxious about their condition in this world, and deemed it their duty to consider little, whether the road was rough or smooth, provided there was a blessed home at their journey's end. The idea is well conveyed in a note to a friend, written in June, 1836:

"I often ride past a house now in quite a ruinous state. I ask, Why is that man content and happy now in such a wretched and dangerous dwelling house as that? The answer is, He has a *new*, and safe, and *superb mansion*, just ready to receive him. Say to *him*, 'How can you live in that hovel?' He replies: 'Oh, it is only for a few days; my house is nearly ready!' I too have a house; not building, but builded—not with hands, not to last one or two centuries, but *for ever*. John xiv. 2: 'I go to prepare a place for you; and if I go and prepare a place for you, I will come again, and receive you unto myself, that where I am, there ye may be also.'

B. C. C."

But we return to Dr. Cutler's journal:

"*Sept.* 26.—God has been giving my people a spirit of liberality."

"*Oct.* 10.—Yesterday I preached at Flatbush, from 'Woe

unto them that are at ease in Zion.' I prayed that God would afford me help, and I obtained it. To Jesus I go, when I want aid, refreshment, or rest. In my parish, for the last month, I have felt more enlargement and love. Oh, that God would comfort me in Christ among this people, according to the years that he hath afflicted me. For two years I have been ill at ease, and now I see what keeps me humble and prevents my setting my heart upon things below. I have had a conversion on the death-bed—I believe a sincere one. Oh, what a joy to meet him (T. Perry) in heaven! God appears to be hearing my prayers. Twice I have preached in Flatbush, and think not in vain. I believe I shall hear in heaven, of one of my sermons preached there."

"*Oct.* 17.—Last week, my dear mother, who is staying with me, was very ill, and brought near to Death's door. Sunday I preached in the morning from the words, 'Though your sins be as scarlet, they shall be as white as snow.' One man came into the vestry with the cry, 'What shall I do to be saved!' O Lord! may it become general."

Dr. Cutler's letters to various friends, during this year are extremely interesting, but by the extracts already given, his devotion to his people is sufficiently demonstrated. His correspondence with others prove how unalterable was his Christian friendship, and that he clung to his friends when poverty, persecution, or any trial whatsoever befell them.

TO THE BISHOP OF KENTUCKY.

"My Venerated and Beloved Bishop—I received, with much sorrow, and yet with joy, the letter of our dear friend. I grieve for all you have suffered, but I cannot but believe it will all result in an increase of glory and happiness to our gracious Saviour, and to the sufferer. I would fly to you on the wings of love, and sit beside you, or at your feet, at your Convention, but I have work to do here. Three of my parishioners have desired to join me in suffering with you at this time of pecuniary trial. Please accept the enclosed, and say nothing.

"With much love, I am yours, B. C. Cutler."

TO THE SAME.

"BROOKLYN, *July* 26, 1836.

"MY BELOVED AND VENERATED FRIEND—I fear your feelings have been much wounded at the course which the *Churchman* has taken. But tarry thou the Lord's leisure. I wrote a letter to the editor, and read it before Drs. Milnor and Eastburn. It was, however, concluded that this was not the best course to be adopted. Every person I have seen, has expressed but one sentiment on the subject of your trials. Of this be assured, that there doth not exist in the State of Kentucky the *power* of blasting the character of its Bishop with the people of the East. 'Know all the Jews which knew me from the beginning.' That Bishop might say, They all know my manner of life from my youth up. We do know it, and bless God for it. . . . . In due time, all will be well. . . .

"I attended the funeral of Bishop White. . . . President Colton has resigned. Mr. ——— resigns Troy, and I suppose many others, if they were to attend much to little discontents.

"St. Ann's is at peace, I believe; on many accounts it was never more prosperous. So say some who know. There is no excitement, but I believe the Holy Spirit is operating, like leaven.

"With all my heart, I am yours, B. C. C."

Thus did Dr. Cutler prove that his friendship was one for hours of darkness, as well as for hours of sunshine. In his own parish it was abundantly demonstrated, through a long course of years. The shadow of God's upraised hand of chastening often darkened his own pathway, and he could administer a balm to many a distressed heart, which none but an experienced hand can ever appropriately give. Through cross to crown, he daily felt was the direction for life's onward journey, and relying on the promise of an unchangeable Jehovah, he knew, and could declare to all,

"Till thy spirit is set free,
As thy day, thy strength shall be."

CHAPTER VIII.

MINISTRY AT ST. ANN'S CHURCH—CONTINUED.

1836–1840.

IN the autumn of 1836 the shadow of death was over Dr. Cutler's household. His venerable mother, who had been residing with him for a short time, was ill for several weeks with inflammation of the lungs. On the 26th of October the struggle with disease was over, and she entered into rest, aged seventy-five years. She was a native of Georgetown, S. C., and was the daughter of Esther, the only sister of Gen. Francis Marion. Combining a noble simplicity of character, with high-toned and ardent feelings, she won the respect and esteem of all who knew her. The intense love she showed for her children was reciprocated by them all, and by none more fully than by this son, from whose home her spirit took its flight to a better one above. An affecting record is found in Dr. Cutler's journal, under date of

"*Oct.* 31, 1836.—On the 26th inst. my beloved mother departed this life; she gradually sank into the sleep of death, breathing her last with her head upon my heart. *There* will her remembrance *last* so long as that heart continues to beat.

"Thirty-eight years of unchanged and fervent affection have I experienced from that mother, and now she is no more! No more shall I see that eye lighted up with joy to meet me when I approach; no more see that maternal smile; no more hear that much loved voice, witness those maternal benedictions, or grasp that maternal hand! Farewell! farewell, my dear beloved mother! Peace be with thee! Tears of affection now fill my eyes; grief—a tender but living grief, an endless grief—dwells in my heart. Here lives, and shall live, thy image. Here will I tell over thy sweet and precious acts of love.

'Time shall tear thy image last from me.'"

"After the funeral," he wrote to a friend, "I opened many volumes of poems, hymns and funeral dirges; but alas! save from Cowper, I could find nothing written to the memory of a mother. So I selected one of Cowper's hymns, beginning,

'In vain my fancy strives to paint
The moment after death.'

And one from Bishop Heber:

'Beneath our feet and o'er our head
Is equal warning given;
Beneath us lie the countless dead,
Above us is the heaven.'

With these I went over to Bond Street to have a season of prayer, etc., and to breakfast with all our family.

"The first hymn we sang. I read 1 Thess. iv and v, and then a large family circle united in prayer. These are precious moments, and with a little attention to 'times and seasons,' they are grateful even to the children. They all welcomed their uncle most cheerfully, as they have from their cradles. But, my dear friend, the mind of the young, and the gay, and the prosperous, has depths in which *huge* sorrows may be sunk."

For a long time, Dr. Cutler declared, tears were his meat and drink, and that half his ambition was destroyed when his beloved parent descended to the tomb. Who can but honor him for a love which never knew diminution from the hour of its dawn? He loved his mother with a deep, devoted affection through life; and when she was dead, like Joseph, he wept bitterly, and embalmed her in his heart. He was ever a crown of rejoicing to her; and often was she fed with that meat, the world knows not of, by this beloved son; and it was enough for her to sit under his preaching, to be refreshed by his prayers, and to see his walk with God. If there was any thing of peculiar interest about Dr. Cutler, he derived it from his mother. His Sister L—— writes: "From her he inherited his warm imagination, and that sensitiveness which enabled him 'to weep with those who weep, and to rejoice with those who rejoice.' His mother descended from an old French Huguenot family, and possessed the traits that characterized that people; these my brother inherited so thoroughly, that even the severe, stern New England education of other days could not root them out. His French blood kept all in for future service."

His sympathy with others, combined with his desire to benefit them, was abundantly evinced during the very week of his trial.

TO MRS. MARY CHUBBUCK, OF QUINCY, MASS.

"BROOKLYN, *October* 29, 1836.

"MY DEAR SPIRITUAL CHILD—I have just received your letter of the 26th, giving me notice of the death of your mother. On the morning of *that day* my own dear mother breathed her last. . . . She summoned all her children and grandchildren about her on the 16th, and then received from my hands the Holy Sacrament of the body and blood of Christ, and with the greatest composure took leave of us all. She was full of repentance and faith, and her last end was peace. . . . . Of your dear mother I always had the highest opinion, as a faithful Christian. I wish I had more like her now. Some I have, perhaps, as devoted, but none more so! How could any be more so?

"My dear child, follow her, 'where she followed Christ.' The cares of a family are great, I know; but the trials of a family ought to lead you to God. . . . Think of the souls committed to your care, of which you must give account; and think, just in proportion as you teach them now, just in that proportion they may be holy hereafter. You make confession of coldness and loss of 'first love.'

Read and pray over the second chapter of Revelation. I rejoice that you have not left *the church*. The repose of the heart is indeed the great thing; and the possession of a place in what I think to be the Church which Christ instituted, is not a small privilege. But if I did not think the Episcopal Church was of Divine origin, I would prefer it above all others, on many accounts; and particularly in these times of error, contention, innovation and questionable zeal. My opinions about the church are, however, just what they were when I left Quincy, and just what I published in my 'Century Sermon.' Affectionately yours, B. C. CUTLER."

With a chastened heart Dr. Cutler toiled on diligently for the good of his people, sowing the seed of the Divine Word, though not reaping all the fruit he desired, assured that the time would come, when he that soweth and he that reapeth shall rejoice together. He had many searchings of heart about the decay of religion in some persons of professed piety. "If it is my fault," he says, "let me fly to God, through Christ, that it may be remedied, and that I may wash my garments from the blood of souls." Whenever tempted to despond, and to feel anxious about fulfilling all the duties of his weighty and responsible station, he would chide his soul with Scripture passages, saying: "Who art thou, O great mountain? before Zerubbabel thou shalt become a plain: and he shall bring forth the head-stone, with shoutings, crying, Grace, grace, unto it." His feeble body was often a very clog to his soul and spirit, but he used to say, it served the good purpose of a chain, to chain up tendencies to evil, and to confine his steps in the straight and narrow way. "It has saved me," he declared, "from many of the impertinencies of life; and when I think of my proneness to levity, I feel grateful that I have been much tied to sick beds and houses of affliction; and also, that I have so many infirmities of body."

Whenever Dr. Cutler or any of his family were ill, the noble sympathies of the parishioners were constantly elicited. When his beloved wife was nigh unto death, in February,

1837, nothing could be more touching than the kindness exhibited. To one devoted friend, who was untiring in her attentions, yet at the same time quite unobtrusive, he wrote :

"It is almost in vain, my dearest madam, to keep pace with the kindness of your heart. Permit me to say, that the condescension you have shown to a Lazarus—a poor disciple of Christ, and his family—will never be forgotten.

"I shall learn by it more fully to condescend to men of low estate. Another beautiful lesson your prayers, your tears, and your steps will teach me; that, as my dear wife is now insensible, or ignorant of much that has been done and suffered for her, so am I of very much that, ages ago, was done and suffered for me. How many prayers, how many tears, how many steps were taken, by the Lord of life for the salvation of my soul, when it was impossible for me to know them! But Eternity will unfold all, and then we shall know what obligations others are under to us, what obligations we are under to others, and all of us to *Him*, who, though he was *rich*, yet, for our sakes, became poor, that we, through his poverty, might be rich.

"Yours affectionately, in the faith, B. C. CUTLER."

His diary at this time is not without interest :

"*Feb.* 6, 1837.—This day, thirty-nine years ago, my parents rejoiced at the news that a man-child was born into the world. Oh, when I die, may thousands rejoice that I ever lived!"

"*March* 29.—My soul has been more alive than usual for a month past. Oh that I might arise and shine! Oh that I might become a burning and a shining light, that all who sit under my shadow might rejoice! Make me, Lord, what thou wouldst have me to be!"

Throughout the spring of 1837, the condition of the commercial world was one of unparalleled distress. The state of financial affairs in New York threw a gloom over every thing, and caused "men's hearts to fail for fear of those things coming on the earth," and even the most sanguine were cast down. Dr. Cutler sought to impress on the minds of his people that "trouble springs not from the dust;" and by advice and counsel, endeavored to turn many to God, who, before this chastening, were afar off. With some it was not without avail.

In July, Bishop McIlvaine, of Ohio, was again welcomed at St. Ann's, where he preached two or three times. Dr. Cutler heard him with unfeigned pleasure, and rejoiced in the preaching of his gifted predecessor. He himself had no reason to covet another's gifts, for the parish had been as successfully administered as before, and the diverse gifts of these two eminent pastors God had evidently blessed to the edifying of the church. In his diary of

"*July* 3, 1837"—He says: "I pray God, Bishop McIlvaine's labors may be crowned with success. This, I know: if envy of exalted attainments dwells in our breasts, we cannot enter the kingdom of heaven. If we cannot be happy to have any body superior to us so acknowledged, then we must never expect to behold God and the Lamb; for, if we were the most perfect of saints, we should be compelled to behold angels, and, if the highest angel, we must behold archangels, cherubim and seraphim! Blessed Jesus! own and occupy me in thy work. Place me where thou wilt in the great building—on the foundation or on the superstructure. I feel unworthy of such a station; am ready to go into a much humbler one.

> "'Let me but hear my Saviour say,
> Grace shall be equal to my day;
> Then I rejoice in deep distress,
> Leaning on all-sufficient grace.'"

How refreshing to see a spirit like that of Dr. Cutler, in a world where jealousy, strife, envy and contention prevail. Human nature, when sanctified, is not free from these infirmities, and it is truly a rare thing to see even a Christian rise superior to feelings which pervade nearly every soul, and which can only be overcome by leaning on the bosom of Jesus, and partaking, in some degree, of his meek and lowly spirit.

Never were pastor and people more devoted to each other than in the case before us, and whenever Dr. Cutler was absent from his parish, his numerous letters to his people evinced his ardent attachment to them. Many a word of instruction, too, was thereby brought home to the hearts of his parishioners. From Newport he wrote to one of them (with a few lines from Mrs. Cutler):

"*August* 14, 1837.

"MY DEAR FRIEND—We had a glorious sunset last night. It was gorgeous indeed. I sat watching it from the window of my chamber. It was a fine conclusion of a day in which the gospel in all its richness had been preached to the people of this place. Grand emblem of Christian hope! As I looked at the *sun*, I thought with what different emotions different persons were viewing it. The infant smiled to see its bright light break through the clouds and illumine its nursery; the youth was invited by its re-appearance over the earth to gambol and play. From these what variation and what a gradation, up to the philosopher who knew the composition of its rays, and the arrangement of its power as the centre of the solar system. But how far short of the Christian, he! The Christian looked upon it as only a sun made, with thousands more, by the word of God, and held it but as a mirror in which to behold Jesus, who was the light of the world. He saw him die and sink into the tomb for us, and then arise with new and never to be diminished splendor. Was it not natural, after long reviewing this glorious object, to think of you and yours as probably enjoying, from the front of your hospitable mansion, the same scene? Be assured, that whether in Brooklyn, or in Newport, no new objects can crowd the friends I have left, from my mind—my heart. With love to all,

"For ever your friend, B. C. C."

REPLY.

"*August* 16, 1837.

"MY VERY DEAR FRIENDS—The sight of your handwriting was cheering to my heart. I have called twice at the rectory, and made Miss B. a visit, and was there again after the funeral of old Mrs. Middagh. In the church, part of the service, that is, the sentences and the 15th chapter of 1st Corinthians, was read, and not another word—no music—and the coffin taken out. It seemed abrupt. Old Mr. Moore said, he expected the bells would have tolled for the first Episcopalian that had attended church. I sent the carriage to follow the procession, after Mr. Luqueer's and one other. There were fourteen scarfs. Old Mrs. Sands found Mrs. Middagh repeating to herself, 'Jesus, Saviour of my soul;' she prayed with her, and her end was very peaceful. . . . . For your sake, I am willing to bear the privation of your society, and I assure you it is no small privation to me to know you to be so far off that I cannot run down and pour into your friendly hearts my anxieties and my joys, which, wrong as I have often felt it to be, I could not practice enough self-denial to avoid; it is so comforting to unburden the heart, and feel the deposit is safe, that I fear it has made me selfish. . . . The weather often reminds me of the cholera season, and, crowded with benefits and blessings, oftener a feeling of awe and sadness, than of joyfulness and pleasure, glides through my mind. The uncertainty and insufficiency of earthly things to convey happiness to the immortal spirit, is strongly set before me daily, and I wish unutterable things. . . . Sunday evening I, too, was watching that glorious sunset, and you were not forgotten! Enjoy, while you can, the tranquil comforts around you, my dear friends, but don't stay too long; old people love to see the accustomed face in the accustomed place, and absence is not required to find out how affectionately we love the precepts and advice of a dear pastor.

"Your sincere friend, A. M. P."

Dr. Cutler's friendships were always lasting; his esteem for those whom he loved did not alter with every variation of the weather, or with any removals on their part to a distance.

His friend, the Rev. Mr. Jackson, had this year removed from New York to Louisville, Ky., and, in the fall, Dr. Cutler thus wrote to him, in allusion to the difficulties which had surrounded the Bishop of that diocese:

TO THE REV. WILLIAM JACKSON.

"BROOKLYN, *October* 31, 1837.

"MY VERY DEAR BROTHER—I received your long looked-for favor to-day, and, before I go to rest, I hasten to say how much delight it afforded me.

"Blessed be God that our dear friend is delivered! Now I pray that he may be merciful. To forgive is divine. I marvel at the demand made for your letters. The demand for Mr. Winthrop's secret, stamped the whole affair with the indelible stain of violent anger and utterly unreasonable opposition. But enough! now may the God of peace give you peace always, and by all means!

"Dear Dr. Milnor is moving about, as practically as ever. Drs. Eastburn and Forbes attend the Committee, and all is harmony—not one note of discord has yet been struck. St. Ann's has been improving in every sense, I believe. . . . Some conversions among our people—which has inspired me a little. Sunday-schools and societies go on as usual. I miss you very much; alas, alas! how few there are with whom I can communicate freely. Shut up as I am, I grow more and more dependent upon books and God. May these words be reversed. Silence, circumspection, diligence, study, and zeal in communicating religious truth, are the grand qualifications of a minister. May we all grow in grace, and in meetness for the service of our gracious Lord, and if we meet not here, may we meet and rejoice for ever, hereafter.

"Yours, for ever, B. C. CUTLER."

The last record in Dr. Cutler's journal for this year, shows how earnest he was that his own soul should grow in grace. It was a cloudy and stormy week, but there was sunshine within, and his heart seems to have been calmed with that "perfect peace" which is promised to those whose hearts are stayed on God.

"*Dec.* 11, 1837.—Christ's yoke is *on* me, and it is easy, and his burden is light. When my people are gloomy and unhappy, I know now the cause. I do not preach Christ as I ought. Oh! reveal, reveal thy Son to me, Lord God! I have been reading some of Mrs. Graham's letters written to my mother. They are *sweet* to my taste. They are filled with gospel truth. Christ is her Alpha and Omega. She applies him as a medicine to her sin-sick soul. This is the use to be made of Christ. He is not to be kept at a distance, but brought into contact. Oh, may I thus be united to Christ! 'If I be lifted up from the earth, I will draw all men unto me.' Come *unto* me; not toward me, but come *unto* me."

Dr. Cutler, though a disciple of love, had a remarkable courage in standing up for the right, and when he conceived others to be unjustly assailed he proved himself "a friend indeed."

Thus he addressed Bishop Smith :

"BROOKLYN, N. Y., *December* 15, 1837.

"MY BELOVED BROTHER—The man that has one hundred stabs aimed at his body, by a circle of experienced swordsmen, and comes off with only a flesh-wound, must have on the armor of righteousness on the right hand and on the left! Just write down Benjamin C. Cutler as your thorough, entire, affectionate, and (while God is) your own dear friend—High Churchman as you are. I have only time to say, all things appear peaceful and prosperous in the parish. Last Sunday we had a collection for the Foreign Mission Treasury of five hundred and twenty dollars, and this in a snow storm. Give my best love to my sweet friends, the Jacksons. Had not your trials appeared, we should not have known what had become of the world. It would have been swallowed up in the church. Perhaps we shall live to see the blessed fruits of such sore travail!

"Give us your blessing and your prayers.

"Affectionately yours, B. C. CUTLER."

The friendship between these two persons was formed early in life, and the survivor, the venerated Bishop of the Diocese of Kentucky, has kindly furnished, for this volume, the following :

EARLY MEMORIES OF THE REV. DR. CUTLER.

"LOUISVILLE, KY., *March* 10, 1864.

"In the summer of 1817, soon after being admitted to the holy order of deacon, by that venerable and very remarkable man, Bishop Griswold, I entered, with fear and trembling, upon my first parochial charge, the ancient church of St. Michael's, Marblehead, Mass.

"The clinging feeling of dependence for advice and encouragement, which had bound my heart so closely to my Bishop, and to my late rector, in Providence, R. I., the Rev. N. B. Crocker, soon drew me to the side of the only zealous and earnest clergyman, at that time within my reach, the Rev. Asa Eaton, rector of Christ Church, Boston. Upon occasion of exchanges with him, and not unfrequently at his house, as I passed through Boston, I met a band of young men, whose hearts the Lord had touched, calling them into his ministry, whose equal, in many respects, is rarely met with; Mr. Theodore Edson, now the venerable rector of St. Ann's, Lowell, 'whose praise is in all the churches;' (Mr. B. C. C. Parker son of the late Bishop Parker), who won to himself such high regard as Seaman's Chaplain, in New York City; and dearer to me than either, his cousin, Mr. B. C. Cutler, whose genial nature yielded a warm response to the yearnings of my heart for sympathy and brotherhood. The religious awakenings in Bristol and Providence, of which I had been witness; the claims of Sunday-schools and evening meetings, just beginning to call forth the energies of our zealous young men; the marked solemnity and deep impression which at that time followed the earnest ministrations of Mr. Eaton, in old Christ Church; the advantages and disadvantages of classical and ministerial training, here or there, when, as yet, we had no school of the Prophets of our own; and when a dead formalism in our own church, in most places, was only less to be dreaded than the growing laxity in high places among our Puritan pastors and teachers, afforded inexhaustible subjects of discussion of the liveliest interest and of the greatest import. None but those who knew Mr. Cutler's surroundings at the time; the influences brought to bear upon him; the tenderness of his nature; and the ties he was called upon to sunder, can form any adequate conception of the struggle he underwent, before deciding upon going to Providence for his education, instead of to Cambridge. But, in the instructions he received at St. John's, in his nearness to his beloved Bishop and in the warm sympathies of a noble band of coadjutors, ladies as well as gentlemen, in Providence, in every good word and work, he found abundant compensation and secured greater fitness for his ministerial work. . . .

"His collegiate course ran through the years of my ministry in Virginia, and I have no further knowledge of it than the testimony borne by my old friends, that 'he adorned the doctrine of God, our Saviour, in all things'—in his classes, in social intercourse, in the Sunday-school, and in every method of usefulness open to him. And, in after life, he was always ready to bear witness to the salutary influences of that period over his character, and his practical views of ministerial duty.

"Such was the demand for clergymen at that period, that, high as was the standard of the Bishop and of Dr. Crocker, as to ministerial attainments, young men of promise were hurried into orders, often against their wishes, with the advice to make up for any deficiencies of previous culture, by diligence in study during the early years of their ministry.

"And I well remember with what marked approbation I heard of a condition, under which my sagacious, but modest, young friend, Mr. Cutler, yielded to this importunity; that, during his diaconate, he should be excused from taking a license for preaching the gospel in the Church of God, and should be indulged with the privilege of reading printed sermons, as he had been accustomed to do as a lay-reader. And the manner in which he availed himself of this privilege produced, at the time, a very deep impression.

"At different times, and from diverse sources, I have derived the impression that the ministry of our dear brother in Quincy, Mass., under these circumstances, was as remarkable as any thing in the wonderful history of the revival of our church, in Massachusetts and Rhode Island from the profound depression into which it had fallen, under the combined influences of the Revolution and the decay of piety and departure from sound doctrine, which the orthodox denominations around her had so generally fallen into. It may gravely be questioned whether, during any portion of his ministry, his blameless character, his holy life, his retiring modesty, his loving heart, ever left a more wide-spread and abiding impression, in so intelligent a community, in favor of religion and of the Church.

"Very many more competent witnesses will be better able than I, to testify to what high eminence he afterward attained, as a sermonizer, and a successful administrator of a great parish. I will therefore close what I have to say by alluding to the influence which, in my opinion, all his previous training exerted, in fitting him for the work of the first city missionary in New York. The opportunity has been afforded me, through a long series of years, of watching the efforts toward church extension of the Episcopal and Presbyterian Churches, in that great city; and, to my mind, it is clear that the direction given to our efforts in this behalf, by the Rev. Mr. Cutler and the Rev. Mr. Jones, afford singular proof of the wisdom and goodness of God, in selecting suitable instruments, whenever he has a great work to perform.

"All, even the most distinguished of the Apostles, 'held this treasure in earthen vessels, that the excellency of the power may be of God, and not of us.' None of the children of God felt this more deeply than our dear departed brother, or took greater delight in acknowledging the rich gifts bestowed upon others. And, in the same spirit, I would desire to bring this tribute, and place it upon my brother's grave; while the higher tribute of praise and thanksgiving is rendered to Him from whom all blessings flow. B. B. S."

We have endeavored to enrich this memorial of Dr. Cutler with copious extracts from his journal, and believing they will be neither uninteresting nor unprofitable, continue to transcribe suitable portions.

"*Jan.* 8, 1838.—My desire is to pour out my whole soul in the work of the ministry. A life of prayer, and a close walk with Christ, is my aim ; and to smile, while laying my head on a dying pillow, is my ambition ! Blessed Jesus, who hast power over all flesh, give me eternal life !"

"*Jan.* 29.—This week was marked by the marriage of my nephew, Samuel Ward, Jr., to Miss Emily Astor, grand-daughter of John Jacob Astor. The occasion was a pleasant one. I offered two prayers with the family of my brother-in-law on the occasion. God forbid that I should indulge any worldly complacency, in even a remote alliance, to the wealth of this world. My prayer is that I may be useful to my new friends in a religious point of view."

"*Feb.* 19.—I am too fond of being merely agreeable. . . . . . Lord, give me a tender and solemn interest in every body. May my speech be with grace, seasoned with salt."

"*March* 12.—Last week was one of labor, but, alas! of sorrow. I see that, left to myself, I am nothing. I see, indeed, a law in my members warring against the law of my mind. My only hope is in flying to Jesus, my strength and my salvation. In me there is nothing good, and every thing evil."

"*Easter Monday, April* 16.—I have been carried through much labor and toil. Here I am a monument of Christ's mercy ! Great has been my weariness of body and emptiness of mind ; but, as of old, 'he that gathered little had no lack.' I work for a good Master, and as I supply my servants with fuel and meat that it may be dressed for me, so will my Lord supply the materials on which I may labor for him. . . . . I have been tempted of Satan, I fear, to be impatient under little domestic inconveniences. The Lord forgive and protect me!"

"*May* 21.—I begin to think that, in proportion as a minister is useful to others, he is less satisfied with himself. I desire self-complacency; but I have none, and ought to have none. I must look out of myself and look on Christ; in him is my righteousness and strength. I am a weak, sinful creature, as much in need of a keeper as an infant or a madman. Oh, leave me not, blessed Jesus!"

How single an eye Dr. Cutler had, is shown by a letter to an old friend, about this time:

TO MISS L. MARSTON, OF TAUNTON.

"BROOKLYN, *June* 21, 1838.

"I cannot let H. go without a line. You are still in a world of trial! so am I! and so are all Christians! yea, and so are all the ungodly! The latter have, more than all, our cares, with none of our *consolation*. My dear friend, let us strive to draw nearer and nearer to Christ. . . . . The reason why Christians are dark and gloomy often, is that, in the Scriptures they do not *see* Christ clearly enough, and in conversation they do not *hear* of him enough. When my pious people begin to complain of their dullness and deadness, and particularly of their darkness, I suspect immediately that I have been hiding my light (Christ) under a bushel; so I begin at once and preach from 'The government is on his shoulder,' or 'A man shall be as a hiding-place from the wind,' or 'There remaineth a rest for the people of God!' Christ first, Christ last, Christ in the midst, Christ all in all! Blessed Lord, appear in our poor hearts!

"I remain, as ever, your friend, B. C. CUTLER."

"*July* 23."—He writes in his journal: "I have had a large addition to the communion—the largest, I think, I ever had in St. Ann's. Eight most interesting cases of conversion, I recorded. Oh may this be the beginning of a large harvest!"

"*Sept.* 3.—On Sunday evening, Rev Mr. P——, of Baltimore, preached a most faithful sermon. I thank God for such an instance of his grace. Oh that there were in all our lips, and in all our hearts, such a message! I think, for a very young man addressing an old church of intelligent Christians, a little less confidence would have appeared well; but it was so good and so interesting, and so unmingled with self, that it did me great good. 'You intend,' said he, 'at some future day to be more pious; but that day may be ushered in by a sun that shall shine upon the grassy turf which covers thy narrow bed.' Oh, let me remember what Dr. Scott said: "A life of indulgence makes a dreadful deathbed!'

"My soul at the Communion was in a better frame than usual; but there is so much mere work of the hands to do, that I have but little time to ponder upon the same. Blessed Jesus! I pray thee to feed me while I am feeding others!"

Dr. Cutler thus approached God with childlike confidence, and recognized the eye and hand of his Heavenly Father in every circumstance of life. That Divine Saviour who has said, "according to your faith be it unto you," seemed to be always near him. His servant often shut out the noisy world and listened for his Master's voice, saying, "Speak, Lord! for thy servant heareth," and thus had ways of communing with him, unknown to world-entangled Christians. One may perceive this in his correspondence.

While at Newport, during a few days of summer, he thus wrote his wife:

"*September* 28, 1838.

. . . . "I once thought I should like to spend the winter in Newport, but perhaps I should find it dull. I believe the mind is better when under some pressure from responsibility, and I know we are best where Providence has placed us. God metes out the 'bounds of our habitation.' If he knows where a sparrow falleth, he knoweth where a sparrow builds her nest; and if he knows where a sparrow builds her nest, he knows where I have builded mine; and if he giveth to the sparrow instinct to select the best place, he will not withhold Divine guidance from me. Oh that I could rejoice in the Lord; rejoice in being under his yoke;

rejoice in being counted worthy to labor for Christ! Oh that I could rejoice in lying in his hands, and leaving every event to him! I am perfectly *satisfied to do it*, but I want to rejoice! But 'Pilgrim' was not half as *happy* a man as his young companion. I live daily by faith; God is the immediate source of all my pleasure; that is, I feel that he permits it, and that I hang upon him as an infant hangs upon his mother.

'Keep me, O keep me, King of kings!
Under thine own Almighty wings.'

My prayers are lifted up, morning, noon and night for you, and I feel indescribable tenderness for you. But our dear Redeemer is expressly said to act the part of a shepherd, and as such, 'gently to lead those that are with young.'—Isa. xl. 12. You must select the precious promises which are applicable to you, and plead them, word for word, before God. . . . .

"Your —— —— —— B. C. Cutler."

TO THE SAME.

"Newport, *September* 30.

. . . . "Oh, how miserable the best portion of the worldling appears to me without Christ and his consolations! I had rather be the Shepherd of Salisbury Plain.

"With respect to anxiety of mind, I have to say that that is my inheritance; it was the particular characteristic of my mother. It was the product of early affliction in life, and the incessant infirmities of my body. But what mental or bodily infirmity is there which Christ cannot heal, or, if not heal, soothe and render less burdensome? To him I desire to carry all my infirmities. . . .

"—— —— —— B. C. Cutler."

Whether he was perfectly willing to leave every event in the hands of God, even when sore disappointment was his lot, was fully tested before another year dawned.

The last week in October, 1838, was to him most distressing. He thus speaks of it: "My beloved wife has been very ill, and for two days, insensible; but, blessed be God! she has recovered so far as to know us all, and to inspire us with hopes of her own safety; but we have little hope of the child's life. My heart has been deeply afflicted. I feel like covering my head in my mantle and retiring from observation. Nature must have its way. I mourn, but do not murmur. The Lord liveth, and blessed be my Rock! I have already had a great affliction, and should I have another, I shall know that I have deserved the rod. But oh, spare, my Saviour! spare my sweet companion, my dearest friend!"

Two years previous a daughter was born unto him, but it was not living; and now again, a son was born, November 6, 1838, but it was not living—a grievous loss to so loving a heart; but it was patiently borne, and he knew it *must* be right, because God so ordered. Though a second time living offspring were denied, both parents were drawn nearer to him who hath "borne our sorrows and carried our griefs," and who is now above, ever pleading with ineffable tenderness and compassion for his children, at his Father's throne.

Thus, Dr. Cutler writes:

"*Nov.* 19.—I never felt my need of a Saviour more than I do now, nor did I oftener apply to his peace-sprinkling blood! While preaching about chastisements yesterday, I was, for a moment, entirely overcome. In speaking of a parent who was deprived of every child in one day, the agony of mind, on this occasion, was vented in these words: 'I see the Lord is determined to have the whole of my heart, and I am determined that he shall have it!'"

Dr. Cutler felt it was no chance event, but seemed to hear the Divine voice speaking, "I, the Lord, do all these things." From the depths of his heart he could say:

"We may live to feel 't was best
That God denied our prayer,
And tried, and prov'd, till we confessed
That waves and storms which broke our rest
And toss'd us to our Saviour's breast,
Our richest blessings were."

Let us peruse a few extracts from Dr. Cutler's journal:

"*Dec.* 17, 1838.—Heard Dr. Tyng preach on 'a famine of the word of the Lord;" a most solemn and reproving discourse, discovering great ability and power on the part of the speaker. It was a great soul, speaking to men's souls.

> 'The wise, new prudence from the wise acquire,
> And one great soul can fan another's fire.'

I bless God for the sermon."

"*Jan.* 28, 1839.—I was very languid in my sermon last night. The time must come when all my animation will desert me, and my services no longer be sought; I have labored for fourteen years, with a poor broken body. I have labored to turn men from sin to holiness, and from Satan to God. This is all clear gain, and cannot be taken away from me; but, was ever minister of Christ so unworthy?"

"*April* 5.—I was unable to keep the precious season of Lent as I could wish; any change of diet, even so small as omitting the common additions to my bread and drink, I had to avoid. I have tried it again, and again, but it will not answer for me; my body is like a delicate watch, if wound up regularly, and kept clean, and handled carefully, it will keep regular time, but a very small thing will stop the wheels. This is *my* infirmity; it keeps me humble."

"*May* 7.—. . . My soul is poor and low. Oh, when will ministers learn to live up to the height of our holy vocation? when dig for truth, and fight to save souls, pulling them out of the fire? Gracious Saviour, save and deliver me!"

"*June* 24.—The church here is perfectly filled; every pew up stairs and down taken; the communion large as ever and increasing; the people respectful and affectionate, some exceedingly liberal and attached. Sermons, whether written or *ex tempore*, well received. What more can I ask, as a minister of Christ, in this world?"

"*Aug.* 19.—I am now to take a vacation, but am learning

that my vacations can afford me no pleasure, except God's presence goes with me every step. To my soul, God in Christ is necessary. Go with me, Lord! I beseech thee; to impart tranquillity in travelling, moderation in relaxation, and devotion in solitude."

It may occur to some, on reading these extracts, that there was too much mental introversion in Dr. Cutler; that he too often turned his thoughts inwardly, dissecting, as it were, by a kind of morbid anatomy, his own religious experience, and thereby his spirits were too often depressed, but those who knew him, knew how little he was open to such a charge. The kindlings of joy in his soul were never quenched by any such analysis, and his outgoings of soul toward a personal Redeemer were never thus checked. To the worldling, his language may seem extravagant; but to the believer who walks with God, it is only the natural expression of a soul which is constantly looking into the mirror of the Divine Word, and lamenting its own deficiencies when compared with such a standard. He by no means, like those anatomists of piety of whom Isaac Taylor speaks, "destroyed all the freshness of faith, hope, and charity," by immuring himself in the atmosphere of his own bosom. An unbeliever might say to him, as was truly the case, in October, 1839, "You live in Baron Swedenborg's world." "Indeed," was Dr. Cutler's reply, "one of the Apostles was counted a madman, and some said of them all, when they spoke of the things of God under the influence of the Holy Spirit, 'these men are full of new wine!'"

But to resume the journal:

"*Sept.* 30.—I preached two sermons yesterday from the same text, on Gal. ii. 20: 'The life which I now live in the flesh, I live by the faith of the Son of God," etc. If ever we suppose that God induces such a poor minister as I am, to choose a text, and to write on it for particular persons, I must think he did last week. A Christian, just on the way, through Brooklyn, to enter upon a scene of great temptation, remained here over Sunday; every word appeared written for her—may it prove a blessing!"

"*Oct.* 7.— . . . I feel an unaccountable aversion to that moral preaching, which, in order to its establishment, hides Christ, depreciates spirituality and love to the Redeemer, while it conveys a wrong notion of religion to the irreligious. Begin with Christ; insist upon an inward experience of the love of Jesus, and then spread out and enforce the morality of the gospel, saying, even as St. Peter does, 'If thou shalt do these things, thou shalt never fall!'"

"*Oct.* 28.—I am exceedingly pained at the conduct of a servant—an evil, surmising, ignorant, and presumptuous person. Oh, how am I driven to the Saviour, to keep my character, as well as my life; when I think of the disposition of those by whom a man must be surrounded. All things drive me to Christ!"

"*Dec.* 3.— . . . Have been for some days at the bedside of a valued brother-in-law, and have now seen his remains laid beside those of my sister, in the family tomb. *Vale! longe vale!* Such a death is a loss indeed. He was a man of fortune, and that fortune had been devoted to the comfort of his family; to the relief of his friends; to the wants of the poor, and to the support of religion. What is the lesson I am to learn? First, the vanity of wealth; next, the insecurity of earthly patronage; then, the necessity of personal preparation for an existence in a world of spirits."

The relative to whose death reference is here made, was the late Samuel Ward, Esq., of New York, one of the most eminent and successful of American bankers, who, in life, was beloved, and in death, deeply lamented.

Dr. Cutler returned again to parish duty, warned by the departure of earthly friends that he must cleave more closely to an heavenly one, and determined to hold up, as ever, the Cross of Christ, as the only refuge for perishing men around him. The ties of kindred and friendship were never lost sight of by him, but they were made subordinate to that love to God which the Creator claims from every creature.

To a clerical friend he wrote, with much feeling, in the early part of this year:

TO THE REV. WM. JACKSON, OF LOUISVILLE, KY.

"My Dear Friend—Your welcome letter lies before me, and I was delighted to see your hand. Oh how I miss you, I cannot tell! I dare not tell! But all is right. The idea of true clerical sympathy is rare! You *knock* at many doors, but 'not at home' is, in effect, the reply. . . . You ask about my wife; she is now well. . . . . . I am enabled to say, It is well. . . . . My church was never better filled, and the work of grace seems going on. I think I see more of the excellency of Christ, and more of the misery of man than ever, a pretty good cause for the above effect! . . . . Now I must tell you that I read and hear every thing about our dear Bishop S. with great eagerness. Give our best love to him and his valued companion. What deep waters he has navigated! Men who are lauded in the newspapers are sometimes, in private, deemed worthy of impeachment, while those upon whom the press heaps indignity are jewels, in the eyes of God and of those who know them best. 'Thy praise is censure, and thy censure, praise!' Give my best love to Mrs. Jackson.

"Your friend and brother, B. C. C."

CHAPTER IX.

MINISTRY AT ST. ANN'S CHURCH—CONTINUED.

1840–1843.

IN 1840 Dr. Cutler received a long and exceedingly interesting letter from Capt. Wm. L. Hudson, of the United States Navy, who was connected with the United States Exploring Expedition, and was then at one of the islands in the Pacific Ocean. This gentleman was one of those men who bless the world by the powerful influence of a godly example; a man of sterling integrity, and one with whom Dr. Cutler cultivated a close and cordial friendship. This experienced officer, as Commodore, was afterward put in command of the Niagara, the finest ship in the Navy, in order to accomplish the most difficult enterprise ever attempted by man, viz., the laying of the Atlantic cable, to connect by telegraph the two great Protestant nations of the earth. The depth and reality of his religious life was amply demonstrated in this undertaking, as well as in all his long voyages; and on the quarter-deck of a man-of-war he proved himself a good soldier of Jesus Christ. He was baptized in St. Ann's Church in 1794, and made a public profession of his faith in Christ Jesus at her altar in April, 1831. He thus writes:

TO THE REV. DR. CUTLER.

"U. S. SHIP PEACOCK, ISLAND OF OTAHEITE,
September 18, 1839.

"REV. AND DEAR SIR—I set out on this cruise as a salt-water missionary, with the Bethel flag gallantly flying from the mast-head, and flushed with the pleasing but visionary hope that all would do it reverence. I counted not the cost of the experiment, nor reflected how utterly impotent is poor human strength to keep its broad folds expanded to the breeze. Many on board seemed pleased with its calm and quiet appearance, while it hung in lazy folds against the side of the mast; but it was no sooner opened to the winds of heaven than they beheld emblazoned on its deep blue tints, 'Be ye holy,' while their contracted vision overlooked all its other characters, though fair and full as the sunbeam, 'Come unto me, all ye that are weary and heavy laden, and I will give you rest,' 'My grace is sufficient for thee,' etc. . . . Soon satisfied of my own insufficiency, I called to mind the Master's declaration, 'Without me, ye can do nothing!' . . . . Having no chaplain on board, I endeavor to proclaim the gospel of salvation to this ship's company, though duly sensible I am all unworthy of so high a trust; and why, my reverend friend, should I hesitate to carry out the honest convictions of duty, or follow where the Saviour leads? Will I regret the effort to win a soul, in the hour of death or at the day of judgment? The rolling ocean echoes back your answer, 'No!' . . . .

"I can now readily imagine your situation, placed as you are in the garden of the Lord, where there are many beautiful trees and flowers, which you are zealously endeavoring to prune and cultivate, but find, after all your toil from year to year, there are some who yield neither fruit nor fragrance! Nor is this all, others condemn your zeal, and find fault with the gospel truths you are bound, as an ambassador of Christ, to unfold and explain. You cannot strip the human heart of its various disguises without being charged with adding unnecessary pangs to an already goaded conscience; you are accused of bringing men, out of time, to a scene which throws a cloud over the world's most enchanting prospects, and the 'amen' of your sermon becomes the most pleasing part of it. But there is another class yet—who can kneel at the Lord's table and yet refuse to meet 'where two or three are gathered together in his name,' because in a *less conspicuous place!* Can it indeed be true that the fashion of this world has so far obtained the mastery over Christian feeling in St. Ann's, as to have endeavored to shut out our God from the little chapel in which you occasionally worship? Can such Christians lift up their hearts to God and say,

'Saviour, where'er thy steps I see,
Dauntless, untired, I follow thee?'

"What, oh what! would be the hope of us poor souls who are thrown destitute on the waste of waters, if the Christian's God could be circumscribed within the narrow compass of steepled churches; hear no prayer save that which broke on his ear from within their massive or costly walls? If such were the fact, could we believe for a moment that our God is an omnipotent God? the same unchangeable being who addressed the multitude on the Mount, and from the deck of a ship? whose birthplace was a manger, and who emphatically declares, 'I dwell with the humble and contrite heart?' . . . . In comparison with your labors, dear friend, my work is all plain sailing. It requires no laborious process to reach a sailor's heart; there is no necessity of stripping off layer after layer, as you would to get at a mummy; for it is as transparent as glass.

"Why is it so little has been done for *sailors?* One would think they had nothing at stake! no interest in Eternity! no soul to save! . . . . The island of Otaheite is a truly delightful spot—blessed with a pure and balmy atmosphere, covered with continual verdure! Nature looks smiling everywhere, and all is teeming with life, from the summit of her cloud-capped mountains to where the sea laves its shores. Man only is unfruitful and vile. . . . The missionaries here have done a noble work. . . . If the few missionary laborers in this part of the Lord's vineyard have effected so much under the faint and glimmering light of the gospel, which has but just dawned upon these people, what may we not anticipate when it shall please the great Head of the Church to withdraw the veil through which his word and power is now but dimly seen, and exhibit them, amid a special outpouring of the Holy Spirit, in all the effulgence of noontide glory? He has promised it, and will surely bring it to pass. . . . I fear my long letter has exhausted your patience; but I know your interest in missions and the extension of Christ's kingdom everywhere. What I have seen since I left home, even in this archipelago of coral islands, is but half told; my meeting at different islands with native missionaries has again and again reminded me of the Saviour's beautiful parable, where he likens the kingdom of heaven to the leaven which a woman hid in three measures of meal, till the whole was leavened. The process is going on here; the leaven is reaching from one chain of islands to another. They are, as it were, lifting themselves out of the ocean to look upon the bright rising of the Sun of righteousness! and I pray God he may be seen and worshipped by all! . . . I will now close my tedious epistle, asking a place in your prayers for all who compose our squadron.

"That the Lord may bless and prosper you, with an ingathering of souls, is the wish and prayer of your absent and, I hope, Christian friend. WM. L. HUDSON."

Over such men (those who love the fervent preaching of the simple Gospel of Christ) Dr. Cutler had unbounded influence. He aimed to honor God in all his ministrations; and God honored him with the warm affection of many of his chosen ones, both in public and private life. Read his record in the opening year of 1840:

"*Jan.* 13.—Rev. Mr. S—— preached for me Sunday; but the sermon was sadly deficient in application and in evangelical effect. One quarter of the talent and the time required to compose it, might have produced a much more useful discourse. Why will men omit the weightier matters of the gospel, as much superior to the others, as are the weightier matters of the law. Let me take my stand under the Cross, when I write my sermon."

Dr. Cutler's views of preaching may also be seen from the following extract from a letter to his wife, written from Saratoga:

"I pray God to give me an unction from on high. May Thy word be as a hammer in my hand! May all attempts at pleasing, or purchasing smiles or praises, cease! May I seek only to save souls! I have, according to my measure, spoken faithfully and evangelically to my people. Mr. C—— preached last Sunday here, but his sermon lacked spirituality, though not deficient in scholarship. We are all far too literary. What do people want to know about astronomy and philosophy, in the pulpit? I could not but feel the force of one of Mr. Witherspoon's remarks. After hearing a cold preacher, he said, 'Why, I could have said every thing that man said, in the House of Commons!' We want something out of the *heart* of the pious minister, and about the heart of the Saviour."

"*March* 2.—There is every appearance of a revival of religion in this place. God grant it may not be a delusive promise! I see that it is not learning, nor talents, nor diligence alone, but God's blessing, which maketh rich in spiritual things."

"*St. Ann's Rectory,* 1 *Sands Street, May* 4, 1840.—The parish has built a new rectory. It was commenced in October last, and completed in April. I have consecrated this house by simple prayer, through our great Saviour. We prayed to be made a devout, alms-giving, and holy family."

In the month of June Dr. Cutler went down on Long Island, on a horse-back excursion, with his friend and parishioner, Mr. W. B. C. This kind of exercise he was always fond of, and his devotion to this species of recreation was indeed life-long—it had resulted, in early life, in his physical salvation.

Extracts from his letters to Mrs. Cutler, during his absence, reveal a good deal of his natural humor of spirit. This always showed itself when he was not oppressed with too much care :

"BABYLON, *June* 10, 1840.

. . . . "This is a pleasant town, forty miles from you. . . . I have arrived somewhat fatigued, but we are both well. Mr. Cooper is exceedingly kind, and has omitted nothing which could contribute to my comfort. . . . While we were at Jamaica two gentlemen on two cream-colored horses, with saddle-bags, rode past us. We found them where we slept; met with them as we mounted after breakfast, and dined at the same table. They are gentlemen, and, like ourselves, travellers for health. Our topics at table were temperance societies, abolition, the tyranny of public sentiment, the effects of religion upon character. We go on to Islip to sleep; breakfast and dine in Patchogue; and now, my dearest, I have left all cares behind, and trust by our blessed Lord's favor, to be much benefited, and come home with the '*mens sana in corpore sano.*' Ever your own, B. C. C."

"MORISHES, 15 MILES EAST OF PATCHOGUE, *June* 11.

. . . . "I wrote you from Babylon yesterday. The two gentlemen we met,turned out to be Rev. Mr. D., of the Canal Street Presbyterian Church, and a young lawyer. I took them both for members of the bar, and when we sat down to dinner I asked permission to say grace, to which no reply was madé, and again I returned thanks. Just as we were parting, he said, 'I believe I must introduce myself to you as a brother clergyman.' I said, 'Where do you pass Sunday?' 'At East Hampton.' 'Well then,' said I, 'I hope to hear you preach, for I am now, I believe, *out of the element of Episcopacy.* 'I am very glad of that,' said he, 'I wonder how you could have remained in it so long." To which I merely said, 'that it was difficult to say which was the greatest wonder, that he should be in it so long *to so little purpose*, or the other wonder. . . . The morning was glorious. We were up at 3½ A. M. . . . . Mr. C. and I slept in the same room, and saw the first blush on morning's cheek. It was lovely and sweet. It did not blush because man, made in the image of God, rose from his death-resembling sleep without a morning sacrifice, for we opened our window on the water, breathed the morning air, and lifted up our poor souls to that blessed God and Shepherd and Saviour who had watched over us through the night. At 4½ A. M. we took our horses."

The above notes give us an idea of his pleasantry, but perhaps the extract we give below, to a friend, is equally characteristic of him when in other moods. To a wealthy and kind parishioner, Mrs. Cutler had written :

"I am glad you are to have a change; it will afford refreshment to your wearied frame; but a fine writer observes, 'the harp of the human spirit never yields such sweet music as when its frame-work is most shattered and its strings most torn;' so may it prove with you, my dear Mrs. P."

Dr. Cutler added the postscript :

"After such a dear little poetical note as this of my wife's, my heavy pen, I fear, will appear to plod. I have but one theme on my mind to-day—the misery of man. It was the saying of an ancient, that *one* man is *no man!* so I find it; try me without my interest in the Saviour, and I am nothing. I feel positively a nothing. God makes me feel as nothing; every thing contributes to the same feeling. But when I think Christ is my paymaster, my righteousness, my provider, my guide, my all; when I turn from off myself and look on him, I see enough to make me rejoice. I am glad our friend Miss H—— S——, accompanies you; she has long studied the happiness of others, and must therefore be a valuable acquisition." . . .

Dr. Cutler was often in such miserable health as to depress his animal spirits for days and weeks. But for every infirmity he found a balm in the solace of religion, and the support of the Divine promises.

"*Aug.* 10."—He says: "In the diary of Lady Maxwell I find these words, in which I concur: 'In the time of sickness, I always appear to myself to lose ground, and I seem to sink from God; one reason for this may be, my complaints are chiefly of a nervous kind.'"

Later in the same year he also says: "My health has improved, but my spirits are easily depressed. Without a hope in Christ I should indeed be miserable; in spite of it, I easily sink. Satan has tried hard to destroy my peace, but I am too much accustomed to a certain kind of trouble to be surprised; and so I just touched the hem of the Saviour's garment, and was able to realize that he died for me."

Dr. Cutler enjoyed another trip at midsummer with his friend spoken of before (W. B. C.), and he thus concludes a letter written from Saratoga, in August:

"I find that having somebody else in the room with me takes off from my solitude; I have so long been accustomed to be in society even in my retirement. Mr. C. is affable and easy as a travelling companion. He is now sitting beside me, reading a beautiful little Oxford Bible. I prefer Oxford for *printing*, rather than for *interpreting* the Bible, although I am not informed that all, or most of the Oxford divines are leading the church into temptation. Once more, adieu!"

From Saratoga, he wrote again:

"I am stuffed to surfeiting with politics. We are all Whigs! at least, one hundred and fifty, out of one hundred and sixty! How little do men think of eternity! The next President, not the next world, is the great object. Instead of considering men's vices as the cause of their sufferings, and God, through Christ, as the means of their deliverance, they say, 'Only give us General Harrison, and we shall have good times!' 'O my soul, come not thou into their secret! unto their assembly, mine honor, be not thou united!' Let me be numbered as Moses was, with the people of God, even in their affliction!"

How zealous and disinterested in doing good Dr. Cutler was, is evinced by his letters, when necessary recreation took him away from the personal supervision of his parish. No trouble was spared if he could 'pluck a brand from the burning' and rescue an immortal soul. "'Tis a thousand pities," he writes home from Saratoga, "that somebody could not stop that man you speak of, from taking liquor. Suppose you go and see his wife at the time when he comes home to dinner, and talk with her, and say a word to him about the temptations of this country. Take all my temperance tales and lend them to him; you will find two volumes in the glass bookcase down stairs. A few words might save his soul, and oh what a delivery! how every thing sinks in comparison with that!"

Many a poor, degraded man has this holy man lifted up, with words of kindness, from the lowest depths of wretchedness. Were it not a breach of private confidence, we could specify many cases which might be enumerated, but we are not allowed to withdraw the veil which protects the sacredness of private and domestic life.

The delightful letters Dr. Cutler received from his home circle while he was away, were refreshing to his spirit, yet never was a man more anxious, yea, jealous over his own heart, lest the strongest earthly affections should detract from supreme love to God. Thus he wrote his beloved companion, August 20:

> "I rejoiced in your spiritual expressions; to us, my dear, this life is of small importance; when I think of parting from you, it is indeed painful, but will not God give us dying grace at a dying hour? Oh, let us live as we shall wish we had done, when we come to die."

We find this in his journal of Monday, November 2, 1840: "Friday was the anniversary of my wedding day; eighteen years of peace and happiness in my wedded life, I owe to the good providence of God. Oh for faith to trust him with all. Oh! for sorrow for sin! for entire reliance upon Christ; for the image of Christ on my heart, and the spirit of Christ in my life!"

On Thanksgiving Day of this year (1840), Dr. Cutler preached an admirable sermon suitable to the occasion, which was printed at the request of the parish. His Thanksgiving Sermon for 1835, and his sermon on our National Independence, 4th of July, 1836, had been also printed previously.

A few extracts from his correspondence, on the opening of the year 1841, will prove interesting to our readers. The first is addressed to the mother of a large family, as a New Year's note of congratulation:

"MY DEAR MRS. —— —I thank you most heartily for your kindness and sympathy, and, from long experience, imagine that I have them, even when I have no visible evidence of their existence. . . . . I wish you all a Happy New Year—many, many! You have so many *beautiful barques* which have spread their sails on the sea of life, that you will require a multitude of tender mercies from above. 'Ask and you shall receive.' J—— looked sweetly, when I met her; it was worth stopping my horse and shaking hands with her. Oh that the heavenly simplicity of early youth might be (I had almost said *petrified)* fixed permanently in the soul! 'If thine eye be single, thy whole body shall be full of light!' Tell F—— that we thank her for her good wishes, conveyed in more than words, and in return for her thoughtfulness, would assure her of the richness of the rector's table on New Year's Day. The representative which she sent of her benevolence became the centre of all its sweets. Tell her I have just returned from the wedding of one of the teachers of School No. 2. It was that of Ophelia Rose and Abraham Flowers.

'"Mid winter snows we've Cupid's bowers,
And hail the Rose the Queen of Flowers!'

And a dear little rosebud she was, clad in white raiment. Now if the printers play upon the names of this couple, they must borrow of me.

"Most truly and affectionately yours, B. C. CUTLER."

TO THE SAME, ON THE FORTY-THIRD ANNIVERSARY OF HIS BIRTHDAY.

"ST. ANN'S RECTORY, BROOKLYN, *February* 6.

"MY DEAR MADAM— . . . . Every new token of regard brings with it the sweet incense of thousands which have preceded it, and the cup, just full before, is, by the last drop, made to overflow. Your note recalled all similar favors past, and eight years of kindness came up in remembrance. This day ought to be spent in humiliation and prayer. . . . . My sins and my unworthiness so entirely occupy the ground that is past, that I can but partially enter into any festivity. Still, the native hue and coloring of my thoughts being bright, to all appearance I am rejoicing. Indeed, I have very much to make me rejoice; that for eighteen years my life has been spared to preach the unsearchable riches of Christ, when, four years before I commenced, I hardly expected to live to preach at all. Is this not enough for praise to God? . . . .

"I remain your affectionate pastor, B. C. C."

Dr. Cutler was always incessantly occupied with his parish work at St. Ann's. His journal reads thus:

"*March* 15, 1841.—Last week was one of continued labor and great variety of occupation. Sunday night, a funeral sermon; Monday, a lecture in the chapel; Tuesday, a large wedding; Wednesday, a missionary prayer-meeting. Visited many families in affliction at the close of the week. Yesterday morning, in my own pulpit; in the afternoon, at Williamsburgh; in the evening, at Calvary Church. God still blesses me! I seem to have been for eight years, however, like an officer on the lower deck of a man-of-war in a battle, wadding and firing his gun as fast as he can, and not stopping to see what execution is done!"

"*June* 21.—Last week I went to Philadelphia, with some clerical friends, to attend a meeting of the Board of Missions. On the whole, we had an agreeable time. But I have seen clergy enough for some weeks. When brought together in large bodies there is too much unsanctified sociability, and very frequently much warm blood. After all, if a minister only lives near to the Great Captain of his salvation, and sees his brethren occasionally, it is enough!"

"*July* 12.—Yesterday, and indeed all the week, unwell; but friends supplied my pulpit. It is a trial to me to be so delicate; to have so much ill health. But I am what I am. *He* doeth all things well!"

Dr. Cutler, by resignation and patience under long continued weakness and suffering, proved the adage true, that "great trials make great saints!" and often declared that he was thereby brought into greater fellowship with his suffering Lord. Dr. Octavius Winslow, who has written so touchingly on the subject of Christ's sympathy with man, thus says: "It is in cleaving, by faith, the deep waters, and in climbing the difficult ascent, we reach the firmest footing, and the highest, brightest, holiest elevation in our Christianity—the complete absorption of our will in God's will. The most deeply afflicted, are the most deeply sanctified. . . . . . Before a loving, sympathizing Saviour, I am subdued and melted. I love him, too, because that he, though God, is near to me; near in the valley of tears and suffering; not chiding, but sharing; not crushing, but sustaining; not repelling, but sanctifying my infirmities, feebleness and sorrow! I love him who, while he sorrows with me, encircles me with his omnipotent arms, upholds me with his Divine grace, and perfects his strength in my weakness." How fully did our friend, Dr. Cutler, attest this truth and express such an experience. He was content, too, to wait till the revelations of Heaven should dissipate the shadows of earth and unfold the inner brightness of life's mysteries. The ancient poet could turn to him, as to an obedient disciple of Jesus Christ, and say, with peculiar emphasis:

> "If thou a Christian art, bound to thy lot
> Shall be some cross! It is the load all bear
> Who follow Christ toward heaven. When at length,
> After long bafflings, thou hast found out thine,

Seek not to lose it more. Turn, and in love
Embrace it; for, whatever shape it bear,
It is in truth thy friend. The ease it spoils,
Or the good gifts it seems to hold thee from,
Are nothing to those blessings yet unknown,
Which, in the mysterious orderings of thy fate,
Are knit with it, and it alone for thee!"

Dr. Cutler's continued ill health obliged him to be much in the saddle, and on this account he often, on the approach of summer, took a journey on horseback along the south shore and to the extreme end of Long Island. He was invariably accompanied by some relative or friend, and very often by some parishioner, who was glad enough to enjoy in this way the privilege of social intercourse with him. His counsels and prayers, and his ready sympathy and co-operation in every plan for doing good, were never lost upon these appreciative friends, many of whom are still living witnesses to the pleasures of these seasons of mutual refreshment, and who testify of them, "Ointment and perfume rejoice the heart, so doth the sweetness of a man's friend by hearty counsel."

It was in July of this year that Dr. Cutler took one of the trips to which we have referred, with his beloved friend and parishioner, Whitehead J. Cornell, Esq.

In August we find Dr. Cutler at Saratoga. His letters home from this place are full of interest and incident:

"SARATOGA, *August* 9, 1841.

"MY DEAR —— —. . . . . We have in this house a quiet, genteel, literary kind of company—some little sprinkling of "fashion," who come here for retirement. I wrote you Mr. and Mrs. W., from Boston, were here, and are much with Mrs. McA. Then, one of the Murdocks, and Miss K. of Georgia. Then, Dr. W., Dr. S. and wife, Gen. C. and lady, from Providence; and Mrs. Judge O., from New York; and Mr. and Mrs. L., from Brooklyn. So that, at present, the great aim is to find time for reading and retirement. It is really distressing to me to see men so destitute of mental resources. They are wandering about from room to room, as 'through dry places, seeking rest and finding none.' Oh that we all heard with more delight those words, 'Come unto *me*, all ye that are weary and heavy laden, and I will refresh you!' . . . . I hope you had a good day yesterday. How happy am I that I chose a follower of the Lamb as a companion for life. Blessed be God that I am thus yoked! The determination of Joshua is more and more my own, 'As for me and my house, we will serve the Lord!' . . . . I am well, and, bless God for all his mercies! a more entirely luxurious resting-place one could hardly have. I hope, however, my Bible and my Saviour will be my great luxuries.

"'Make me to love my Bible more,
And take a fresh delight
By day to read its wonders o'er,
And meditate by night.'"

. . . .

"SARATOGA, *August* 13.

. . . . "I gave one man a quietus to-day. He is a young Churchman from Vermont (once a Methodist), a great unfinished kind of body. He said to me, 'So you have got *Stone* down in Brooklyn!' 'Yes,' said I. 'Well, I hope you'll make him straight, for he has never been straight.' Surprised and indignant, I said, 'Are you not sensible of the impropriety of speaking in that way of a man your superior in age, in the ministry, and, as far as I know, in every thing else? It would be but modesty in you to suppose him right and yourself wrong.' He floundered and bristled up, and began to talk very big, but said I, 'You have got an old soldier in hand, so you might as well keep cool.' Now, however contemptuously these young men speak of those who differ from them, when they attack me they must be ready for a reply such as they deserve. I gave this youth no reason to take this liberty with me; on the contrary, I was kind and courteous to him. He will remember me many a day." . . . .

Dr. Cutler was full of ready wit, and excellent at repartee; yet every feeling of this kind was kept within the bounds of Christian moderation. This is illustrated by another incident of this journey:

"SARATOGA, *August* 18.

"I returned to-day from an excursion to Lake George. We started in a stage, and I was the middle one of three on the middle seat—seven persons inside. The gentleman on my right was a 'buck' from Philadelphia. He soon said, 'Sir, I am sorry to say of any man his room is better than his company; but, really, it is so hot and dusty, that I know of no man's society which could repay for the room he would take up.' 'Well, sir,' said I, 'the only material question is, whose name was down first on the stage-book. Now, sir, my name was the first or second down, and therefore I consider you as riding with *me*, not I with you!' This little incident provoked a pleasant and spirited conversation, in which we all took part, and soon we were all on the best of terms. . . . .

"At 2 P. M. we entered the boat and went up the lake. Who should be on board but Mademoiselle Elsler, the dancer, and her train. We were all crowded into a very small place, and compelled, the church and the theatre, to look each other in the face. She has an unfaded face, and dressed plainly, avoiding all display.

"On board the same boat I was introduced to Mr. and Mrs. B——n, of New York, and their niece, from Brooklyn. With these I had a pleasant chat. They are fine specimens of New York Presbyterians—excellent people, pitying the player, enjoying the Christian society, admiring the scenery, and reading the early Indian traditions about the spot." . . . .

About this time the Oxford Tract controversy caused much excitement in the Episcopal Church in this country, as well as in the Church of England.

No one could mistake Dr. Cutler's position in this matter. Frank and decided, without any bitterness or uncharitableness, he, on all suitable occasions, openly expressed his opinion. In clear and emphatic terms he warned his flock against the pernicious influences of those Semi-Romish practices, which some intriguing formalists and other weak and fanciful men had introduced into the Protestant Episcopal Church on this side of the water. The dangers which threatened our communion he pointed out in a masterly manner, in a sermon delivered at St. Ann's on the text, "One is your Master, even Christ."—Matt. xxiii. 10. This discourse is at the close of a volume of Dr. Cutler's sermons published in 1857.

His views on this topic are also made manifest in his correspondence.

TO MRS. CUTLER.

"SARATOGA, *August* 7, 1841.

. . . . "How much time and attention are bestowed on the body and on the comforts of this life! I am struck—when surrounded with comforts and honors, which, however *small*, are more than I deserve—with the fact, that they are only the livery and apparel of Christ's servant. The servant of a nobleman in England is dressed far better than men greatly his superior in worth and property; yea, he is fed better and housed better; and why? not because that servant is a better or wiser man, but because he is 'my lord's man!'

"Dear ——, religion is the one thing needful; indeed, it is. My Bible was much read during my late journey, and I mean it shall be during this. I am now going to the house of God. I expect to meet with some of the 'new notions' imported from Oxford, *via* New York. I saw, this morning, as I passed the door, a gilded cross very conspicuous. Poor human nature! how compassed with infirmities, both priest and people! Our church has points of unpopularity enough, I think, without the addition of things which, although trifles in themselves, and which give me no trouble, yet offend many; nay, most observers. But I go, resolving by Christ's grace, to worship God and to listen to my duty, whether Mr. W—— prays sideways or straightforward, or whether he bows once or a dozen times in the service. . . . .

"*Sunday Evening.*— . . . All the trumpery and foolery of Oxfordism Mr. W—— has introduced, to the loathing of some of the strangers. It is, indeed, contemptible, and will infallibly be followed here, as at Troy, by deserved retribution. Mr. W—— does not only bow, but makes a plain bending of the knees, like a woman who salutes you! Dr. C—— was disgusted both with the preaching and practice; it was, indeed, deplorable! . . . . What reason have any to be thankful who have a clear gospel preacher!"

. . . .

TO THE SAME.

"SARATOGA, *August* 29.

. . . . . "I have just returned from church, alas! most empty. We had a defence of those who adopt the Oxford practices, from the text, 'He that was after the flesh persecuted him that was after the spirit.' The term 'Ishmaelite' was conferred on all who were out of the church! Alas! if I saw the fruits of the Spirit in the lives and conversation of those who thus preached, it might make me think; but when there is hardly a decent morality in some, and a manifest denial of the gospel in others, and a leaning to that corrupt religion which shuts out the light, I can only say, God has seen fit to punish the church with such men. My soul is, indeed, sad! May God help me! No human being has so deep a view of his own deficiencies, inefficiency and want of spirituality as I have; but I must believe that the gospel which you and I teach is the true one. With regard to the intercourse which is to be kept up with such men, I calmly think the coldest and most formal is best. Last week I met one of them, and in return for kindness of manner, which I supposed would induce a return, I met with that which only disgusted and repelled me. 'Really and truly,' as Sargent says, 'if I had to acquire evidence of Episcopacy, or even of the gospel from such alone, I should never have been a Churchman or hardly a Christian.' But God forgive them! If I can only be lifted in spirit above all such things, and live near to God, I shall be contented. Men were sitting in church to-day perfectly uninterested, as well they might be. The laity care little for such things. Oh, where are the solemn, repeated, faithful calls to sinners to repent and believe the gospel? Lord, make me able and willing to make such calls! . . . . I left Mr. W—— and Mr. J—— quarreling about rubrics. After tea, we went into a drawing-room in the house, where a circle was formed, and we conversed for an hour on religious subjects. We had singing:

'To our Redeemer's glorious name;'

a discourse upon Luke xv, and prayer." . . . .

TO MRS. P——T, OF BROOKLYN, ON THE OXFORD TRACTS.

"St. Ann's Rectory, *December* 8, 1841.

"My Dear Friend—I rejoice that your mind is set against 'the novelties that disturb our peace.' I hope that you will 'call no man master;' that, in the matter of your salvation, you will act out the *clear convictions of your own conscience*, and adhere to the ground you have taken, which, I am convinced, is the safe ground of our church, and 'the holy ground,' on which apostles, prophets and patriarchs have ever stood. 'Be thou faithful unto death, and Christ will give thee a crown of life.' To you it must be obvious, that when the mind is but partly dedicated to God, it will be constantly seizing upon something as a substitute for true, vital, soul-humbling godliness. The Sabbath is too *triste*, the Bible too severe, Christians too scrupulous. Let there be some relaxation—the more decent the better; the more like religion the better. But, my dear friend, if we, or an angel from heaven, preach any other gospel, let him be accursed! . . . . May God direct us, for Christ's sake!

"Yours, most affectionately, B. C. CUTLER."

Dr. Cutler's last records in his journal for the year are in unison with all his previous correspondence:

"*Monday, Nov.* 22.— . . . . My soul feels its need of Christ to save it from destruction. I feel that there is but a plank between me and death; but that plank is the Lord, my righteousness. I lie at his feet; I am nothing! He is all my salvation, and all my desire. How much must he bear from me; the lowest place in heaven is far too good for me! My soul lies humbled in the dust! I feel the need of Christ, but I have not that sweet consoling sense of his presence which I desire. O Lord, I am thine; save me!"

"*Dec.* 20.—I am full of gratitude to God for his mercies, and for the wide door opened to me to preach the gospel, and the place in which I live, although deeply grieved at the Popish inventions around us. Lord, cleanse my foul heart, and lead me not into temptation!"

We give a few extracts from his journal for 1842:

"*Jan.* 3, 1842.—I am a monument of God's mercy! I have all things, and abound in temporal blessings; all I want is more grace to live near to God, and to work more faithfully for Christ and immortal souls. What have I to do but to bless God and serve Christ?"

"*Jan.* 10.—Alas! I am living at a poor, dying rate. Again and again have I sought the fountain for sin, that I might bathe in it, and only in that way could I find peace. O my Saviour! have mercy on me; draw me, and I shall come after thee."

"*Jan.* 22.—I have set apart this day for self-examination, prayer, and thanksgiving for the mercies of life. In 1815 I publicly gave myself to God, in Trinity Church, Boston, in the supper of the Lord. I then took up my cross to follow Christ, exercised faith in the word of God, believed that he is the rewarder of those who diligently seek him ; set to my seal that God is true, and that if a man seek first the kingdom of God and his righteousness, all things will be added unto him.

"Since that time more than a quarter of a century has passed away, and I am now in possession of all things which make this life desirable, and yet the thought of leaving it and of going to heaven is far from painful. 'I have all things and abound,' in the apostolic sense. I have no fortune, no wealth, but I have a hope of salvation through the merits of Christ. I am in pretty good health ; am out of debt, and have a salary which puts me above all want, and permits me to be generous to the poor. My church is full and in peace, and my labors are acceptable to the people in general. And now I subscribe my hand that God has been true to his promises. 'Them that honor me, I will honor.'

"B. C. CUTLER."

"*April* 18.—My dear friend Edson has been with me a week. God has had compassion on me and sent him to cheer me up. We have taken sweet counsel together. May God bless us! He is out of health, and I think I can see in his trial, mercy and sanctification. Oh! why can we not trust that all things will work together for good?"

He had another "most refreshing visit" from his friend, Rev. Dr. Edson, of Massachusetts, in June. He visited the same friend in August, and they returned together to Brooklyn, and set off on a horseback journey along the shores of the Hudson, intending to cross the Green Mountains, and travel thence down the Connecticut River.

From Poughkeepsie (seventy-five miles from New York city) he wrote to Mrs. Cutler a glowing account of his journey. He had often said at home, "I never feel like a well man, never feel hearty and sound, unless journeying on horseback. There is always something the matter with my lungs or stomach, and I have a great sense of lassitude and fatigue." But now he wrote to his wife :

"I am without pain, or ache, or weariness, having the sensations of a perfectly well man. We have had the usual varieties of a long ride—rain and sunshine, good and bad taverns, agreeable and disagreeable company. Our conversation has been most pleasant. How could it be otherwise? Every pious feeling in my heart finds a response at all times in that of my friend, and every advantage that education, religion, experience, and great sagacity can afford, without restraint, I find in Mr. E. Religion, the church, theology, philosophy, politics, agriculture, education—all, have been employed to enliven our ride, and to add a charm to every beauty of nature we have seen. But after all, the health that I feel is the great *pearl* of the journey. In riding, I lose every trace of morbid feeling."

Dr. Cutler, however, was still reminded that he was "in the flesh," and a few days later he was taken ill at Bennington, Vt., from which place he returned home alone. The first entry in his journal, after reaching home, was :

"*Aug.* 29.—I took this journey to avoid being sick by travelling in public conveyances, but it is the will of my Saviour that I should not have that robust health which I so much desire. 'I was with you in weakness, and in fear, and in much trembling,' said St. Paul, and so say I to the Christians of St. Ann's. Let but my Master be with me, and all will be well! O Lord Jesus, forgive my sins ; intercede with me, and bless me!"

We close this chapter with one or two extracts from the journal and letters which show his affectionate spirit and attachment to friends and parishioners :

"*Sept.* 12, 1842.—Last Monday my brother's only son came down from Avon to join my family. He was named for me, Benjamin Clarke Cutler. I received him to educate and bring up. I commend him to God, through Christ! I have placed him at school with a pious man, Mr. Davenport. May God bless the relation between this boy and my household! may he make him a child of God, a minister of Christ, and an heir of glory!"

"*Oct.* 3.—Dear Bell (Miss I. G. Boyd) was with us all day yesterday. She is a sweet child to me."

TO MRS. P——T, OF BROOKLYN, AFTER RECEIVING FROM HER A DONATION FOR THE POOR.

"*September* 15, 1842.

"Your kindness, my dear madam, is like 'oil.' Circumstances often compel a mode of communication which is constrained and savors of the world, but I feel, when I receive the fruits of your pen, and when writing to you myself, as if there was nothing to interrupt a stream of religious thought. . . . . Your enclosure comes very opportunely for a poor sick widow who is in want—such an one as I always assist with real pleasure, because I think they are the best objects of charity—a widow (with small children) professing godliness, and who has seen better days. Of course, there is a little shiftlessness. If it were nor for this, or some other little infirmities and faults, we should have few, if any objects of CHARITY in this world.

"Every thing about —— ——— is as interesting to me as it can be to a pastor. I think of her, and love her, as I suppose God intended that a spiritual guide should love his children. 'From the first day until now,' my acquaintance with her has been a source of pleasure. . . . I am now ready for Sunday. How much better it is to take time by the forelock. May I, long before the time, be prepared for my change from life in this world, to life in the world to come. I have a hope that when my 'appointed time' comes, I shall experience a loss of the love of life and the fear of death, and shall desire to depart and be with Christ.

"I have not yet congratulated you upon the happiness of your son. . . May he be the founder of a family as much distinguished by Divine grace, as its ancestors have been for patriotism and virtue! With Mrs. Cutler's best love, and my own, to you and yours, I remain, most affectionately,

"Your friend and pastor, B. C. CUTLER."

TO MISS L. M., A FORMER PARISHIONER.

"BROOKLYN, *November* 20, 1842.

"MY DEAR FRIEND—You have been much in my thoughts today. I have been going over and over the early scenes of my ministry in Quincy. The blessing of your conversion to Christ, and your subsequent aid to me in the parish, have been spread out from the store of memory. I have rejoiced, yea, and will rejoice, at your subjection to the gospel. My dear friend and sister in Christ, may more grace continually be given you! He is '*rich* unto all that call upon him.' What rich blessings we may have by calling on the name of the Lord'—'Ask and receive, that your joy may be full!' . . . Pray for me! At 6 o'clock, Sunday morning, let us meet at the Throne of Grace. I meet others at that hour—some whom, no doubt, you will meet in heaven! A blessing seems granted to my labors here. Still, I sow little, and I reap little. Your valued letter was received.

"Your affectionate brother, in the best of bonds, B. C. C."

How few such pastors there are in these degenerate days? How few like Dr. Cutler hide themselves behind the cross, and strive earnestly for the spiritual welfare of every one with whom they come in contact. How few, with tender love follow up in private intercourse the instructions and counsels which are weekly given in the sanctuary. And how profound, too, was the *humility* of our friend, combined with a strong assurance of faith! The extracts already given from his journals, show us how beautifully and perfectly these two traits were united in him. Though treading oft the vale of humiliation, he never lost sight of his completeness in Christ; and, on the other hand, the closer he clung to Jesus, and the stronger his sense of forgiveness, the more softly did his spirit walk before God, the more lowly did he ever appear. The heavy-laden vessel sinks deeper into the water; so the soul, the more it is filled with Divine grace, sinks the lower in its prostration before the Giver of all grace!

The Christian's progress will ever thus be chequered, till he reaches the land of unmingled praise! This invariably marks the life of the true believer—the humility of the man "after God's own heart" sinking himself to the lowest dust, under the sense of the evil of his heart, and again his holy and joyful aspirations, after the salvation of his God. His highest notes of praise, united with the deepest expressions of abasement, forming that harmony of acceptable service, which ascends "like pillars of smoke" before God.

CHAPTER X.

VISIT TO ENGLAND.

1843.

"What scenes of beauty, glory, wealth and power
Their halo o'er the living landscape throw!
Lo! haven and bay; church, abbey, feudal tower;
Cities on high, and sunny vales below—
These are the scenes that line the British coast,
Fair freedom's bulwark, and the patriot's boast."

THE spring of 1843 found Dr. Cutler still at his post of duty, abounding in pulpit and parochial labors. Ten years of faithful duty had been performed at St. Ann's, and it was no matter of surprise to his friends, that, under the pressure of increased parish labor, his health was again seriously undermined.

Within the limits of the city, six or seven new churches had been organized, all of which were offshoots of St. Ann's, since the rector of this parish came to Brooklyn in 1833. Of course, the ever-increasing population of a growing city like this, made the call for new churches an imperative necessity, and as fast as this became apparent, those members of St. Ann's who were living at a great distance took suitable steps for the formation of new parishes. Thus, a nucleus of interest was made, about which, in several sections, gathered a thriving congregation. The rector of St. Ann's always rendered his hearty aid in all these enterprises, and often unduly exceeded his strength in rendering his assistance and co-operation.

In his own parish, the weekly or monthly meetings for

missionary societies, and other benevolent purposes, were sustained with their usual vigor and interest. A profitable and delightful missionary gathering was held at St. Ann's in January; and in February, at a still larger meeting, at St. James' Church, Philadelphia, Dr. Cutler, as a member of the Foreign Committee, addressed the audience. Oppressed with many difficulties, and a depleted treasury, the question of retrenchment had been raised. To this, Dr. Cutler would not consent, and in a spirited address portrayed the real difficulty in the case, and assured his hearers that the self-denial of the church had been by no means reached. He would stand by the colors he had chosen; and would say in this conflict with trial, what Lord Nelson once said, when, in the battle off Copenhagen, the signal was thrown out by the commander to withdraw from the enemy, "I do not see the signal; keep mine for closer battle, flying; nail mine to the mast!"

This was Dr. Cutler's spirit in every thing he undertook; even feeble health did not cause him to shrink from grappling with difficulty or opposition, and not till probable death stared him in the face, would he cease temporarily from constant labors.

His journal reads thus:

"*April* 4, 1843.—For two weeks I have been very unwell, and have suffered much for months. The winter also has been uncommonly severe. I expected to have to flee this week and leave my charge for a time. Perhaps I shall have to do so yet; but if I am kept by the mighty power of God, all will be well.

"If Christ strengthen me, I can do all things.

"If Christ weaken me, I can bear all things.

"If Christ be with me, death is life.

"Come, Lord Jesus, into my heart!

"I had an offer this week from Capt. F—— to go to England, free of expense. I almost wish I had gone."

"*Brooklyn, April* 10.—Preached all day on Sunday with apparent blessings. On coming out of the pulpit I was called into the robing room by a young man, who said, 'Sir, what must I do to be saved?' Oh that this might be a drop which precedes a shower! Lord, visit thy Church, for Jesus' sake! . . . . I have tried every expedient to remove the pain in my side. I at length prayed to the Lord Jesus Christ, and am better. 'Ye believe in God, believe also in me!' I have been hardly able to bear up, but through grace I have got through. May I not hope to come off more than conqueror, through Christ, over sin, death and hell?"

"*April* 25.—Last week I labored as usual, though suffering from exhaustion. A sea-voyage has been proposed by my physician and friends. My vestry passed a resolution, last evening, which allows me to go to Europe, have all my expenses paid, and my pulpit supplied in my absence.

"But I have greater news than this to record. The Spirit of God appears to be moving on the minds of the people in this parish; and oh that it may come down as a mighty rushing wind, and I may see many souls added to Christ as seals to my ministry!"

"*May* 1.—Yesterday I was so feeble that I verily thought it would be my last day of labor before going away."

All doubts about his course of duty were now removed, and it was obviously necessary for him to take a sea voyage for the restoration of his health.

The Lord evidently was pleased to open his way before him, and as he had always acknowledged him in all his ways, so now that same Divine Guide directed his path. Every arrangement was duly made for an immediate departure for England.

We find a most affecting record in his journal, made early on the day of his sailing:

"*Brooklyn, May* 15, 1843.—My beloved wife and I are about to embark; now may He who made the sea go with us! May the great Angel of the Covenant go before us, and the God of Israel be our rereward!

"I go amid a multitude of prayers of both young and old, rich and poor. The cry of the poor is certainly not against me. I have ever remembered them, and I know I have their blessing. Into thy hands, Lord Jesus, I resign my spirit!"

Dr. and Mrs. Cutler sailed for Liverpool on the 15th of May, in the packet-ship "Stephen Whitney," accompanied down the harbor by numerous friends and parishioners. Before he was fairly out at sea, he wrote a farewell letter to his flock, although a few days previous he had delivered a solemn and affecting farewell discourse:

"SANDY HOOK, *May* 15, 1843.

"MY BELOVED FRIENDS—The feelings which I experience in leaving you and the shores of my native land are mingled. I feel humbled to the dust when I consider the high and awful responsibilities which have been entrusted to me, and compare them with the manner in which they have been discharged. If God had not taken compassion and poured out an undeserved blessing, I should have sunk under my own reflections. It is the language of my soul; 'If thou should'st be extreme to mark iniquity, O Lord! who shall stand?'

"I feel grateful for the many marks of friendship and affection which, in the course of my ministry of ten years, I have enjoyed. They are too numerous to be mentioned, and will continue to endear the bestowers of them to my heart until death.

"May God reward all who have given even a cup of cold water to the writer, in the name of a disciple! I feel also great confidence that many who have not as yet joined themselves to the Lord's people, will remember, when I am gone, the words which have been spoken, and, if I reach heaven, will meet me there, through the abounding grace of our Redeemer!

"With respect to my voyage, I feel it's absolute necessity, and I have a calm and imperturbable conviction that it is the Lord's will. I have not undertaken it without much consideration and prayer. May I not hope that during my absence you will, one and all, support St. Ann's Church, by every means in your power, and be united in every good word and work?

"At the foot of the cross of our Redeemer I now address you, firmly believing in his omnipresence and atoning death; and there I pray you may by faith ever live, and there, with joy and triumph, die!

"Let me close with the following words, as our united motto—the inscription on our banners, 'To live is Christ; to die is gain!" Jehovah—Father, Son, and Holy Ghost, be with you all!

"Most affectionately yours, B. C. CUTLER."

During this voyage he kept a journal in detail, written in the form of letters, for members of his household who were left behind. This valued collection of his experience on the sea, is still treasured up in his family, and has now become, more than ever, a precious memento of "the days that are past." The trip could not but be pleasant, as far as companionship was concerned, as they had over twenty cabin passengers, all intelligent and agreeable people. England, Scotland and France, each had their representatives in this social group, and, with a good sprinkling of Americans, a varied and delightful circle was formed. Urbanity, harmony and kindness prevailed. The United States Chargè to Brussels, the Rev. Mr. Nott, of Schenectady, the Rev. Mr. Sewell, of Quebec, and Mr. Anstis, of St. George's Church, New York, were among the passengers. Divine service was held in the cabin, and also in the steerage (where were a large number of passengers) on each Lord's Day. Every opportunity for doing good was eagerly embraced by Dr. Cutler, and he freely distributed the Testaments, books and tracts, large parcels of which he had brought on board with him. His second letter he closed with this language, "I hope and pray to be able to save some souls yet, before I reach port!" and in the Irish Channel, when near his destined place, he writes: "We do not doubt that this voyage will be marked with the salvation of some souls."

Meetings for prayer and praise were often held in Dr. Cutler's state-room, which, as he said, strengthened and consoled his soul, and made him feel at home, even when, as the latitude and longitude taught, he was far away.

In his letter marked "No. 11," we see how he turned every event and every fact, however trivial, to his own spiritual good, or to the edification of others.

"FRIDAY, 11 A. M., *June* 2, 1843.
Long. 10¼ West; Lat. 50.

. . . . . "One thing has struck me forcibly, and continually awakened my surprise. It is that so few ships are seen. For three days we have not seen one inch of white canvas on the deep, and now, though at the entrance to the Irish Channel, we are apparently entering alone that mighty arm of the sea. God grant us gentle and favorable breezes in ascending, as it were, that hazardous passage. But why fear now? Fears may be tormenting.

'Awake our souls, away our fears,
Let every trembling thought be gone;
Awake, and run the heavenly race,
And put a cheerful courage on!'

"What a type of the vastness of the Creator's attributes is this ocean! How many thousand ships might have performed this voyage in company with us? Yet we have been alone, or nearly so. So it is with the Christian. He embarks on the attribute of God's mercy alone. Thousands might embark with him. It is wide enough and deep enough for all mankind, and yet the Omniscient eye sees but here and there a voyager on that mighty sea, of which St. Paul, in contemplation, exclaims, 'Oh! the depth, and length, and breadth,' etc.

"Yes, and God's mercy like the ocean, never wears out! How many keels have cut their way from one continent to the other, since Columbus first landed on the western side of this great ocean, and sang '*Te Deum laudamus*,' to the God who heareth prayer and accepteth praise!

"Our morning and evening sacrifices to God seem to be more and more acceptable to the worshipers. May they become more and more so to the Saviour to whom they are addressed! . . . My sick man assured me to-day, that my few words occasionally spoken had not been in vain. Some think he will not live to reach port. He seems touched to think God has raised up so many kind friends. Will not God always raise up friends for his people? *He doeth all things well!* . . . . Present to the Sunday-schools the most affectionate remembrances of their pastor. Love to each, and all, of our dear friends in Brooklyn.

"Most affectionately yours, B. C. CUTLER."

The ship was becalmed off Holyhead, but after a trial of patience for two or three days, she entered the port of Liverpool on the 6th day of June, after a passage of twenty-one days.

Dr. Cutler had been furnished by Dr. Milnor and others with letters to many distinguished personages in England, and to many choice spirits in the English Church and other religious societies. He rather desired, however, to keep out of the busy world, and in the retirement of Christian society to find the rest and soothing influences his impaired health so much required. The Bishop of the Diocese of New York, in addition to public credentials, gave him private letters, warmly commending him to the love and cordial hospitality of English Christians. He did not avail himself of all the proffers of kindness so earnestly pressed upon him, but whenever he chose to present his "epistles of commendation," as the Rev. Mr. Carus said of him, "he amply verified all the declarations of his friends."

Dr. Cutler and lady proceeded to London, where they were cordially greeted by some of their parishioners who had gone to Europe previous to their own departure. They took the usual routine of travelers, visiting the chief places of interest in that great city—the Tower, the British Museum, St. Paul's Cathedral, Westminster Abbey, etc., etc. The latter seemed to fill them with the most sublime emotions, and scarcely any place in England impressed them with so much wonder and awe.

St. Mary's Woolnoth, where they attended Divine service, was also a place of thrilling interest, from its associations with that eminent man of God, the Rev. John Newton! Here, for many long years, the author of "The Cardiphonia" broke the bread of life to a devoted flock, and beneath the chancel lie his mortal remains.

On the 11th of June, they had the pleasure of hearing an eloquent discourse at St. John's, Bedford Row, from the

Hon. and Rev. Baptist W. Noel. This church is the one where the Rev. Mr. Cecil and other godly men, whose names are dear to every lover of evangelical truth, had preached the Gospel of Christ. Among them all stands foremost the name of the Rev. Daniel Wilson, D.D., the late Bishop of Calcutta.

On the 13th of June, Dr. Cutler breakfasted with the Rev. Josiah Pratt, whose faithful ministry at St. Stephen's, Coleman Street, and especially his unwearied labors in the Church Missionary Society, had made him known and esteemed on both sides of the Atlantic. On the following Sunday, Dr. and Mrs. Cutler passed a delightful day with Mr. Pratt and his family. It was one long to be remembered, such as Christians love to put away in memory's store, and bring it forth, again and again, in after years, to be dwelt upon with ever-recurring interest. True, unaffected Christian intercourse was enjoyed with the various members of the household. Dr. Cutler preached for Mr. Pratt, and visited his Sunday-school. The latter gave his guests many interesting reminiscences of " John Newton," with whom he had been associated as curate in early days. In a note to Dr. Cutler, a month later, Miss Pratt thus alludes to this visit:

" I feel thankful for this opportunity of expressing the great pleasure we have all derived from the intercourse, short as it has been, which we have lately had with yourself and Mrs. Cutler, and trust that the savor of affectionate zeal and piety thus communicated to us may long be cherished and found fruitful in the great work in which we all delight to be employed."

Dr. Cutler also enjoyed a missionary meeting, held at Islington, in the month of June, where he made an address. He was also gratified with visits to other kindred spirits in and around London, among whom was the Rev. Mr. Noel, who entertained him at his delightful residence at Walthamstow, seven miles from London.

After remaining three weeks, visiting many celebrated places in the environs of the city, Dr. Cutler went to Oxford, taking Windsor Castle and Eton College in his route. In a little embowered cottage, in old Windsor, they dined with the Bagsters, a most worthy family of dissenters, whose piety, hospitality and loyalty to their Queen, did not fail to interest and attract them.

English friends had gladly proffered letters of introduction to eminent men at Oxford, where the party were kindly received. The Rev. Dr. Richards, of Exeter College, and others, showed them every attention, and they availed themselves of the opportunity afforded to attend the " Commemoration" at the University. Among the degrees conferred at that time was that of LL. D. on Mr. Edward Everett, then United States Minister to England, who was present on the occasion. After a few days profitably spent at this place, so full of historic associations, they returned to London, where invitations to visit Brighton and other places awaited them, but which they were obliged reluctantly to decline.

The party set off again, in a day or two, for Cambridge, where an American friend, then resident there, met them, and rendered their stay very agreeable.

On the 4th of July, they dined with him, meeting American and English acquaintances, and partook of the feast under the folds of the English and the American flags.

The colleges, rich in architecture, particularly " King's College," interested them much. The ancient relics of bygone days were all eagerly viewed, while the extensive grounds and shaded walks, which ever render Cambridge so attractive, also absorbed much attention.

They were often musing in many a sequestered nook, where the cultivated mind, which loves retirement from the noisy haunts of men, would be naturally led to look up to God, and realize that

"The calm retreat, the quiet shade,
With prayer and praise agree;
And seem, by thy sweet bounty made,
For those who follow thee."

In this place, above all others, the Christian's heart would be kindled with new emotions, as he remembered that here, beneath these trees, the evening breeze often wafted to heaven those communings of soul which the devout Martyn poured forth, long before he sailed for India's shores. Here were the name and deeds of that devoted missionary recalled. But there were also *living* men at Cambridge upon whom the mantle of his spirit had fallen, and who, in singleness of heart, were laboring for the same Lord and Master, who is rich unto all his servants that call upon him in every age.

The hand of Christian fellowship was warmly extended by such to Dr. Cutler, and by none more cordially than by the Rev. William Carus, of Trinity College. As the biographer of the late Rev. Charles Simeon, he has since been widely known and honored in many religious circles in both countries. "I feel honored in being with so holy a man, and he was exceedingly kind (wrote Mrs. Cutler). He invited us to breakfast and tea at his rooms. I have heard him preach three times. This evening he was upon his favorite theme—Christ our Saviour. It was the same, but varied, impressive, faithful, heavenly! He came and took a most affectionate leave of us with prayer, and we parted, I presume, for ever!"

What could be more gratifying to a Christian man of Dr. Cutler's fine sensibilites than the following note, received a few hours after reaching Cambridge:

"TRINITY COLLEGE, *July* 1, 1843.

"MY DEAR SIR—Allow me to give you a hearty welcome to Cambridge, even before I have had the pleasure of seeing you. Had I not been going this moment to the Regius Professor of Divinity, I should have come to your room and begged you to make my study your resting place this evening. Can you, however, give me the favor of your company to breakfast in the morning at quarter past nine? and we can then go to church together, as dear Dr. Tyng did with me last year, and good Bishop Meade the year before, and beloved Bishop McIlvaine some years before that. . . . .

"Believe me, yours most truly, in Christian regard,

W. CARUS."

Dr. Cutler's allusion to his visit at Cambridge, in a letter to a friend in London, indicates his hearty appreciation of the kindness he had received.

In acknowledgment of the receipt of a letter addressed by the St. Stephen's Coleman Street Sunday-school girls to St. Ann's Sunday-school in Brooklyn:

TO MISS PRATT.

"DURHAM, *July* 11.

"Thank you, kindly, my dear Christian friend, for your attention to my request. I was quite delighted to find on my arrival, a few moments ago, the promised letter. I shall pray over it, and prize it, and shall expect some immortal soul may be made better by it. There is a great importance in making first impressions, and I am not without hope that from what shall strike the young and lively mind, in this new mode of exhortation, something may ultimately result, for which both you and I may give glory to God. . . . .

"To-day brings me a kind letter from Mr. Waddington, and one from the boys' school to my own. . . . I addressed, last Sunday, the Sunday-school of the Rev. Dr. Marsh, with whom Mrs. Cutler and I passed a sweet Sunday. . . . .

"At Cambridge we had a most delightful visit, chiefly in the company of Mr. Carus, with whom we took 'sweet counsel,' sweet indeed! Every circumstance conspired to draw out his heart; and whose heart could resist when Mr. Carus poured out the cordialities of his? There were at times but one stream made by our thoughts, communings and prayers. One almost sighs to think of such solitary '*fellowships*' as those of Cambridge.

"With Mrs. Cutler's best respects to your venerable father, your excellent mother and family, I remain yours, most affectionately,

"B. C. CUTLER.

"P. S.—We expect to embark August 1st, for New York; will you give us your prayers?"

Dr. Cutler always spoke with delight of his meeting with this valued man of God, Mr. Carus, who, in 1851, was called away from Cambridge, and became a canon of Winchester Cathedral. How fully his kindly feelings were reciprocated, is apparent in a note to the writer of this memoir, dated

"WINCHESTER, ENGLAND, *May* 30, 1864.

"MY DEAR SIR—I have been deeply moved by your kind letter about our beloved, and now sainted, friend and brother, Dr. Cutler. Never shall I forget that visit of his to Cambridge, and the blessed intercourse I was permitted to enjoy with that eminent man of God.

"It was one of the richest privileges of my life. Would that I could furnish you, as you desire, with some memorials of our Christian fellowship, during those happy hours at Trinity College. But I fear it is *now* out of my power to furnish them. . . . My large mass of papers have remained unassorted for years which I have not had leisure to arrange. . . .

"Yours most sincerely, W. CARUS."

It is rare that such congenial spirits meet on earth; and if such are the foretastes of heavenly love, what, indeed, will the reality be, when the friendships formed here below shall be consummated, purified and made perpetual in the presence of Christ above?

Dr. Cutler left Cambridge (hallowed for ever in his memory) on the 7th of July, for Durham. He passed through a rich country, replete with loveliness and beauty; regretting he could neither stop at Northampton, the residence of Dr. Doddridge, nor turn aside to reach Olney, made famous by the Christian poet. At Leamington he was introduced into the bosom of a delightful family, that of the Rev. Dr. Marsh, one of the most devoted clergymen of the Established Church. After treading on the soil consecrated by traditionary associations of Queen Elizabeth, at Kenilworth, and visiting other famous places in the neighborhood, he went on to York, and thence to Durham.

At the latter place Dr. and Mrs. Cutler were cordially received at the residence of G. T. Fox, Esq., with whose son they had a previous and long acquaintance in New York. One can readily imagine how delightfully a week was spent at Durham, especially with such hospitable friends. Dr. Cutler here met many clergymen and distinguished authors, through the constant kindness of Mr. Fox. At a dinner party given by the venerable T. Gisborne, prebendary of Durham, he was gratified to meet the Rev. Dr. Waddington (well known by his Church history), the Rev. George Townshend and other clergymen of note, including the Bishops of Durham and Chester. The latter produced the same impression on Dr. Cutler's mind which he never failed to produce on his own countrymen. A general favorite of all classes, and one who received all the honors bestowed upon him (even when afterward he became the Primate of all England) with unaffected grace. His lordship held an ordination at Durham Cathedral at this time, when over forty candidates were admitted to holy orders.

In a letter to his nephew, Mr. Charles Bancroft, then at Brooklyn, Dr. Cutler thus writes on the occasion :

"It was a solemn and interesting scene. . . . The Bishop and his examining clergy are holy and learned men, and such as any church might well desire to honor. What a blessing such a number of heralds may confer on a sinful and lost world. I thought of Henry Martyn, of Bishop Heber, and of Daniel Wilson, and offered my poor petitions that a rich spiritual anointing might follow this great act of public and authoritative separation for the ministry.

"At 10 o'clock the congregation assembled for Divine service. Two Bishops were present—the Dean of Durham, a tall, dignified man, in his white surplice and scarlet hood. The sermon was preached by the Rev. Prebendary Thomas Gisborne, from the words, 'God has not given us the spirit of fear, but of power, and of love, and of a sound mind.' The preacher was over eighty years of age; but he delivered a most excellent discourse, showing the true character and spirit of a minister of Christ. He took the opportunity to bear his testimony against the Oxford heresy. . . . At 6 P. M. the Bishop of Chester preached in his robes; his text was, 'Now then we are ambassadors for Christ,' etc. His sermon was evangelical and spiritual; not about the authority of the priesthood, but about the responsibility of the treasure of the gospel. His preaching is like Bishop Eastburn's.

"I have been struck with the ease with which the rubrics sit upon the clergy. They seem to form an easy, flowing robe, which is never laid aside, but which gracefully becomes them. I have never heard bishop or priest repeat the collect: 'Grant, we beseech thee,' etc., just as it is in the Prayer Book. The Bishops of Glasgow and of Chester altered it; and every other man Sunday after Sunday has altered it by a word or phrase. Almost every church sings different psalms and hymns, and some sing no psalms. They sing between the second lesson and the creed, or after the first two collects; the latter custom prevails in Westminster Abbey. Indeed, they do not appear to speak of such trifles. For my part, I like to see a minister correct. I am so myself in the service. But I think, with many here, that to have our religion consist in a close attention to trifles, is belittling to the soul; to make a great fuss about little things is a sorry way of serving God.

"Last week your aunt and I had you much in mind, and often united in prayer for you, that the Holy Spirit would seal your ordination and make you his own. Take care of flattery, especially from other ministers. God setteth up and God putteth down. Depend upon it, your best friends are the best friends of Christ; the most devoted and spiritual Christians! I know this; I am sure of it. Therefore, take heed:

'The vulgar, fickle are and frail,
The great, dissemble and betray;
And, laid in Truth's impartial scale,
The lightest thing will both outweigh.'

"I do not expect to come home until October 1st. . . . May God bless and keep you, prays

"Your affectionate uncle, B. C. CUTLER."

Allusion is made in the preceding letter to the ordination of Mr. Bancroft. This gentleman was a nephew of Mrs. Cutler, and much loved by Dr. Cutler. He was born in Montreal, and was sent in early youth, by his parents, to Dr. Muhlenberg's celebrated institution at Flushing. He afterwards graduated at Columbia College, New York, and while at college, and during his theological course, enjoyed the friendship and counsel of his loved relative. On the

25th of July, 1843, he received holy orders at the hands of the late Lord Bishop of Montreal, administering the Diocese of Quebec, and was appointed in charge of the chapel of St. Paul (at Quebec), to commence his duties in the following October.

The *interim* was spent at Brooklyn, and the parish of St. Ann's gladly secured his services during that period.

Before his ordination he had been at the rectory in Brooklyn, and at the time of Dr. Cutler's departure, was especially useful in the various departments of parish labor. It was wisely and kindly ordered that at this juncture he was at hand to facilitate every plan in connection with his uncle's temporary absence, and we know nothing was more grateful to Dr. Cutler, standing as he did, almost in the light of an adopted son to both Dr. and Mrs. Cutler.

Dr. Cutler, while in Europe, constantly received tidings of the condition of his church and Sunday-schools from this relative, as well as from others in the parish.

The summer of this year was made famous in the annals of the Episcopal Church in the United States, by the "Carey ordination," when Drs. Smith and Anthon protested, in the midst of the public services on the occasion, against the admission to orders of a late graduate of the General Theological Seminary, who had been accused of holding some of the doctrines of the Church of Rome. The excitement which was awakened throughout the church was unprecedented, and the baneful influence of Tractarianism was becoming more and more apparent.

This explains the following extract from a letter Dr. Cutler received, from his Sunday-school Superintendent while he was in England :

. . . . "The papers will no doubt give you the particulars of the doings in St. Stephen's. The stand that Drs. Anthon and Smith have taken is approved by all sound Churchmen, inasmuch as the time had come when a stand must be taken in regard to the errors that are spreading among us. . . . Things are rapidly coming to a focus with us in regard to the Puseyite heresy. . . . Our missionary meeting in Boston was well attended. It was determined to discontinue the mission to Crete, and reduce the expenses of that to Athens. The Constantinople mission with Mr. Southgate, was continued at the earnest solicitation of Bishops Doane, Whittingham, and Ives, though the Foreign Committee pressed very strongly the removal of Mr. Southgate. . . . May you enjoy the kind favor and protection of your Heavenly Father during your absence, and be returned to your people in the fullness of the blessing of the gospel of peace!

"In bonds of Christian love, yours, F. T. PEET."

Dr. Cutler, though absent, took a deep interest in all the details of the above mentioned ordination, and all the minutiæ of the affair were forwarded to him while in Devonshire. He attached great significance to this and other like matters, regarding them as occasional developments and outlets of those deep undercurrents of error, which he feared were undermining the stability of the Church.

But we must follow the routine of our friend's journey. After leaving Durham, he returned to London and spent another fortnight. Dr. and Mrs. Cutler were soon off again, however, for Devonshire, visiting Bath, Bristol and Clifton; thence they proceeded to "Fremington Vicarage," near Barnstable, where they arrived on the 7th of August. Here in a sequestered rural spot, with refined, intellectual and pious friends, they were entertained for weeks with that generous hospitality which is so characteristic of retired English homes. The passing traveller who is simply absorbed in sight-seeing in England, or taken up with the whirl and excitement of the great towns and cities, sees nothing of the rural charms which adorn many a place hid from the busy thoroughfares; nor can he know that genuine, frank and cordial hospitality, which attracts so many cultivated minds to the interior of those delightful Christian homes, where heart meets heart, and every noble sentiment of the soul meets with a suitable response. In such a home, under the roof of the Rev. William C. Hill, Dr. and Mrs. Cutler found an agreeable resting-place.

A slight link of connection with a relative of theirs in America had first brought them to each other's notice, and now, after some correspondence, long anticipations were to be realized, and the promised visit made.

We have an interesting account of their sojourn, in a letter from Dr. Cutler to his nephew, Mr. Bancroft:

"FREMINGTON VICARAGE, DEVONSHIRE, *September* 1, 1843.

"MY DEAR CHARLES—For the last three weeks we have been staying at this quiet place. It is on an arm of the sea called Barnstable Bay, and the tide comes up nearly to the house. Nothing can exceed the kindness and hospitality of the Rev. Mr. Hill and his lady—the counterpart of our two friends at Athens of the same name (and, by the way, we received a letter this week from Mr. Bracebridge, of Warwickshire, inviting us to pass a few days at 'Atherstone Hall.' This was through the kindness of our friends at Athens). My health is slowly improving. . . . I have preached two Sundays, and assisted Mr. Hill every Thursday evening. I have also addressed the Sunday-school, and the children have sent many messages to our own schools. . . . We have now been about three months in England, but we remain unchanged in our love of home, and say now as when we left you, 'Thy people shall be my people.' As it respects the reigning heresy of incipient Romanism, my mind is firmly fixed. I look upon it as fearful in its consequences, and deep and deadly in its injurious effects on the truth. . . . .

"Mr. Parker's letters are received by his kind friends here with very great pleasure. They fondly dwell on the thought that one day they shall see Mr. and Mrs. Parker. . . .

"I am anxious to hear about your ordination. Stir up the gift that is in you, and study; approve yourself unto God, a workman that needeth not to be ashamed. We have just had the weekly lecture. It was fully attended, and at the close it was a very affecting scene—the villagers praying God to bless us and give us a safe journey. I was cheered by the singing—so much sweetness and sincerity. 'Come ye that love the Lord,' was sung to the tune of Shirland. Surely, such scenes are the home of the soul.

"'Speaking to yourselves,' says St. Paul, 'in psalms and hymns and spiritual songs.' . . I have planted a fine honey-suckle near the garden wall, that it might remain as a memento after our departure. . . You will like to hear about the preaching in England. What I have heard, in every case, is more plain, more scriptural, more evangelical, and more doctrinal, than what would be termed good preaching among us. It is far from being as elaborate as the better part of ours, but it has more of a scriptural cast. The preachers aim at building men up in the most holy faith. Human depravity, conversion, the influence of the Holy Spirit, etc.; these are the ingredients of which the preaching is compounded. There is too, a bold and open, and very solemn rebuke of the new Romish sentiments of the Oxford Tract men, not a looking that way, not a hint, not a fear expressed in general terms of the tendencies of the times, but a charge of false doctrine, and a soul-destroying corruption of God's truth. I was glad to learn that Lord Wellington said, when a female relative of an Archbishop said, 'Why will not your Grace interfere and protect that good man, Dr. Pusey?' 'Poh, poh! he has been let alone too long!' There will be a dreadful upheaving of the laity here, I am well convinced. . . . But I must close, and send my love to all my dear friends in the church and Sunday-schools. Who shall I name? Where shall I begin? They know. Our love and salutation to your Aunt S., to dear H. and Ben. Also to Mrs. Francis and the Doctor.

"Yours, most affectionately, B. C. CUTLER."

At Fremington, Dr. and Mrs. Cutler enjoyed every comfort and pleasure that the most considerate thoughtfulness could devise, and the inmates of the vicarage became endeared to them for life. When they came to leave, it was with real regret, yet mingled with gratitude to the Giver of all mercies for this "spring by the way." The correspondence between these friends, in after years, was a source of unfeigned pleasure, and ended only with life. Time and distance could not separate them in spirit, and now these two ministers of Jesus pour forth their united praises in the eternal home where partings are never known.

The letter of Dr. Cutler to Mr. and Mrs. Hill, after leaving their residence (written partly at Exeter, and partly at London), we fail not to transcribe.

"EXETER, *September* 2, 1843.

"MY VERY KIND FRIENDS—The *fragrance* of your friendship is still fresh on my mind, and in my meditations this morning it came over me like a soothing and pleasing dream. May God reward you for all! . . . . This morning has opened very finely, and we have the prospect of a charming ride; but we want another Sun to make us happy, the light of his countenance, who is the Alpha and Omega of the Church, in heaven and on earth. May he be with us all! Adieu!"

"LONDON, 13 CECIL STREET.

"This blessed day has found us, my dear friends, in the great city of sin, and salvation, too! Here we may take our choice of a hundred Christian temples, in which to worship God. For worship, after all, is the great object for which the true Christian waits upon God in his courts. Mrs. C. wants to go to Westminster Abbey. I had rather go to Bedford Row, to St. John's Chapel. . . . . . I had no opportunity to do good in the cars yesterday, save by a battle with a kind of Puseyite; but, alas! this is a wretched mode of doing good. I am every day more and more averse to religious controversy, and yet I fear that on reaching home I shall be compelled to take up the sword. But shepherds make poor swordsmen. I have been for a quarter of a century floating on the kindlier sentiments of men, yea, and of babes, and I shall make a bad hand at fighting giants. But if I fight at all, it must be with prayer and the sling of truth. . . . . I have been reading some of Keble's Christian Year. The poem on 'The Gunpowder Plot' should be republished.

2 P. M.

"The choir at Westminster Abbey was full, and we went to St. Margaret's. The sermon was a good one for *me*, but a poor one for those who do not hear the gospel. St. Margaret's is a nice church; the window over the altar is superb stained glass, the subject of which is the Crucifixion.

"'Yet faith's pure hymn, beneath a *shelter rude*,
Breathes out as sweetly to the tangled wood,
As where the rays through painted oriels pour
O'er marble shaft, or tesselated floor;
Heaven asks no pomp around the heart that feels,
And all is holy, where devotion kneels.'

"With love to Mrs. H., I am yours, most affectionately,

B. C. CUTLER."

After returning to London, Dr. Cutler went to Brighton, and then, crossing the Channel, went to Paris, where he preached for Bishop Luscomb, the English chaplain there. In a fortnight they were in London again. From thence Dr. Cutler wrote a few lines to his nephew:

TO THE REV. CHARLES BANCROFT.

"13 CECIL STREET, LONDON, *September* 26, 1843.

"MY DEAR CHARLES—I sincerely congratulate you on your ordination and upon the favorable auspices under which your ministry is commenced. Who ordained you, however, is a matter of small importance, compared with the question of your fidelity. 'Be thou faithful unto death, and I will give thee a crown of life!'"

"LIVERPOOL, *October* 3.

"Mr. T—— says, in a letter, that you are much approved, and that he hears you are inclining to High Church doctrine, which he admires not the less. This he said, I suppose, to tease me. However, high or low, you must now take the consequences; but, after all you have seen, if you side that way, I know you will do it against your conscience. You must preach what you believe. Never utter a 'saying,' or urge upon men a duty, which you do not perform or thoroughly comprehend. You had better be thought a babe in Christ, than preach one whit more than God has taught you by his Spirit. . . . .

"I am sorry to say my side is not free from pain. In this body I 'groan, being burdened.' The Lord grant that I may be clothed upon from heaven. Pray for me. . . . . Don't be worried about my attack on your High Church. I don't think so highly of the *depth* of such young gentlemen's notions as to quarrel about them. Puseyism is, in my view, the 'dandyism' of the church. Indeed, it is something very much worse. Love, in abundance, to your dear mother. . . . .

"Your affectionate uncle, B. C. CUTLER."

Dr. and Mrs. Cutler visited "Atherstone," and thus acceded to the urgent request of Mr. and Mrs. Bracebridge (the warm friends of the Greek Mission), but regretted that, owing to delay of letters, they could not visit Tutbury, Burton-on-Trent, the home of the Jacksons, whither they had been so kindly invited.

They left the shores of England in the ship "Sheffield," Capt. Popham, October 5, 1843. The voyage home was boisterous and protracted. In the Irish Channel they were overtaken by a violent gale, and afterward encountered a succession of westerly gales; but the unfavorable state of the weather was counter-balanced by the society of their fellow-passengers. They were favored with all that intelligence, urbanity, piety, and harmony of feeling could afford. The captain was devoted to the entertainment and comfort of all his passengers. Public worship was held twice on Sunday, and prayers daily in the ladies' cabin.

On the 10th of November they approached the shores of their native land, and on the morning of the 11th they were furnished with a pilot, who held out the cheering hope that in a few hours they would be amid the greetings of friends at home.

But God's ways are not as man's ways. At noon of the same day the ship struck at Romer Shoal, at the entrance of the harbor of New York. Who can describe the scene of consternation? Hearts but a moment ago buoyant with hope were now filled with gloom and dismay. Despair was on every face, and night soon added its horrors to the scene. The rain fell in torrents, and the wind blew strong and high.

The captain told Dr. Cutler that their Christianity was now to be put in practice, for they were in a howling storm on a desolate shoal, and their vessel was fast going to pieces. Twelve hours of heart-rending, smothered agony were spent upon the wreck. When it was nearly midnight, Dr. Cutler delivered a short and appropriate discourse to his hearers assembled in the cabin, from the text, "As Moses lifted up the serpent in the wilderness, (were they not in a waste, howling wilderness of sea then?) even so must the Son of man be lifted up; that whosoever believeth in him should not perish, but have everlasting life." Doubtless, many were enabled to look to the Saviour at that hour and hear his voice, amid the howling blast, whispering to their souls, "Peace, be still!" The hope of life departed from nearly every breast; but at the very last moment a steamer came to their assistance (having perceived the blue lights and rockets which were sent up from the sinking ship, as signals of distress). A hymn of praise arose from these voices, just now mute with despair, which bore upward to God the gratitude of every heart. They were soon transferred to the steamer, and six hours later they were at home.

Our readers will find a most interesting, detailed account of this shipwreck in a little book called "Twelve Hours on the Wreck," containing a narrative of the disaster, prepared by Rev. Dr. Cutler.

It was like a resurrection from the grave, when, with the first rays of the morning sun (on Sunday, November 12), Dr. Cutler beheld not far off the tower of old St. Ann's Church. Friends gathered at the rectory, but Dr. Cutler, after having been, like the apostle, "a night and a day in the deep," retired immediately to rest. In the afternoon the shepherd was amid his flock again. At 2 o'clock the Sunday-schools met their restored pastor in the chapel. What joyful emotions filled his heart and theirs can be better imagined than described. "A Hymn of Gratitude," written for the occasion of his return by a teacher in the Sunday-school, was sung by the choir on his entrance.

Several hymns had been written by persons connected with the schools, or by their friends, to welcome the rector's return, which were all sent in to him, as tokens of continued respect and affection.

How expressive of the feeling of every heart was a piece called "The Greeting," an extract from which we here give:

"There's gladness in the fold once more!
And gushing hearts rejoice;

Thanks to our God! our waiting o'er,
We hear the shepherd's voice.

"Foremost to join the joyous strain
The cherished lambs would come,
And praise the Power that brings again
Our own dear pastor home."

Dr. Cutler brought with him various letters from England—one from Mr. Edwin Hough (who was connected with the Evangelical Alliance), addressed to St. Ann's Sunday-school. Also, from the Superintendents of Rev. Mr. Pratt's schools, in London, which was subsequently read to the Sunday-schools of the parish. Letters had been transmitted during the previous summer, from the same school, to that of St. Ann's. *

After Divine service, in the evening of that Lord's Day which found him at home again, Dr. Cutler received the congratulations of the parish; with great eagerness, the people pressed forward to the chancel rails to greet him who had been set over them in the Lord. The signal deliverance from the jaws of death which Dr. Cutler experienced, was not allowed to pass away unimproved. On the last Sunday of November he preached an appropriate discourse from Psalm xl. 1, 2, 3. "I waited patiently for the Lord, and he inclined unto me, and heard my cry. He brought me up also out of an horrible pit, out of the miry clay, and set my foot upon a rock, and established my goings. And he hath put a new song in my mouth, even praise unto our God; many shall see it, and fear, and shall trust in the Lord."

On each returning anniversary of the day of the shipwreck, he gathered his friends about him (some of whom were his companions on that fearful night), and spread a feast to commemorate the goodness of the Lord, mingling with the amenities of social life, interesting and profitable religious exercises.

* See Appendix C.

On Thanksgiving Day he preached a sermon from the text, "Prove all things; hold fast that which is good;" describing his experience in England, and comparing the educational and religious advantages of the two countries.

From friends scattered over all portions of the land came cheering letters to him, during the remaining weeks of the closing year, hailing his safe return with profound gratitude. From old England, too, came tributes of love and sympathy and thanksgiving from many hearts. The friends at "Fremington vicarage," wrote:

"DEAR AND BELOVED FRIENDS.—What an astonishing instance of Divine goodness and power was displayed in your preservation! May it prove the spiritual life of many; not only of those who were with you in the ship, but of those who hear what great things the Lord has done for you. 'Bless the Lord, Oh my soul! and all that is within me, bless his holy name!' . . . . . . I can but faintly conceive your situation; the trial of your faith and constancy, surpassing any thing I have ever experienced. . . . What a scene God, in his love and mercy, hath carried you through, since you left us! Praise to his holy name! he hath done wondrous things for you, whereof we rejoice. . . . It must, indeed, have been a trying time to yourselves, and to many; yea, I hope, a blessed time! Every one's refuge must have been tried; many, doubtless, prayed as they never prayed before. We cordially join with you in wishing to take our place, also, at the feet of our Redeemer.

"What a lesson does this shipwreck teach us also! How loudly does it call to us to have our loins girded, and our lamps burning, when our Lord shall come, and when he shall say, 'I come quickly,' to answer with a desire to be in his presence, 'Amen, even so come Lord Jesus!' Amen, prays, dear friends,

"Your ever affectionate, W. C. HILL."

A few years later, and the writer of the above lines, found with his lamp trimmed and burning, was called home to the heavenly feast.

The Rev. Mr. Pratt ,of London, also sent a gratifying communication.

TO THE REV. DR. CUTLER.

"LONDON, 15 FINSBURY CIRCUS, *December* 15, 1843.

"MY DEAR SIR—The intelligence of your shipwreck has awakened our sympathy and our thankfulness. Finding you ultimately saved from death, we rejoice that you are spared yet to labor for Christ, and the good of precious souls. . . . At that fearful season of darkness and tempest, it must have been consolatory to you, my dear friend, to feel that amidst the weaknesses of the Christian, you had labored to render the passage across the Atlantic (which you were just bringing to a close), a blessing to those who sailed with you. Had you been all irrecoverably lost, as to this world, we may hope that your labors would have been instrumental in preparing some for eternal glory; and we now hope and pray that the long-suffering of God, in sparing sinners for repentance, and believers for lengthened and increased fruitfulness, may have its full influence, through the grace of the Holy Spirit, on the hearts of all. . . . . Take courage, then, my dear friends, that you may stand for truth and love with still more boldness and zeal, in this disordered world and distracted church. If the pressure of that resistless hand, which restrains 'the unruly wills and affections of sinful men,' be in judgment and in wisdom lightened still more and more, elements of evil and anarchy and death, which are struggling to throw the world into confusion, will spring into dreadful action. Our one consolation is, that all the evil which is and may be permitted to oppress the church, and to ravage the world, will be restrained within the limits of its commission, and will be made to serve the spiritual and everlasting interests of every child of God, and the glory of Christ, in the ultimate establishment and enlargement of His kingdom. . . . . My family unite with me in very kind remembrances to yourself and Mrs. Cutler. Believe me, my dear sir,

"Ever faithfully yours, JOSIAH PRATT."

The Rev. Mr. Carus also penned a most affectionate letter, and sent it, by a private opportunity, at a later date.

A sojourn in a foreign land had by no means allowed the friends of Dr. Cutler in America to lose their hold on the affections of his loving heart, as this concluding epistle will show :

TO THE REV WM. JACKSON, LOUISVILLE, KY.

"BROOKLYN, *December* 22, 1843.

"MY VERY DEAR FRIEND—I thank you for the expression of interest and sympathy which your late letter conveyed. Such Christian congratulation is one of many good fruits which our dear and Divine Redeemer has caused to grow out of my late affliction. There are some indications of fruit in my heart which is yet humbled and softened within me. Oh, I wanted a more solemn and spiritual frame of soul! And what was more fitted to procure it than going down into the grave, with all my thoughts about me, and coming up again? I have been baptized with death, if not 'for the dead.' Jonah hardly felt more separated from the living than I did. And Jonah never felt more happy than I did on Sunday morning about daybreak to land on the shores of Brooklyn, and to walk up the hill while the rays of the bright sun were gilding the tower of my church. . . . . The letter of your dear sister, from Tutbury, I received just as I was embarking for home, at Liverpool. . . . . I cherish your image and that of your dear wife. . . . . I say, I cherish your united image near my heart. Who did you leave (when you removed to Kentucky) that would come over from the city of New York and sit together with us in heavenly places? Who, I inquire? Who is like minded? Dr. Shelton and wife are the only substitute, and they are truly good and 'nice,' as your countrymen say. Every thing is 'nice' with the English. But don't think that I felt like criticising; far from it. I was delighted with my visit. But it will last me all my life. When I landed, and met my brother-in-law, Capt. Bancroft, I made over to him all my right and title to all the oceans, seas, channels, gulfs and straits in this round world. I wipe my hands clear of all, save the Ohio River, and a few others, on which I shall place my foot with considerable diffidence.

"Neptune said to Ulysses (at least so Pope says in his translation of the Odyssey), when escaped from shipwreck:

'Whate'er thy fate, the ills my wrath could raise
Shall last remembered in thy best of days.'

"Now, dear Mr. Jackson, I make over to you and your dear wife, and to your heirs for ever, all my right and title to all England, Scotland, Ireland, yea, and France. America is good enough for me. 'I love Cæsar well,' but I love—no, I don't love Rome—but *home* more! England—rosy, green, merry Old England—with her 'fairs' and her harvest homes; lovely old England, the queen of the seas, I love to think of, —— but her princely young daughter, with her blooming cheeks and buxom form, and numerous and noble offspring, is my delight:

> 'In nature's most delightful scene,
> My happy portion lies.'—Ps. xvi. 6.

"Bishop Berkeley says:

> 'Westward the course of empire takes its way—
> The four first acts already past,
> A fifth, shall close the drama with the day;
> Time's noblest offspring is her last!'

. . . . . *Vale, vale!*

"Yours, B. C. CUTLER."

CHAPTER XI.

MINISTRY AT ST. ANN'S CHURCH—CONTINUED.

1844–1849.

"The Christian warrior—see him stand
In the whole armor of his God;
The Spirit's sword is in his hand,
His feet are with the Gospel shod.

In panoply of Truth complete,
Salvation's helmet on his head;
With Righteousness, a breast-plate meet,
And Faith's broad shield before him spread."

DR. CUTLER did not experience that renovation of health he so much desired, by his voyage to Europe. Indeed, the trying scenes through which he passed at the time of his shipwreck, seem to have neutralized the good effects of previous rest and change of climate. There must have been, however, some slight improvement in his physical condition, or he could hardly have lived twenty years longer to accomplish so much good on earth. But in spiritual things he had evidently been blessed. There was apparent, to all observers, a new measure of the Spirit bestowed and a ripening of Christian graces, which, as years increased, gave a mellowness and charm to the whole man, and like "the full corn in the ear," was the result of much care on the part of the Divine Husbandman, and a due proportion of sunshine and rain upon this "plant of his keeping." All his desire was, that the blessed Redeemer should fill his heart "with his image and his spirit."

Thus he writes in his journal:

"*Feb.* 5, 1844.—This has been a year of trial, frequent indisposition, and some seasons of despondency. But my soul has become more alive to God, and my interest in Christ is greater. I am driven to him oftener, and feel more deeply my need of him. To those who believe, Christ is precious. He is all in all to me. My voyage was one of spiritual dependence upon Christ. I was reading of him, praying to him, and working for him. I rejoice that I went abroad, and am still more rejoiced that I am at home. He doeth all things well; 'he maketh both the dumb to speak and the blind to see'—dumb ministers to speak of Christ, and blind ministers to behold his beauty!"

Dr. Cutler engaged in his parochial duties, after his return, with his usual activity, and before the month of February (1844) closed, sixty persons were confirmed and added to the communion.

His health became more enfeebled as spring approached, and the vestry, as well as the rector, were soon convinced that an assistant in the parish was indispensable in order to preserve his valuable life and secure his earnest labors for this church.

The minds of both parties were turned to the Rev. C. Bancroft, who would ere long conclude his year of promised labor at St. Paul's Chapel, Quebec; and it was with no small degree of pleasure that Dr. Cutler wrote to this relative and offered him the post. It was soon accepted, though he could not commence its duties until summer.

Not many months elapsed since Dr. Cutler penned the interesting letter which concludes the previous chapter to his valued friend and brother in the ministry, Rev. William Jackson, ere the latter was suddenly called from his earthly toils to his heavenly rest. His own loss was great, but he wrote immediately to the bereaved widow.

TO MRS. WILLIAM JACKSON.

"BROOKLYN, *March* 1, 1844.

"MY BELOVED AND AFFLICTED FRIEND—A few hours ago I heard from Louisville the distressing intelligence of the death of your dear husband. I need not say how deeply grieved I am at this stroke, nor how much I sympathize with you in your inexpressible sorrow. Our gracious Saviour alone can support you, and I doubt not he has prepared your mind, in a measure, for the trial. Still it is and will be great. But you must look forward to a reunion in a better world, where death shall be destroyed.

"Think how long you were permitted to enjoy his society, and what a length of time he was spared to labor in the church, and in various ways to promote the cause of Christ. He labored almost to the last, and then safely entered the desired haven, as we trust and believe.

"'No more fatigue, no more distress,
Nor sin, nor hell, shall reach that place!
No groans to mingle with the songs
Resounding from immortal tongues.'

"Accept, my dear afflicted sister, the warmest sympathy of both my dear wife and myself. Be assured of our prayers in your behalf, and trust, I beseech you, that, however dark the cloud, you will yet be able to say 'it was good for me that I was afflicted.' . . .

"With our most affectionate sympathy, B. C. CUTLER."

Deep was the void and wide was the breach which was made at Louisville at the decease of this honored servant of God. Though the workman was removed, the work of God must still go on, and the parish of St. Paul's, Louisville, hoping to mitigate their sorrow by filling the place of the departed with a dear friend of his, soon proffered a unanimous call to Dr. Cutler. The Bishop of that diocese, and others of the clergy, urged upon him the acceptance of this call, but the parish in Brooklyn could not think of separation from their much-loved pastor, and he felt, for various reasons, constrained to decline.

We find in his journal:

"*May* 6, 1844.—I am nervous and feeble. Never more

so. This is my infirmity. It is of the Lord. Its end is known only to him. Oh, may his grace be sufficient for me! Blessed Saviour, may I kiss the rod and bow my head! Oh, forgive me and wash me, for thine own sake! Draw me near to thee! Lord, undertake for me! Condescend to order my footsteps by thy word and spirit!"

"*May* 20.—I arose with this text of Scripture on my mind, 'Be still, and know that I am God!' I arose and read the 46th Psalm. It is called Luther's Psalm. I read it in a shipwreck, November 11, 1843. It is a psalm for trouble, deep trouble. I am better than I was, but weak. I am at God's disposal. One thing only I am anxious about—that my union with the Lord Jesus Christ, as a branch to the vine, may be ensured. I must give diligence to make my calling and election sure. There appears to be a great trial before me—uselessness, poverty, perhaps death! But none of these things move me. How I lived, not how I died, will be the great question—not that my life will save me. Oh, no! I have never done a single action, for which I have not reason to ask forgiveness of God. But, in judging whether I am a true believer in Christ, I must be governed by *fruits*. 'By their fruits, ye shall know them.'"

"*May* 27.—My assistant has arrived, and has preached, very much to my satisfaction. With such help, my spirits may rise and my health improve. Yesterday was communion day, and six new members were added to the church, and six more from other churches. May the ministers of St. Ann's be visited with a blessing from on high, and may sinners turn from the paths of death, and live! Oh, let it be my whole aim to live for the service of Christ—no more for the world!"

It was well for Dr. Cutler that his dearly cherished relative, a very son in the spirit, should becomes his coadjutor at this critical period.

As the fine weather appeared, he used every means of

building up his health and strength, especially by exercise on horseback. In June he rode up and down the length of Long Island, in company with Mr. M——, of his parish, traveling in the saddle nearly three hundred miles. In July and August we find him at Saratoga, using the mineral waters from the springs which have made this place so noted. The last note in his journal before going was :

"Blessed Jesus! add thy blessing to the springs ;

"Thou seest me waiting at the pool ;
I would, thou knowest I would, be whole ;
Oh, let the troubled waters move
And minister thy healing love!'"

While absent from home he preached occasionally, distributed tracts, and attended meetings of the Bible Society, or gatherings of a kindred character. He always realized his responsibility as a minister of God, and acted accordingly. At Saratoga he wrote out new sermons, and "took sweet counsel with Christian friends from various quarters of the land." Here he met his attached friend, Bishop Eastburn, and wrote to his assistant in this strain :

"My communion with Bishop E—— was really a blessing. Only think of being two weeks together, sitting up till 11 o'clock in the most deeply interesting conversation on the whole range of topics, literary, social, sacred and ecclesiastical. . . . . He has been called out by his Massachusetts duties, and is in full blast against the Romish party. By the by, how modest it is for a presbyter to say, 'There is no cause for this opposition to Romish error!' when nearly every Bishop in England has awoke, and charged his clergy against it. The goose, when she put her head into the wall, saw no danger! I trust that the pastoral letter of the House of Bishops will speak decidedly against this leaning to Rome. The Anti-Puseyites want to know whether they have been alarmed without cause, and the Puseyites, whether they are right. All eyes in the church, and out of it, are looking to the Bishops. Bishop Chase has said much already. Oh that he might not lack firmness now! His best friends expect from him something explicit. . . .

"Yours in the strongest bonds, B. C. CUTLER."

We give an extract from a letter of an earlier date, addressed to the same, in which allusion is made to the same topic:

"Coming up here, I fell into conversation with a gentleman from Baltimore and another from New York. I find that the exclusive and ultra views of the church, maintained by the Romish party in our church, are doing great mischief, and creating great disgust and even animosity against us! How can it be otherwise? What is there in our numbers, piety or zeal, which justifies the ground they take, viz., that no other ministry is valid? Indifferent spectators might say that almost all ministries might be valued BUT ours, from the fruits. Our good Lord, deliver the church from this deplorable leaven!" . . . .

To a parishioner he wrote:

. . . . "Bishop E—— soon joined us. . . . . His taste is truly formed on the Anglo-Saxon model, or, more truly, on the English. . . . . But I have found tastes in the good Bishop far worthier of admiration than this, however good it may be. He is truly and thoroughly awake to the errors of the times, and preaches in a most faithful and edifying way."

Happily, Dr. Cutler and his assistant, and the bulk of his parish also, held similar views on the topics of discussion which then agitated the church.

"*Sept.* 9."—He says: "My dear son (referring to his assistant) preached faithfully on Christ our righteousness; the Lord bless him! he is all that I could desire."

Toward the close of this month he had the pleasure of uniting in marriage his assistant (the Rev. C. B.) and Miss Ellen Smith, of Philadelphia. While Mr. B. was absent on his wedding trip to Montreal, Dr. Cutler wrote to his relative:

"BROOKLYN, *September* 29, 1844.

"I hope you will come home refreshed, and with your '*cara sposa*' resolved to serve God. Oh that a new unction might be given to you and to me! How tame and cold my sermons appear! Oh for words that breathe, and thoughts that burn! Oh for a pen of fire! that I might BURN IN the awful truth, that men are in danger of everlasting woe.

"But a pen of fire may not convince them so much as a pen of Christian love! We have preached the simple gospel to ——— and said little about the terrors of the law, and yet she appears deeply convinced of sin. God will own his truth. It is mighty and will prevail. Study it and preach it, my dear C——, and may God give you many happy seals of your ministry, as crowns of your rejoicing. . . . . . With much love,

"Your affectionate uncle, and co-laborer,

"B. C. CUTLER."

The records of his journal show how constant was his love and zeal in the cause of Christ, and the extension of his kingdom:

"*Dec.* 9, 1844.—I took my family, yesterday, over to St. George's Church, New York, to attend a farewell meeting for the missionaries to China. It was a glorious meeting. My prayers have been answered; the church has arisen and shines in the star-like lustre of a clear sky. O Son of Righteousness, arise! The night is far spent; the day is at hand. For twenty years have I prayed to see such a sight as I saw last night. Glory to God in the highest, peace on earth, and good-will toward men!"

"*Dec.* 17.—Bishop Johns preached last evening. It was wonderful, sweet and strong. The Lord reward him! Oh that his mantle may fall upon us ministers! My soul was satisfied, as with marrow and fatness."

"*Dec.* 20.—Rich privileges during the last Sabbath. My mind, however, is absorbed in church with my duties and occupation, but my heart, on which God keeps his eye, is too often cold and dead.

'Heart thou art ice, or why this long delay
To melt in streams of liquid grief away?'

I want to love God with all my heart, and soul, and mind. Oh that with the old year, I might throw off all old sins and follies and put on the Lord Jesus Christ! Thy grace is sufficient for me, O Lord!"

The trial and subsequent suspension from office of the Bishop of the Diocese of New York, at the beginning of the year 1845, gave Dr. Cutler much sorrow. Conscientiously adhering to his sense of duty, he expressed his opinions with much candor and firmness, and for the good of the diocese, acquiesced willingly in the decision arrived at by his peers. In later years, however, when age and suffering had brought his diocesan near the end of life, and unfeigned repentance had been unquestionably exhibited, Dr. Cutler was one of the very first to ask for a remission of his sentence, and to desire those in authority, after the injunction of Scripture, to "restore such an one in the spirit of meekness," if it could be with propriety accomplished, and without interfering with the rights of the Provisional Bishop.

His comment at this time was:

"*Jan.* 13, 1845.—Oh what a temptation is high health and spirits in any thing like a high place in the church! It is through much tribulation that we must enter the kingdom of heaven. Oh for a tender conscience, a broken heart, an humbled mind, and a constant preparation for death!"

Let us read a few more extracts from his journal:

"*March* 17.—My spirits droop, and my left side is still painful. I am beginning seriously now to think of giving up my charge. Lord, undertake for me! I need wisdom, grace and patience.

'Behind this frowning providence,
Thou may'st hide a smiling face.'

We have not an high priest which cannot be touched with a feeling of our infirmities."

"*March* 31.—Much wearied and discouraged on account of my health, yet not quite in despair; 'as dying, and behold we live!' I feel like an afflicted man. Yet I am kept up like a person in deep water, whom some one keeps from drowning, by placing his hand under his chin. 'Hold thou me up and I shall be safe!'"

"*April* 7.—'Every branch in me that bringeth forth fruit, he purgeth it, (*or pruneth it*) that it may bring forth more fruit.' I have been well pruned, and I needed it.

"Rev. John Fletcher said: 'I keep in my sentry-box till Providence removes me. My situation is quite suited to my little strength (then aged fifty-four). I may do as much or as little as I please, according to my weakness; and I have an advantage which I can have nowhere else in such a degree. My little field of action is just at my door; so that if I happen to overdo myself, I have but a step from my pulpit to my bed, and from my bed to the grave. If I had a body full of vigor, and a purse full of money, I should like well enough to do as Mr. —— does, but as Providence does not call me to it, I readily submit.' *

"I have suffered for twenty-five years from weakness of body. A state of valetudinarianism is unfriendly to piety on account of the self-indulgence which is fostered, and the selfishness which the attentions of others increases; but to be in the state in which I have been is *safer* than to be in robust health. A man like me, and in this parish, has no time and no temptation to trifle; no opportunity for foolish talking or jesting, but many an one, for giving of thanks and for prayer.

"I am now forty-seven years old, and twenty-eight out of these have been years of languor and infirmity. God has kept me near the borders of the grave, that I might be delivered from a miserable, light and trifling spirit."

Amid all the personal and relative trials of this year, how refreshing and encouraging to Dr. Cutler's spirit must have been the epistle which came over the waters from the halls of Cambridge, and reached him in the month of April. We subjoin it almost entire:

* See Fletcher's Life by Cox, p. 154.

TO THE REV. DR. CUTLER.

"TRINITY COLLEGE, CAMBRIDGE, *March* 27, 1845.

"MY VERY DEAR FRIEND AND BROTHER—Often have I been purposing to send you a few lines, but my incessant engagements, enormous correspondence, and often infirm health, have actually obliged me to postpone my good desires. But I wished to tell you how affectionately I hold you in remembrance, and shall not forget, to the end of my days, that brief but blessed visit with which you favored us in Cambridge. How is your own health? I feared much for you; you were, indeed, very feeble, whilst sojourning here; and then, what a trial, just as you were reaching your own dear home once more! Surely, you can now say with the apostle, 'in perils in the sea.' What a mighty deliverance! Truly, the landing of Paul at Melita was not more the work of our gracious Lord, than your preservation from the deep water-floods. No sooner did I hear of this, than I offered up my poor praises in your behalf, as I had before, my prayers. . . . . Now, happy and grateful indeed should I be to have a few lines from you, whenever it may be in your power to find a few moments for an affectionate, though distant and unseen, friend and brother.

"I often think of all the heavy troubles with which your branch of Christ's Church has had of late to contend, as well as *our* branch here. But we know who shall prevail, though for past neglect and unfaithfulness, and coldness and pride, we may be called to suffer shame and loss, for a season. These storms will break off all branches which are withered and unsound; and though the stem may be rudely shaken, it will only cause the roots to take stronger hold. Oh, may He who is the truth, and life, and love, keep and bless us! Excuse this most hasty and unworthy note. I am obliged to write in a great hurry, and am weary. But, sir, believe me, with true Christian regard to yourself and lady,

"Your most affectionate brother in Christ Jesus, W. CARUS."

Another friend, the Rev. Josiah Pratt, had been called to "the rest that remaineth for the people of God" during the previous year, and the number of Dr. Cutler's correspondents in England were decreasing, so that the above letter was especially cheering to his soul.

But a heavy loss now fell upon the Church in the United States. The sudden death of the venerable Dr. Milnor, the rector of St. George's Church, New York, on the 11th of

April, 1845, produced deep sensation throughout the length and breadth of the American Church, and startled, like an electric shock, the whole community in the cities of New York and Brooklyn. He had long been a personal friend of Dr. Cutler, and the latter delivered a highly appropriate sermon upon his decease, from the text, "For though ye have ten thousand instructors in Christ, yet have ye not many fathers."—1 Cor. iv. 15.

An extract from this sermon appears in the Memoir of Dr. Milnor, by the Rev. Dr. Stone, and every word of this discourse might, with equal force and truthfulness, have been delivered eighteen years later to the multitude of people who were weeping over the loss of a spiritual father at St. Ann's, Brooklyn.

The following letter shows us how deeply Dr. Cutler felt the departure of Dr. Milnor:

TO BISHOP EASTBURN.

"BROOKLYN, *April* 23, 1845.

"MY DEAR BISHOP— . . . . I am glad to get a line from you,—your feelings are mine entirely. I was called upon on Saturday to draft the resolutions about Dr. Milnor, for the Foreign Committee; and last night, before I read them, prefaced them by an *ex tempore* address of the same order with your letter. How wonderful the dispensation! Where shall we find the man to take his place? . . . . May I be found more faithful, more self-denying, more willing to sow beside all waters.

"I was not aware how rich a contribution might be found in his character! He was a pillar—a Corinthian column in our temple! nay, of the Composite order! But whoever dies, the Lord liveth; Jesus is alive for evermore, and has the keys of death and of hell. He opened the grave; let us submit. He said to our Moses, 'Go up into the mount and die.' He said, on that eventful night:

'Soldier! lay thy weapons down,
Quit the sword and take the crown;
Triumph! all thy foes are banished,
Death is slain and earth is vanished!'

. . . . .

"Your afflicted but affectionate brother, B. C. CUTLER."

His assistant, the Rev. Charles Bancroft, was now called away to St. Thomas' Church, Montreal, carrying there the savor of the same earnest and devoted spirit which he had manifested at St. Ann's. His ministerial career, Dr. Cutler followed with deep and paternal interest, as he was transferred thence in 1847, to the rectory of St. John's, and in 1858 back to Montreal, where he became the incumbent of Trinity Church. He had already, in 1854, been appointed one of the canons of the cathedral. His degree of D.D. was received successively from Columbia College, New York, and the University of Bishop's College, Lennoxville, Canada. The office of assistant, now vacant, was soon filled by the Rev. A. W. Duy, a graduate of the Theological Seminary of Virginia (as were all the successive assistants of the parish, with one or two exceptions).

We give here an extract or two from Dr. Cutler's journal:

"*June* 23, 1845.—Last week the Board of Missions met, and the annual sermon was preached by the Rev. G. Burgess, D.D. It was excellent. The addresses at Ascension Church were also good. The cause seems flourishing, and I now believe the tree of Foreign Missions is rooted in the church. Great minds are now engaged in its nourishment. A river of water now flows hard by its roots, and my own beloved church is, I think, engaged for life in the work—blessed be God! Domestic missions are as important as foreign, but they will always receive attention where there is a spark of piety."

"*Oct.* 26. *Sunday.*—I baptized two infants—twin children of R. B. and E. G. D.; they were five months old, and both on one arm—to-day. Lord, before thee I am a little child! Hold me on thy everlasting arm, and baptize me with thy Holy Spirit!"

"*Nov.* 18, 1845.—This day was observed as a day of thanksgiving for the deliverance of my wife and myself from shipwreck in November, 1843. The 11th day of the month was the one to be observed, but parish duties prevented. To-day was spent in solemn, humble and grateful recollection. In the evening, about twenty communicants of the church were invited to spend an hour with the rector, at the rectory, in social prayer and praise."

In April, 1846, Dr. Cutler met with another loss in the death of his assistant, Mr. Duy, who departed this life under the parental roof in Philadelphia, aged twenty-three years. Thus was removed, in the morning of life, one of the brightest lights which God has ever given to our church. Suitable resolutions were passed by the vestry of St. Ann's, and Dr. Cutler delivered two discourses in connection with this solemn event, and published an interesting obituary notice of his fellow-laborer in the Church papers.

In June, he took his annual excursion down the island on horseback with the same companion who accompanied him the preceding year, the Rev. Mr. D——.

Before the end of the summer, he happily secured the services of the Rev. G. D. Miles, as assistant minister of St. Ann's. "Thanks to a gracious God!" he says, "I have an assistant who promises well, a good man and true; now that we have our work before us, all we want is more grace, more holiness, which I take to be equivalent to being more wrapped up in Christ!"

The Tractarian controversy was still disturbing the Church at large, and Dr. Cutler could not be silent on the subject, as we see from some of his correspondence of this year:

TO MISS P——, OF LONDON, AFTER THE RETURN OF THE BISHOP OF CALCUTTA TO ENGLAND.

"BROOKLYN, N. Y., *May* 2, 1846.

. . . . "Your favor of the 21st of March reached me a few days since. I made an examination of my letters and papers and found your father's letter. I send it as copied by my dear wife. We are glad to hear that you intend to prepare a memorial of your sainted parent, and hope that we shall be among those who will be favored with its perusal. We have enjoyed the visit of the Bishop of Calcutta, *by faith;* 'we have seen it afar off;' we rejoice that from the lips of one high in office all 'reserve' is removed. May his precious life be preserved! But, alas! if I did not look above and beyond the life of any man, or all men who are good and true, my soul would sink! The enemy is coming in like a flood, and I look to God to lift up a standard against him. Oh, the infatuation of our clergy! What but a delusion from the unseen world could have so blinded them? With our Romanizing brethren here, no 'developments' seem to have weight. Like men intoxicated, the more they drink, the less they perceive their true condition. But our laity judge in a good degree for themselves, and those gentlemen find it hard to get employment. And why was I kept from this delusion?

'Oh, to grace how great a debtor!'

"Present our most Christian regards to your mother and sister, and brothers, one of whom we know not in the flesh, but hope to know, when all separation of Christians shall for ever cease. I am preaching and laboring as usual. I have now been thirteen years in this parish, ... and have been twenty-four years in the ministry! Alas! how many sins and imperfections have I to lament! 'Lord, weigh not our merits, but pardon our offenses!' These would be my dying words. . . . .

"I remain yours, B. C. CUTLER."

TO THE REV. MR. ——, LE ROY, N. Y.

"DEAR SIR—God be praised that some minister of Christ in our church is found to 'lift up his voice like a trumpet!' . . . Oh, the unfaithfulness that abounds! The fear, the time-serving, the abominable connivance with deadly error! I tremble for the ark! I tremble for myself! If we of the clergy will hold our peace; if bishops refuse to 'contend earnestly' for the faith once delivered—not to Rome, but to the saints—the very stones will cry out! women and boys will rise up to shame us to courage and conflict! The Lord be with you! Yours, B. C. CUTLER."

Dr. Cutler could never be accused of judging others or condemning them with undue severity, while he failed to look inwardly upon his own heart and life. Indeed, his watchfulness and circumspection was quite unusual, and few have ever been equally faithful.

"*Monday, Nov.* 30, 1846.—I tried to keep the Sabbath holy; but alas! how sinful is my heart at best! I say, 'will this heart ne'er be clean?' Here is the smell of sin still. All the perfumes of Arabia will not sweeten this little heart! I am surprised myself at the motion of sins which I have no desire to gratify. The tree is cut down, the root remains! Oh that it might be rooted out!

"I cannot rest till pure within,
Till I am wholly lost in Thee."

Faithfulness in his ministerial life was also his chief aim. Read the following, addressed to a parishioner:

"St. Ann's Rectory, *February* 19, 1847.

"My Dear Friend—The upholsterer yesterday sent home my sofa. It is repaired in the neatest manner possible, and will probably endure, unless burned up, until my weary body shall find a permanent resting-place in the grave. I thank you for thinking for a moment of my comfort. I will try more than ever to think of yours, and that of the precious immortal souls entrusted to my charge. But how different the true method of doing this, from what the world may suppose. It is by preaching God's word so faithfully that it will wound, and then pointing out Christ who will heal. It is by urging to labors and sacrifices, and a wearisome attention to duties, and then pointing to Christ for rest. And oh! if through my poor instrumentality, you alone shall find Christ as balsam to a wound, and shall retire to him as to 'the shadow of a great rock, in a weary land'—if I shall succeed in grafting your soul alone into Christ, I could not regret my choice of a preacher's life—so full of duties, of abasement and humiliation, compared with that of a merchant, or a scholar, or any other man. The Lord grant me this success at least, and reward all my benefactors. With Christian love to your household, I remain

"Your friend and pastor, B. C. Cutler."

In May, 1847, he took another excursion, on horseback, down the island with Capt. Bancroft, his brother-in-law.

It was just on the eve of this journey that he wrote to a friend, then in England, a letter expressing clearly and pointedly his views on the Tractarian controversy :

TO MRS. WILLIAM JACKSON.

"BROOKLYN, *May* 25, 1847.

"MY DEAR FRIEND— . . . My saddle-bags are lying on the floor, and my good wife is stitching up my riding-dress; so, you see, I take one precept of Scripture literally, '*Ride on*, because of the word of truth, of meekness and righteousness.' It is that word which alone is worth living for.

"Blessed be God, for at least twenty-five years that I have endeavored to preach and teach it, and that after an evangelical manner. But who can tell how oft he offendeth? I often wonder why I am preserved. But 'when the fruit is ripe, the sickle will be put in'—immediately too! . . . I thank you for the pamphlets, etc. We had a collection for the Irish of three hundred dollars, which goes out by the frigate 'Macedonian,' 'now in the stream.' Poor, politically-ruined, Papal-ruined Ireland! Dead! twice dead, I fear, to be plucked up by the roots. . . .

"Now you want to know how I am about Oxfordism. I say as Bishop McIlvaine says in an introduction to Mr. Simeon's life, just published here, 'I take pleasure in the opportunity of reiterating my protest against what I abhor more and more as a covert denial of the gospel and the very soul of the Romish anti-Christ—the Oxford views.' Amen. From all such heresy, good Lord deliver us! It is spreading slowly but surely, and we have the prospect of a 'good fight of faith.' Let him that hath no sword sell his garment and buy one. Jesus, under thee we conquer. Dear ———, at the feet of Jesus, with all our sins, let us rest, repenting and believing.

"Yours for ever, B. C. C."

Dr. Cutler's natural independence of spirit always exhibited itself whenever he felt called upon to protest against errors injurious to the Church. In the practical workings of her plans for the extension of the cause of missions, also, he fearlessly set forth his views, and labored strenuously for what he deemed the best interests of the church.

At a meeting at St. Bartholomew's Church, in New York, in October, 1847, there was a large assembly of Bishops and presbyters, and many laymen. A division of opinion occurred on the subject of the mission to Constantinople. Dr. Cutler was among the number of those whose opinions were overruled, and whose counsels were rejected. Bishop ——— charged those whose views coincided with those of Dr. Cutler, with deadly hostility to the mission. His remarks were interpreted to mean that he now felt released from all obligation to treat their opinions with any consideration, and he was opposed to their voting again on the subject. In commenting on this, Dr. Cutler says in his journal, "This was so violent an assault, and he was so conspicuous in his attack upon the foreign committee, of which I am a member, that my spirit was roused, and I, in an equally violent manner, called upon him to explain himself, and said I would not sit still under so outrageous a charge. I also called Bishop ——— to order, for persisting in calling us enemies, when all we asked was, that the Constantinopolitan mission might be supported by its friends. . . . I am humbled and abashed that I gave way to my feelings; and though I consider it was an overflow of indignation and not of anger, yet I do not justify or defend it. I have been praised and blamed for my rebuke of a Bishop. I like neither the one nor the other. I desire not the distinction of a rebuker of Bishops, and deeply regret that the thing took place. I pray God to keep my heart in future."

February 6, 1848, marked the fiftieth anniversary of his birthday. These seasons, as they recurred, were always set apart for special humiliation and devout gratitude to God. On this occasion a parishioner sent him some impromptu lines, and the reply was as follows:

TO MRS. F——.

"St. Ann's Rectory, *February* 6, 1848.

"My Dear Friend—I have read over and over again your very kind, but too flattering lines. I am, indeed, celebrating my semi-centennial birthday, but I cannot fully realize it. My body is indeed benumbed and besprinkled with the frost of time. But my heart is nearly as young as ever, and forces my head to its daily tasks. As it respects my profession I have but one thing to say; by the grace of God, I am what I am. . . . . Oh, if the Saviour will but manifest himself to me, as he does not to the world, then I shall confer not with flesh and blood, either my own or another's. . . . . With best respects to your husband, I remain most affectionately yours, B. C. CUTLER."

In the same month he penned a touching letter of consolation to a much esteemed friend:

TO BISHOP EASTBURN.

"BROOKLYN, *February* 17, 1848.

"MY DEAR BISHOP—We were all very much surprised, as well as grieved, to hear of the death of your sister—I am almost sure your twin sister. Alas! what a lesson is taught us! What is life? What is death? What are we? How many lessons we repeat to others, but with what weight do they not come when we have been made to feel them? Death has been more busy here than ever before. All ages have fallen before it. . . . . But, my dear Bishop, to die, to the Christian must be gain. We must gain many relations for one we shall have left! We must gain the clearest and loveliest views of Christ, for at best but cloudy apprehensions; and must receive a reward for our past labors, which as yet has not been visibly dispensed. I trust that your sister was prepared, and then I must suppose she was taken away from the evil to come.

'Can the laborer rest from his labors too soon?
He worked all the morning and rested at noon;
We gather the flower when full in its bloom,
When brightest in color and best in perfume.'

We think of your mother's affliction, and pray God to support her.

"Our friend, Mr. Miles, leaves me on April 1st. A successor I want. I may be compelled to draw another nail out of your house. Don't be impatient. I may in time pay you all. . . . .

"Most affectionately yours, B. C. CUTLER."

The Rev. Mr. Miles now went to Wilkesbarre, Pa.; and, after some delay, Dr. Cutler was enabled to procure another excellent man, the Rev. F. S. Wiley, to fill the vacant post. Dr. Cutler wrote on this topic to Mr. W.:

"I shall confer with your Bishop. He is an old and very kind friend of mine, and one who knows by experience what it is to be wounded in his Master's service. He has just taken from me a valuable man in priest's orders. How can he complain if I can obtain a deacon from him?"

Still later, he wrote a pointed letter to his friend on the subject of sermonizing, which might be of great avail to every youthful minister who may happen to peruse it, as it stands here:

TO REV. F. S. W.

"BROOKLYN, *July* 27, 1848.

"MY DEAR SIR—I hear that you are to be ordained on the 30th in Philadelphia. May you receive the Holy Ghost to fit and prepare you for the great work in which you are to be engaged. God, by his ministers, will lay his hand upon you. May you be thenceforward a holy and happy servant to the best of masters.

"We are very desirous of having you in Brooklyn. . . . On the subject of sermons, I would suggest a thought or two. In the first place, I would advise you to write them in a large hand and on lines far apart. Don't mind the expense of paper, for freedom in delivering your sermons is of more worth. We want your eyes on the congregation; we want you to see how much your words affect our hearts. As iron sharpeneth iron, so do the countenances of a congregation their minister! Again, begrudge no time before preaching in becoming very familiar with your sermon. A very plain sermon, if perfectly familiar to the speaker and delivered with simplicity and a moderate fluency, will always command attention and do good; while an elegantly composed sermon, a deeply conceived one, or an eloquent and argumentative one, if mumbled out or blundered over, is an abomination to the people, if not to the Lord.

"Select for your first sermon some general subject of evangelical religion. Brother Miles took, 'First the blade, then the ear,' etc.; and because he was plain, evangelical, experimental, and somewhat in the parable style, he was much liked. Scriptural, experimental, and spiritual truths, which cluster around some object—such as a vine or a head of wheat, or leaven, or a lost sheep, or a lost son, or fire, or water, or building, or sowing, or reaping—will always command respectful attention from all classes of hearers, except conceited romance readers and empty-headed 'Review' admirers! I had rather preach before Daniel Webster, and Henry Clay, and

Edward Everett, than the Noahs, Daniels, and Jobs of the weekly Lyceums—gentlemen who, as Dr. Johnson said of certain members of parliament, are 'silent in the *house* and loud in the *coffee-house*.'

"But, be assured, you have nothing to fear from the critics of St. Ann's. They have been long accustomed to downright simplicity and straight-forward dealing; but they are apparently hungry for any mode of preaching the truth as it is in Jesus. Learning, argument, exposition, exhortation, will not be lost upon them. Every good gift and every perfect gift they think to come from above. They admire to hear the youthful champion of the Cross; they loved Mr. Bancroft, and Mr. Duy, and Mr. Miles, and my belief is, and prayer will be, that they will also love the brother soon to be with them. To him I beg to convey assurances of high esteem, and am his in the holiest of bonds.

"B. C. Cutler.

"N. B.—An introductory discourse should always be rather short, say twenty-five minutes!"

It was in this year that a clerical prayer-meeting was formed, composed of some of the Episcopal clergy of Brooklyn and vicinity; they met every fortnight at the house of each in rotation. The rectors of St. Ann's, of Christ Church, Holy Trinity, St. Peter's, etc., etc., and others were present, and Dr. Cutler and his assistants always found these meetings a delight.

Another excursion was taken in July, with his nephew, F. M. McAllister, down the island, on horseback.

Shortly before this, he wrote a letter to the widow of a valued clerical friend then in England. It had been a long-tried friendship, and we transcribe the letter to show what a spirit of tenderness he had toward the children of sorrow:

"Dear Sister—My heart was tenderly alive to your last letter. I understand and sympathize with every word. May Jesus make up himself what you have lost, and fill the aching void. I say may he, but he will not, and according to the laws of nature he cannot. He made those very fountains from whence gush often the silent tear. He caused them to flow. He created those affections which he commanded us to exercise toward a wife or husband, and though we are commanded to do this in moderation, yet twenty years moderate loving of a holy, generous and devoted friend, forms habits not easily overcome! No! weep we must, suffer we must, smart we must; religion itself cannot prevent it (Read Henry Martyn's Diary); only let us learn to submit; learn to hope; learn to anticipate; above all, learn to love Jesus Christ. . . . Jesus is worth ten thousand husbands, ten thousand fathers or mothers, or brothers or sisters, and just as much of himself as we have eyes to see, and just as much as we have ears to hear, will he in general manifest. . . I grieve for you; I lament with you; I tremble when I think what you have suffered, what an eclipse of the sun! O Jesus, prepare me, prepare all for the *cup* bitter, bitter indeed, but medicinal and richly deserved, and by and by to be rejoiced in! . . . . I rose at 4 to-day; took a shower-bath; poured out a cup of tea over my study lamp; rode two hours in the saddle, and returned at 7 to breakfast. . . . .

"Your sincerely affectionate brother in the Lord,

B. C. CUTLER."

His correspondence was by no means confined to merely local matters, or to letters of consolation. He often wrote to gentlemen of his acquaintance, in regard to their spiritual welfare, and since his decease, most decided and affectionate testimony to the value of his influence and letters has been given. One case may be cited: a friend of his, who was a lawyer in the city of Baltimore, wrote to him in 1846, "What you have said to me has not been washed off the rock; you have done me much good; I am ignorant and feeble in these matters, and I want you to continue your interest in me."

Again, in 1848, this friend wrote:

TO THE REV. DR. CUTLER.

"MY DEAR SIR—Do not think that I have lost my interest in the subject that first led to our correspondence. This, my letter, is the result of the review of the past, in connection with the Communion this day received, at the hands of our mutual and kind friend, Dr. Johns. A past, with which you are permanently and pleasantly associated. . . . . I recognize the grace of God in the earnest desire that I have, to draw nearer and nearer to him in prayer, which must be the greatest joy and the greatest blessing of which our nature, in this life, can be susceptible. And I believe that, in his own good time, he will grant the prayer I daily offer to him for a livelier faith, a truer and profounder repentance, and a more confident assurance. If your experience can aid me, write to me as a friend, freely and fully. . . . . . I dread the tendency of the times amongst us. These trifling innovations are trifles in themselves, but tend to the rebuilding of that wall between man and his Maker, which the Reformation threw down. I deprecate, most truly, the parties of high and low church. The difference between them is a stumbling-block to many. It is a scandal, and worse. But one is obliged to side with one or the other. Write to me about this matter, also; for, although I have been in Oxford since I saw you, and in sight of Dr. Pusey's door, I came away uninfected.

"My letter has, as you will perceive, no other object than to extract from you a reply; to renew an intercourse which was of service to me. I wish, if you ever come to Baltimore, that you would take up your abode in my house. . . . .

"Ever, most truly yours, J. H. B. L——"

Another extract from a letter received this year (1848) from a clerical friend, then at Chester, in England, though afterward transferred to Durham, will conclude this chapter:

"My Dear Friend—Your letter reached me safely, and did my heart good. It restored me to old times and old friends, to hear from you; very often do I long for some sweet communion with you, as one of the dearest pilgrims I have ever travelled any part of the road with, toward the Celestial City! . . . . Mr. Sands will have told you the severe affliction I have experienced in the loss of my father. . . . . It is a great thing to have the late Bishop of Chester made Archbishop; he shines in his high station, and it has not spoiled him in the least; see how nobly he came forward at the Church Missionary Society, and the Bible Society, to throw his new influence in the right scale. . . . . . What a church we might have, if men so pure, so faithful, so devoted as he who is now at its head, were common!" . . . .

"Yours, G. T. F."

"To the Rev. Dr. Cutler."

CHAPTER XII.

MINISTRY AT ST. ANN'S CHURCH—CONTINUED.

1849–1855.

IN the years 1849 and 1850, there was little of sufficient importance to note either in Dr. Cutler's personal history, or in the unvarying routine of his parish. His heart was, indeed, gratified by the large numbers of additions to the Communion. In 1849, no less than sixty persons were confirmed. His Sunday-schools were constantly increasing in numbers and influence. How could it be otherwise, with a careful and judicious pastor, devoted superintendents, and an indefatigable band of teachers? They all diligently toiled in waiting hope for the Divine blessing, and many plants carefully nurtured in the nursery of the Sunday-school were annually transferred to the fold where, as communicants, they could sit down together with more experienced pilgrims, at the table of the Lord.

In October, the vacancy in the assistantship, made by the removal of the Rev. Mr. Wiley to Honesdale, Pa., was supplied by the Rev. F. C. Clements, of Philadelphia. We make one or two extracts from Dr. Cutler's diary here:

"*Jan.* 7, 1849.—I again set up my stone of help. Oh, why can I not please God? why live so low! why yield to my depraved heart! Lord, I am vile; save and sanctify me! Long experience has taught me that self-denial is bitter for a moment and sweet for an hour! self-indulgence is sweet for the moment and bitter for hours and days! When Esau sold his birthright for a mess of pottage, what a type was he of ten thousand other members of God's visible Church! O Lord, keep me, and finally save me, through Christ!"

"*March* 26.—Rev. Dr. Smith, of St. Peter's Church, New York, died yesterday. He fought a good fight! He was once rector of St. Ann's, and his death has made me feel my mortality. But God is the same:

'For ever and for ever Lord,
Unchanged thou dost remain;
Thy word, established in the heavens,
Does all their orbs sustain.'

God's word has sustained upon nothing all those glittering orbs, calling them all by names, and kept them in their places in all regularity for six thousand years. Oh, what should shake our faith in his promises of support!"

Dr. Cutler made the discovery, early in life, that the shortest way to be happy, is to make others happy; and he was constantly endeavoring, not only to do others good, but also to make them happy. When he could do no more, a volume was loaned, or a few kind words spoken, or a letter penned to some distant friend. Read the following letter he addressed, about this time, to some former parishioners then residing at Bristol, R. I.:

TO THE MISSES M——.

"MY DEAR FRIENDS—My beloved wife and I desire to greet you, as old and tried friends. We long to see you, and to inquire about your present and eternal interests! We should be greatly refreshed with a true Christian epistle from dear L——, unfolding her and your experience of the goodness and severity, I had said, but would prefer *faithfulness*, of the Lord, for, whom the Lord loveth he chasteneth. I would like much to know how the seed of God's word, which I, perhaps, sowed, has been growing up—not outwardly but inwardly. What is the faith, the hope, the charity, the sense of sin, the humility, the dependence on the Saviour, the experience of unbelief, hardness of heart, emptiness and misery?

"I would like to compare notes with one who, more than twenty years ago, parted company from me on the journey! For myself, dear friends, I can only say this: 'by the grace of God, I am what I am.' What there is of religion in me is, by the grace of God. I feel as much as ever, or more, the need and virtue of prayer. I adhere to God's word, and all false ways I utterly abhor. I loathe Romanism in the Church. Still you know what I am—not an ultra Low Churchman; I aim at being a *charitable* Churchman. . . . If you were to see and hear me, I am afraid you would say, 'He is just the same as he was in Quincy.'

"Yours, B. C. Cutler."

Perhaps a still more characteristic letter is the one written to an absent Sunday-school Superintendent of St. Ann's, then at Hartford. This gentleman was also a very warm-hearted personal friend, with whom he often took sweet counsel:

TO G. D. M., ESQ.

"*June* 15, 1849.

"My Dear Friend— . . . . I am sorry to have you out of sight, but out of mind, you are not. I am happy in your enjoyment amid cool shades. I hope our blessed Saviour is your shepherd, and that he is leading you in green pastures and beside still waters—by that beautiful river of your native State. What a sweet, noble, rich valley that river fertilizes for more than a hundred miles! Just now, the ride along its banks must be a rich treat. This, my eye hath seen. But there is a sweeter and more beautiful river, with richer banks, more splendid 'mansions,' and more fertile and blooming and fragrant fields! It is more than one hundred miles long; and, as we ascend to its fountain, we shall find it larger and larger, diminishing, more and more, as it rolls from its source.

"Sweet and pleasant has been our intercourse, my friend—a long summer day, without a cloud—*esto perpetua amicitia!*

"Yours, B. C. Cutler."

The following original lines we find in his journal of the following year:

"*Jan.* 28, 1850.—In writing my sermon on Saturday, these impromptu lines flowed from my pen:

What are earthly pomps to me,
If my soul my Saviour see?
Chief of all my joys thou art,
Christ is cordial to my heart.

More than music to my ears—
Jesus Christ can calm my fears;
More than friends or riches, He—
Christ is heaven—is heaven to me!

Let these two last lines be the motto on my banner."

"*March* 18, 1850.—My soul seems low and insensible, although, thanks be to God, I am sensible of my insensibility! My heart is cold, and I need a solemn, tender, devout, and watchful spirit. I have wandered like a lost sheep. I hope I have begun to return. O Lord, see me afar off—a great way off; have compassion on me, and draw me near thee, for Christ's sake!"

Dr. Cutler's English friends at "Fremington Vicarage," were gratified to hear tidings from him this summer. We give an extract from his letter to them:

"BROOKLYN, *May* 24, 1850.

"MY DEAR CHRISTIAN FRIENDS—This month of May makes me feel very English. There has been a beautiful verdure all around us, but a great deal of the cold chilly air of an English spring. How are you both?—agitated, no doubt, with the fury and folly of the church, in some quarters. But, after all, not only is Satan chained, but so is every other one that would assault or hurt the body of Christ! All will yet be well! It would give me unfeigned satisfaction to preach the gospel on the subject of regeneration before some people. But this is a vain wish. How do all you Gorhamites expect to preach under the ban of your Bishop? I suppose he does not invade your private cures; if he does, I hope you will open your mouths wide, and God will fill them. To me, his course seems like madness or monomania. The church teaches us not to believe her, and St. Paul teaches us not to believe an angel from heaven, if he or she should preach or teach any thing contrary to God's written word. . : . When you next write, tell me all about your church and schools. . . . Our green miniature park or close is very sweet now. Under the trees, all our Sunday-school gathered the other day, four hundred or five hundred children. It was a lovely sight. May you and we see all the saints, little and large, under the trees of life!

"Affectionately yours, B. C. CUTLER."

In August, Dr. Cutler took his tenth annual excursion down the island, with his nephew, B. C. Cutler, Jr.

In October, his assistant (Rev. F. C. C.) left him, having been called into a neighboring diocese. Of his farewell sermon, Dr. Cutler says, "It was most excellent. May the Lord bless that young man!" His place was supplied in January following by the Rev. G. L. Platt. At Christmas season, a suitable offering was made to the parish by one of her noble-hearted members, and Dr. Cutler sent this reply:

"ST. ANN'S RECTORY, *December* 28, 1850.

. . . . "In the name of the congregation of St. Ann's Church, I return you our sincere thanks for the two silver sacramental cups which you presented to us on Christmas Eve. I beg to remind you that however costly this gift, it will be considered as an offering to the great Head of the Church, and he has assured us that such benefactions shall not go unrewarded. The best reward I can wish you, is that those cups may be to all of your household 'cups of salvation,' and that, whenever you approach the sacred feast, you may taste the 'sweet mercies' of Christ's love, and be strengthened and refreshed.

"Affectionately yours, B. C. CUTLER, *Rector*."

The year 1851 was marked in the history of the parish by the decease of Mrs. Ann Sands (widow of the late Joshua Sands). She died July 17, aged ninety years. She had been for more than sixty years a burning and a shining light in the church, and her pastor mourned for her with sincere sorrow. His love and veneration for her was great, and he felt that her prayers were beyond price, and often thanked God (to use his own language), "for having seen such excellence." To her superior character, as a "mother in Israel," his predecessors in St. Ann's, Bishop McIlvaine, of Ohio, and Bishop Henshaw, of Rhode Island, bore ample and honorable testimony. Like Anna of old, she served God with fastings and prayer, night and day. She had been the succorer of many, and the support of many eminent prophets of the Lord, who had in their turn, ministered to her in holy things. And now her present pastor was to consign her to the dust. This he did with much emotion, and also made a suitable address.

He afterward delivered two highly appropriate discourses with reference to the event, which were ere long published. In his note of reply to a member of the family, soliciting a copy of the sermons for the press, Dr. Cutler took occasion to thank him as one of those mainly instrumental in introducing him to that most saintly lady, he says, "whose acquaintance and encouragement in my parish labors for eighteen years, I esteem one of the greatest blessings of my ministerial life."

In a letter to a friend, in July, 1851, Dr. Cutler thus gives his views on a topic in connection with the baptismal office, which has been much discussed in the Episcopal Church, and which has been productive of some uneasiness to extremely scrupulous consciences. The view here given it would be well for all such to consider—it is substantially the same as that of the late Rev. Mr. Simeon, of the Church of England. The extract read thus :

"Our beloved church is now in the furnace! Her true sons feel deeply the apostasies and desertion from her ranks. Still, their faith fails not. They believe that which is despised of men may be chosen of God and precious. As for leaving the church, I should ask, to whom shall I go? I am for reforming, not quitting, the church! What is there against her constitution? what against her articles of faith? what against *a* form of public worship? what against nineteen-twentieths of our form? what in that remaining twentieth, which cannot be reformed?

"For my part, the objectionable collect after baptism, if used as the language o charity, as it is of faith, may be objected to, but who can give to its affirmative proposition a denial? who can say that the infant is *not* regenerate? If it should die shortly after baptism, who would not believe it would go to heaven, and if it go to heaven, it must have been born again. For peace sake, I wish the collect away. But in the sense in which it was, in my opinion, composed, I, for one, find no trouble in using it."

1852 and 1853 witnessed an unusual ingathering of souls into the fold of St. Ann's, nearly eighty persons having been confirmed, and, under the persevering labors of the rector, brought into full communion with the church. Dr. Cutler, as far as man is instrumental in bringing forth such precious fruit, plowed deep, planted with care, and watered abundantly, waiting in hope for the Divine blessing. And he did not wait in vain. Great caution should be used in analyzing such subjects, yet we may say of the fruit of his labors, It was not as the apples of Sodom—fair to the eye, but deceitful; it still buds, and blossoms, and ripens for the harvest-home.

The pastor's warm heart was often made to thrill with more intense delight by receiving written testimony from members of his flock, to the good he had, under God, accomplished. This is evident from a reply to a note of this kind dated—

TO MRS. WILLIAM H——Y.

"BROOKLYN, *January* 22, 1852.

"I cannot better express the great pleasure your letter gave me this morning, than to say that the receiver fully appreciated the kind motives which actuated the writer. I thank you more than I could possibly have thanked you for the richest and most gorgeous gift presented this season. The happiness of doing good is great; that of knowing you have done good, is greater; and the gratitude of those whose souls you have benefited is most blessed of all. God grant you may not have cause to change the tenor of your communications while I am permitted to call myself

"Your pastor, B. C. CUTLER."

His private pastoral intercourse with his people was always faithful, yet tender and affectionate:

TO MRS. C——R, A VALUED PARISHIONER.

"ST. ANN'S RECTORY, *February* 28, 1852.

. . . . . "I admire your bouquet very much, and thank you kindly for it. Of flowers I never get tired. They always cheer and benefit me. They speak so lovingly and sweetly of the Giver of all good, that I set them before me all day long. I carry them up stairs when I study, and take them down stairs when called to my table. . . . . As you take care of your flowers, so may the Lord take care of his flowers that are growing up within your dwelling, and may he cause them to flourish and blossom, and may you present more than one such bouquet from them, to delight and bless the heart and house of the receiver.

"Most affectionately yours, B. C. C."

From his flock, the grave received another trophy this year, in the person of Capt. Charles C. Berry, commander of the steamship "United States," who died June 21. He was a personal friend of Dr. Cutler, and over his cold remains, the latter delivered a touching address to a very large audience.

Dr. Cutler's journal at this time exhibits his usual clearness, simplicity, and withal a quaintness of expression, which reminds us of the old divines. A few extracts:

"*July*, 1852.—Heard Rev. Dr. ——'s sermon; too showy and pedantic; where is the *gospel* ministry? Christ is made at the feast what he has made his ministers in the world—a salt-cellar, occupying one corner only of the table; something we can't do without, but nothing for us and others to glory in."

"*Aug.* 28.— . . . I was in a good frame of mind and was edified. I made a discovery yesterday and never before, that means of grace were, after all, but MEANS, and not grace. When they did the most, they did not do enough! Direct application to Christ is *the thing*, frequent, fervent, and affectionate; even then, that will not make us whole! We shall still be poor sinners. To be saved from first to last, that is, at last as at first, by the atonement, the merits, and through the intercession of Christ. In that way, I can conceive that I may and can be saved, and in no other. There is no other name for me but Christ, no other Saviour will answer for me. I want all of Christ to supply my deficiencies. BENJAMIN CLARKE CUTLER."

In connection with this view, we extract from his journal a record he made at another time:

"Romaine says, 'Christ does not give us a stock of grace, and expect us to improve it by being faithful to grace given. No, no! that is not his way.' He does not so feed our bodies. He gives us for them daily bread. They must hunger and be empty every day, and more than once every day, and then depend on the bread that perisheth to sustain them. And so with our souls: they must live every hour, every moment, upon Christ. And this is our happiness, to hunger and thirst after Christ; for we shall then be filled, have all in Christ: a beggar in myself, but rich in my connection with Christ!"

After the death of the Rev. F. C. Clements (who fell asleep in Jesus at Trenton, N. J., December 18, 1852), Dr. Cutler preached a funeral sermon on the occasion. He had once labored with much acceptance at St. Ann's, and he could not be allowed to pass from earth without a tribute to his worth, from both the pastor and people. It was truly a remarkable providence that took away, in the morning of life, two such men as Mr. Duy and Mr. Clements. Thus, Dr. Cutler interpreted these events, and upon his own heart he endeavored to fix the lesson God designed to teach.

Thus closes his journalizing for the year:

"What lesson is to be learned? The importance of constant preparation for death; the mysteriousness of the ways of God, and God's sovereignty! 'Shall I not do what I will with mine own?'"

In March, 1853, his assistant (Mr. Platt) left him; not, however, without conveying, by letter, a sense of his thankfulness for all the kindness and consideration of both the rector and the vestry, and making happy allusion to all their reciprocal intercourse.

At midsummer, a new assistant was elected to fill the vacancy, the Rev. J. F. D. Cornell.

Another of Commodore Hudson's excellent letters reached Dr. Cutler early in 1853. It was written from Valparaiso, while Capt. Hudson was on board the "Vincennes." It is a matter of regret that no more of their interesting correspondence can now be obtained; but, grateful for the preservation of the smallest portion, we subjoin an extract from the letter to which allusion is made; [another extract from the same letter was made in Dr. Cutler's address at the funeral of Com. Hudson in 1862]:

TO THE REV. DR. CUTLER.

"*June* 26, 1852.

. . . . "I need not say how deep an interest I feel in St. Ann's Church, and all that pertains to you and your pastoral charge. If I mistake not, I have been longer under the teachings of her various parochial ministers than any other male member of your congregation. The present church was my spiritual birthplace; and oh, how many things that I have heard from you and others, which made no impression at the time, have since come vividly to my remembrance, and so operated on the mind, as to show they had made a lodgment in the heart (though I knew it not), and through the effectual working of Him who doeth all things, in his own mysterious way, after years of forgetfulness, are made to germinate and give life, as it were, to the dead!

"Though far away from the sound of her (St. Ann's) church-going bell, the voice of her ministering servant, and the sanctuary privileges she offers to all within her reach, I have not forgotten daily to carry you all to the foot of the mercy-seat, and plead with our Father in heaven, that each of you may be washed, purified, and made meet for an inheritance among the saints in light; and that he would abundantly bless your labors with an ingathering of souls that shall fill your church to overflowing; and while your own soul is rejoicing in the work, you may feel like Paul of old, it is God alone who gives the increase! . . . . Passing years admonish me that I am hastening to the allotted span of human life; that winding up of all I shall have done on earth; that solemn hour, when the spirit shall be summoned from its tenement of clay, before the God who gave it, to answer for the use and abuse of all its powers and privileges!

"Oh what a glorious feeling it must be, in that hour of the soul's trial, to find our sins blotted out and cancelled in our Redeemer's precious blood, our names written in the Book of Life, and our souls transformed and made meet for all the bliss of heaven. Well may we all desire to die the death of the righteous, and have our last end like his. The thought of this subject quite unmans me, and I must bring this scrawl to a close, assuring you I am heartily tired of seeing the world, under so many different phases; feel there is no place like home. long for the return of domestic joys, the solace of wife and children; and to hear once more (I beg pardon, while I so call it) the not over clear or melodious sound of St. Ann's old church bell! That you and yours, with a large and pious flock, may long live to gather under its sound (or that of a better one), is the earnest wish and prayer of your absent, and, I trust, Christian friend, WM. L. HUDSON."

At an annual meeting of the Board of Directors of the American Tract Society, held May 11, 1853, Dr. Cutler was unanimously elected a member of the Publishing Committee, in the place of the Rev. Dr. Stone, who had removed to the vicinity of Boston. When, ten years later, he was called away from all earthly toils, this society put a highly appreciative minute on their records, showing how justly they valued his unwearied labors in their behalf.

On the 8th of May, we find Dr. Cutler at Philadelphia, where he listened with great pleasure to the ministrations of the Rev. Dr. Stevens. He made a note of this, and was especially pleased with the preacher, who discoursed with so much sweetness and with so much unction "on the Saviour."

August 18th, Dr. Cutler preached a funeral sermon on the death of an interesting and exemplary youthful member of his flock, which has been incorporated into a little volume, by the Rev. G. D. Miles, entitled, "Memorial of J. G. Fuller." In October, Dr. Cutler (with his wife) took a journey to Boston, visiting many old friends and scenes in that vicinity. From thence he wrote to his sister-in-law:

"TREMONT HOUSE, *October* 20, 1853.

. . . . . "My old military company of cadets dined in this house last night, and kept up a pretty noisy jollification. I gave them a wide berth.

"I took a stroll to-day down on the wharf, where I spent my early youth; saw riches and stores of wealth all around, and questioned myself whether I regretted leaving the world for the sake of Jesus Christ. Not one regret tenants my bosom! My only desire is to grow in grace, to live nearer to the Saviour, and to do more good.

"Most faithfully yours, B. C. CUTLER.

"P. S.—Tell E—— I rejoice with her on the arrival of our dear Samuel from England."

Who could have a regret when his life had been such a blessing to others? Not long after this, the wife of Dr. Cutler received a letter from a friend, in reply to one she had sent, inclosing a contribution (for the light-house in Ireland) from St. Ann's Sunday-school, which indicates the extent and value of the many influences which emanated from Dr. Cutler's dwelling at Brooklyn; and oh! how many can emphasize with truth every word of this communication:

"RECTORY OF THE CHURCH OF THE NATIVITY,
"PHILADELPHIA, *December* 8, 1853.

"MY DEAR MRS. CUTLER—I received the contribution with more than ordinary pleasure, arising from my former connection with the parish. . . . . The reference to the past brought back many happy hours of social intercourse, fraught with much profit to myself. In the start of a new profession, much, far more than we are willing to allow, depends on the influences which surround us. In this respect, my first efforts in the ministry were most happily conditioned. The blessed results of such influences acting on me in the spring-time of my profession, will be known only in the light of Eternity. More obligations are resting on me, toward you and Dr. Cutler and Miss B——, than I can well express. A grateful remembrance will ever mark this period, when I was privileged to reside under your roof and call myself a member of your family. . . . .

"Most sincerely yours, F. S. WILEY."

The testimony of this esteemed clergyman is of intrinsic worth, and much of tender interest gathers about it now, since both Dr. Cutler and his former associate have met in the ranks of the Church triumphant!

During the whole period of the year 1854, Dr. Cutler

was much tried by ill health, as the extracts from his journal show:

"*Jan.* 23.—I have been unwell, chiefly from mental perplexity. But all things work together for good to them that love God. Jacob said, 'all these things are against me,' but they were all working for his good. Yet what an amount of suffering did not Jacob endure! When Joseph was lost, he said, 'I will go down into the grave unto my son mourning.'"

"*March* 6.—How much I have suffered from nervous irritability and depression, God only knows. I am in trouble and heaviness, and I have been calling on God. It is good to wait the Lord's leisure!"

"*March* 16.—I am weak, depressed, and afflicted. I ought to change the scene, but Jesus knows best. Riding on horseback is my best resource, and faith, my chief support of mind. My eyes are lifted up to the hills, from whence cometh my salvation. Cast down, but not destroyed. I have cast my burden on the Lord."

A journey to Washington had a beneficial effect, though not to the extent desired. While absent, he addressed a letter to a friend then at Milwaukee, which is not without interest:

TO MRS. JACKSON.

"WASHINGTON, *April* 1, 1854.

. . . . "We are on a tour of relaxation and mental refreshing, and during the journey have both thought and talked of you; of your residence at Chestertown, Md., of which you used to speak so often, and the time you spent in Virginia. It is a long time since we heard from you; but the printed sermon you sent to me, proved that you were still a tenant of this vale of tears! Dear friend, we also are, and greet you most affectionately; and with true, tried and sincere Christian regard, we think over all you have endured, and pray that all may be sanctified to your good. . . . My precious wife has been spared to me, and is an unspeakable earthly support. . . . . If I did not dread the sea so much, I should go to Europe this summer. . . . . You will ask, how is the cause progressing? I reply, parties in religion, as in politics, are disintegrated. Our Bishop will not indorse the Seabury School nor the School of the Recorder! The consequence is that nobody knows where to find men! I like Bishop Wainwright, and rejoice at his election, and am entirely content with his proceedings. He does not require me, nor expect me, to adopt his *specialties*, and, in generals, I can do very well. True religion does not seem to be gaining ground. The Church may say:

'The world and worldly things, beloved,
My anxious thoughts employ.'

"Great prosperity, and great leaning to externals, and a great taste for 'visibilities,' all conspire to make the people restive under that plain, bold and emphatic preaching, which says, 'Behold the Lamb of God, which taketh away the sin of the world!' May that Lamb of God bless and keep you, convince you of his presence, and satisfy you with his consolation here, and with his personal presence hereafter!

"Your brother, in heart and mind, B. C. CUTLER."

In May, Dr. Cutler was again compelled, by the state of his health, to take another journey, which was extended as far as Cincinnati. He wrote to a friend, this summer: "I have every thing *but* health or strength. But there must always be a BUT! I feel the rod, and know who hath appointed it. May it have its perfect work!"

In June, his sister left New York for a temporary residence in Europe.

"*June* 14.—My beloved sister, Mrs. McAllister, with her husband, daughter and son (Marion) sailed in the steamship "Pacific." May the goodness and mercy of God be over them!"

This relative has favored us with an extract from her own journal, of this same year (1854): "Heard my brother at Dr. Bedell's church, in New York, a building to me, full of past memories. His text was, 'We have an advocate with the Father.' He spoke of Christ in heaven, as interceding for us, showing his wounds, his agonies to the Father, in testimony that our debt was paid. . . . . Going down stairs, this morning, I heard a voice, and, as I approached the parlor door, found my brother was reading of Christ's interview with Nathaniel--reading aloud to himself. What a picture of a holy man! It was very sweet to hear his earnest voice. I remained a moment at the parlor door, and felt that I was in a holy atmosphere. When he had finished, I opened the door, and was greeted by that smile of welcome that always went to the heart." "I can see him now," she writes; "those visits are never to be forgotten. Truly, I can say, I thank God for every remembrance of thee, my beloved brother."

Dr. Cutler's failing health was, indeed, a heavy cross; one which the robust and hearty can never fully understand. His own view of it, as well as his strong fraternal affection, is presented in a note to his elder sister, Mrs. Dr. Francis, dated

"*August* 6, 1854.

"DEAREST SISTER— . . . . Life is so full of business, that little is left really for pleasure, that is, the calm pleasure of fraternal friendship, and pure, simple, plain, inexpensive social intercourse. It is bustle, excitement, expectation or disappointment. Amid all, however, I see and appreciate the noble and generous impulses of unbounded philanthropy, and can pray for a thousand blessings in return. I thank you for a thousand kind feelings to me and mine, and to ten thousand other persons. Although at a distance, and perhaps apparently frigid, I feel keenly every thing connected with my family. Their joy is my joy, and their sorrow is mine also. God has apportioned to me a peculiar trial in my bodily constitution. It is to me what the Jews were to St. Paul, a 'continual heaviness.'

"I have nearly all the time, just enough of bodily trouble to remind me that I am in, and must be out of, the body. But whether in the body, or out of the body, I have given myself to my God, through Jesus Christ. I therefore commit all, body, soul and spirit to him, and go on from day to day, living by faith. Heaven bless you! prays your affectionate brother, B. C. CUTLER."

His trial, great as it was, only furthered his advance in the spiritual life, and tended, as all could see, to his entire sanctification; yet we find him saying, "I am a poor, cold-hearted sinner, but Christ died for sinners, and I trust in him for every thing. He is all in all to me. To do good is present with me, but how to perform it I know not. Lord, help me! I aspire to the saintship of the gospel—not of poetry or Popery; but I aspire to be holy—a vessel fit and meet for the Master's use."

We do not err, we trust, when we use the experience of God's holiest servants (with care and caution), for the edification of his Church. And if any would hesitate on this topic, let them look to the records of Scripture. There is presented the awe-inspiring intercourse of Moses, when he talked with God; there is the heart of Hannah laid open before us; there, in Gethsemane, too, poor dying sinners can gaze with wonder on the exceeding sorrow of their Redeemer, when, in agony of prayer, he prayed the Father, "Let this cup pass from me!"

But we pass from the diary of Dr. Cutler to his correspondence. Surely, every afflicted one may find comfort in reading a letter like this:

TO MRS. M——, HIS NIECE, AFTER THE DEATH OF A CHILD.

"*August* 16, 1854.

"DEAR A—— —It does not seem to me best, to speak to the distressed in the moment of their bitterest woe.

'Leves loquuntur,
Ingentes stupent.'

The loss of an only son can be poorly consoled by words. God alone can heal the wound which his hands have made.

"I write this to assure you of my sympathy, and to offer a few thoughts by way of improvement. Yesterday, at the funeral, though in the carriage with you, my lips were sealed. God had spoken, and the Church had just been speaking in the service for the departed. 'Let all the earth keep silence.' When our Lord Jesus was suffering he spake little. Your affliction is great, and the more I think of it, the greater it appears. But think of Job, who lost all his children in one day, and not one of them died in comparative innocence like yours! Think of the innumerable sufferers like yourself, who have lost their only sons. "I will restore your son to life, if you will point out to me three persons of your own age who never grieved," said an Eastern sage to an inconsolable king:

> 'The path of sorrow, and that path alone,
> Leads to the world where sorrow is unknown.'

. . . . God has taken away that boy, that you and ——— may set your affections on things above. He says: 'My son, and my daughter, give *me* thine heart.' It is well with the child. He is provided for, in Paradise; but you are yet in the world, among thorns and briers. Labor and sorrow are before you both; but rest and joy are to be ensured through Christ our Lord. This, it would seem, God is beginning to prepare you for, in his usual way, by putting you in his common school of affliction. 'Whom the Lord loveth he chasteneth or afflicteth. He seems to say, 'Be still, and know that I am God!' . . . . Not a sparrow falleth to the ground without your father, said our Lord; your little darling, could not, then! If God took him, it was for his good and for your good, and what you know not now, you shall know hereafter. That you may yet say as David did, 'It was good for me that I was afflicted,' and that you and your husband may receive a large return for this treasure you have paid back to the Lord, is the prayer of your absent, silent, but not unmindful nor unsympathizing

"UNCLE."

In the autumn of this year (1854), the writer first met the Rev. Dr. Cutler, being introduced to him by a mutual friend. Then commenced a friendship, the comfort, pleasure, and profit of which, no language can adequately express. Unreserved confidence, true affection, and intense sympathy, produced a bond, not unlike that which bound in such harmony David and Jonathan of old. In this case, however, the younger is left without the solace of his friend's counsels and love, to say from the depths of a sorrowful heart, "Very pleasant hast thou been unto me, my brother!"

The allusions to this friendship found in his journal, it is not necessary to record. We pass on to "the anniversary of the shipwreck," upon which he comments:

"*Monday, Nov.* 13, 1854.—This day I have set apart for

remembering God's mercies on the *deep*. Sunday, the 12th, I could not properly celebrate any private and personal event. It is the *Lord's* Day. To-day I call my mercies to mind, and have called my friends and neighbors together to rejoice with me."

In a note of invitation to Mrs. Pierrepont, November 11, he says: "This has been a counterpart to Saturday, November 11, 1843. How good is God! How grateful ought we to be! There is a vast difference between the 'blackness of darkness' on 'Romer' and the light and comfort of this our dwelling place!"

The death of the Rev. Dr. Spencer, a distinguished minister of the Presbyterian Church, in Brooklyn, about this time, filled Dr. Cutler's heart with sincere grief. They had long been intimate friends, and were of the same age; and being sufferers from severe physical pain for years, they could enter into each other's feelings with unusual interest. He had lived and died a good soldier of Jesus Christ, and his friend and cotemporary, bearing the gospel standard in another communion, was now, with similar fidelity, carrying it onward, till the great Head of the Church should also call him home, and the solemn dirge should announce another soldier fallen from the ranks, and gone—to rest!

In the ministrations at St. Ann's at this period, Dr. Cutler was assisted by a clerical friend then staying with him. Before the year closed, the vestry elected the Rev. William Huckel to fill the assistantship, which for some months had been vacant.

The rector's heart was made glad by many substantial offerings from parishioners and friends at Christmas. From the neighboring metropolis he had evidence that he was not forgotten, as this note bears witness:

TO MRS. DR. FRANCIS.

"ST. ANN'S RECTORY, *Christmas Eve*, 1854.

"Many thanks, my dear sister, for your kind remembrance of me and mine. What a large and loving heart you have; it is a perfect fountain of kindness! . . . . Alas! I have no presents to give; nor do I repine at the want of worldly wealth. Allow me to transcribe for you and my kind brother, the Doctor, a beautiful passage from Sir Humphrey Davy's 'Consolation of Travel:'

"'I envy no quality of the mind or intellect in others; but if I could choose what would be most delightful and, I believe, most useful to me, I should prefer *a firm religious belief* to every other blessing; for it makes life a discipline of goodness, creates new hopes when all earthly hopes vanish, and throws over the decay, the destruction of existence, the most gorgeous of all lights; awakens life, even in death, and from corruption and decay calls up beauty and divinity; makes an instrument of torture and of shame, the ladder of ascent to Paradise; and far above all combination of earthly hopes, calls up the most delightful visions of palms and amaranths, the garden of the blessed, and the security of everlasting joys! . . . where the sensualist and the skeptic view only gloom, decay, annihilation and despair.'

"Most affectionately, your brother, B. C. CUTLER."

In Dr. Cutler's life there was a practical illustration of the truth contained in the above quotation; amid all toil, all pain, "he endured as seeing Him who is *invisible*," laboring on for his Divine Master, strengthened often, when ready to sink by the way, by a cordial from the hand of an unseen but abiding Friend, and stayed by those Divine promises which never fail. He was now about to enter upon the untried path of duty for another year. While his earthly tabernacle began to give evidence that it would not many years longer restrain his panting spirit from soaring to the bosom of his Lord, he looked upward for strength from on high, and for new measures of grace; the angel on the right hand of the Throne seemed to assure him of a sufficiency of grace and strength unto the end:

"Onward, courageously; 't is but for awhile
Lasteth the warfare and struggle of life;
Then the warrior shall lay down his weapons and cease
From the fears and the fightings, the conflict and strife."

CHAPTER XIII.

MINISTRY AT ST. ANN'S CHURCH—CONTINUED.

1855–1858.

AS years rolled on, Dr. Cutler withdrew as much as possible into the retirement of his own parish. He kept himself aloof from all strife, and, with great care and patient toil, fed his own flock. Above all things, did he cultivate a holy walk with God. The fire of youth was abating, and the holy calm which results from close communion with an unseen yet precious Saviour, seemed to descend from above and settle upon his spirit.

He initiated a new plan for private life. Rising very early, before 5 o'clock, at times, and retiring to his study, he kindled his own fire, and after some simple refreshment, spent an hour in devotion and reading the Scriptures. He then took his daily exercise in the saddle, while the greater part of his fellow-men were slumbering. These rides were almost always seasons of communion with his God, ejaculatory prayer, and devout praise to the Creator of all the earth. How familiar was his appearance in the early dawn of morning upon the outskirts of the city, wandering, with his docile steed, over the fields or through the lanes or along the shore of the Bay, the people of Brooklyn can bear witness. On his return, he often breakfasted with a parishioner, who lived at a distance from the great central thoroughfares, where he was always cordially welcomed. . . . . "I shall never forget," writes this friend and parishioner, "our morning rides, when we were travelling together. It was an hour of the day in which he seemed most happy and genial. During the past fifteen years he has always breakfasted with us, upon his return from his own (solitary) morning ride, at intervals of two or three weeks, when his coming was hailed with delight by every member of the family. His manner was always so genial and affectionate, that so far from inspiring fear or awe, my children all loved him, and religion was always presented to them in the most attractive form by him, and there is now not one of them, from oldest to youngest, who does not love and honor his memory. His loss to me, personally, will never be made up." . . . .

The first hour of each day was devoted to God, and he allowed nothing but severe illness to interfere with the path of duty he marked out for himself. How truly was it demonstrated in the daily history of our friend, that from a secret source the believer in Jesus draws his life—the morning portion of the Word; the morning prayer; the morning meditation; these are "the stolen waters" that keep him green all day! Thus was he sustained; thus was his soul nourished by heavenly manna; thus did he abide in the fear of the Lord; and thus was his heart fixed on the fountain of all real enjoyment, on God himself! He feared no evil tidings; as the beloved of the Lord he dwelt "between his shoulders," and was kept in perfect peace. He had been trained in the school of sanctified sorrow, and leaning upon the bosom of his Lord, he received inward strength. Comforted thus himself by Jesus, he was eminently qualified to lead others to the same Divine source of consolation. His wounds were often healed by the Saviour's sympathy, and who so well fitted to lead bleeding hearts to him? And he constantly used this gift. With the opening year of 1855, there fell a blow upon the household of his sister, Mrs. Francis, which shrouded, not only the family circle, but many others in deep sorrow.

On the 20th of January, John W. Francis, Jr., the eldest son of Dr. Francis, died at his father's residence, in New York, aged twenty-two years. He fell a martyr to his heroic labors and unwearied vigilance, in attendance upon a case of typhus fever. Full of promise, it was fondly hoped he would remain to wear the mantle of his distinguished father; but just on the threshold of his opening manhood, the fell destroyer marked him as his victim, and after two weeks' illness, life departed, and his remains were laid away in the silent tomb, amid most impressive obsequies.

Literary friends and numbers of the medical fraternity were plunged into inexpressible grief. The hearts of strong men were smitten in a moment; and the prevailing sentiment was, "I was dumb; I opened not my mouth, because Thou didst it!"

The heart of Dr. Cutler was deeply touched. In addition to a letter written to his brother-in-law, immediately upon the sad event, (which has been published in the "Memorial of J. W. Francis, Jr.") he addressed a few lines to the bereaved mother:

"BROOKLYN, *January* 28, 1855.

"MY DEAR SISTER—We are thinking of you day and night, and the more I think, the greater the loss appears to be. What is the blessing of having children (I say to myself), if they are to be taken away just as they can be useful and companionable to their parents? But who are we, to reply against God? Shall the thing formed say to Him that formed it, 'Why hast thou made me thus?' Shall not the Judge of all the earth do right? How can he possibly err in his doing?

"The experienced mariner cuts away one of his masts, valuable as it is, if by this means he can save the ship. The difficulty is that we do not realize, as we should, that this is not a life of pleasure, but of probation; that this life is a school time for eternity; that man is in a fallen and condemned condition, and his great business is to recover, through the Saviour and by the influences of the Spirit, the favor of God, and to ensure his calling and election in Christ.

"Our business on earth is simply, first to obtain pardon of sin, and next, to grow in grace, and become meet for the inheritance of the saints in light.

"Give my most sincere sympathy to the Doctor. I cannot express how much I feel for him. John was such a treasure; you know I delighted in him. Dear John! 'if I forget thee, my right hand will forget her cunning.'

"Most affectionately and sorrowfully, your brother,

B. C. CUTLER."

Some of his correspondence with his parishioners during this year will show how he availed himself of every incident to promote the spiritual welfare of his flock:

TO MRS. WM. B. C——, ON RECEIVING A BOUQUET—A STORMY DAY.

"*February* 14, 1855.

"Many thanks, dear Mrs. C——, for your pleasant foretaste of spring. . . . . All around is cold, and wet, and winterish; we are shut up in the house, and cannot get out; and to-night again we can have no meeting. But let us have patience. These very clouds which are now sowing in tears, shall reap in joy. Laughing skies and blooming fields, and fragrant flowers and fruitful trees, and long, long days of sunshine, and open doors and windows, and visits of friends, all will return, and we shall forget these icy streets and shivering frames.

"Now, your bouquet is only a chapter in my Bible. I read in it the kingdom of heaven is at hand; that paradise is to take the place of our present earthly prison, and one glorious, unending summer is to succeed the present weeping and mourning season of sin. May you and yours, and I and mine, see it, and see it together, for Christ's sake! Amen.

"Affectionately yours, B. C. CUTLER."

Both are now together, where earth's revolving seasons are not known, but where eternal sunshine gladdens their immortal souls!

How touching was this to the same friend:

"ST. ANN'S RECTORY, *March*, 1855.

. . . . . "In return for your brilliant bouquet, please accept a little violet, or 'heart's ease,' from me, and be assured that I never should have found it growing up in *my* bosom had I not lived in the neighborhood of the Cross of Christ, my Lord. He alone has said, 'let not your heart be troubled.'

"Affectionately yours, B. C. C."

TO MRS. H. S. H——, A VERY DEAR PARISHIONER.

"*August* 15, 1855.

"DEAR S—— —I cannot see that you are called to hear any man preach whose doctrines you consider erroneous. . . . . As for your neighbor's unbelief, I suppose she would not believe in any other world, unless she could make it what she pleased. Such people are simply infidels, or more truly skeptics, or nothingarians. 'How can ye believe who receive honor one of another?' They are full of this world, and its literature, and its good things; but it would be a thousand times better to be a Lazarus, than such a Dives! . . . . I send you the *Protestant Churchman* and intend sending the *Recorder* with a sketch of Henry Martyn. Give my love to E——. Now for the angels, big and little! the little one, you say, is changing color! I hope he will be an angel of light, not of darkness. I shall expect to hear him say his catechism when I see him. . . . .

"Your ancient friend, B. C. C."

TO G. D. M——, ESQ., ON THE DEATH OF A PARENT.

"*October* 4, 1855.

"Many thanks for the admirable engraving of your father. . . . I should esteem such a portrait of a parent as beyond all price. I can fully appreciate your grief at the loss of your father; and I rejoice that you can with so much reason anticipate a reunion with him in the habitations of the blessed.

"To the sailor, the land and the sea form but one great highway, and to him it is the same thing, as far as fear is concerned, whether he is on the one or the other. So to the Christian, the church militant and the church triumphant are all *one;* and all the difference is, the head of the column has entered and conquered, while file after file is following on.

"Accept my thanks for your donation for the poor, and believe me, Your friend and brother, B. C. CUTLER."

His interest in the missionary cause was undying. In November a large gathering of the friends of missions was held in the Church of the Holy Trinity, Brooklyn, and some of the missionaries were present. Dr. Cutler thus comments upon it in his journal:

"*Nov.* 5, 1855.— . . . . Dr. Tyng spoke most eloquently. Blessed be God for the prosperity of the missionary cause in our church; and blessed be God for the address I heard last night from Rev. Dr. T——. Such lifting up of Christ I have rarely heard. Speak the word, Lord! and great shall be the company of such preachers."

"*Nov.* 25. *Sunday Evening.*—We had one of those full and fine mornings at St. Ann's, which have been our joy and rejoicing. It has been a solemn and laborious day. The same fate awaits an earnest ministry now, that ever did. Some admire, some love, some hate, and others mock or make light of it; but use us, O Lord, to convert souls!"

Dr. Cutler always deemed it best for ministers to be at work in their calling, yet he never forgot the saying of our Lord: "I will have mercy and not sacrifice." Seasons of rest (the limit of which each individual conscience must decide) are certainly necessary to the faithful laborer in God's vineyard, as is intimated to us by our Master himself, when he expressly said to his weary disciples: "Come ye, apart, and rest yourselves awhile."

A remark of the late Bishop Corrie, of Madras, in connection with this point, seemed exactly to coincide with the views of our friend, who says in his journal, he was "much struck with it." "You and I have both erred in excess of labor; we might have served our generation more effectually by simple dependence on the promised blessing—on quiet, unconsuming labor!"

A note to his nephew is in point here:

TO THE REV. C. BANCROFT.

"*December* 25, 1855.

. . . . . "I was glad to receive your letter of the 17th, and grieved to think of dear Brother Smith. What a pity you ministers would not be entreated to take up your Cross, and *sit still* and have mercy on yourselves! A merciful man is merciful to his beast or animal. If you young men were to treat your horses as you often do your own bodies, all around would cry out, Shame! But the goodness of God can overrule in various ways, even such cruel zeal, for good, and I expect he will in dear Joseph's case. . . . I am about to publish a volume of sermons. They will be out at Easter (God willing). I am moved thereto by the passage from Scripture, on the title-page, 'Moreover, I will endeavor that ye may be able, after my decease, to have these things in remembrance.' . . . .

"My people, particularly Mr. M——, Mr. G——, Mr. H——, and the M——s are as generous as ever. . . . .

"Your affectionate uncle, B. C. CUTLER."

In speaking of publishing his sermons, Dr. Cutler wrote another friend: "In case of my death, I should still be preaching to my people. 'Though dead, he yet speaketh!' and my remembrance would not be clean gone!"

Whether it *can* pass away from the minds of the present generation, let the people of St. Ann's witness!

In very few instances is the tie so strong, or the intercourse so generally delightful and reciprocal, as existed between the pastor and people of St. Ann's, Brooklyn. Dr. Cutler never entered any dwelling, within the limits of his parish, without receiving a cordial welcome. He was the same faithful pastor to all, high or low, rich or poor, giving to each a due measure of attention. He loved to minister to the poor, "rich in faith," yet he never, with pharisaic or self-righteous pride, held himself aloof from the mansions of the prosperous and wealthy; knowing that it required more grace to follow the meek and lowly Saviour in an exalted position, than in a more obscure one. His influence for good he hoped would penetrate all the habitations of his flock; and happy indeed was he, when he could lead any soul into the green pastures of Christ's fold, or cause them to find refreshment by its still waters.

Let us read some of his correspondence with his parishioners.

TO MRS. T. M——.

"St. Ann's Rectory, *January* 4, 1856.

"My Dear Mrs. M—— —Though I have seen you since Christmas, yet I cannot refrain from acknowledging my grateful sense of your kindness and generosity. . . . .

"The friendship which Providence has permitted us to cultivate with your large family circle, is now among the most pleasant circumstances of our life. The hope, too, of being of service to you all, in the best of causes, is also cheering; and the good which we see performed by so many in your domestic circle, draw our hearts peculiarly toward you, and dispose us to rejoice and to weep in whatever concerns you. In the hope that, however we may pass the waves of this troublesome world, we may meet in a better and happier, I remain

"Your obliged pastor and friend, B. C. Cutler."

TO G. D. M——, ESQ.

"Philadelphia, *January* 22, 1856.

"My Dear Friend— . . . . . You see I am four times as far from home as Irvington is.

"On Monday I received a telegram announcing the death of the late Capt. Bancroft's widow. His only child (now an orphan) sent for us to be with her; and, as it is the part of pure and undefiled religion 'to visit' such, my wife and I came on. . . . I should be happy to make another of those visits to you, in which, at our leisure, we can go over the whole ground of our temporal and eternal interests. How little of religious conversation, strictly speaking, is common, and yet iron does not sharpen iron more surely, than one Christian does another! In old times they that feared the Lord spake, and spake 'often,' one to another. They spake no doubt much as David spake in his Psalms; and I love to think on Sunday, when in church, and responding in our Psalter, that, that is religious conversation between Christians. But when shall we think and speak of Him who loved us and gave himself for us, as if he were in our hearts, and our hope of glory? What a privilege to have an Almighty Saviour who is so touched with our 'infirmities' that we can address him concerning them at all times, 'Lord, thou knowest all things!' If we are Christians, Christ will soon be the absorbing theme of our songs, and we shall then wonder how we could have lived at our present poor dying rate! . . . .

"Affectionately yours, B. C. Cutler."

Dr. Cutler fully appreciated, as we see, the devoted kindness of these and other parishioners. We find in his journal:

"*Feb.* 7, 1856.—I have received two letters from Mr. G. D. M——, and Mrs. P——, which were comforts to me in my labors; also, a present from my dear friends Mr. and Mrs. H——.

"My chapel was crowded last night.

"Rev. Dr. Muenscher is staying with me, and I find his company very agreeable.

"My soul is rising up to God through Christ, and solemn thoughts are passing through my mind. Blessed be God for health of body, and ability to speak in his behalf!"

St. Ann's Church was much blessed at this season, by the addition of forty-four persons to her fold, and her pastor, we see by his diary, was rejoicing over this ingathering of souls.

While laboring for the spiritual good of his people, their pastor's heart was often made glad by their ministering unto him of their temporal things. In 1856 some of his more special friends, of ample wealth, presented him with a horse and carriage, and the vestry increased his salary by the addition of two hundred dollars per annum. Other substantial favors were also received at the rectory.

Early this year Dr. Cutler received tidings of the death of his friend in Devonshire, England—the Rev. W. C. Hill. To his widow he thus wrote:

"*March* 23.

"My Dear Afflicted Friend— . . . . What can we think but that Jesus is touched with a feeling of your infirmities; not merely merciful to pardon your sin, and to intercede for you at the Throne of his Father, but he is '*touched*' with your sorrows, with your bereavement, with your desolation, and he is saying by his Holy Spirit, to you in particular, what he is saying to the churches: 'Let not your heart be *troubled.*' Weep not, *I* will never leave thee nor forsake thee.' . . . . Now, the just shall *live* by *faith.* Others live by *sight;* the first do *not.* A poor man and a small tradesman, have all their fortune before their faces, but a millionaire may have loaned all his to his sovereign, and have only *some pieces of paper* as his security! But who can doubt which of the two is the richer! If the 'unsearchable riches' of Christ are worth any thing, I trust you may have the richest of righteousness, the richest of mercy, the richest of consolation, the richest of support, the richest of defence, and the richest of glory! Your dear departed husband preached to you these unsearchable riches, though he esteemed himself less than the least of all saints! You must say to that Saviour:

> 'Whilst thou art Sov'reign I'm secure,
> I shall be rich till thou art poor!'

"I have read with great interest 'The Farmer and his Family' (which you sent me), and think that one thousand copies of it will be circulated in this land. . . . .

"Most affectionately yours, B. C. CUTLER."

The arms of his love and of his affectionate interest, extended far and wide to friends at a distance, yet he drew them more closely, perhaps, about his own flock. The two following letters are samples of anxious solicitude about the youthful members of his congregation:

TO F. C. T——, ON LEAVING HOME.

"ST. ANN'S RECTORY, *May* 2, 1856.

"MY DEAR F—— —I feel an irresistible desire to write you on this occasion. Your mother was, and ever will be, cherished near my heart; her image is before my mind, and I expect to meet her in another world, long before you do. Her first question to me will be, 'Did you feed my lambs?' Now, F——, you are just making an important change, and one that has been the ruin of millions; *you are entering the world as your own master.* If you do wrong, there will be no one who has a right to say, 'Why do you do so?' Let me beseech you, then, to walk in the ways of God's commandments. Forty years ago I was just in your condition; I chose to serve God, and here I am alive and well; while, perhaps, every boy of the score or two who were my early companions, and who chose to walk in the way of wickedness, is dead. Disease contracted by dissipation ended their lives, and they lived and died in debt and despair!

"God made you, my dear boy! God has a right to your service.

God can reward you, both here and hereafter; and God can kill your body, and after that, can cast you into hell!

"You have openly given yourself to God in his church, before many witnesses. I beseech you, then, first—to keep holy the Sabbath day. Never swear; never pass a day without prayer and reading the Bible. Remember *now* thy Creator, in the days of thy youth, and when you are old, and when you need him most, God will remember you. It is said in Genesis, God remembered Noah—remembered him in the ark, and saved him alive, while all other families were lost. So, if you do as Noah did in his youth, if you remember God, he will remember you for good. I need not say that the sin of licentiousness is one to which young men are peculiarly exposed. It ruins the body and ruins the soul! Flee youthful lusts. If any one would tempt you, read devil and damnation in that person's face. I look upon you as pure and virtuous, and I have no words to convey my abhorrence of the individual who should lead you into vice—a vice, too, which he knows he would give all he has, if he were able to conquer, but he cannot! He is gone; he is sold, a slave to Satan, and his fate is probably sealed.

"Be honest. Speak the truth and follow the pure precepts of Jesus Christ, who died for you. Then may you expect the favor of God, both here and hereafter. Our prayers shall attend you, and I remain your friend and your father's and your mother's friend and pastor, B. C. CUTLER."

TO T. H——, AFTER A WONDERFUL ESCAPE FROM DEATH.

"ST. ANN'S RECTORY, *June* 9, 1856.

"MY DEAR YOUNG FRIEND—Your recent and most happy preservation from instant death, by drowning, has caused me many serious thoughts? What would have been your appearance before God? Where would you now have been? In happiness or in misery? What tongue can describe, nay, what mind can conceive, the nature and extent of the suffering or the enjoyment which, in a moment, you would have entered upon, had not your strength held out? Consider this as a loud call to you, to give God your heart. He is certainly saying, 'My son, give me thy heart!' Think how kindly and wonderfully God has provided for you! When father and mother forsook you, the Lord took you up! and now, when your only means of safety was overturned—when heart and flesh were failing, 'God was the strength of your heart.' May he be your portion for ever! It is not necessary that you speak much about your deliverance; but it is necessary that you *think* much about it!

When alone, ask yourself, What am I? Where am I? Whither am I going? . . . .

"Never join in any ungodly merriment, in making light of God's word or name, but from this time cry unto him, 'Thou art the guide of my youth.'

"Faithfully and affectionately, your pastor and friend,

"B. C. CUTLER."

We recur again to his journal. In all its records we see how he was filled with an absorbing desire to do God's will in all things, and to be what he would have him to be. His standard of Christian character was high, and the distance between that and his life, caused him often to touch the note of grief.

"*June* 2.—I love to be where God's blessed name and law, and Son and salvation, are the staple of the talk! I hate vain talk, but thy Word is my delight. My thoughts wander, to my sorrow, and I am distressed and disappointed. Lord, thou knowest all things; thou knowest that I love thee!"

As he advanced in life, however, though he was occasionally cast down in spirit, on the whole, his strain was changed into one of joyous thanksgiving. The Saviour who had redeemed him, would keep him to the end; and, constantly fixing his thoughts on him, he was changed into the same image, as by the Spirit of the Lord.

"*July* 13.—I was interested in an excellent sermon from young R. B. P——t. It was a deeply interesting scene to have him preach for me, and to preach so faithfully. His parents were present—his father being the senior warden of St. Ann's."

"*July* 20.—Mrs. P——r, a member of the church, died yesterday, aged eighty-five! She has often longed for death, and wept for it. Now, I trust, she is with the Lord!"

"*Aug.* 1.—I spent part of the week with Mr. T. Messenger and his family, and the second week at Saratoga."

It will be noticed that Dr. Cutler had discontinued for a few years his annual excursions on horseback down the length of Long Island. His strength was now hardly equal to this, and, as a substitute, he usually went to Saratoga Springs for summer recreation, and then, before the season closed, he always visited "Clarence," the summer residence of the parishioner referred to above, at Great Neck, L. I.

The whole-souled hospitality, and the free, unrestrained intercourse with the extended circle there, often refreshed and invigorated his weary spirit. All welcomed him with cordial delight, and he became the centre of all interest and pleasure—alike to each of the group who thronged about him, father and friend, counsellor and guide—a sharer in the happiness of all, yet the revered and chosen pastor who

"Allured to brighter worlds
And led the way!"

How he did this we all know, as few ever can, and still fewer ever do—faithfully, patiently, *judiciously*. Either in person or by letter, he sought to reach every heart in his family circle, in the church, in the community at large—wherever he could speak a word for his Master. Indeed, if any one ever knew what the Latins call the "*mollia tempora fandi!*" those favorable opportunities to speak, when hearts can be easily, and softly, and wisely touched, surely it was he, for he knew more than most, how to reach various classes of mankind, and was observant of the shifting phases of their varied and varying experience.

Some may think that the tender sentiments were too often touched, but quite enough of sternness was in the composition of his nature to offset any extreme tendency in that direction. How full of pathos was the note to his brother-in-law, Dr. F——, who was bowed down with sorrow:

"*June* 15, 1856.

"Many thanks, my dear Doctor, for the memorial of our dear John. We all think the engraving inimitable, and the likeness perfect. It fairly took possession of my mind for a day and night after I received it—the image was all the time there. I paid a visit to John's grave this morning, early, and saw that all things were as they should be. The flowers which abound in other parts of Greenwood I wished were there. The willow is growing up and thrives. But what are all these? What is any thing on earth to compare with *life?* Speaking of flowers, I committed these beautiful lines to memory lately, from a poem of Mrs. Hemans:

'Bring flowers, pale flowers o'er the bier to shed
A crown for the brow of the early dead;
For this, the white rose through her green leaves burst;
For this, in the woods were the violets nurst;
They slept in their graves, through the wintry hours,
They burst forth in glory—bring flowers, bring flowers!'

"Ever yours, B. C. CUTLER."

A true lover of flowers, as the creation of a Divine hand.

TO MRS. C. H——Y.

"Many thanks for some of the last roses of summer and other sweet flowers. I do love flowers, and love to think that God made them, and made us capable of admiring them. The love of the beautiful is no small capability, there are so many beauties to admire here, and, above all, so many to admire in the paradise above. *There* are roses without thorns, whose bloom never withers. With every desire for your happiness and that of all your friends, I am, very truly and affectionately,

"Your pastor, B. C. CUTLER."

How replete with Christian sentiment is the following:

TO MRS. JACKSON, ON HER DEPARTURE TO ENGLAND.

"SARATOGA, *July* 3, 1856.

. . . . "Amid the guests here, I found a Christian man, and conversed on the 'great things,' this morning; but still how to find one who can tell me what Jesus has done for his soul, is the hard task! I love to hear such an one talk. Oh, there is a hidden life, and that is the best life! There is a whole world within a man, which savors of heaven, and when two such meet and interchange thought and feeling, there is a great confirmation of faith and hope. May you find such an one on your voyage, and take sweet counsel together! Present my respects to your dear friends beyond the flood, and be assured that he who made a way over Jordan and through the Red Sea will make a path for you through his mighty waters.

"Yours, B. C. C."

The following note to an aged parishioner contains a beautiful allusion to our missionaries to Africa:

"What may be said to every mortal, may be said with especial emphasis to our African missionaries. 'What is *your* life? It is even a vapor that appeareth for a little time and then vanisheth away!' They give good evidence that they are followers of those who 'through faith quenched the violence of fire, and out of weakness were made strong.' 'My strength,' saith Jesus, 'is made perfect in *weakness!*' Capt. Vicars, who fell before Sebastopol, it may have been thought, ought to have been spared, and to have exchanged the sword of the flesh for the sword of the Spirit; but his early death, and the memoir which has chronicled it, will do more good to the world than his preaching could do; and so the death of that lovely flower, Mrs. Virginia Hoffman, that 'blossomed as the rose' in the wilderness of Ethiopia, will diffuse its fragrance now through the world. Surely we can say:

'’Tis e'en as if an angel shook his wings;
Immortal fragrance fills the circuit wide
That tells us whence *her* treasures were supplied.'

"Yours and theirs in love and sympathy, B. C. CUTLER."

TO THE SAME.

"*August* 26, 1856.

"MY DEAR MRS. P—— —Many thanks for your letter, and for the specimen of growth and decay at so high an elevation as three thousand feet above the sea! . . . . Your visit and description of the Catskill Mountains have created in me the first desire I ever felt, to see that extensive prospect myself. Mountains, I confess, have never had attractions for me as a summer retreat. They are difficult of ascent, cold in the morning and at night, and hot at noonday. I have therefore preferred the sea shore or a champaign country. Indeed, my life and bodily tendencies have led to repose rather than to exposure and fatigue; and as I have long looked upon life as a '*valley*,' and heaven as a mountain, I have postponed my ascent until a *new body* shall be given me! It is, you know, a mark of old age to be afraid of 'that which is high;' but I am glad so much elasticity remains in you. . . . . Our sympathy to the afflicted ones. Yet a little while and all separations will cease. Assuring you of the true Christian regard and affection of a pastor,

"I remain, dear madam, yours in Christ, B. C. CUTLER."

In October of this year, the General Convention met in the city of New York. Dr. Cutler rejoiced to gather about his table as many of the clergy as would favor him with their presence at Brooklyn; and no one delighted more in such opportunities of Christian intercourse. Interviews with friends from east and west, and from various sections of the country, were heartily enjoyed, and they were generally closed with prayer. How many who will read these lines will look back upon those delightful reminiscences of the past and say, "When shall we see another like him?" "How oft he has refreshed me!" and the silent tear will flow from many an eye; yet may our faith wipe every tear away, and look forward in anticipation to a more blessed and lasting intercourse with him, in the land whither he has gone! Does he not watch us now with eager eye? Does he not beckon to us to follow him as he followed Christ? And does he not assure us that, through infinite grace, we shall meet again?

Through the long lapse of years, he still clung to his earthly friends. At this very time he speaks with pleasure (in his journal) of "meeting L—— M——, an old and highly esteemed friend and parishioner, at Quincy, Mass."

Nor were the strong ties which bound him to new friends and parishioners ever weakened, because he occasionally wove another strand about the chain of early friendships. Clasping often the links which bound together the cords of friendship, along the whole course of his earthly life, he united them all to a heart free from envy, jealousy, or any like imperfection, and only prayed that the Saviour would bind them in one "bundle of life" together, and present them all at his Heavenly Father's feet as the fruits of his soul's travail!

Read the following, addressed to one of the parishioners of St. Ann's, then sojourning at the White Mountains—(the note is full of vivacity and playful humor):

TO D. H——, ESQ.

"MY DEAR FRIEND—Your favor is at hand, and I was interested in all you said, especially about the Sunday services. I can truly say, that many and many a Sunday morning I have come from our services at St. Ann's, and said, 'blessed are your ears,' etc. I am no great zealot for any changes in the Liturgy, a little more liberty merely in the use of the Prayer-Book, or its parts, is all I ask. . . . . We shall be glad to see you back. Mrs. Cutler and I have been at Saratoga, in *a crowd* and in *a jam.* We went for a change, and we had it with a witness. By day and by night it roared about us like Niagara! But then it was a *change! and it cost money*, and you know both of these are delightful to us New Yorkers!

"Your mother left last Saturday for the grand tour. Whether we are to have one volume or four, as the result, I don't know, but abundance of observation, reflection, inspection and conversation we must expect from such travellers. My poor prayers attend them. . . . I learn that Mrs. T—— is better, and is resigned to the will of God. Why should we not all be? How can God err? And if we are his children, 'heirs of God,' and if we have already had so beautiful a world as this to enjoy, why should not our imagination and faith, going hand-in-hand, spread out for us a 'blooming paradise' as our next remove—where the sweetest, richest, purest, most heartfelt happiness awaits us, and departed saints, and angels, and Christ who is God over all, and all they can do to make us perfectly and for ever happy. Dear, dear friends, let us *all* aim to meet there!

"Yours, most affectionately, B. C. CUTLER."

The following is the last note in his journal of 1856: "This day a quarter of a century ago, I opened my ministry in New York by preaching, at the Mission Church in Vandewater Street, from these words: 'Unto me, who am less than the least of all saints, is this grace given, that I should preach among the Gentiles the unsearchable riches of Christ.' I preached to-day from Philippians iv. 13: 'I can do all things through Christ which strengtheneth me!' On Saturday, I walked around my old field of labor, where, twenty-five years ago, I began to labor for Christ in this part of his vineyard. It is much changed, but *Christ is the same!*"

"*Jan.* 1, 1857.—My motto for this year is, 'Christ is all and in all.'"

As another year opened before him, Dr. Cutler received a testimonial of regard and esteem from a few gentlemen of the parish, to whom he sent the following reply:

"St. Ann's Rectory, Brooklyn, *January* 20, 1857.

"My Dear Friends—You can easily imagine the gratification which your letter of the 12th inst. afforded me. Had it been unaccompanied by a most generous offering, it would of itself have been a testimonial which of all others I should value, more especially if I could hope that it was merited. But the enclosure of two hundred dollars, accompanied with a box of one hundred volumes of my sermons for my own distribution, together with the remaining five hundred copies in Philadelphia, and the expense of publishing the work, form, unitedly, an expression of kindness and regard which I could not and did not expect. But, aside from all this, the Christian sentiments advanced in the letter, the pious wishes which it breathes, and the evidence which it affords of your own salvation in Christ, would fill me with joy. That I have, in any material measure contributed, through God's assistance, to the sending forth into Christ's vineyard of so many laborers, who have the means and the will to do good on a large scale, is a reflection too flattering to be indulged; and yet I am encouraged by your letter to hope for this.

"But, all other considerations aside, the possibility that the book you have so generously published, may, in the end, be the means of saving even one soul from everlasting death, is enough to fill to overflowing the heart of its author. With profound thankfulness,

"I am your obliged brother and pastor, B. C. Cutler.

"To Messrs. Thomas Messenger, Harry Messenger, Joseph W. Greene, John Halsey and George D. Morgan."

We insert here a few passages from his journal:

"*Jan.* 11, 1857.—When a man goes to church with a deep

sense of his own unworthiness, his thoughts will not wander as they do when he goes light-hearted."

"*Jan.* 25.—The sermon I heard to-day on 'Be not conformed to this world,' was a qualification of the command not called for by the state of things. The apostle did not *qualify*, why should we? Young ministers had better be thought too strict than too lax! Most thinking people really want ministers who will co-operate with their *consciences*. They know when they do wrong, and like the man best who agrees with their conscience. Young men often make such mistakes; I think I may have myself, when first setting out."

"*Feb.* 1.—Mr. J. A. G—— staying with me; I like him much. Oh that we had many like him!"

"*March* 8.—I fear I have been cross and irritable, but I have been very tired. What is man? How unlike his Saviour! Shame and humiliation follow such folly. Oh, when shall I be free from sin?"

Mutual greetings and kind notes were exchanged at New Year's between pastor and people. Various members of his flock also sent substantial tokens to the rectory. There was a circle of devoted and appreciative friends who never failed, as oft as this season recurred, to give of their temporal substance, to him who was "set over them in the Lord," and, so faithfully broke the bread of life to them. His replies to some of their kind remembrances are as follows:

TO W. B. C——, ESQ., A WEALTHY PARISHIONER.

"BROOKLYN, *January* 13, 1857.

"MY DEAR MR. C—— —As usual, I received your generous gift of this season, and as usual, I return my thanks. I look upon you now as a blessing about to be taken away from me; but it is not true that 'the blessing brightens as it takes its flight!' Your friendship is like the bird of paradise, whose beautiful plumage appears to best advantage when the bird is *in repose!* I love you and your wife, and all your children, and from every one, for many long, long years, I have received nothing but kindness. I value and prize you as an officer of the church, and am rejoiced that our church has such to support and sustain her among the laity. Now let me only beg you to hold fast to the fear of God, and your profession of the faith of Christ. Remember that it was the '*world*' that crucified Christ, and not the profane and vulgar, but men of high life! 'The common people' heard him gladly! It was the great and self-constituted wise, who hated him. Remember that Jesus Christ coveted not palaces, but was content with a cottage! and oh! above all, remember that 'God manifest in the flesh,' said, 'How hardly shall they that have riches enter into the kingdom of heaven!'"

"Most affectionately yours, B. C. CUTLER."

TO T. M——, ESQ.

"*January* 13, 1857.

"MY DEAR FRIEND—I thank you for your present. This is a handsome sum for a minister to receive. . . . . . . My family *in* doors is not large, but out of doors, it is pretty extensive, and I am not quite sure that all you raise on your farm at Great Neck, would be enough to put food into their mouths! I never think of rising from my dinner-table, without laying down, twice the cost of my own dinner, for the poor, who will come at 3 o'clock! Nor would twice this sum supply my needs for the objects of charity who daily apply to me. So much for ways and means. I am rejoiced to see your increasing interest in good things—*things which perish not in the using.*

"It would take one sting from death for me to know that when I am gone, there will be men left who will defend the gospel in the church; and the church, for the gospel's sake; and both, because of that glorious Saviour, whom they ought to hold forth and hold up. There is indeed, nothing in religion to compare with the name or power of Christ; him first, him last, him in the midst, him all in all.

"Affectionately, your obliged pastor, B. C. CUTLER."

Every year Dr. Cutler received from one member of his flock a watch-chain, woven together by her own hand. Other gifts, noble and large came also, from the same household where generous hearts loved to share with others, of the bounty with which God had blessed them. The pastor's affection is fully exhibited, in a note, dated—

TO MR. AND MRS. H. M——.

"*January* 13, 1857.

"The pressure of duties has prevented my acknowledging your accustomed generosity until now. The silken chain, emblematic of the bond of Christian affection, was just in time to take the place of the old one that had become weakened by use. Emblems do but imperfectly answer their object. Time only brightens and strengthens the chain that binds Christian hearts together, and twenty years of Christian fellowship and affection have not weakened the bond that binds me to you. The 'Expedition to Japan' is a valuable work. . . . . Commodore Perry's expedition may be the opening wedge to the whole empire, and what is begun in the 'flesh' may end in the 'Spirit.' God will overturn and overturn until *right* shall be *might*, and the upper world shall be filled with his glory. My dear R——, I shall bear you and your little family especially in mind. . . . .

"Affectionately, your obliged pastor, B. C. CUTLER."

His own birthday was noticed by another kind parishioner with a congratulatory note and memento, and Dr. Cutler, in turn, ever kept hers in remembrance. His note to this individual, in 1857, was excellent:

"Allow me to add my best wishes to the many offered you on this day. May this be the happiest of all your years. You have plowed up and sowed carefully ten large fields. It is now time to see the fruits. May you have all the joys of the 'harvest home!' May you gather all your golden sheaves into the garner of the Lord, and at the great day be able to say with triumph, 'Here am I and the children which thou hast given me!' and may the 10th of March, 1858, find you still flourishing and bearing fruit to the praise and glory of God's grace.

"Your affectionate friend and pastor, B. C. CUTLER."

In June of this year, a new assistant minister was procured for St. Ann's, Brooklyn, the Rev. W. W. Sever (the previous assistant having removed some months before, to St. Ann's Church, Morrisania, in the neighborhood of New York). As a faithful watchman on the walls of Zion, he upheld the hands of his elder fellow-laborer, and esteemed it a privilege to be thus associated with Dr. Cutler.

In August, we find Dr. Cutler at "Clarence," visiting his beloved friends and parishioners at their summer retreat. From thence he wrote to a valued parishioner, then absent with his family in Europe, a letter which, perhaps, exhibits the real spirit of the man as well as any letter in the whole collection of his correspondence.

We give an extract:

TO MR. AND MRS. D. H——, LONDON.

"*August* 2, 1857.

. . . . "I presume you see any number of '*Amerikins*.' 'The periodical flight of American clergymen' to England took place before you left, I think. What the Bishop of London thinks now, I know not; but he said to me in June, 1843, 'This is about the time for the periodical flight of American clergymen!' *Geese*, no doubt, were in his mind! But really, when we get worn out, what do we more than they? We fly to the Continent; so do they. We can't go South, and there is nothing to be seen North, and so we go East. I suppose we are great bores! Whether I shall ever trouble London again is doubtful. By the by, Mr. Messenger handed me a letter on Saturday which he received from 'Lambeth Palace' from the Archbishop, which begins as follows:—'Lambeth, June 1: Dear Sir—I write to thank you for the volume of valuable sermons by Dr. Cutler, which you have kindly sent me,' etc., etc. You must not suppose that I approved of sending such a present to the Archbishop, for I had nothing to do with it. Little has transpired since you left. We have been out of town two weeks.

"The Sunday cars vex my soul. Such is the noise on a Sunday evening, I almost dread to go back, and think of securing a room in some house in a quiet part of the city to flee unto, as the heart to the water-brooks! But enough. This (Mr. M.'s place) is a fine *location*, as the Americans say. Long Island Sound and a bay compose half the circle round the house. Woods and cultivated fields, flocks and herds dot over the whole scene. Our friends are all heart and hospitality—and what with six horses and six cows, and five times six geese, and ducks and fowl of every kind, and abundance of fresh food from garden and larder, we cannot sigh for Egypt! The little children like their pastor, catch his favorite hymns, and sit up to hear him lecture. This is pleasant, as I am fast reaching the last decimal division of human life. When you next see me, I shall have but about *ten years* to live before I arrive at the station-house.

. . . . I bless the Lord that I have labored forty years in promoting the kingdom of Christ; in so poor a way, however, as to shame me and doubtless provoke him. But I know that I have all this time desired the prosperity of his kingdom, and been continually doing something for it. I am striving to get a fixed '*joy*' to be ever before me.—Heb. xii. 2.

"I don't want to think of the grave, the coffin, or the shroud, but of Christ, and God, and glory! I try to fancy 'the moment after death'—the beautiful gate of heaven, the golden streets, the smiling saints, the approving Saviour, the white-robed crowd, the golden harps, the enrapturing melody, and the transporting sound, 'Well done, good and faithful servant!' I am waiting for the word of command:

'Soldier, shout! the war is done!
Lo, the hosts of hell are flying!
'T was thy Lord the victory won,
Jesus conquered them by dying!'

"Take care of yourselves. Live *on shore*, so that if you should be brought into trouble *at sea* you may not be ashamed to meet Him at his appearance; so that you may say, Lord, when I was well and at ease, I remembered thee—oh, remember me! I kept thy Sabbaths, I lived above the world, I contended for thy honor, and now I rely on thy faithfulness and truth. God is not unrighteous to *forget*, man is. The Saviour fold you all there to his bosom, prays

"Your old friend and pastor, B. C. CUTLER."

It is easy to see by Dr. Cutler's correspondence, and indeed in all his daily course of life, his piety beaming forth with the naturalness of transparent childhood. His religion was not a superficial layer upon the mere surface, but an integral portion of his being. Christ Jesus was known to him not by abstract definition, or vague theory, or even by sublime conceptions alone, when the soul would mount on the wings of faith and survey the scenes of heavenly glory, which at times thrill the believer's soul with ecstatic pleasure, but he was known as a man knoweth his friend; known by the hourly wants he supplied, by every apprehension which he relieved, and every temptation he enabled him to surmount. The love and sympathy of a Divine Saviour were his constant refuge, and each of the many minute cares and perplexities of life became only a fine affiliating bond which drew him closer to that Almighty Friend. As years rolled on, he found in every situation, in every trouble, from the lightest sorrow to that which wrings the soul with agony, that Jesus was equally present, and his gracious aid was equally adequate; and thus his faith grew strong, seeming to change gradually almost to sight, and Christ's care and love were to him more *real* than any other source of reliance, and multiplied trials became only new avenues of acquaintance between him and his God.

His journal (after a time of trial) attests the truth of these remarks:

"*Sept.* 20, 1857."—He writes:

"'Guide me, O thou great Jehovah!
Pilgrim through this barren land,
I am weak, but thou art mighty,
Hold me with thy powerful hand.'

"I feel exactly like a little child in religion, all my prayers and labors, and faith, and feelings are those of a poor little child! Christ is great! I am less than nothing. I owe ten thousand talents and have nothing to pay."

In a note to his sister-in-law, several months later, he expressed similar sentiments: "God can make every thing sweet, while a thousand sweets may be wholly embittered without him. I go to God, just as a young child runs to its mother, a great many times a day, though I don't stay a great while at a time. I believe in him, and trust in him, and refer all things to him, through Christ."

In his journal, under date of November 8, 1857, he thus expressed his gratitude to God:

"When I consider that forty years ago I was broken down in health, and could not read a page aloud; that I was thought to be in consumption, and was told that I could not live to graduate from college, how little did I anticipate my present age, nearly sixty years old, and I now preach twice a week. Glory be to God for his goodness, through Christ Jesus! Let me thank God and take courage!"

This year in Dr. Cutler's history was one of great trouble in the financial world; seldom has there been known "a monetary crisis" of such unparalleled severity. Prominent firms and merchants of unusual sagacity and foresight, both in Europe and America, found themselves in great pecuniary distress. The business community in the large cities and great commercial centres felt the shock most keenly, while gloom, like a heavy pall, was spread over all future prospects.

To a dear friend, engaged in large business transactions, Dr. Cutler wrote in this strain: "We are shaking here for the earthquake we expect you will have over the river. But it must needs be that it burst. Things will not come right, I suppose, until the bubble is broken; the great imposture must be lanced! Alas! I feel for those who must know the '*sorrow of the world!*'"

A few weeks later, he wrote to the same friend:

TO G. D. M——, ESQ.

"*November* 7, 1857.

"MY VERY DEAR FRIEND— . . . . I have not visited you, nor troubled you recently even with a letter, during these 'monetary struggles,' inasmuch as I was well assured that you knew the way to 'the great refuge,' without my direction, and also because I knew that your time would now be much taken up. . . . . I have no fears for you and yours. These are times, however, which must 'try men's souls.' I have my mode of interpreting the providence of God in them, and I suppose others have theirs. That *God's hand* is in them I am sure; and that his voice is crying to every man in the city, cannot be doubted. If ever that great city was 'given over to idolatry,' it was within your memory and mine; and it is 'for covetousness' sake,' which is idolatry, that the wrath of God cometh on the children of disobedience. I pray that its present trials may be sanctified to its good, and that you and all God's children may have peace, though the war of lusts should rage still longer. . . . .

"With love to your family, I am your obliged and affectionate

"Friend and pastor, B. C. CUTLER."

To an absent friend at Tutbury, in England, who was preparing a valuable biography for the press, Dr. Cutler thus wrote:

"*December* 27, 1857.

"MY VERY DEAR FRIEND— . . . . The panic has put a stop to all printing of new works by the E. K. S., and you will therefore have abundance of time to prepare your work. In order to write the letter you have requested, and my own heart would dictate, I only want time for calm retrospection. God willing, it shall come. . . . . . . As to civil matters here, we are in an evil case; a vigilance committee is almost needed in New York. I often wonder when I visit a lunatic asylum and see forty maniacs together, and I expect havoc and death; but he who keeps them, knows that they never have their paroxysms at the same time. So our metropolis mad-house, having English and Irish, German and Dutch, Swedish and French, and American inmates, these are played off, one against the other, and we keep alive. . . . .

"In church matters we are still; except that our friend, Bishop ——, has been exposed in his unguarded loyalty to his patriarch!!! Who could have been so little his friend as to publish that letter in the *Christian Observer?* Some people do not know *how to trifle*, nor who to trifle with.

"India, dreadful India, is in all our thoughts; we have mourned, and lamented, and prayed. Missions here are at a low ebb. Our annual collection at St. Ann's, however, came off just before *the dark day*, and was as large as usual.

"I have a truly evangelical curate, Rev. W. W. Sever, a graduate of Harvard University, and of the Theological Seminary of Alexandria, a young man of faith and prayer. My parish church is just as full as ever. My Sunday-schools number six hundred names on the books, and my field in this poor part of Brooklyn is large.

"The M——s are still great comforts to me. Christmas has just gone, and presents come in as usual. . . . . I admire Dr. Livingston's work, though I should not admire it less, if it had more of *salvation* in it. Salvation! what can compare with that? Oh the joyful sound! . . . . .

"Affectionately, your brother and friend, B. C. CUTLER."

These were dark days for many who were engaged in mercantile pursuits. Some of Dr. Cutler's parishioners, however (faithfully taught as they had been for years), did not give less of their earthly substance than before to benevolent and charitable objects, nor did they withhold the hand of bounty from the Lord's suffering poor. For this, Dr. Cutler was grateful, yet was he faithful, too, as the last letter he wrote in the year 1857 well attests:

TO T. M——, ESQ.

"*December* 29, 1857.

"MY DEAR FRIEND—For your liberal response to many calls of suffering humanity, through me, I return my own thanks, and, I must believe, those also of many others. Whatever may become of your fortune in time to come, upon a pretty large share of it you may be able to reflect with satisfaction. My hope and prayer is that it will never be diminished; but that the more you give, the more you may receive; and that with your means, you will give also yourself, body and soul, to Him who gives power to get wealth and who does more than this—who gives the power *to enjoy what he bestows.*

"It is folly to expect all things to go smoothly at all times. There must be night as well as day, winter as well as summer. There certainly is death, as well as life. Let us all then lay hold upon God while he is near to us, and we are drawn to him by His goodness, and let us honor him while we have honor from men. Piety of soul is the great secret of happiness. With love,

"I am yours, faithfully, B. C. CUTLER."

In what light Dr. Cutler considered earthly riches, all could see from his personal example, his household arrangements, and his public teachings; these were in perfect harmony with each other. His opinion on this topic could be expressed in few words. Wealth, to be received with thanksgiving, if love to God was supreme; hoarded up, it became like an alabaster box, of no avail, except as a mere ornament, and imparting little or no happiness; but if broken and scattered and poured out as precious ointment upon the body of Jesus Christ, in the person of his suffering children, it was exhaling rich fragrance around, and returning, in the grateful benedictions of others, the richest aroma to the Dispenser himself.

Some may prefer, however, to read his own written testimony on the ability of mere wealth to afford happiness. It is clearly expressed, in one of his letters written to his beloved wife, in the following language: "The happiness of earth at best is momentary, and generally as incomplete as it is momentary. The rich, for the most part, know less about it than those who have neither riches nor poverty. I was thinking to-day, that the rich were always striving to increase *the means* by which they expect to be made happy, while the wise were constantly cultivating dispositions which could produce happiness from the smallest means! It is needless to say which course would insure the most independent and permanent happiness. Take from the merely rich their riches, and you cut off all happiness from them. Take from the wise their riches, and you dry up only one source, and perhaps the smallest source, of happiness. But take from the Christian every thing which can make the rich and the wise happy, and you have not touched his '*mountain*.' Thanks be to God, the happiness of the Christian is independent of all creatures and things!"

CHAPTER XIV.

MINISTRY AT ST. ANN'S CHURCH—CONTINUED.

1858–1861.

THE year 1858 was marked by a "revival" of special religious interest throughout the United States; the previous year had been one of temporal losses, and now, as God ordered, in his manifold wisdom, it was followed by a season of spiritual gain. Men found their earthly idols crumbling into dust, and their worldly props suddenly breaking away, and many hearts were thus forced to look up to God for refuge, as their only sure and safe abiding-place.

In many places, the outpouring of God's spirit was truly remarkable, and the Church of Christ rejoiced in large accessions to her fold. The churches in New York and Brooklyn were sharers, in no small degree, in this baptism of the Divine Spirit.

Meetings for prayer and praise were multiplied, and, as is always the case at such times, a remarkable spirit of union and harmony prevailed among the ministers of Christ, of every name. Dr. Cutler entered heart and soul into the good work. In his journal and letters, at this time, frequent allusions are made to it, as we shall perceive.

We give a few extracts from the former:

"*Jan.* 3, 1858.—I am nearly sixty years old. This is a high point of land to reach; it is a place to look down from, and above all, to look up from. Ten short years more and my lease expires (the life of man is three score years and ten). They are to be employed in drawing near to God and in doing good. Draw me, O Lord, with the cords of love, and with the bands of a man!"

"*Feb.* 6.—This is my birthday. I am sixty years of age. I rose at 5 A. M., and thanked God for the past, and prayed that I might live nearer to him than I have heretofore. I have read my journal for last year; it is an account of moderate and steady labor, and of God's mercies. Ten years will make up my life, but, ten months, or even ten days, may not remain. I am humble, and peaceful, and hopeful, builded up on the foundation of the apostles and prophets, Jesus Christ my chief corner-stone!"

"*March* 26.—Continued religious services have been held at St Ann's."

To a friend and parishioner, then in London, Dr. Cutler wrote at this time:

"*March* 22, 1858.

"We are now in the midst of a great revival of religion. It would be better worth crossing the water to see it, than to see either the Crystal Palace or the picture gallery at Manchester. I have just attended an interesting meeting at the Church of the Ascension (Dr. Bedell's)." . . . .

To another friend in England, he also wrote:

"We are having a delightful refreshing from the presence of the Lord, all around us; we have a prayer-meeting at St. Ann's, immediately after church in the afternoon; our wardens and young male members pray and make short exhortations; the congregation generally go into the chapel. I saw Dr. H—— at a meeting at Dr. Bedell's, where Dr. Dyer, Mr. D——, and I, spoke. 'Poverty makes strange bed-fellows,' and revivals make strange fellowships. . . . . Now about the American Tract Society. Thinking has become a passion in New England; every body thinks *hard*, and as every body differs from every body, so opinion is the bloodless field of strife. If a great man forms a strong opinion, woe betide the luckless wight who opposes! Now, it is the opinion of ——, that to insult the Southern people is the duty of the American Tract Society at any rate. However, feeling predominates at the South, and practical common sense at New York (near the centre), and hence, when the vote to approve came up, about one thousand against two hundred was the result.

"Your brother, in faith and love, B. C. C."

In April of this year, Dr. Cutler presented to the Bishop for confirmation sixty persons—a noble accession of both young and old from the extensive parish of St. Ann's to the ranks and service of Christ. Dr. Cutler gave all the praise to God, while he humbly acknowledged his own deficiencies, even in the midst of so much labor and such blessed fruit.

"*April*, 1858.—I have lived and labored in Brooklyn twenty-five years. What a long period, and how much of deficiency appears? What labor I have bestowed, has been chiefly bestowed on this parish, and God has apparently blessed it, and glory be to his great name! Thus the Lord has led me on; less than ten years to live, and very much land 'remains to be possessed!' But I must trust in him who has fed me all my life-long, and who knows that, forty years ago, I left Egypt and entered the wilderness, bound for the heavenly land. Ever since, I have felt as a stranger and a pilgrim on the earth, and that here I have no abiding city! I can say with another, 'I am so unworthy I suppose I ought to fear, but I do not; my trust is in God.' We have a glorious revival of religion, on all sides, and in all parts of the land; such a season America has rarely seen! Oh that grace might be poured into my heart and into my lips, and that God would bless me for ever!"

In May, 1858, Dr. Cutler preached his quarter-century discourse at St. Ann's. It was divided into three parts, and delivered on successive Sundays, and was soon printed, in accordance with the earnest desire of the congregation and of many other friends. For twenty-five years he had fed this flock, and now, fully aware that his connection with his beloved people must be severed by death before many years should pass away, he analyzed before his people the principles upon which his ministry had been conducted, and exhorted them to hold fast to the truth as it is in Jesus. Seven hundred and seventy-five new members had been added to this church during that period, which was indeed an encouraging token of the Divine blessing. The rector had performed one thousand three hundred and eighty-two baptisms, five hundred and nine marriages, and eight hundred and twenty-three burials, and preached one thousand eight hundred sermons. Such was his resumé of parochial labor. He had acted steadily upon the resolution of the apostle, "not to know any thing among you (his people) save Jesus Christ, and him crucified," during all this period. The secularization of so many of God's ministers in these latter days, he earnestly protested against; the time for a minister's own special work was too short, the immortal soul too precious, and Christ's command too urgent, he thought, to admit of "saluting any man by the way." Thus he declared his views: "The association of ministers to so great an extent with mere men of letters, which unfits them for converse with their flocks, subtracts a very large portion of time that really belongs to those flocks, wears out their own strength, and shortens their ministry and their lives. The additional celebrity and literary cultivation which they gain, are no equivalent for the loss the people suffer. . . . I cannot wonder that men of talents and learning, and of fascinating powers of oratory, do not relish the conversation of the humbler portion of their flocks. . . . I wonder not at the preference of these cultivated men, for the information, the enlightened criticism, the brilliant repartee, the pungent satire of the *literary coterie*. But I blame them for becoming pastors or *shepherds* of Christ's flock, whose duty it is, as they know beforehand, to *feed the sheep and the lambs*. If a man is ordained to this office, a large share of his time ought to be taken up in supplying the spiritual wants of the flock. I therefore offer no apology for not being placarded along our streets, by the side of all the secular announcements of the day; and I confess that though I love letters well, *I love the gospel more;* and I would rather preach one gospel sermon than make an exhibition of the greatest learning on earth."

He closed this valuable discourse in brief and pointed language: "Twenty-five years more, and the greater part of my adult hearers will have been transferred from the busy haunts of men, to the shades of our rural cemetery. Think of this, dearly beloved, and delay not to make all preparation for the great change. Think of this, and firmly resolve, that in a truly Christian sense, the world shall be benefited by your brief residence in it! Think of this, and seek for nobler and more enduring monuments than are obtained from the hand of art—even those of *immortal souls*, saved and beautified by Divine grace. Oh that I might fire your breasts with a holy ambition to rise above the low pursuits of earth, and to run the race for a *heavenly and eternal renown!*"

One of Dr. Cutler's most characteristic letters, full of the strongest and deepest religious sentiment, yet with a playful expression, gleaming like a silver thread here and there throughout, was addressed this summer to a parishioner absent in Europe. She had been baptized, presented for confirmation, and married by Dr. Cutler:

TO MRS. D. H——.

"BROOKLYN, *June* 10, 1858.

"MY DEAR FRIEND—Rivers overflow their banks, and then we have a rich alluvial. Three papers from you, of various dates, lie before me, containing sundry questions, etc. What a delightful frame you must be in! . . . . The Bishop of —— I see is a favorite with you. I hear of him often as an eloquent man. But I must confess, that unless a minister of Christ preaches *a full-orbed gospel*, and one as free as full, I cannot be satisfied with oratory. I feel sick of sin, there is no health in me, and Christ alone is the only and the all-sufficient medicine for my sickness. I want to be directed at once to Christ. I want my sins, my infirmities, my backslidings, my coldness, my foolishness, taken for granted: and I wish to be addressed as a poor, weak-hearted sinner, needing a Saviour always, every moment, as much as the lungs want air! Give me Christ or I die! I am perishing with hunger, give me Christ! I am parched up with thirst, give me Christ! I am in doubt about many things, give me Christ!—then shall I have 'wisdom;' he will correct all my mistakes. . . . . I told you, years ago, not to trouble yourself about afflictions, they come fast enough; if God sees it best for you to be without them, rejoice and praise him!

"I fear the slave trade will be renewed at the South. I am anti-slavery to the back-bone; but I do not sympathize with the extreme abolitionists! In one of the light works of Harry Lorrequer there is the sentence, '"They are poor-spirited creatures," said one, "they won't vote!" "Not they," said another; "they are as decent boys as any we have; they are willing *to wreck the town* for fifty shillings' worth of spirits!"'

"John Bull's boats have been playing the mischief with our commerce. John had better haul in his horns; he has neither the time nor the money to fight, this side of the Atlantic. Besides, young Bull is getting quite too large for old Bull to manage. But I suppose it will end in a kind of Pickwickian explanation. What a happiness that we have this safety valve!

"I am thinking often of the pleasure you will have in the company of Gen. and Mrs. T——n. They are delightful anywhere, but quite too much for *you* in London; you are so afraid of prosperity!

"June, the 'belle' of the whole twelve moons, is now smiling sweetly upon us; her thirty days seem like thirty minutes! She comes with flowers and fruits, and is received with open doors and windows and is hailed by hospitalities, by warm suns, and clear heavens, and long days. I love June. I breathe the external air day and night. I get up at 4 A. M., read and pray, breakfast, and get on my horse at 5½ A. M, and away I ride, over the hills and far away. Then I come back to bless my household at 7 A. M. But there is a better land than even this, and a better month than June, and a better *sun* than ours, and better fruits, and all without sin or suffering, or fear of any. 'Set your house in order, for thou shalt die and not live,' said God to good King Hezekiah. Who does not require this change? Whose house is in *order?* Who is quite ready to receive the Master? We have a house, perhaps we have it furnished, but it is out of order to die; it is only in order to live. Set it in order then. Put things to rights, wash and sweep the house, still the unnecessary noise, and quiet the carking cares! *Take down the map of the new place and study that.* Talk about

Christ's coming and your going. Think what you will say when he comes and knocks at the door. Oh, that we were all wise; that we understood this, and would consider how frail we are! Love to my dear friend (your husband), a kiss to Charlie, and keep for yourself the affection of a father, for a kind of child.

"Two sheets, from your busy friend, B. C. C."

In this month, a very kind parishioner had sent her pastor an offering from her garden in Myrtle Avenue, and the following was his reply:

TO MRS. K——.

"St. Ann's Rectory, *June* 23, 1858.

"Dear Friend—I return you many thanks for your rich and sweet bouquet. As I look at it, it represents to my mind your own dear family group, all growing in the garden of the Lord, and, to my eyes, all blossoming under the beams of the Sun of righteousness. There is moral beauty, and variety, and harmony in the household of faith. I cannot but hope that such a 'bunch' of flowers is as grateful to God as these perishing ones are to the receiver. Commending the 'Rose of Sharon' to you all,

"I am, in love and truth, your pastor, B. C. Cutler."

While at Saratoga, in July, he wrote an interesting letter to a parishioner in Europe, from which we make an extract:

. . . . "The fashionables come here to saline the inner man not until after the 20th, and they leave by the 10th of August for the sea shore to salt the outer man. But with all this care they are not a long-lived race; they lose by night what they gain by day, and whatever invigoration their system receives, their supplies are so abundant and expensive to digestion that the account is balanced at the close of the visit. Still, it is hard to realize that it is not a great blessing to be rich; there is the carriage to drive in, there is the bowing of the host and hostess, there is the best room in the house, and the best coat in the town; all this is nice, a sweet morsel to roll under the tongue! But has the humble Christian no bright side to his character? He has *the peace of God;* rest of soul on Christ; a hope of heaven; a sense of the favor of God; an 'inheritance, incorruptible, undefiled, that fadeth not away—

'Riches above what earth can grant
And lasting as the mind.'

"A poor Christian fears God, and in general, a rich man does not; and I think the great distinction is, between them that fear God and them that fear him not. The 'revival' had passed through Saratoga before we arrived, and all we can perceive of its effects is *quietness* It was a blessed visitation, and one which will leave its savor behind it." . . . . .

How constantly Dr. Cutler suffered, hardly any one outside of the family circle could realize. The records of his journal show how keenly he felt "the thorn in the flesh:"

"*Aug.*, 1858.—I am more delicate in body, and more susceptible to cold than ever. I am growing old and inactive. I feel the decay of fervor in public prayer. I am easily fatigued, and wearied, and out of patience. God knows that for more than forty years I have been wearied and humbled with a weak and sickly body. *I am, still.* I pray that he may sanctify my infirmities and crosses. I have discontinued set self-examinations, for after proceeding in the same way for forty years, I found myself no better, but rather worse, and like the woman in Scripture, I tried to touch the hem of Christ's garment. On the whole, however, I prefer to go back to my old practice of plain and simple self-examination; not to find any good in my wicked heart, but to find out what it really is, to humble myself on account of it, and to apply more earnestly to the blood of Christ, which taketh away the sin of the world.

"I can perceive in myself the infirmities of age. The old are impatient, irritable, suspicious, timid and torpid. These infirmities I must watch against. Jesus Christ is my only refuge from my sins and myself. In him may my righteousness be found. I feel the dull, cold effect of *age* on my heart! What a prayer, what a hymn is that:

'Come, Holy Spirit, Heavenly Dove!'

In August, a venerable member of St. Ann's died, aged ninety-two years. As a shock of corn fully ripe, she was gathered into the heavenly garner; and the many branches of a large, wealthy and influential family, of which she was the respected and beloved head, were called to mourn with sincere sorrow. Her pastor and the church felt the loss hardly less deeply. For sixty-six years she had been a communicant of the ancient parish, and was identified with much of its past history. At the open grave of Mrs. Sarah Cornell, the faithful pastor addressed the children and the children's children, and a multitude of descendants, in an earnest appeal, beseeching them, in expressive terms, to lift up their hearts to God, through the great Mediator, and say, as they bid adieu to the precious remains, "Farewell, oh, my mother! thy people shall be my people, and thy God, my God!"

His annual "shipwreck thanksgiving," as he termed it, was celebrated on the 12th of November. Some of his vestrymen and other friends were present, among whom were Mrs. Maxwell (a fellow-passenger), Mr. and Mrs. Harper, and Capt. William L. Hudson, United States Navy. It was fifteen years since the event, and Dr. Cutler took for his subject of remark on this occasion, the reprieve of King Hezekiah, when his lease of life was extended for the same period of time.

Among the changes in Dr. Cutler's family circle, none gave him more pleasure than the advancement of his beloved nephew, from St. John's to the incumbency of Trinity Church, Montreal. Thus he writes:

TO THE REV. CANON BANCROFT.

"BROOKLYN, *November* 2, 1858.

"MY DEAR CHARLES— . . . . I hear with much satisfaction of your success. I suppose you do not expect to please *the world.* I hope you do not try to do it. You may be counted a 'babbler;' so was St. Paul! Let the world hate you, so much the more will Christ love you. But don't let it despise you! Let it feel the weight of your arm, and let it be awed by your holy and blameless conversation. . . . . I have written my sermon for next Sunday.

It is an open and downright defence of dealing with men as sinners, and opening to them *the way*—the philosophy, the nature of salvation; not merely proclaiming salvation itself, or the possibility of salvation, but the way, the new way, the living way, the straight way, the narrow way, viz., justification by faith alone. . . . . .

"Your affectionate uncle, B. C. CUTLER."

Christian experience, in some of its most holy and lovely phases, was pre-eminent in Dr. Cutler's religious life and correspondence. His life was an Emmaus-like journey, walking with Jesus all the way, and his heart often burned within him as he talked with him by the way. In his letters to other Christians, also, we see the holy flame of love to Christ kindling in his heart and moving his pen, diffusing a glow and warmth of expression over all his correspondence which could not fail to stimulate the reader to admire, to appreciate, and, if possible, to imitate a seraphic piety like his.

The inmates of the vicarage at "Fremington," in Devonshire, hailed with delight the letters which occasionally found their way from St. Ann's Rectory, over the bosom of the Atlantic, to the inner shrine of their retired home. How cheering must such a letter as this have been, at this time, to the sorrowing widow of Dr. Cutler's friend, the Rev. W. C. Hill:

"BROOKLYN, N. Y., *December* 17, 1858.

"DEAR CHRISTIAN SISTER AND FRIEND— . . . . I notice in your last letter you speak of Queen Elizabeth and the Reformation. I enter fully into the rejoicings of the 17th of November. My confidence in the gospel increases continually, and my expectation is that we shall be compelled to contend earnestly for it. Human depravity and Protestantism are enduring antagonists! True Christians everywhere, and at all times, must protest, and go on protesting to the end. Why, I protest against the decisions, at least the desires, of my own heart, daily. I am protesting against the errors, new and old, of my own church, and my soul is vexed with every day's report of this sinful world. My soul is a stranger and a pilgrim. I feel it fully at this moment. My comfort is, that the Lord reigns. My text for my Christmas sermon is, '*The government shall be on his shoulder.*'

"In Oriental countries an immense key was laid over the shoulder of him that had the power of life and death; and my rejoicing is that, while various locks confine men and inclose them in political apartments from each other, Christ has a key that opens them all; and to change the figure, but not the word, his hands cover all the keys of earth's great instrument of human governments, and play a '*gloria in excelsis*' in spite of all their opposition. Dear sister, it is written unto us, a child is born—a child in our old age—a son to support and defend us is given. And what a child! and what a son!

'Jesus shall reign, where 'er the sun
Does his successive journeys run.'

Jesus holds the key of the grave. He openeth, and no man shutteth; he shutteth, and no man openeth. I am continually preaching *Him!* I wish I could say, breathing more and more of his Spirit, and following more and more his example.

"Surrounded, as I am, with Christians, I find few who talk freely of Jesus. We have lectures and public prayer-meetings, in which clergymen and laymen lecture, and exhort and preach of Christ; but sitting down to have some pleasant discourse on the preciousness of the Saviour's love is mournfully rare in my circle. I went last evening to a tea-party, where nearly all were Christians. I had some religious exercises, but all the rest was chit-chat about horses running away, children having whooping-cough, the health of neighbors, the evil of smoking cigars, etc.! Alas! if our hearts were full of the love of Christ, would not our tongues speak? Could we keep a bottle of musk or of otto of roses in our pockets and not betray the secret? I am very lively, and tell a good many anecdotes, and love cheerful society; but I love above all fragrance and all sociability, heartfelt converse about Christ. . . . . O Lord Jesus, comfort my sister and friend by night and by day, in life; and when bodily life is giving way to eternal life, be thou the strength of her heart and her portion for ever!

"Most affectionately, your brother in Christ,

B. C. CUTLER."

At Christmas, one of the youthful members of his flock sent to Dr. Cutler a token of regard made by her own hand; the reply was just such a one as an appreciative pastor would make to an appreciative parishioner.

TO MISS K——.

"*December* 27, 1858.

"When I look upon your beautiful work, and think how many stitches you have taken, I feel as if I ought not to expect such attention. But I look upon the offering as made to the servant of the Lord Jesus Christ, and as such, I am both happy and thankful to receive it. In the path of professional duty, where all 'the world' is really in opposition to your work, there is, and must be, many a thorn. But in 'God's world,' there is generally something to counterbalance the pain. It is a thorn with roses, and it is suffering with a refreshing odor to help you bear it. Nothing is more refreshing than the friendship of his flock to a shepherd. May we all meet, dear L——, on Mount Zion, and sing the song of Moses and the Lamb. Affectionately, your pastor, B. C. CUTLER."

Much in the same strain were the touching expressions of regard to another loved parishioner, who failed not to send her customary annual remembrance of a *watch-guard* of silken cord:

"DEAR R—— —You still fulfill your promise in keeping the chain that *ties me to time* strong and new! Still, there is somewhat mournful in its sable color. But what can a minister's life be but dark and anxious? His whole happiness comes from looking to the tie that binds him to eternity; that is golden and bright, and his Saviour has promised that that shall never break! Oh, the happiness of an assured hope! It is an anchor of the soul, both sure and steadfast! With best wishes and prayers, I am your obliged and affectionate pastor, B. C. CUTLER."

To a valued friend at Irvington (a former Sunday-school Superintendent at St. Ann's), whose whole family were members of the church, Dr. Cutler wrote, ere the year closed:

"MY DEAR FRIEND— . . . . What a favor has God granted you in your family! a whole household in the ark, and this in the midst of riches! Wonder of wonders! . . . . We thank you for your valuable present. On Christmas Day, several new communicants united with us. Oh that my labors may be blest! I have no children in my own house, but oh, that I may have many in God's house, to rise up and call me blessed! I note what you say of your children and St. Ann's. They certainly got no harm there, but I must attribute all instrumentality to their parents.

"Such a sight as our Sunday-school now makes would rouse the heart and the hands of any but a dead pastor! Do come and spend Wednesday with us, and see our celebration. It is a temple which you had a great hand in building. Adieu! with love to all. From your obliged friend, B. C. CUTLER."

In January, 1859, his cousin, the Rev. Benjamin C. Cutler Parker, A. M., Chaplain of the Protestant Episcopal Church Missionary Society for Seamen in New York, was removed by the hand of death.

Dr. Cutler delivered a suitable funeral discourse, which was repeated in St. George's Chapel, and in the Church of the Ascension, New York, and afterward printed at the request of the Seamen's Society.

The first breach was now made in the circle of the three fast friends, who from boyhood had known and loved each other. The strongest was taken hence, while the youngest (Dr. Cutler) and the oldest (Dr. Edson, of Lowell) remained. Dr. Cutler's record in his diary reads thus:

"*Jan.* 30, 1859.--How I want to be alone! What thoughts crowd upon me; my reverend friend and brother is no more! I have great searchings of heart. Here is my old companion gone, and it gives me a feeling of solemnity and awe!"

Again:

"*Feb.* 13.—My friend and parishioner, Mrs. W. B. C——, died on the 10th. I have felt her loss very much; another valued parishioner, Mrs. P——, is very ill."

These losses of friends only quickened Dr. Cutler in the path of duty. He diligently improved the hours of the day of life, knowing that "the night cometh, when no man can work. Truly, he was "steadfast, always abounding in the work of the Lord."

He once met with a young lad from England who was

seeking some situation in business life. He took him into his household and gave him a home at this particular juncture, which, as it afterward proved, was of incalculable advantage to him, in a spiritual point of view; the youth had returned to England, and was now about to enter the ministry in the church of his ancestors. This kindness to a stranger, in a strange land, was like "bread cast upon the waters," and after many days it yielded a rich return. The father of the youth, rejoicing in the influences which, through Dr. Cutler's instrumentality had been brought to bear upon his beloved child, thus wrote to Dr. Cutler:

"DEAL, ENGLAND, *February* 28, 1859.

. . . . "Allow me, my dear sir, to thank you from my heart for all your kindness to him, for which he is truly grateful. He often very often, speaks of it, and any thing Dr. Cutler did must be right; he is very strong on the subject of America—perhaps after awhile he will think better of us Britishers. You have been, indeed, a kind friend to him, and I trust that the gracious Lord, who ever regards his waiting people, will bless you, and make you a blessing. We seem to want here such an outpouring of the Holy Spirit as has been vouchsafed to you. . . . .

"Yours thankfully, in the best of bonds, H. H. D——."

In March, Dr. Cutler and his wife went to Irvington to spend a few days at the country-seat of a much esteemed friend. This was one of the places Dr. Cutler loved to visit, where hospitality, congeniality and ardent piety, combined to make it a most delightful resting-place to the Christian pilgrim journeying Zionward. Here he was truly refreshed in body and soul, and none had a stronger hold upon his heart (though there were a few, equally beloved) than the friends here, who so often loved to welcome him to their mansion on the banks of the Hudson. Of these friends he writes in his journal:

"*March* 21, 1859.—I know of no man in greater prosperity, in this world: every member of his family a communicant, too! Perfect health and great success; a more unlimited influence at forty years of age I have rarely seen. Mr. —— seems aware of it, and is generous indeed. O God, I pray thee to keep him and his! Make them to excel in virtue, as thou hast made them to exceed in prosperity!"

Before the summer came, Dr. Cutler was pleased to welcome home again his sister and her husband and daughter, who arrived from San Francisco, where many of the family had taken up their residence, and on the 14th of June, he united his beloved niece in holy matrimony to her cousin Samuel W. Francis, M. D.

The tie which bound Dr. Cutler to all his family connections was unusually strong, and he used this as a lever to advance (if possible) their spiritual interests. To his attached brother-in-law, Dr. J. W. Francis, he thus wrote:

"*July* 7, 1859.

"MY DEAR DOCTOR—I read with more than common interest your excellent remarks at the Typographical Society's rooms. It seems as if age had ripened and rendered more prolific your mental resources. I suppose you are now considered 'the sage of Bond Street,' and that your present abode will be sought after and visited by curious travellers when your sons, with gray hairs and well-earned reputations, will possess, protect and point out the precious relics! But a pin for all this, compared with that reputation which you will yet enjoy, I trust, of honoring God, and of being honored by him, as an open believer, supporter and defender of the faith of his only-begotten Son. This would be a fame as enduring as the sun, and indeed would shine with greater brilliancy than the sun ever did, millions of years after the sun and the moon shall be no more. Yours, affectionately, B. C. CUTLER."

His heart beat warmly also toward his parishioners, in every varying circumstance of their lives. One of them was at this time threatened with blindness, and to her husband he wrote:

"MY DEAR FRIEND—We were all made glad by the receipt of your note just before dinner. I rejoice with you and Mrs. F—— at the termination of the experiment . . . . The particulars you entered into (which always form the cream of a letter), were as interesting to us as to you, and we shall keep this object of your and our solicitude before our minds, and hope soon to hear the joyful news of a recovered vision. It will be almost like Noah coming out of the ark. . . . . . Believe me interested in your welfare and happiness. This is a cold world and a selfish one, and its exterior may chill you, but there is an *interior* as well as an exterior, and that may be of a different temperament! It is said the farther you dig down in the earth, the greater the *heat* becomes!

"Most affectionately, your pastor, B. C. CUTLER."

Besides family relatives and endeared parishioners, many other friends shared his affection, and often gathered about his table. One cherished friend spent many weeks at the rectory during this season, and with the warm benedictions of this man of God, he bade adieu to his native shores and went to a foreign land to recruit his health. As the vessel passed down the harbor, a steamer passed her, coming into port, having on board another friend, who in a few hours received the heartfelt greetings of the rector's household, after her long absence. Thus was Dr. Cutler ever welcoming to his heart every congenial spirit, and beneath his roof they often enjoyed together foretastes of what we must believe is "the communion of saints above!"

As years increased, Dr. Cutler, while still loving earthly friends, seemed to give his supreme and strongest affection to God. His sister was now (in August) preparing to return to San Francisco, after the marriage of her only daughter. Though absent from New York, Dr. Cutler could not allow her to depart without a farewell line which he penned from

"SARATOGA, *August* 2, 1859.

"MY BELOVED SISTER—. . . . . I am truly thankful to have seen you, and to have enjoyed the great event which unites by a new and sacred cord, what God had even before joined together, two loving families. . . . . What can I say 'more,' except what I have said an hundred times?—God is the source of all happiness. 'Every good gift and every perfect gift is from above and cometh down from the Father of lights;' that God, who formed the almost invisible *insect*, and provided for all its wants, who originated the most delicate of all the perfume the garden yields, and made it to please both rational and irrational creatures, whether they could return gratitude or not; that God, who knows every thing; that God, through Jesus Christ his Son, is to a Christian, *all in all!* Oh that we loved him with all our hearts! What then could exceed our happiness?

"Life with me is drawing to a close, and God appears greater than ever, and is drawing nearer. God is every thing! My motto is, I and all I have done are nothing, but God in Christ is all in all! Forty years I have deliberately and steadily, though feebly and unworthily labored to restore a rebellious race to him as their rightful sovereign. I feel that my reward is sure! I am every year requiring less and less in quantity of what this world can afford. . . . God bless you! prays

"Your affectionate brother, B. C. CUTLER."

Let us turn to his journal:

"*Oct.* 9, 1859.—I lost much of consolation to-day by my own want of firmness. Obedience is sweet and sin is bitter. My mind was in a serious frame, and I felt the need of a Saviour; the one I preached. Indeed, I am a lost soul without Jesus."

"*Nov.* 6.—Distressed at the absence of the officers of the church from their places. But any thing to drive me to think of God, my Almighty friend, whose presence is better than any or all men. It is better to trust in the *Lord*, than to put any confidence in *man!* I came out of the world to serve the Lord Jesus Christ, and him I try to serve, and to him I look for comfort."

"*Nov*. 10.—Mrs. Pierrepont died, aged seventy-five. A great loss!"

We see how in every phase and circumstance of life, even in the most trivial events, he made constant reference to God. He encouraged others to do the same, assuring them that earth's chief happiness could be found only in him.

Truly comforting to one of his parishioners in a time of trial was the following note:

TO MRS. K——L.

"Many thanks, my dear sister in Christ, for your flowers and for your note. The flowers were beautiful to the eye and are the greatest ornament to our house; but the note was more fragrant, in Christian faith and submission. 'All things will work together for good to them that love God.' If you have not your portion in this world, so much more will you have in the next; and should you be afflicted ever so much, you would still be at a great distance behind him who was '*made perfect through suffering!*' Be ever 'looking unto Jesus, the author and finisher of your faith. He is able to do exceeding abundantly above all you can ask or think,' both for you and yours; both for time and eternity. To him be glory for ever and ever!

"Affectionately yours, B. C. CUTLER."

Ever the consoler of the afflicted, Dr. Cutler wrote to a cousin in Boston, who had just met with a severe loss in the death of her husband:

TO MRS. T. W. PHILLIPS.

"BROOKLYN, *November* 13, 1859.

"MY DEAR COUSIN— . . . . Your affliction is certainly very great and very hard to bear. But is there any thing too hard for the Lord? 'Through Christ, who strengtheneth me, I can do all things,' says St. Paul; and why cannot you say so? Your venerated mother, when *a widow*, no doubt said so. I was with her at the time, and know how wonderfully she was supported under her accumulated trials. She was, indeed, a wonder unto many. Many a prayer did she offer for you, and now, I hope, they will be answered. You have good health, she had ill health. You have two fine sons who may be the props of your age. You have travelled and seen the world, and now you can live quietly among your once loved and loving circle in friendship, and in the cultivation of that 'holiness without which no man can see the Lord.'

"I hear you have quite an eloquent preacher at St. Paul's, and I hope you will find great comfort in hearing him. Mrs. Frances Parker would be a most valuable visitor for you, if she can go out. She has tasted of the cup that you have tasted, and knows how to speak a word to them that are weary. May our gracious Saviour be near to comfort you, and may you yet have grace to say, 'He doeth all things well.'

"Affectionately yours, B. C. CUTLER."

No pastor ever received more constant and kind attentions from his people than Dr. Cutler. The offerings this year were more abundant than usual, and while he was grateful to all these devoted friends, he never failed to recognize the hand of his Heavenly Father in the least event that made his heart glad. A beautiful and appropriate remembrance from a devotedly attached parishioner in Pierrepont Street, elicited the following reply:

TO MISS C——L.

"*December* 1, 1859.

"MY DEAR FRIEND— . . . . I cannot refrain from repeating my grateful acknowledgments in a more formal manner. God has placed the ministry of his Son on the best footing. The clergy are to be dependent upon the laity for support, and the laity on the clergy for the ordinances of religion. The first arrangement is intended to humble pride, and the last to increase reverence for things sacred. Whenever either of these conditions are changed, it is for the worse. It is good for 'us of the altar' to depend upon the people, to be stripped of this world's goods, and to be 'considered highly' only for Christ our Master's sake. In ourselves, alas! we are sinners, and often deserve to take the very lowest place in God's house, perhaps not to be there at all! It is good also for the laity to express their gratitude to the Master by acts of kindness to his servants. It is all right! God leads all his servants 'by the right way.' Whenever we look at that beautiful covering for our social board, we shall think of the friend who spread it over it, and took such delight in making us happy.

"Affectionately, your pastor, B. C. CUTLER."

What an interesting review of his past life is given in a letter written, toward the close of this year, to a friend in England, whom he had visited in 1843:

TO MRS. W. C. HILL.

"*December* 13, 1859.

"MY DEAR SISTER IN CHRIST—Your letter and the almanac came safely to hand, and I sent your inclosed letter to Mrs. Parker. . . . . My family, consisting only of Mrs. Cutler and her elder sister, are well. I have labored now for sixteen years since I saw you, and am better able to labor to-day than when I saw you. I am thankful to God, though overwhelmed with my unworthiness. . . I am now just about entering on my sixty-third year. Pray that I may be prepared for glory. Forty-two years ago I cut the cord (or God did) that tied me to a vain and ungodly world, gave up secular business and secular wealth, and gave myself to Jesus Christ to save souls. I believed that he *could* repay me for any sacrifices I made; I believed that he *would* repay me. I believe that he keeps account of every thing, whoever else '*forgets*.' God is not unrighteous to forget our work; not that I *deserve any thing* but wrath! But he promised; I accepted, and treasured up his promises. Exceeding great and precious they are. I will send you by this mail a description of our inheritance in a tract." . . . .

The tract, to which reference is made above, was a special favorite with Dr. Cutler. It was entitled "The Christian's Inheritance," and was very often distributed by him among his friends. How often have we heard him read it aloud to others, and then descant in glowing terms upon the blessedness of the saints in heaven! Those glorious realities are now his; and while we are amid shadows here, and are enabled to say of him, with the Shunamite of old, "It is well," we long to follow his faith up to the land of vision and of bliss!

With the new year came a new assistant to St. Ann's, the Rev. A. M. Wylie; a man vigorous in mind and body, who delighted, as did all Dr. Cutler's assistants, to hold up the hands of the rector. In a letter to the Rev. W. W. Sever, his former excellent assistant, Dr. Cutler thus alludes to his associates: "Assistant No. 11 is liked. He throws all his power into the composition of his sermons and their delivery. He seems to have visited all the gardens of classical learning, and to have culled a good many bright thoughts, as No. 10 seemed to have visited all the picture-galleries of the world and treated us with illustrations by the hundred. So we go; what one has, another has not—all for the edifying of the body of Christ."

The people of St. Ann's have always treated their assistant ministers with true kindness and regard, while both parties invariably loved to do honor to their chief pastor who was set over them in the Lord.

On the anniversary of the rector's birthday in 1860, a dear parishioner, who had been often in "the furnace of trial," sent to him some original verses which gave him much pleasure. Expressive as they are, we transcribe them, together with his reply, below:

To Our Pastor.

Another year! another year!
  The day we celebrate has come;
Time waves his passing pinions here,
  And points to nearer views of home.

How often, by the Spirit's power,
  Hath thy o'erflowing heart in prayer
Asked grace for us in trial's hour,
  So that not one be missing there.

We thank thee! Thou hast led the flock
  Through soft green valleys up to heaven;
And oft, beneath the sheltering Rock,
  Drink to the weary ones hath given!

And some are lost in sorrow's night,
  Crushed down and stayed with heavy hand,
While thy firm foot has reached the height
  That overlooks the promised land.

Does thy quick eye discern the souls
  That won our heart's devotion there?
Have they escaped the tide that rolls
  For ever on, in black despair?

Silent! all, all is mystery!
To do, and bear our Father's will,
Thou to the Cross hast bid us flee,
And every warring pulse is still.

Pastor! for love, that Time endears,
We'll weave fresh chaplets for thy brow;
Till Time is lost in countless years
And Love Divine, thy crown bestow.

REPLY—TO MRS. F——.

"St. Ann's Rectory, *February* 14, 1860.

"Many thanks, my dear friend, for your birthday poem. It brings a crowd of thoughts to my mind. First, in order, is my own unworthiness of any such notice, and next, your persevering regard, and your almost unparalleled afflictions—the loss of children, the loss of health, and the loss of sight.

"I preached a sermon, February 5, on the text, 'The Captain of our salvation made perfect through suffering.' I have not heard that it did my people any good, but I am sure it did the preacher! I am thinking of myself as a soldier whose business it is to fight, and to continue to fight to the end. Not to 'dream that the way is smooth;' not to hope 'that the thorns will be roses.' But, putting on the whole armor of God, to stand! nay, to fight the good fight of faith! If God made his son perfect through suffering, let *us* not repine.

'The path of sorrow and that path alone
Leads to the world where sorrow is unknown.'

"With love to Mr. F——; your affectionate pastor,

"B. C. Cutler."

So much parish work and outside labor, in connection with various religious and benevolent societies, absorbed nearly all his waking hours, and we find every record in his journal, during the latter years of his life, very brief:

"*May* 13.—My assistant has gone to Bridgeport, and I have heard the Rev. L. W. Bancroft preach on the texts, 'We who believe do enter into rest,' and 'Behold I stand at the door and knock;' good sermons and true—short and impressive."

"*June* 3.—A glorious Sunday, and I have much for which to thank God. I am able to write, preach and visit. I have a regular appetite, sleep well, and can take horseback exercise. I have a large charge, and a strong and able curate to assist me; a boundless field of usefulness—boundless as the globe, lasting as eternity. Parish, pulpit, press, religious and secular, tract and missionary fields wide open. Glory to God! To-day I have given up my pulpit to two young friends, Rev. R. B. P—— and Rev. S. B. Dalrymple. It may be a day of rest—a breathing spell. May the Lord be with me!"

The youthful clergyman (Rev. S. B. Dalrymple) referred to above, was one of the most promising ministers ever known in our church; after a short but blessed career, in which time he won many souls to Christ, he was called home to the presence of Jesus, whom he had here so faithfully and lovingly served, surviving Dr. Cutler only a few months.

It was affecting, indeed, toward the close of their lives to see, how eagerly they both, the youthful champion of the Cross, and the more advanced soldier of Christ, looked forward with joyful anticipations to their heavenly rest, giving blessed evidence of the strength of their faith. Diversities of gifts they had, indeed, but the same *spirit*.

Under date of June 17, 1860, we find this record in Dr. Cutler's journal:

"'My rest is in heaven, my rest is not here,
Then why should I tremble when trials are near?
Be hushed my sad spirit, the worst that can come
But shortens the journey and hastens thee home.

"'With a scrip on my back, and a staff in my hand,
I march on in haste, through an enemy's land,

The road may be rough, though it cannot be long,
So I'll smooth it with hope, and cheer it with song.'

"'So *I'll* smooth it.'"

September 13, 1860, was a day of happy memories to Dr. Cutler, for it witnessed the consecration of the new stone edifice, erected by the parish of Christ Church, Quincy, Mass., and another link was added to the chain of associations which connected him with this ancient and now thriving parish.

The revolutions of time conducted his footsteps in the evening of his pilgrimage to the same place where, in the morning of life, he first trod the hallowed courts of the Lord as the priest of the Most High, and here, on this very spot, he preached the consecration sermon. As his friend, Mr. Brackett, declared, his efforts here had "always been gratefully prized," and to see his face again, and hear his well-known voice, was gratifying indeed. It was true, there were many changes among the people, and "the good pastor" had himself changed in appearance; the rosy hue of youth had faded from his face; the stout frame had become attenuated through sickness and age; but the same benign expression, the same glow of holy love, illumined his countenance and nerved his spirit, and when he spoke of Jesus and his righteousness, all could see that an *unchanged heart* beat warmly within that earthly tabernacle.

It was soon to be freed from its imprisonment here below, and the tabernacle of flesh dissolved, but, to the very end, Christ and his cause and his people were dear to his heart.

Let us watch his onward course, as life was drawing to its close. The current of all his affections was strongly set toward God and was deepening and expanding, catching from above the loveliest tints, till mortals could behold it no longer, and the imperfections of earth gave way to the clearness and fullness of heaven.

To a Christian friend across the Atlantic, in whom he took much interest, Dr. Cutler wrote, about this time:

"*September* 18, 1860.

. . . . "I am still a poor, sinful, weak mortal, but I keep drawing near to my Saviour; trying to be lost in him; trying to look on him as a great rock, and to crawl into the cleft of that rock and to hide myself in him. Sweet is the rest in Christ, so he giveth his beloved sleep! I cast my burden on the Lord, day by day; heart burden, sin burden, body burden—life, death, and ministerial burdens—on the Lord Jesus; not merely lay them down and take them back again, but cast them away! Oh for more of the knowledge and love of Christ!

"We have just published in our American Tract Society, the life of R. Knill, which is sweet and precious. I see something of Devonshire in it, and many references I understand. My dear wife sends love, and my afflicted cousin, a double portion.

"P. S.—Monday next is the anniversary of the Fulton Street Prayer-Meeting. I have been requested to preside on the occasion. Why, I know not, except that I approve of these meetings and enjoy them. I am sorry they did not select a more fit man; but a more *willing* one, who is as unworthy as I am, they could not find. I shall open with that hymn of Montgomery's on prayer, 'The path of prayer thyself hast trod.' Adieu!

"Most affectionately, yours in Christ, B. C. CUTLER."

The Fulton Street noon-day prayer-meeting was a source of delight to Dr. Cutler. Here, with Christians of every name, he loved to meet; his catholic spirit did not weaken his loyalty to his own branch of Christ's Church, but only expanded his heart, so that he could *act* on the expression of the apostle, "Grace be with all them that love our Lord Jesus Christ in sincerity." Wherever he saw the image of his Divine Master he cherished it, under all circumstances and in every condition, and no frigid rules of mere ecclesiastical routine could fetter his spirit, or bind down his soul. He had preferences without prejudices, and "the communion of saints" was to him a living, tangible reality!

The touch-stone of all his friendships was a personal interest in a Divine Saviour!

With what true simplicity and earnestness did he counsel others to cleave to Christ? A beautiful instance of this is found in his letter to a young parishioner, who had gone to the Seminary at Alexandria to prepare for "holy orders:"

"*October* 13, 1860.

"MY DEAR FRIEND— . . . . I take up my pen to exhort you to continue in the faith. Take care of your personal interest in Christ. Live by rule, and make your rules in the fear and love of God. I repeat it, your great business at the Seminary is the catholicon of *piety!* If you should be pious and live near to God, you will study, as a matter of course. Every thing around you will cry, Study, study, study! Let my voice come from home to you at all times; be pious, be devout, be zealous, be gentle! I am glad you enjoy the Professor's meetings, I have often thought I should like to attend one.

"There is a great deal of good done in an indirect way, and a great deal done in an easy and familiar way. Said a late writer to his sister (an authoress): 'You would be more really *instructive*, if it were not for your *determination to instruct!*'"

"Live much, dear Thomas, between the two lids of the Bible; you will not lose your reward!

"Your friend and pastor, B. C. CUTLER."

On the anniversary of his wedding-day, Dr. Cutler made this entry in his journal:

"*Oct.* 30, 1860.—This day, thirty-eight years ago, I was married to Miss H. B——, in Christ Church, Boston, by the Rev. Asa Eaton, and in the evening, I married my dear sister, Louisa Charlotte Cutler, to M. H. McAllister, Esq., of Savannah. The ceremony was performed at Quincy, Mass., at my mother's residence, near Madame Miller's. What mercies have I received and enjoyed! All four of us are living and have been greatly blessed. May we express our gratitude by our lives!"

We find another record of a later date, this year, which

we do not omit, as we wish to present the character of our beloved friend in its true light. If he had no infirmities where should we see the victory of grace? Says Mr. Carus, the biographer of Mr. Simeon, of England, "It is of great importance that the infirmities of eminent servants of God should ever be faithfully recorded, in order that we may learn what trials and conflicts they had to endure, and how they gained power and strength to have victory against the Devil, the world, and the flesh! Thus shall we be the more led to magnify God for his grace bestowed upon them, and at the same time, derive comfort and hope for ourselves, when endeavoring to subdue our own besetting sins."

If religious biography came nearer to the Bible standard, as does the life of Simeon, in a good degree, it would generally be more interesting and much more instructive. The church militant is truly bound together by common feelings, common sympathies, common imperfections and sins, and looks for a perfect pattern only to its great Leader! Its most devoted members, like Dr. Cutler, have often to mourn over inward departures, and are constantly striving to subdue sin, the moral virus of which, will never be utterly destroyed, except with the dissolution of the body.

Thus, our friend found his experience like that of many other of God's holiest servants:

"*Nov.* 19, 1860.—I have given way to impatience and irritation, which I have read of as not uncommon in old age. I am accused of this, and am distressed and humbled. It is true, and I have nothing to say but 'God be merciful to me, a sinner!' Blessed Saviour, I would wash in thy fountain! I pray for thy spirit, and I would keep my eye on thy example. Be thou my ruler and guide!"

Again he writes: "I have much to humble me in my own experience of infirmity and weakness."

Records like these indicate great faithfulness with himself, and yet he sought for more grace, knowing that God giveth grace to the humble.

While, with careful introspection, Dr. Cutler thus searched his own heart, testimony from others often poured in upon him, showing the blessed influences that fell upon all around him. Thus, after the marriage of his assistant and friend, he was surprised by a note (enclosing the fee) which read as follows:

"St. Ann's Rectory, *December* 4, 1860.

"Reverend and Dear Father in Christ—With many sincere thanks and kind remembrances of the social and religious benefits you have conferred upon one who has stood in great need of your example, and who feels deeply grateful to God that in his all-wise providence he has placed me under your influence. Most of all, I thank you for your prayers.

"Your affectionate brother, in Christ, A. M. Wylie."

Christmas of this year came and went, with the usual offerings to the cherished rector of St. Ann's, and as the year closed, Dr. Cutler penned two appropriate epistles, written in his own peculiarly happy style:

TO MRS. H. M——.

"*December* 31, 1860.

"My Dear Friend—Your Christmas present of valuable books, together with your invariable 'guard,' came to hand, and caused much rejoicing at the rectory. . . . . I suppose the custom of making presents at Christmas arose from the best and highest example. God gave us his Son! (See John iii. 16.) Now, if God gave you and me his Son, he *gave* him, not lent him, not showed him, nor only let us handle him for a moment, but *gave him* outright! What a gift, you may say! I have got Christ; he is all mine, my own. I have an atonement for my sin, an advocate with the Father, a perfect righteousness, a sovereign protector, a certain purifier. Indeed, when God gave me Christ, he gave me *all things!* I am rich, unspeakably rich! I count all things but loss for Christ! Draw largely on this gift for grace—for yourself, and for all your household, and for me; and believe me,

"Your affectionate and obliged pastor, B. C. Cutler."

TO T. M——, ESQ.

"I return you many thanks for your generous present, and for the pleasure I enjoyed at the annual banquet at your hospitable mansion. Of such reunions there are not enough; of heartless and fashionable gatherings there are too many. I am convinced that the whole community would be happier and better if there were more true sociability. I hope you were present to see the display of youth and beauty of all kinds at St. Ann's yesterday afternoon. To me it was the happiest possible sight, and I went to rest, with my mind, at least, upon a bed of roses. Our Superintendent and teachers deserve well of their country! There were over seven hundred children in the three schools, and over three hundred dollars was collected for missions. In these little, bright faces, you see the future supporters of St. Ann's Ghurch, and, I trust, *the future sons and daughters of God Almighty!* With kind regards to Mrs. M—— and your family,

"I am, my dear sir, your obliged pastor, B. C. CUTLER."

Dr. Cutler's allusion to his Sunday-school, reminds us of a record in his journal:

"My spirits low to-day, but the sight of the Sunday-school is enough to cheer all hearts. Blessed are the eyes that see such a school!" and, we may add, with perfect propriety, Blessed is the church that has such a pastor: "*O si sic omnes!*"

CHAPTER XV.

MINISTRY AT ST. ANN'S CHURCH—CONCLUDED.

January, 1861, *to August*, 1862.

DR. CUTLER lived just long enough to see his country in the deep waters of trouble. The year 1861 was, indeed, a gloomy one for the United States. All the bitter feelings which sectional pride, jealousy and hatred could stir up, were fully developed in open antagonism between the North and the South. Several States of the Federal Union (led away from their allegiance to the Government by ambitious and unscrupulous politicians) attempted to separate themselves from the other States, thus virtually declaring war against the old flag which they had sworn to protect. The violence of political parties could not be restrained, and the popular fury and blind frenzy of extremists on either side (of anti-slavery and pro-slavery), soon brought the matter to an open issue, and civil war was the result.

In this crisis, Dr. Cutler, while he was conservative in his principles and moderate in the expression of opinion, showed himself a true patriot, and stood by the Government and the Constitution with unflinching loyalty. While gloomy forebodings often filled his heart, he looked up to heaven, saying, "God can help us, and that right early." He wrote a friend: "The American Union is sick unto death; all her physicians may well despair; but the Lord liveth, and blessed be our Rock. I can only lift my eyes upward; if I look around upon the waves, my spirit sinks."

Death, too, at this time entered his circle of clerical friends, and one after another were removed from the land of the living. When the Rev. Dr. Anthon, of St. Mark's, New York, was called away, Dr. Cutler made this entry in his diary: "My valued friend and fellow laborer died January 5th. Alas, alas! the righteous perisheth and no man layeth it to heart, and merciful men are taken away from 'the evil to come;' they enter into rest."

Sorrow in private circles, and the great trial which had befallen the country, elicited the following touching and appropriate note to one of his earliest friends in Massachusetts:

TO THE REV. THEODORE EDSON, D. D.

"DEAR BROTHER—As friend after friend leaves us for another world, our minds turn to the few that remain. Death has been busy among us, and we expected him in our circle. Dr. Francis has been unspeakably low; if he is raised up, it must be by prayer, and not human skill, or by a combination of both.

"But even this has been swallowed up in the sickness of the country, the death of the Union!

"In thinking of John Adams and his co-patriots, these words have been continually on my lips: "*O terque, quaterque beati, qui ante ora parentum, sub altis mœnibus Trojæ contigit oppetere!*" But we are all in God's hands. My text on Christmas Day was, 'King of kings and Lord of lords;' Christ holds the reins after all.

"Let us sing, to the praise and glory of God, the ninety-eighth selection of Psalms, 'To Zion's hill I lift my eyes,' etc.

"My health and strength hold out, and I labor steadily and regularly; but I am kept a good deal '*under glass*.'

"Yours, as ever, B. C. CUTLER."

Amid the strife of such a period, Dr. Cutler's peace-loving spirit was much disturbed. With the poet, he could say,

"My ear is pained,
My soul is sick with every day's report;"

and he gladly sought a place of rest and retirement for a few days, at the house of a former parishioner residing at

Irvington. To the privileges and pleasures of such a Christian home, he made a brief but pertinent allusion in a few lines addressed to another parishioner:

TO T. M——, ESQ.

"MY DEAR FRIEND—I have just returned from a most pleasant visit to our beloved Mr. and Mrs. M——. . . . . . I feel deeply grateful to the memory of your brother for his bequest to our Sunday-school, and will do my best to see its provisions carried out. . . . . I hear you and Mrs. M—— are to pass next Sunday at Mr. M——n's . . . . all I can say is, if you both enjoy as pleasant a visit as we did, you will be abundantly repaid for the journey.

"'Blest is the pious house, where zeal and friendship meet,
Their songs of praise, their mingled vows, make their communion sweet!'

"With Christian love, I remain, your friend and pastor,
B. C. CUTLER."

On the 8th of February, 1861, Dr. Cutler was called to mourn over another breach made in the family circle, by the death of his brother-in-law, John W. Francis, M. D., of New York. Science mourned the loss of one of her most distinguished sons when Dr. Francis was numbered with the dead; for as Dr. Cutler said, in his appropriate address at the funeral (held at St. Thomas' Church, New York), "There was in the departed a remarkable combination of genius and learning, of industry and enthusiasm."

We find an allusion to the sad event in Dr. Cutler's journal:

"*Feb.* 10, 1861.—Here endeth the life on earth of a man of ability, activity, genius, learning, and philanthropy. He was a genial and generous spirit, whose name and memory will go down to posterity as one of the literary lights of this Western world. To the full development of his powers, the extension of his usefulness, and the preservation of his property, his wife contributed most essentially, by giving her whole time and thoughts to him and his interests—a woman of uncommon ability, a rare specimen of disinterested benevolence, and one much beloved by all. She was in the world, but not of the world. I owe her much more than I can ever repay. She has been a mother to her brothers and sisters, and to their children. My prayers for her and her husband and children, have been offered, morning and evening, for more than thirty years!"

Dr. Cutler, thus admonished by the passing away of relatives and friends, and spared himself to scatter around him the golden fruit of his rich and matured experience, devoted himself to his parish duties more earnestly than ever, looking anxiously for the Divine blessing upon his pulpit and parochial labors. Fifty-three persons were admitted to the full privileges of the Church at St. Ann's in the month of March! and great was the delight of their spiritual father, to see blessed evidences of a work of grace all around him.

His assistant left him after Easter, to labor in a distant parish, to the rectorship of which he had been elected, and the vacant place was now supplied by the Rev. Mr. Syle and others, till a new assistant minister was obtained.

Extracts from Dr. Cutler's journal at this time are not without interest, as they relate to matters of importance:

"*April* 21.—The war which we have dreaded has come, and it threatens to be like all civil wars, of the worst kind. I prayed to-day in church, for the country, and for our soldiers."

"*May* 1.—Yesterday, Bishop Onderdonk expired in the seventieth year of his age. A man hardly used by the church. He was suspended from office (and kept so till death) about sixteen years! In 1859 he petitioned the General Convention to remove his suspension, but was refused! How much of gospel mercy, and how much of worldly policy there was in it, I shall not decide. Rev. Dr. Vinton, Dr. Hawkes, Dr. Tyng, and B. C. Cutler, advocated the removal of the suspension in the Diocesan Convention.

"This is one view of the matter; in the light of heaven there may be another. Let me not be high-minded, but fear."

"*May* 19.—The country is more calm, the South have thought better of their plan to take the Capitol. The flag of the Union never stood higher, and never had warmer friends. May God avert a long civil war, but if it must come, may he bless those of us who have adhered to a lawful government, long and well established, and who hate wrong and robbery to and of the African race!"

In June, 1861, Dr. Cutler and his friend who has compiled these memoirs, took a trip to Saratoga, for recreation and rest. Here a week was passed in the most delightful manner; the morning prayers, the morning rides, the intimate and confidential intercourse of each day, are still hallowed in the remembrance of the latter, who had been greeted by him on his return from Europe, a few months previous, with almost a father's love, and could he have known that only one more precious interview was to be enjoyed on earth, still more carefully would he have treasured up his paternal counsels, and listened to his sparkling and edifying conversation.

After a few weeks of continued labor in the summer, Dr. Cutler suffered much from debility and nervousness, the cause of which he could not trace.

Again he went to the Springs to recuperate his system. From thence, he wrote to Mrs. Francis, who, with Judge and Mrs. McAllister, was then at Newport:

"*August* 3, 1861.

"MY DEAREST SISTER—We came here on the 29th ult., and hope to stay a week. On one account I much regretted not going to Newport—that is, your presence there. I am growing *avaricious* of the hours with my dear sisters; I would not lose a moment, life will soon be over. But my system is in such a state, that sea-air would be too strong. At this moment I am suffering from cold, but I hope to recruit. I am thinking much of Mr. McAllister, and praying daily for him; may God restore his health and sanctify his troubles to his good! I have now been three months without a regular assistant, and have not engaged one yet. My health is about as usual, and I have accomplished as much work as usual; still I feel that I am growing old, and in various ways am trying to set my house in order. But while my own strength is growing weaker, my trust in my Saviour is growing stronger. I think I see him everywhere, and in all things. . . . Love to dearest L——, and believe me,

"Your own affectionate brother, B. C. C."

A few days later, he writes in his journal at home: "My soul is dull, and deservedly so. Oh, Lord, help me, and deliver me from all mine enemies, spiritual and temporal! It is good, to feel good for nothing—to be low, with my mouth shut, and to think of nothing but Christ, and him crucified; it is good to be as I am."

Patiently did he wait, till the good hand of the Lord gave him deliverance from all bodily evils, which so often oppressed his spirit; but he was to consign the mortal remains of many chosen friends to their last resting-place, before he should himself go hence.

On the 15th of August, Mr. Joseph Sands, the Junior Warden of St. Ann's Church, was called from the service of his Lord here, into his immediate presence and joy above.

An exemplary, unostentatious Christian, and a consistent and devoted member of St. Ann's, was thus called away; a communicant for thirty years; a vestryman for twenty-five years, and for the last eight, a warden. For a long term of years he had lived a "life of faith, upon the Son of God," and was an Israelite indeed, in whom there was no guile! Dr. Cutler keenly felt the loss of such a man, and yet, there was a peace and serenity about his latter end, that tinged the deepest sorrow with chastened joy. How truly did Dr. Cutler say, at the funeral service:

"The sweet remembrance of the just
Shall flourish when he sleeps in dust;
His hands, while they his alms bestowed,
His glorious future harvest sowed;
Whence, he shall reap wealth, fame, renown,
A temporal and eternal crown!"

"This church has met with a loss which cannot easily be supplied. In this age, when the dividing line between the world and religion is becoming less and less defined; when, too, you can with difficulty discover truth from error, it is a great loss to the Church when a man dies who can clearly discriminate between the precious and the vile, between the pure Gospel of Christ, and one of its many miserable adulterations. . . . . Oh! with what interest have I, for years upon years, seen him enter and take his seat in the sanctuary! What devotion was evident in his manner! What attention did he pay to God's word! Whoever was in this place, proclaiming the truth as it is in Jesus, he was sure to be fed, as with marrow and with fatness! Would you know the secret of his success in the Divine life? *His Sabbaths were well kept, his Bible well read, his prayers unceasing, and his charity undying!* These, like the rivers which watered the Garden of Eden, four branches from one great river of God's grace—these were the means that ripened him for glory!"

We committed the earthly remains of Mr. Sands to the grave, in the sure hope of a glorious resurrection at that great day, when "those who sleep in Jesus" will God bring with him.

Not long after this, Dr. Cutler received from a clergyman in England, who had known Mr. Sands in New York in former years, in most intimate business and social relations, a letter, in which allusion is made to this private sorrow, and to the public grief through which our country was passing.

"DURHAM, *September* 30, 1861.

"MY DEAR FRIEND—I was very much obliged to you for sending me your address after Mr. Sands' death. I feel that I have lost an old friend, one highly valued, though I have seen so little of him for many years. I often wish to come and take a look at my surviving friends in America, and you amongst them. If I put it off, a few years longer, the gaps will indeed be many. . . . . How I mourn over the sad state of things on your side. . . . You have made England more conservative than ever, and if you go on fighting for three years longer, we shall want no more slave-grown cotton. How I wish your Northern politicians had erected the anti-slavery flag at the outset! Mrs. H. B. Stowe does not do us justice, when she complains of our want of sympathy. So long as it is merely a domestic quarrel, you can't expect to develop much sympathy; but make it a question of Freedom *versus* Slavery, and you have the hearts of all philanthropists the world over. My own sympathy, however, is not lacking, and all my feelings are with the North. I trust that our gracious God, who makes the wrath of man to praise him, and educes good out of evil, may yet cause this mischievous war, to redound to his glory, and the good of man. But we cannot see how. It is a dark dispensation; and I sympathize especially with your church, dependent as it is on the voluntary support of the people, and which must be fearfully crippled by the present subversion of spiritual interests.

"You will often have to call to mind that central and fundamental truth—the Lord God omnipotent reigneth, and be driven to take refuge under his wing, and lean on his arm for support and comfort, in this day of adversity. . . . .

"Your affectionate friend, G. T. FOX."

About this time, in so hopeless a state were the affairs of the country, that the Chief Executive of the nation appointed a day for special fasting and prayer. The services at St. Ann's, Brooklyn, on this occasion, were of a remarkably interesting character.

In a friendly letter to his cousin, Mrs. B. C. C. Parker (then residing at Newton, Mass.), Dr. Cutler makes allusion to these services, and also gives his views about preaching and other ways of doing good, which must commend themselves to the approval of all.

"ST. ANN'S RECTORY, *September* 27, 1861.

"DEAR FRIEND—We had services yesterday morning, and I preached from Psalm xxxix. 7th and 8th verses. At 3½ P. M. we had divine service, and afterward a prayer-meeting, in which my senior warden prayed, and my oldest superintendent prayed, and also my assistant. I addressed the meeting from Ephesians iii. 8. I can but hope that the prayers offered up by so many Christians as were collected together in the United States will be heard. We are all much as usual. . . . . I met Rev. Mr. H——, of the Seamen's Chapel, last evening. He is an extraordinarily good preacher—most evangelical and intellectual; but I am afraid he will be drawn away from the mission by foolish people, who tell him his talents are buried there! A city set on a hill *cannot be hid.* If he stays, he will do great good.

"I wish you could get out to hear Mr. Sever; he is as thoroughly an evangelical preacher as I know. I am glad he visits you. I wish I were near enough, for it is in the sick man's room, in the house of mourning, and in free conversation with a Christian friend, that more true religious preaching can be found now-a-days, than in the pulpits! Here, our thoughts are like *fine ladies in full dress*—artificial, oratorical, rhetorical, logical, scientific. We talk about 'subjective and objective religion,' etc., etc. God forgive us! It is not, however, enough to use great plainness of speech—men may be rough and cold too; no, it is tenderly, and solemnly, and sweetly, and in a saintly manner, to dispense gospel truths! It is only THEN, men will wonder 'at the gracious words' which proceed out of our lips! My neighbor has just returned from Boston. I said 'Did you hear any preaching that did your soul good?' 'Oh, yes,' she replied; 'I met a dear, good, pious woman, and I was refreshed by hearing her conversation!' Try to preach in your chamber, dear Frances, and to pray with and for others, and 'for me, that utterance may be given me.' The Lord be with you! Amen!

"Your brother, B. C. CUTLER."

On the 18th of August, 1861, the Rev. L. H. Mills, of New York, a recent graduate of the Theological Seminary of Virginia, preached at St. Ann's, and on the 22d of the same month, Dr. Cutler addressed to him the following note:

"REVEREND AND DEAR SIR—The vestry of St. Ann's Church have, by a unanimous vote, this day, authorized me to call you as assistant minister of this parish for one year. . . . . I am most happy in being the bearer of such a call, and earnestly hope you will accept it. I will do all in my power to make you happy and useful.

"Affectionately, your brother in Christ, B. C. CUTLER."

The call was accepted, and the new assistant entered upon his duties September 1. Thus, Dr. Cutler's mind was entirely relieved of all anxiety on this point, by the timely aid of a valuable and efficient helper.

All parochial affairs being settled to his satisfaction, Dr. Cutler now enjoyed a short period of rest, and, by change of air and scene for awhile, endeavored to recruit his energies of mind and body for another season of continued labor. First he went to Clarence, then to Irvington, and last, but not least, we find him with his two sisters, Mrs. McAllister and Mrs. Francis, at the hospitable abode of the latter. This visit was "very grateful" to his heart, as it was seldom he could meet these beloved kindred together, and the removal of some of those near and dear to him to a distant land, necessarily caused their interviews to be less frequent.

But, let us recur to the journal:

"*Sept.* 22, 1861.—Rev. Mr. G—— was with us last week, and sociability prevailed. . . . . He is a man after my own heart; I would like to live near him."

"*Oct.* 20.—I was unwell on Thursday and Friday, but better on Sunday. Mercy-drops came down through the day to my soul, and I felt cheerful amid the services."

"*Nov.* 19.—Shipwreck anniversary. A week ago was the right day, but I was compelled to defer it. Eighteen years of mercy have dawned on me and faded away, and here I am, and here is my beloved wife, both, monuments of God's mercy! I remember my peril, my prayers, God's answers, and my deliverance; and I set apart this day, and I call my friends and my neighbors together to rejoice with me. O Saviour of the body and of the soul, be with me, be with us all!"

"*Dec.* 25.—A mere mistake about music to-day occurred, to ruffle my mind at the Communion, and, after having labored hard to prepare a useful sermon and struggled with a hoarse cold, all enjoyment was gone. Yet I was thrown directly on my Great High Priest."

But the record of this year should not be closed without a notice of the substantial kindness, the delicate tokens, and the affectionate offerings, which friends and parishioners were gratified to present to their devoted pastor and friend. His high appreciation of the slightest token of regard, and grateful recognition of every favor, is beautifully exhibited in his letters of acknowledgment:

TO G. D. M——, ESQ.

"*October* 4, 1861.

"VERY DEAR FRIEND—Your basket of grapes, with the letter and enclosure of a check for a hundred dollars on the Bank of Commerce, and eight dollars for the poor, came safely to hand yesterday. I return you many thanks, and pray God to reward you. Let me ask, Is not God *now* repaying you for your goodness to the poor in times past? While other merchants are becoming impoverished, you are becoming rich. But whatsoever you give now, and in time to come, will he not also repay you? Forty years ago I began to prove God in this way, and I can now read the eighth of Deuteronomy with great pleasure. . . . . I am glad you are coming nearer, and hope oftener to see you.

"Most affectionately, your obliged friend, B. C. CUTLER."

How precious must a note like the following have been to a new parishioner, who had estimated aright his rare worth, and vied with others to do honor to this chosen servant of the Most High:

"*October* 21, 1861.

"MY DEAR MRS. C—— —It would be necessary for you to live thirty or forty years longer, to know how grateful such a kind note and pleasant offering is to the heart of *an old pastor*. There are histories and experiences which are indissolubly joined to long life; and let the young days be ever so light and bright, yet even Solomon warns us to prepare for the days of darkness. Oh, how I thank God that he broke up all my worldly expectations very early in life, and thus compelled me, for happiness and peace, to seek him out, and through Christ to find him, and *to build a nest for my heart*—a soft and safe one too, in the secret place of the tabernacle of the Most High! Did not you do the same? You have always looked to me, as if you did. Did not that rugged nurse, '*sorrow*,' wring from your young heart some early and bitter tears? Come then what may, we are safe.

"Flowers have long been my delight. I regret, sometimes, that I have not turned aside from my particular profession to look with the curiosity of a botanist, and with the eye of a philosopher, upon the *floral world*. It is said of Wordsworth, that, in looking at the humblest of these unfallen servants of God, the daisy, he had emotions too deep for tears; and of Mungo Park, that when lost in the deserts of Africa, the sight of one little flower set his soul on fire and renewed his strength: 'Does God take care of that flower, and will he not of me?'

"But though no botanist and no philosopher, I can look at flowers as a child of God, and see in them *God's beautiful pictorial Bible*. I see wisdom, power, and goodness, instruction, encouragement, and consolation. These I have also in the written Word, but I have *here* the thoughts of God *in full dress*. Solomon himself was not arrayed in such glory. They come, like angels who have toned down their too dazzling splendor, and taken the richest colors and dresses that mortal eyes can bear to behold, and visit us." . . .

Who ever received from a cherished pastor a more encouraging note than the one we here subjoin? The parishioner to whom it was addressed, counted it her highest joy, next to serving God and bringing up her household to fear him, to "hold up the hands" of God's devoted, but often weary servant, and most fully and cordially she did this:

TO MRS. H. M——.

"*December* 26, 1861.

"MY DEAR FRIEND—I return you many thanks for your Christmas present; and however many and various and valuable have been your remembrances, the sweetest of all, is the existence and influence of piety in your life and conversation. 'Now we *live*, if ye stand fast in the Lord!' I know that we ministers ought to hail the coming of one *sinner* to our churches more than the coming of ninety and nine Christians!

"But certainly we want some Christians to hold up our hands and to help us do our work to sinners. May grace ever be given you to bring up your household in the fear of God, and may you and yours be, to the end, burning and shining lights in the world.

"The world at this moment seems to be heaving with great events. Our Ship of State is in a heavy gale, and is hard pressed; we have not only a tempest from one quarter, but now there is threatening another from the opposite quarter. The waves of the sea are mighty and rage horribly, but God who dwelleth on high is mightier. 'Jesus, Master, save us, or we perish.' 'And he arose and rebuked the wind and the sea, and there was a great caim.' So may it be now!

"With best wishes for you and yours, I am

"Your obliged pastor, B. C. CUTLER."

Thus did he counsel and encourage the different members of his flock in their manifold phases of Christian experience, using every passing event, not indeed "to point a moral or adorn a tale," but with the higher motive to lead their affections heavenward. His convictions of the truth were so strong, and his sense of the preciousness of the Saviour was so great, that every thing else seemed trifling compared with the interests of the soul, and his pen traced no lines without a word that spoke of a world to come.

The following record, on the sixty-fourth anniversary of his birthday, is too important to omit, as it is a faithful review of his past life. While his remarkable self-humiliation makes it an almost painful scrutiny, one cannot fail to see how he was still hungering and thirsting after righteousness, finding his chief joy in serving and proclaiming to others, the Saviour of sinners.

"*Feb.* 6, 1862.—For sixty-four years the Lord has led me on; for forty-seven, I have professed to fear and serve the Lord. I was baptized, confirmed, and communed in Trinity Church, Boston, the church of my ancestors. Bishop Parker (then Dr. Parker) baptized me, Bishop Griswold confirmed me, Dr. Gardiner admitted me to communion. Bishop Griswold ordained me deacon at Quincy, Mass., and priest at St. Ann's, Lowell, in company with my dear brother, Rev.

Theodore Edson. For nearly forty years I have had a parish. What an amount of mercy I have had! I very gradually became serious in youth; very gradually yielded to high motives, and renounced the fashionable world; very gradually had my eyes opened to see evangelical truth, and have been approaching very gradually the central point of religion in my preaching—the Cross of our Divine Lord and Saviour.

"I was not worthy to be called to be a minister. I am now less than the least of all saints, and should God's grace be given me, I shall end my life with a sincere confession, that of sinners I am chief. I feel compassed with infirmities, chargeable with faults of temper and spirit, and I am sensible that I am but dust and ashes, and sinful in soul. All my hope is in Christ. Christ Jesus came into the world to save sinners. This is a faithful saying, and worthy of all acceptance. I accept it.

"Six years more will bring me to the allotted span of human life. How shall they be spent? In drawing nearer and nearer to that great Saviour who came to save sinners. My soul, draw nigh to God, and he will draw nigh to you—nigh, very nigh in prayer, particularly in prayer! I will commit all, and *all*, and ALL my interests to Christ, and cast all my care upon God!"

When we read such extracts from his journal, and see such clinging to God, such earnest desires to know more of his grace, and to be filled with all the Divine fullness, we cannot refrain from the poet's exclamation:

"Haste thee on from grace to glory,
Armed by faith and winged by prayer,
Heaven's eternal days before thee,
God's own hand shall guide thee there;
Soon shall close thy earthly mission,
Soon shall pass thy pilgrim days;
Hope shall change to glad fruition,
Faith, to sight, and prayer, to praise."

His span of life was extended only a twelvemonth more. How delightful was the last letter he received from his aged friend in Devonshire, England, pressing on (like himself) in her heavenward journey, full of faith and hope.

TO DR. AND MRS. CUTLER.

"3 UNION TERRACE, BARNSTABLE,
DEVONSHIRE, *January* 27, 1862.

"MY BELOVED FRIENDS—Your kind letter of November 29 should have been answered long ere this, but partly from my impaired sight and partly from my enfeebled health, I have thus long delayed; but you, with other dear friends, have been much upon my *heart;* especially at a throne of grace has it been my privilege to remember you. I need not say how delighted I should be to see you both once more! A week or two ago I sent you a sermon by Archdeacon Law, upon the death of Prince Albert. My dear friends at Weston, who heard it preached, sent me a copy. There was not a dry eye in the church on the occasion of its delivery. It is said that the Prince on his death-bed repeated that sweet hymn, "Rock of ages cleft for me;" that he desired the most faithful preaching, and that both he and the Queen ordered their domestic servants to be allowed alternately to attend the "revival meetings," when in Scotland. . . . How interesting and solemnizing must be your love feasts to commemorate so great a deliverance (from shipwreck), and such an answer to prayer! The Lord has reserved you, dear friends, for much which will be your crown of rejoicing hereafter! His Providence directs *every* step you take. He is at the helm in the stormy tempest! He can say, 'Peace, be still,' or enable you to outride it, or take you out of it. All, all is well! I am too prone to look to circumstances and second causes; but when I get a glimpse of Christ's power and love, I desire to leave all in his hand, and I have great peace and comfort in casting my care upon him. Oh, if I had done so, what trouble and anxiety would have been spared me in times past. I am now, at my advanced age, only beginning to do so. I see in 'the Link and the Rivet,' and in the 'Ragged Homes,' marvellous instances of Divine grace, under most excruciating pain; one case is mentioned of a person who was for sixteen years unable to be turned in bed, without money, with a small amount of food, with little fire and no light, and only the ability to move one thumb, yet the voice of praise and thanksgiving sounds forth from that afflicted one. It gladdens one's heart while it covers one with shame! Through deep affliction we shall see glorious ones arise, who by prayer and enduring patience have turned many to righteousness; whom the world knows not, but who are very dear to Him who deals with them in *love*.

"I beg my warmest love to my dear cousin; and with much affection must conclude,

"Yours, most truly, F. E. HILL."

As years grew apace and labors multiplied, we notice that the letters of Dr. Cutler were much more brief than formerly, though not less frequent, to his valued friends.

We insert extracts from one or two notes at this time, the expressions and style of which are so eminently characteristic of the man:

TO MRS. JACKSON.

"*March* 21, 1862.

"MY DEAR FRIEND— . . . . I am not as well as usual; indeed, I must take a respite, and travel, as soon as spring opens. Forty years have been spent in the ministry. I am trying to draw nearer to God; to press on until I find and feel him all around me, and my prayer is that my last days may be my best, and my last hours my happiest.

"I am writing, and preaching, and laboring for societies, just as much as ever: but I do not visit so much, as I am wearied so soon.

"My assistant, Rev. L. H. Mills, is very acceptable. He is a close student, and labors on his pulpit preparations. . . . . St. Ann's was never so flourishing. May our Divine Master comfort you and all his children, last and least, *me*."

TO A PARISHIONER.

"*April* 22, 1862.

"MY DEAR FRIEND— . . . . I was out when your letter arrived, and have been in attendance on the dying hours of a young and beautiful mother since midnight. . . . . With all my cares, and still another death in the parish, I have been so wearied, that if I should attempt to write what I want to say to you, I should fail; anon, you shall hear from me. . . . . You can hardly feel too deeply the importance of maternal influence; it is the seal to the soft wax. As God's minister, I may baptize her, and add her name to the records of the church, and draw down a blessing upon her; but this is *once only*. You may baptize her soul daily with piety, truth, and love, and arm her against sin, the world, and the Devil. Most affectionately, your pastor, B. C. CUTLER."

In his journal he writes:

"*Easter Eve*, 1862.—I was never better satisfied with St. Ann's Parish than now. It is really in a flourishing state, in every respect. Eight or ten persons propose to join our church to-morrow. Thanks be to God!"

His sister, now about removing from New York to Newport, received from her beloved brother a parting note:

TO MRS. FRANCIS.

"I wanted to come over and give you a parting blessing, but was necessarily detained by parish duty. Your departure is almost as if all New York had departed. Who is there now for me to visit, when I can run over? It is forty years now since the 'Cutlers' came to that great city, and all but Susan are out of it now. '*Sic transit gloria mundi!*' I am now getting to that period when all places are alike to me; that is, all are unsatisfactory but *home!* . . . . Henry Bancroft, from Montreal, is staying with us, which delights us. He is unwell and needs rest. I am glad I can entertain him. Give my love to S—— and H——, and believe me,

"Your affectionate brother, B. C. CUTLER."

A few months of suffering and weariness intervened, and the nephew referred to in the preceding letter, finished his course, and went to join the glorified spirit of his dear relative before the Throne.

There seems to have been a prophetic significance in the few lines addressed to a youthful parishioner at this time:

"ST. ANN'S RECTORY, *June* 21, 1862.

"DEAR FRIEND—Many thanks for your beautiful present, and for a bouquet from your dear mother. It is a sweet thought for a Christian, that, although his dusty pathway through life may *not* be strewed with flowers, he yet may die in a bed of roses, and awake in a world of glory. May this last, at any rate, be our happy lot!

"Your affectionate pastor, B. C. CUTLER.

"Mrs. L. V— N——."

The old parish of St. Ann's had now for many years been blessed with unexampled temporal and spiritual prosperity.

The labors of the rector and his various assistants, had evidently received the Divine favor and blessing. Multitudes had been gathered into the fold of the church, and believers walking in the fear of the Lord and of the Holy Ghost were multiplied.

The present faithful assistant minister was about completing the year of his promised engagement, when he was re-elected for another year (to September, 1863), and thus the vestry secured his services, which (as it afterward proved), were as indispensable as they were useful.

On the 1st of July, Dr. Cutler was summoned to Newport to attend the funeral of his niece (by marriage), the wife of Capt. Julian McAllister. Neither youth, health, beauty nor affluence, could save her from the grave, and a pall like that of midnight suddenly overspread a sunny household. Dr. Cutler took as the basis of his remarks on this occasion, that appropriate passage of Scripture, "Verily, every man at his best state is altogether vanity," and delivered a most touching address.

He returned home with Mrs. Cutler on the 8th of the same month. On the 9th he was taken ill at midnight with severe diarrhea, but so far recovered as to be able to preach at St. Ann's on Sunday, July 13, 1862; he also assisted in the celebration of the Holy Communion and baptized a child.

None could realize that this was his last sermon within the walls of St. Ann's, where he had so long and so faithfully preached the Gospel of Christ.

The effort proved to be too much for him in his weak state, and produced a relapse. For a few days he was quite ill, and had two physicians in attendance. By the 25th, however, he was able to drive out and see his friends, but his recovery was very slow.

"Thus I have had," he writes in his journal, "a season of solemn meditation, and I pray God, it may do me good!"

The glorious truths which had fallen with so much fervor, from the lips of this honored servant of Christ, in the pulpit, were now to be repeated in broken fragments, as it were, from a couch of weariness, or reiterated in those many epistles, in which he loved to tell his people how gracious were the Lord's dealings with his soul. Thus he gave renewed and most impressive testimony to the value of the Gospel, and to the power and love of a never-failing Saviour, who was with him each hour as he went down, step by step, to the banks of Jordan, and refreshed and strengthened his fainting spirit, for its passage over the dark river.

CHAPTER XVI.

LAST DAYS.

CONTINUED ILLNESS—DEATH—FUNERAL, ETC.

August, 1862, *to February*, 1863.

"How beautiful it is for man to die
Upon the walls of Zion! to be called
Like a watch-worn and weary sentinel,
To put his armor off, and rest—in heaven."

DR. CUTLER'S public labors were nearly over. A few months more, he was to linger on the threshold of another world, while the growing spirituality which gleamed through his conversation and correspondence, seemed but to be a reflection of the deepening glory into which he was so soon to enter. The weary wheels of life were moving slower and slower, and as the child sighs for home, or the weary soldier longs for victory and rest, so he yearned to depart and be with Christ.

On the 7th of August, being yet quite feeble, he set off, with Mrs. Cutler and a nurse,(accompanied also by a kind friend and parishioner, Mr. H. P. M——n,) for Saratoga Springs.

His appetite had failed, and he was wasted to a mere shadow, but his spirit was kept in perfect peace. He wrote to his sisters, who were both at Newport, "God is good every day, and every hour, and every moment, and through my glorious and gracious Saviour, my mind is as calm as a summer sea."

Slowly led back, as from the confines of another world, he was not only to be the recipient of new joys in intercourse with various children of God—a blessed foretaste of communion with the church triumphant, which he should ere long enjoy—but, he also imparted heartfelt happiness to others by his letters, and scattered around him the fruits of his rich and matured experience, before he passed away to his eternal home.

The gleanings we give cannot fail to be treasured up by many hearts; and tears will flow from eyes unused to weep, as they read these precious records—precious indeed to his parishioners, now that for awhile, he was not permitted to see them "face to face:"

TO MRS. H. M——R.

"SARATOGA, *August*, 1862.

"MY DEAR SISTER IN CHRIST—God has been scourging me for my good, and has also dealt very graciously with me. I have never been conscious of making such struggles, (not voluntarily though) as within a month. Why I was not taken I know not. It has pleased God to spare me some time longer, I trust, to review my long life, repent, and submit. I am living on the promises, the exceeding great and precious promises of God.

"As far as a choice of a profession is concerned, I rejoice that I have been for nearly fifty years, (certainly more than forty) actually working for God, in the service of his dear Son.

"I love his work, and his word, and his house, and his people of every name. By this I know that I have passed from death unto life, because I love the brethren. I know that Christ's kingdom, and power, and glory, and universal dominion is my delight, my great delight, and all my hope. I feel I love him so little, that I am unworthy to be called a child, and yet I know I love him above all this world, over and over again.

"Pray that Christ may manifest himself unto me more and more—more nearly, more tenderly, more lovingly, more compassionately—pitying my infirmities, and taking me for what I would be, not for what I am. Give my love to your family, and thank your husband for his kind offer. Most tenderly do I daily think of the kindness of your brother Thomas and his wife.

"God bless you all! Amen! B. C. CUTLER."

With a heart full of Christ, he penned the following to his former parishioner and cherished friend, then in Europe:

TO G. D. M——, ESQ.

"SARATOGA, *August* 26, 1862.

"Many thanks, my dear friend, for your letter from Switzerland. . . . . You see I am at Saratoga. I was brought very low by an attack of my old complaint. 'I was brought low and He helped me.' God has visited me with a rod, but this has been with scourges. It is good for me, and blessed be his name.

"I hope you will stay another year by all means. Our country is still in the midst of war, and I think will be for some time, but the result is not doubtful. The confederates have had nothing but a succession of victories they say; still they have lost almost every place of importance, and are on their last legs. They will be punished for their rebellion against God (in the best Government in the world).

"St. Ann's has a new warden, Mr. Cooper, in the place of Mr. Sands, and Mr. H. Messenger, a new vestryman. Our parsonage is just painted. Mr. Mills is very acceptable. I do not expect to preach for two months yet. . . . . Indeed, what God has in store for me, he only knows. Forty years this summer, in the pulpit, has he borne with me. My short-comings have been great. Some good, I hope, I have done. ONE DEAR FRIEND I have made, whose family are very dear to me. God bless you all, and return you in safety!

"Prays your old friend and pastor, B. C. CUTLER."

This friend returned ere a year had passed, but only to stand at his grave, over which the winds of spring and summer had already swept.

Dr. Cutler's natural playfulness of spirit still manifested itself, as other letters show :

TO MRS. H——N, AT THE WHITE MOUNTAINS.

"SARATOGA, *September* 1, 1862.

"What has become of the lively, and agreeable, and affectionate friend I had in the mountains? and what has become of her admirable husband, on whose mind the beauties of Nature leave indelible impressions? Do let us hear.

"Many thanks for the last letter, and the good news that one sinner had been brought to repentance by my sermons! I have now been here three weeks, and have improved beyond my expectation. . . . . Hosts of friends and parishioners have been here all this time, paying us every attention.

"Truly, God has been good to us; mercy and truth have followed us. I have had opportunities of doing good by 'tracts' and conversation, and many more of getting good from most wise and excellent Christian people. Several hundred persons have been in these two houses, opposite each other, since we have been here. Mrs. Cutler joins me in love, and I am still, to all intents and purposes,

"Your old, and steady, and fatherly friend, B. C. CUTLER."

We find in one of his letters the following allusion to one of his friends, during this sojourn at Saratoga: "Our friend, Rev. H. G——, is here. We were delighted when he and his sisters came."

How fully the interviews, on this occasion, between these friends are daguerreotyped upon the heart of the survivor, can hardly be told. Even then, struck with his altered appearance, we looked forward with anxiety and sorrow; for every lineament of his face seemed to be stamped with death. These forebodings, expressed at the time to others, were in a few months sadly realized.

During this absence from his parish, the beloved pastor continued to receive many affectionate letters from his people. The parish itself was virtually under the care of the assistant Minister, who with indefatigable industry labored for its prosperity, and with such aid as he could obtain from others, the pulpit was well supplied.

The earnest desires of the flock to see their faithful shepherd were well expressed in the following original verses, sent to him by a parishioner, who never failed to appreciate the privilege of having such a pastor:

"'Come Home.'

"A cloud is resting o'er the camp by day—
No nightly fire illumes our onward way;
Lingers our leader up the Holy Mount
To gather vigor spent on our account,
And then to us, the shining face to bear!
We miss our pastor—miss him everywhere!

"There came an answer on a passing leaf,
Where many look for solace in their grief:
'He whom thou lov'st is sick,' was the reply,
With the sweet promise, 'He shall never die!'
Hope and solicitude inspire our prayer;
For oh! we miss him—miss him everywhere!

"In labors oft for us, his heart was pained
To note the fearful power that sin had gained,
But hoped that grace within the barren soil,
Compassed by weeds, might yet reward his toil.
Though vain all strivings to requite his care,
The house of sorrow ever found him there.

"But now, we miss his voice in our distress,
His guiding hand uplifted but to bless,
Where hearts bereaved, bemoan their lost in vain,
And at the couch of sickness and of pain.
So happier homes, that feasts of joy prepare,
Await the pastor, and his blessing there.

"The memory of his life-devoted years,
Of joys too few—too much of toil and tears,
Forbids the ungrateful thought that any breast
Would rob him of one hour of needful rest;
Rather we'd guard that rest with jealous care,
And every member all his sufferings share.

"If but to bid us love each other more,
Come, and may God to thee all joys restore.
The Cross in sweet companionship we'll bear,
That we with thee, a heavenly crown may wear,
Though well supplied and fed with faithful care,
We miss our pastor—miss him EVERYWHERE!

"ST. ANN'S PARISH, *August*, 1862."

On the 16th of September, Dr. Cutler had so far recovered, that he was enabled to leave Saratoga and journey to Boston, passing a night at Albany, N. Y., on his way thither. He still suffered, however, from his cough, though able to be in the open air each pleasant day. It afforded him much gratification at this time to be present at the marriage (in Roxbury, Mass.) of one of his parishioners, who was also a vestryman and a valued friend. It was a happy occasion, and as he wrote one of his friends: "All Nature opened her store of sunshine, fruits, and flowers; a fine day, and every body happy; it was a success; and really, for the moment, you would hardly think this a fallen world!"

A kind Providence afforded Dr. Cutler the pleasure of meeting other kind friends (Mr. and Mrs. K——) at the "Tremont House," in Boston. The cold east winds which prevail on the coast increased his cough, and it became more distressing and of a spasmodic nature. The whole party of friends now went to Springfield, Mass., in the interior, and after a few days there, Dr. and Mrs. Cutler reached the parsonage at Brooklyn on the 29th of September. He was able to be out of doors now, as the weather permitted, and could give attention occasionally to parochial duty.

A letter, very refreshing to his spirit, now arrived from Europe, in which was conveyed the greatest comfort that a faithful minister can possibly desire. It was from a friend (to whom allusion has often been made) whose heart so full of cordial friendship and Christian love, often beat in unison with his own:

"PARIS, *September* 16, 1862.

"MY DEAR PASTOR—I was glad to learn, by your kind letter of August 26, that your health was improved. . . . You are very dear to us, and we count Mrs. Cutler and yourself as our true and precious friends. As I tried to read your thoughts in reading your words, my mind went back over the past, twenty years ago, when I remember your faithful words and prayers for us, and now, twenty years afterward, six of those who, through your ministry, blessed by the Holy Spirit, trust they have a home prepared for them above, are in Paris praying for your health and peace! Oh, how much I might say about the peace and joy of casting all our care upon Jesus! I have found no rest but this. Am I a sinner? I have told it to Jesus. Am I weak? I have told it to Jesus, and then have I been strong. Do my infirmities come back to me? I have told Jesus. Do sorrows press upon me? I have told it to Jesus, and to no one else; and I feel that he has answered me: 'My child thou art mine. I have spread out thy path, not one unneeded sorrow shall come to thee. You must walk in the narrow way. I must lead thee by a way often dark to thee, but be satisfied to trust all to me.'

"When I was at Brussels I saw in the Royal Gallery a painting that left a deep impression on my mind—Jesus, bearing his cross up the hill of Calvary, had fainted, and was upon his hands and knees; his mother was wiping his forehead, and Cyrene (or Simon) was in the act of relieving him of his load. It showed me of his sufferings and troubles before the crucifixion, and made me think more of his earthly life. Oh, how hard when the world is flowing on like a full river, to walk humbly with God! How difficult to see the pride and worldliness of our own hearts! It is only when sorrow comes that we get under the shadow of His wings.

"I want you to give up all care about preaching, for a year or more, and prepare to come out to England next spring. . . . . Let St. Ann's do what we long ago did for Dr. Creighton. He is provided with an assistant at each of his churches, and their salary is regularly paid, with the understanding that the Doctor is never to preach unless he desires, and to go and come when he pleases, and he to choose his assistants.

"St. Ann's has a large fund, and should do this gladly, and you should accept it cheerfully, for it is your privilege, and God has blessed your ministry, and the church is in temporal prosperity. It is your right to be ministered unto, for the rest of your days with the fruits of these temporalities.

"My dear pastor, rejoice that for forty years you have been permitted to speak for Jesus; look not within for deficiencies, but upward to him who covers us with the garment of his righteousness.

"Most sincerely yours, G. D. M——."

Once more at home, Dr. Cutler conducted the general affairs of the parish. Many clerical friends, who were at this time in New York, in attendance upon the General Convention, rendered him such aid as was in their power.

On the first Sunday of October, his nephew, the Rev. F. M. McAllister, from San Francisco, preached for him; and on the second Sunday he was glad to welcome his old friend, Bishop Eastburn, to the pulpit of St. Ann's. His own impaired health allowed him only to assist in the ministrations of the sanctuary. Thus, he often appeared in the desk and chancel, though not quite equal to pulpit duty. His record in the journal is: "I progress slowly; yet, sick or well, weak or strong, I am in Christ's hands."

He now heard of the death of Mrs. Mitchell, of Philadelphia, and lost not a moment in writing to one of the family circle with whom he had intimate acquaintance. He had travelled with the family from some point to another during the summer, and had made "a lasting impression" on their minds.

The mother of the deceased afterward wrote to Mrs. Cutler, that the letters of Dr. Cutler (though not addressed directly to her) "had soothed and touched their bleeding hearts," and were very precious to herself. They distinctly pointed out the only refuge in sorrow, and were full of heavenly consolation, as we are privileged to see:

TO MRS. CADWALLADER, ON THE DEATH OF A NIECE.

"BROOKLYN, *October* 3, 1862.

"DEAR MRS. C—— —I have only just heard of the new affliction which has come into your circle. I feel so deeply and sincerely the loss to her friends, and to the world, of that lovely and charming spirit that has fled from us, that I cannot help sending a few lines expressive of my grief. I had never felt so great a regard for one whom I had seen so little of, as I did for Mrs. Mitchell. She seemed a gem, a dew-drop, a pure, unsophisticated being, who acted her part without an effort, and that part a most important one.

"Her new relation only exalted her, and my last recollections of her, in her husband's office, when I called, is that of a perfect and entire character, just placed in her allotted sphere. But she has gone! May God sanctify her loss to the larger, and especially to the smaller circle, of which she was the central light.

"I write not to elicit one line of response, but really as a positive relief to my own mind.

"Very respectfully and very sorrowfully, I remain, dear Mrs. Cadwallader, Yours, B. C. CUTLER."

Rarely has a more beautiful or appropriate letter ever come from the pen of any minister of Christ than this one, addressed

TO THE SAME.

"BROOKLYN, *October* 9, 1862.

"DEAR MRS. CADWALLADER—I feel the sacredness of the correspondence you have so kindly submitted to me, and return it by mail the same hour I received it.

"I am very near my last stage in the journey of life. I am near three-score years and ten, that is, I am within five or six years of it, and my life for fifty years has been one of Christian reflection and observation. The result of the whole is, that it is impossible to find happiness for the immortal mind in this world. You must give up, wholly give up the idea. Your heart must by some means be *broken;* your whole plan of life deranged, and, taking your place in the procession which is following *the Man of Sorrows*, you must have regard only to 'the joy that is set before you.'—Heb. xii. 1, 2.

"If you have riches, *you must have the antidote*—you must have *inward* trials.

"I must acknowledge, however, that I think Dr. and Mrs. Elwyn's affliction has been very severe. But WHO is the physician that prescribed that terrible remedy? It is the Great God who made that darling child, and who redeemed her with the death and sacrifice of his only Son. He gave his Son up to death, that her sins might all be pardoned and she admitted to Paradise, to be eternally happy.

"In such profound grief as that in which you are all plunged at this moment, *words* are poor comforters. Silence is perhaps the most expressive kind of sympathy in *present friends*, but the absent must at least salute their afflicted and bereaved friends,—the dear afflicted parent and husband! 'Whom the Lord *loveth* he chasteneth, and scourgeth every son whom he receiveth.'

"It is to such bitter bereavements as this, that saints in glory look back from heaven to earth and say,

"'Oh! had'st thou left me *unchastised*
Thy precepts I had still despised;
And still the snare in secret laid,
Had my unwary feet betrayed.'

"Very respectfully, and with sincere sympathy,
"I remain your friend in Christ, B. C. CUTLER."

Though he was slowly improving at this time, his health was precarious, and he almost feared to leave home, even for a night! Thus he wrote a dear parishioner at "Clarence:" . . . . "In joy and in sorrow, I have been so accustomed to see you and Mr. M——, that I have been planning a one-day visit, ever since I came home; but I fear we must give it up for the present. . . . . Coming in to-day from a ride, I saw your rich present of grapes, and joyfully ate part of a cluster. Many thanks for your kind remembrance." . . . .

He was able to attend three funerals in his parish, within three weeks after his arrival home. In one case, especially, he felt deeply the loss of a long-tried friend. Thus he alluded to it:

"*Oct.* 19, 1862.—My health is improving, though I have a lingering cough. I expect to be free from pulpit labor this winter. May God give me grace to take rest wisely, and help me to improve every opportunity of doing good. The death of Commodore Hudson is a solemn warning to me and to all. Though sixty-eight years old, he was to all appearance hale and hearty. 'There is but a step between me and death!'"

Prophetic, indeed! though he was to linger awhile near the portals of another world!

His much-lamented friend was buried, with military honors, from St. Ann's on the 18th of October. A great concourse of citizens filled the church, and a large military *cortége* stood without, and accompanied the remains to the grave at Greenwood. The presence and remarks of the Rt.

Rev. Dr. McIlvaine, of Ohio, greatly increased the interest of the occasion. After his eloquent address, Dr. Cutler followed, in his own fervent style. In strong and forcible language, he reviewed the life of this distinguished officer, dwelling on his remarkable piety, and concluded with a glowing appeal (which found its way to many hearts) as follows: "Gentlemen of the profession of which our departed friend was an ornament, a standard-bearer has fallen. Is there not one here who will now throw himself into the fight and raise that standard again? Through the grace of Christ, he too will come off conqueror, and say, Thanks be to God which giveth us the victory through our Lord Jesus Christ."

In the midst of his sadness during this week, Dr. Cutler was called, on the 16th, to celebrate the marriage of one of his parishioners (Miss R. P. G——), with the Rev. Mr. Henshaw, of Providence, R. I. It was, with one exception, the last time he officiated on such an occasion. Thus was he performing the rites of the church, for and among his chosen friends in his latter days.

Joy and sadness were closely interwoven, at this period, in his own experience, and in that of friends around. The greetings connected with the nuptials just celebrated were scarcely over, when death entered the same family circle, and sorrow shrouded also the home of one dear to himself. Mr. and Mrs. J. A. G—— were called to part with a darling son on the 27th of October, and in their beloved uncle they found not only a devoted pastor, but a sympathizing friend and relative. The mother had, before her marriage, resided for a long time under the roof of Dr. Cutler, and he ever regarded her as a choice spirit, and now that she was in affliction, a double measure of kindness and tenderness he gladly bestowed. It is affecting to remember, that the last time he pronounced those solemn words, "earth to earth, ashes to ashes, dust to dust," it was over the precious remains of the child of this relative, "Walter Cutler Greene."

The time was not far distant when their voices would blend *together* in singing hallelujahs to the Lamb in Heaven.

He was not called home himself, however, until he had counselled, succoured, and sympathized with many more of the perplexed, tried, or sorrowful children of God. Thus he writes:

TO MRS. FRANCIS.

"DEAR SISTER—I have often thought of some expressions in one of your last letters respecting your *inward* anguish, hidden under outward submission! If you ask what the remedy is, I answer, It is *not* from us mortals. No mortal can ever know the sufferings which I doubt not you have endured. How then can any mortal alleviate them? God, in Christ, is the only comforter of such sorrows. We, your nearest and dearest friends, have implored his presence with you and support for you. But still, even Divine consolations do not always extract '*the thorn*' from the wounded soul! No! not when a Paul himself prays, and prays for himself, 'No affliction is for the present joyous, but grievous.' Jesus says, 'My grace is sufficient for thee.' 'I know your sorrows are hard to bear, but I will give you grace to bear them.' I visited poor Mrs. Commodore Hudson yesterday. Her husband went to bed well and joyful, after reading a chapter in God's holy word and making a long prayer, and in two hours was called home! . . . . Capt. H. died of a spasmodic cough like my own, only much more violent, yet he was out, and looked, and felt well. But 'he was not, for God took him!'

"I have not preached a regular sermon yet. But my cough has almost gone, and my appetite and strength are returning. I may spend the winter in the Southern cities, if God will. My vestry have been most kind and generous, and say I must take a year's rest, and go to Europe, if I desire. . . . . .

"Believe me, most affectionately, and with continual intercessions for you, Your brother, B. C. CUTLER.

"P. S.—I received dear Louisa's letter."

He thus endeavored to administer comfort to an afflicted parishioner:

TO WM. H——, ESQ.

"ST. ANN'S RECTORY, *October* 20, 1862.

"DEAR SIR—The wet weather of last week, and afterward the sudden death of Commodore Hudson on the 15th inst., prevented my calling on you since the funeral of Mrs. Tucker. This morning I set out on my horse, but was compelled to turn back, in consequence of the cold wind which aggravated my cough. I have thought daily of you all, and we have all prayed that your great disappointments and severe bereavements may be sanctified to all concerned. God saw your benevolent intentions, and I trust will reward them, although not in the way you expected. Happy is it for those dear little motherless children, that you and Mrs. Halsey stand so nearly related to them. It is possible they will hardly feel the loss of a mother. May God spare your lives, and reward all your kindness, both here and hereafter.

"Oh, my dear sir, if we only make Jesus Christ our Master, he will be our Friend, the Saviour of our souls, and will admit us at death to that glorious rest which is prepared for the people of God! I beg to be particularly remembered to Mr. Tucker, and to send him my sincere sympathy. With love to all my dear friends in your house and circle, I remain very faithfully,

"Your friend and pastor, B. C. CUTLER."

On the 30th of October, the vestry of St. Ann's Church passed a resolution by which the rector was granted leave of absence for six months, in order that his health might be restored. His salary was to be continued, as usual, and the pulpit supplied at the expense of the vestry.

Great solicitude was felt among the people, and every thing within their power was freely offered for the benefit of their beloved pastor.

They besought him to take entire rest, and gladly offered any pecuniary facility which would attain the desired end.

The anniversary of his shipwreck now recurring, he made the following record:

"*Nov.* 12, 1862.—This morning, nineteen years ago, I was delivered from the perils of shipwreck; Mrs. Cutler, Mrs. Maxwell and I reached this house, taken from a sinking ship (the Sheffield). I have kept this season ever since, but at this time, am not well enough to call my friends and my neighbors together to rejoice with me. I have, therefore, given to the poor what my feast would have cost me, and look back upon the day with thankfulness, and forward with hope. Thanks be to God who hath delivered me!"

On the 18th, after having dispatched a line on business affairs to Thomas Messenger, Esq., he addressed a note to Mrs. M—— (who was in the country), in which we see how his warm and loving heart flowed out toward his affectionate flock:

"DEAR MRS. M—— —We are still lingering here. . . . . I am occasionally troubled with my cough, but it is a small matter now. Still, I take great care of myself, lest it should be provoked to come back. Mrs. Cutler and I think of spending a few days with our relatives, the McAllisters, at the New York Hotel. . . . . I shall be glad to get a glimpse of you both on Thanksgiving Day, if I am in these parts. You and yours are ever in my mind and will be. I think sickness softens the hard heart of man, and those friends who are kind, stamp their whole image and superscription on the suffering soul.

"My mind is at peace, and I am effectually *at rest* in body and spirit, as my kind vestry wish me to be. A few cold words poorly convey the warm current of my heart.

"Your affectionate pastor, B. C. CUTLER."

His beloved sister, Mrs. McAllister, and other relatives, urged him to give up all superintendence of parish affairs, and go over to New York, where they could enjoy that intercourse with each other, which circumstances had hitherto denied them all. He accordingly yielded to their solicitations, and passed a week with them. His sister, Mrs. Francis, was still in Newport with her children, and from his temporary resting-place he thus wrote her:

"NEW YORK HOTEL, *November* 26, 1862.

"DEAR SISTER: H—— and I came over yesterday to spend a week with Louisa and the Judge. I am very glad I came, although it seems almost folly to spend thirty-five dollars a week for board when you are not thirty-five minutes' ride distant from home.

"But change of air is recommended to me, and this I get, with every other comfort, by just crossing the East River; and why should I not spend my sovereign a day in America, as well as in England or France? Besides, I have been so busy and so much occupied these last thirty years, that, with the exception of you and your precious circle, and also of the Bishop and a few of the clergy, I have seen nothing of New York or of New York people, or New York places or 'lions'—sacred or secular.

"My cough still hangs on, but is evidently a natural concomitant of pectoral weakness and torpor of the system.

"I expect to spend a month or two in Philadelphia and Baltimore, unless forced to Havana by my cough. I am beginning to enjoy my rest and freedom from professional cares. One reason why I came over here was, that while in Brooklyn I am mixed up with 'the ups and downs' of the parish.

"During the six weeks I have been at home, I have baptized sixteen children, married six couples, and buried six of my people! Another wedding, too, if I will stay till after Christmas!

"I have been reading over Baxter's 'Saints' Rest' with real delight, and my thoughts are radiant with heaven and its glories. Read it! Love, *love*, LOVE, to all, from UNCLE B."

How fast was he hastening to, and ripening for, those very glories and blessed realities on which, in imagination, he was now feasting!

He had no anxiety about the future, as we see by a few lines addressed to a friend in Europe:

TO G. D. M——, ESQ.

"*November* 28, 1862.

"MY DEAR FRIEND— . . . . I left my rectory on the 25th inst., and began my pilgrimage by encamping first at the New York Hotel. Judge McAllister and family are here, also his son (Ward) and his family. We have a suit of sunny, airy apartments, by ourselves—five or more adjoining rooms, and here we can collect, morning and evening, our family circle to sing the praises of the Lord.

"My cough is better but not gone. How I shall bear the cold of this North Atlantic seaboard, I know not. I may have to take the wings of the morning and fly over the ocean, but I would rather not. The most favorable opinion is, that as my strength increases my cough will fade away; perhaps so—but come what will, *so long as my Saviour comes with it*, all will be happiness to me.

"I have not preached for four months. . . . . St. Ann's is as flourishing as ever. Mr. Mills is increasingly liked, and our congregations are good. . . . .

"Yours, most affectionately, B. C. CUTLER."

He returned home somewhat improved in health, having much enjoyed also these last interviews with his beloved sister. She and her husband soon sailed for their home on the Pacific coast, not dreaming they should see his face no more.

To a dear parishioner who had made inquiries (by letter) after his health, he penned the following reply. She had had varied and peculiar trials, and "through much tribulation" and physical suffering, like her pastor, was walking the pilgrim's path which leads to the Celestial City. Very often had her pastor's sympathy and heartfelt kindness cheered her fainting spirit, and now he gave her a parting word of encouragement, while experiencing himself (as it seemed to be) foreshadowings of the coming glory.

TO MRS. B——.

"ST. ANN'S RECTORY, *November*, 1862.

"DEAR SISTER IN CHRIST—Yours of the 19th was received. You ask about my health. It is not confirmed yet, and it is not yet decided what is to be done. I propose still to spend some months in more Southern cities. Yet I may still be driven to sea by my cough.

"'While place I seek or place I shun,
The soul finds happiness in none;
But with a God to guide our way,
'Tis equal joy to go or stay.'

"I am in the hands of our adorable Master. I hope I am on his heart; if so, all will be well. My sister is in New York; her husband is in a deplorable state of health, and they hardly know where to go; so you see we all have our trials. But I am so near seventy years, that how I spend, or where I spend, the last five years is a very little matter. I am daily striving to draw near, more near to Jesus Christ by faith, and also to acquaint myself with all that can be known about the glories, and joys, and delights of *the new world* into which I am expecting to be borne.

"God took me and brought me into this preparatory world, and I am expecting him to keep me by his power, through faith, to the day of my transition, and then to take me out of my present dark and helpless state, and usher me into a world of light, and joy, and peace!

"'Where the saints of all ages in harmony meet,
Their Saviour and brethren transported to greet.'

"My long known and beloved sister in Christ, and also sister in suffering, I call upon you to rejoice that Christ has counted you worthy to suffer in the sight of the saints, and called you to the field of patience and submission! Let us both glorify him there; let us try to 'rejoice in tribulation,' and however we may suffer, let us lift up our heads, for our redemption draweth nigh!

"I have not preached for four months, yet I could preach, if it were necessary; but my vestry have provided a young substitute, and still give me my support. When God opens my mouth I shall preach, and I hope he will fill it. Our dear, blessed Lord, be at your right hand!

"Your affectionate friend and pastor, B. C. CUTLER."

Dr. Cutler now consulted an eminent physician in New York, about the feasibility of a proposed plan to take a trip to Cuba. After examining his lungs he advised him not to go, and thought that entire rest in some inland city would be all that was necessary. It was therefore decided that he should go to Philadelphia. Before his departure he penned two letters, extracts from which we think well worth recording here:

TO MRS. FRANCIS.

"ST. ANN'S RECTORY, *December* 7, 1862.

"DEAR SISTER— . . . . God is very gracious to me, and this period of rest will result favorably, I doubt not, to body and soul. I needed a release from close professional confinement and responsibilities, and I can get much good from reading. Thompson's Elysium, I can almost attain, viz., 'an elegant sufficiency, content, retirement, rural quiet, friendship, books, ease and alternate labor, a useful life, progressive virtue, and approving heaven.'

"The speculations and sportings of such men as Thompson may *aim* at truth, but a Christian alone can *reach* it. Cowper can incorporate Christian experience in golden verse. Oh what a blessing to be taught of God! to be converted by the Holy Ghost! It was worth all Cowper's affliction. The darkness and gloom of Cowper was only superficial; his soul was settled deep in the Rock, Christ Jesus, and those winds that blew over him, and those waves that covered him, dispersed and disappeared, and he 'walked with God,' as he wished.

"My church seems in a very healthy state, and I can easily be spared. Oh that I might have the Saviour to lean upon, as I go down to the valley of rest and repose!

"With Him, I hope for all joy; and
"With Him I fear no evil,
"How far soever I go.

"Love to H——, and her husband and her children.

"Yours, most affectionately, UNCLE B."

TO MISS M. C——.

"*December* 9, 1862.

"MY DEAR FRIEND— . . . . . You speak of preaching the gospel. I long to be once more at that glorious work, and yet I am entirely submissive to Providence, and very thankful to my people for allowing me to rest. . . . . I expect it will turn out that I shall do better to remain in my own country, than to make a pilgrimage to foreign lands. In the hope of meeting you soon again, and in a better and more glorious hope of living eternally with saints now living and those departed, in glory,

"I remain most affectionately your pastor and friend,

"B. C. CUTLER.

"Best love to Miss Catharine."

The same day he baptized a granddaughter of his senior warden (Julia Maria Taft), and the next morning set out with Mrs. Cutler for Philadelphia. Soon after his arrival in that city, he wrote to his nephew in Montreal what proved to be his last letter to him, and full of precious counsel it is:

TO THE REV. C. BANCROFT, D. D., MONTREAL.

"PHILADELPHIA, *December* 12, 1862.

"DEAR CHARLES—Your choice of topics will determine your usefulness. Always take a rich gospel text, handle it so as to convert sinners, and throw your whole soul into it. Then, whatever of human learning or eloquence there may be in you, must and will come forth, and while trying to glorify Jesus Christ you will become glorious in the eyes of saints and angels, and of God himself. 'Let the dead bury their dead.' . . . . . 'But go thou and preach'—what? The kingdom of God, of grace and of Christ's glory! Let it all be royal—kingly in its conception, kingly in its accomplishment, and royal in its magnificence. I love those royal words, 'I will and you shall.'

"I trust my trial may be sanctified to me. I have not preached since July 13, except at funerals, etc. I am very delicate, and have had an obstinate cough, but that is almost gone.

"Best love to all, from UNCLE CUTLER."

He enjoyed very much every means of grace now available to him, especially the noonday prayer-meetings, held very near his hotel. Often did he step in and refresh his spirit here, when too feeble to do any thing more. He eagerly embraced every opportunity to attend missionary or prayer-meetings in various churches of the city. In a note to Mrs. Francis, under date of December 16, he thus alludes to these privileges:

"I have attended a prayer-meeting to-day in one of the most beautiful Episcopal churches in this city, viz., 'Holy Trinity,' Rev. Mr. Brooks, rector. Eleven ministers were present, and we had first a short service, and then other prayers and addresses. I never expected to see such zeal in the Episcopal Church when I entered its ministry forty years ago!

"With such pious and evangelical ministrations, the Puritans in the days of James I, would never have left the church; and John Wesley and Whitfield would not have rent it! Surely I can say, 'Lord, mine eyes have seen thy salvation!'"

A few days later, he wrote another consoling letter to a relative in Boston, who was in deep affliction:

TO MRS. PHILLIPS.

"PHILADELPHIA, *December* 20.

"DEAR COUSIN—We heard to-day with deep sorrow of your unspeakable loss. It came unexpectedly upon us, for we supposed your excellent son was restored to health. But God has seen fit to take him to himself, and what a chasm has been left in your heart! H—— and I have been musing over this great and strange work, and what can we say but this, that 'whom the Lord loveth he chasteneth,' and 'scourgeth every son whom he receiveth?'

"Your good mother's prayers were daily offered for your salvation and sanctification, and God is certainly taking the most effectual way of weaning any heart from the world. I mean, by withdrawing her son from a widowed mother. I heard of a widow like you, with two sons, both were drowned in one day, and what did the mother say? 'I see the Lord is determined to have the whole of my heart, and I am determined that he shall have it!' Our prayers shall be offered daily for you, that you may be supported under this severe bereavement, and that we may all at last meet in a world where all tears shall be wiped away.

"Affectionately, your cousin, B. C. CUTLER."

On Sunday, the weather being intensely cold, he did not dare to venture out in the morning. The following record is in his journal of this date:

"*Philadelphia, Dec.* 21, 1862.—I am travelling for my health, and experiencing, if not enjoying, perfect rest. I am slowly improving, if at all. But I have time given me, to look back upon my past ministry of forty years. Imperfection and unfaithfulness seem to stare me in the face. One in a thousand of my sins, I could not excuse. Lord Jesus, help me to make the scrutiny!"

In the afternoon of this Sunday, he attended divine service at St. Andrew's Church. On Christmas Day he assisted the Rev. Dr. Goddard at St. Paul's Church. It was a sad and lonely day to him, and his thoughts were often wandering back to Brooklyn and his dear parish.

His assistant and other friends were at the rectory of St. Ann's, anxiously awaiting almost daily tidings from him. To his devoted sister-in-law, he wrote on Christmas night:

TO MISS B——.

"DEAR SISTER—This has been a very dull day to me; my thoughts have been in Brooklyn all day. In the morning, heard Dr. G—— preach, and the remainder of the day I have been in my room. I have so long associated the day with festivity and social joys that solitude was strange. I have preached every Christmas, beginning with 1822 to 1862, except on two occasions, 1829 and 1862, and I was perhaps able to preach on these days, but was away from home; first in Savannah, and next in Philadelphia. . . . . So far, it augurs well about my wintering in America, instead of in Europe or Cuba. Give my love to Mr. Mills, and tell him our prayers are constant for him; also, give my love to all my people you meet, and tell them I find it difficult to content myself away from them, and from the work in which I have been so long engaged. . . . . I continue to enjoy the daily prayer-meeting; and cold, dry, ordinary pulpit '*reading* of sermons, without fervor of spirit, falls unprofitably on my ears. Fine writing, or attempts at Lyceumism, prevail here as in New York! The Lord have mercy upon us, and 'incline our hearts to keep' to *his gospel*, both in matter and manner. Jupiter, Julius Cæsar, ancient Egypt and Rome, bespangle our pulpit productions, to the delight of the weak and foolish, while God's people go hungry away. . . . . Adieu! H—— sends much love, and I too.

"Your affectionate brother, B. C. CUTLER."

Much in the same spirit he addressed a letter to one who had often enjoyed seasons of delightful intercourse at the rectory. She was now at a great distance, but still looked forward to many future seasons of happy greeting with these cherished and long-tried friends. But, alas! Infinite Wisdom had ordered otherwise.

TO MRS. WM. JACKSON, MILWAUKEE, WIS.

"PHILADELPHIA, *December* 27, 1862.

"MY DEAR SISTER IN CHRIST—You have heard that it has pleased God to reduce my strength to almost nothing. But I am slowly recovering part of what I have lost. Why God has not cut me off I know not, except it is, to give me time to repent and do my first works.

"Very close application to business of any kind, for a long period of time, is unfavorable to growth in grace; attending to every body's vineyard, our own is neglected; and yet it would not be fair to say that I did not lay down rules for the cultivation of personal piety and keep to them after some fashion. The relish for all Christian acts has never been lost. Still I am glad of time to set my house in order, to celebrate the praises of my Redeemer, and to recommend Him to *poor sinners* and to *poorer preachers!* Oh, how I long for the plain, simple, and spiritual preaching of *Cooper's* sermons or of Ryle's harangues!

"Literature, brilliancy, smartness, and oratorical efforts in the pulpit, fill churches and the pockets of the preachers; but, alas! for poor, stupid sinners!

"Lord have mercy upon us, and incline our hearts to preach and to love thy sweet, sure, sanctifying gospel. Oh for a thousand tongues to sing my great Redeemer's praise! The Lord bless you!

"Your brother in Christ, B. C. CUTLER."

His letters at this time, like the unfoldings of a panoramic picture, followed each other in rapid succession, and show the gradual workings of his mind, week after week, in a far clearer light than any mere statements which his biographer might make; and no apology will therefore be necessary for laying before our readers so much of Dr. Cutler's correspondence.

We recur once or twice more to his journal:

"*Sunday Eve, Dec.* 28, 1862.—I went this morning to St. Paul's and assisted Dr. Goddard. His sermon was on the text, 'The fashion of this world passeth away.' He told an excellent anecdote about a man on the point of committing suicide, converted to a philanthropist. . . . . Returning from church, I engaged in conversation with a stranger about the sermon.

"At 3½ P. M., I went to the 'Church of the Epiphany.' The Sunday-school celebration was held this afternoon. The rector (Rev. Dr. Newton) preached on Canticles v. 1—

our blessed Lord coming into his garden. The church was full to overflowing. . . . . Dr. Newton preached Jesus as I wish to hear him preached—plainly, spiritually, holily, boldly. Jesus must be the Alpha and the Omega of preaching, to satisfy my longing, sinful, languid, lagging heart!

"'How sweet the name of Jesus sounds
To a believer's ear!'"

Cheering letters from friends and parishioners came in, during the days intervening between Christmas and New Year's, some of which contained substantial tokens of kindness. An interesting reply to one of these is below:

TO W. B. C——, ESQ., BROOKLYN, N. Y.

"CONTINENTAL HOTEL, PHILADELPHIA, *December* 29, 1861.

"Many thanks, my dear friend, for your Christmas present and kind wishes. They were very cheering, for a duller Christmas I have not spent for scores of years. I have now been here nearly three weeks; the first week I lost ground, the second week I began to improve, and have continued gradually to gain a little. I have every kind of attention from friends, and this house is so central and so much esteemed, that I see the most interesting society now in motion. . . . .

"I find the Episcopal Churches are flourishing. . . . . Philadelphia, with two genuine bishops, and a large staff of evangelical clergymen, together with a Divinity School, under such instructors as Bishop Potter and Bishop Stevens, Drs. May and Stone, and with a heavy Episcopal purse ready to back them and to build churches, promises well for our Zion!

"I wish the nation was in as fair a way of improvement! I happened last week to hear the opinion of two extreme men, 'Parson Brownlow' and my friend the Hon. Mr. Randall, about the probable result of the whole contest; and though at sword's points in politics, they (separately) agreed! . . . . The 'Parson' was not very *polite* in handling your friends, the Democrats.

"The late Secretary of War, Mr. Cameron, Gov. Curtin, Mrs. President Lincoln, Gen. S——, and others of similar stamp, have been in the panorama before my eyes, and with most, I have been in conversation. I have both eyes and ears open, though I decline politics, and make speeches only at the noonday prayer-meeting, and at Sunday-school celebrations—by far the purer atmosphere!

"Give our love to Mrs. C—— and your family, also to my good old friend, Mr. R. S. Tucker, who, I hear, did not forget me at Christmas. . . . . I wish to live brimful of compassion and charity for all men, and burning with zeal only for my Master, who is King of kings! . . . . Adieu!

"Your obliged and affectionate friend and pastor,

"B. C. CUTLER."

The last note of the year was written to his niece (at Bordentown, N. J.), who had forwarded him several interesting books to beguile his weary hours:

TO MRS. M——

"PHILADELPHIA, *December* 31, 1862.

"MY DEAR ANNIE— . . . . I have done with Mr. M——'s books. 'The Gorilla' (in Du Chaillu's Africa) haunted me day and night. It is a frightful object, but I do not see why there may not be a progression upward, from small to great, in the monkey tribe, as in the *cat tribe!* I am not disturbed, as many are, by the external resemblance of the monkey to *man*, for I look at man's mind as the standard, not his external temple of dust! . . . . We think a little of going home to a wedding on the 8th of January, but it will depend upon both my health and the elements. I am still very sensitive to cold; am hoarse to-day, and have taken a little cold, with all my care.

"I was glad to hear from your Aunts Eliza and Louisa. . . . .

"There is no comfort for me in looking at the external form of *our political body*. It is a 'gorilla,' too! My comfort is that the Lord, who made us all, reigns, and he alone can make men 'to be of one mind in a house.' Your loving uncle, B. C. CUTLER."

A few more letters to beloved parishioners, and one parting line to a valued clerical friend of his early days, and his pen was laid aside for ever.

Could he have foreseen how soon he would be done with Time, what more appropriate language could he have uttered, than those quaint words so oft repeated by old Andrew Fuller, in his last days:

> "Go fearless, then, my soul with God,
> Into another room;
> Thou, who hast walked with him here,
> Go, see thy God at home!"

In tracing the course of his history, we now arrive at the commencement of a new year; but, in fact, we are called upon to contemplate in his own closing life, a rich autumnal sunset; "the sere and yellow leaf" is falling thick and fast, but there is a lingering freshness and bright glow upon the spiritual landscape that deepens every hallowed feeling, and with mingled admiration and awe, we approach to watch the scene, where mortals may not too far intrude. As we gaze at it from a distance, through the rifted clouds which in heavy folds skirt the horizon, gleams of light beam forth, and gradually those clouds themselves roll up, showing us somewhat of their silver linings, and revealing a radiance reflected from heaven itself, only to give way to the dawn of that eternal morning, where the ransomed spirit is to be "for ever with the Lord!"

The effusions of his pen at such a time, must not be passed by without notice.

See how his affectionate spirit beams forth in this congratulatory note to a parishioner.

TO MRS. H. M——.

"PHILADELPHIA, *January* 1, 1863.

"MY DEAR CHRISTIAN FRIEND—I received by mail to-day a watch-guard, and sit down to thank you for it, and to wish you, your dear husband and large family, a Happy New Year! I trust you all had a Merry Christmas, which I did not have. But since Christmas, many letters and tokens of kindness have come in to make me cheerful. But, as a general rule, I am *at heart* always cheerful. I expect nothing here below, but food and raiment, and that I can *trust* that God will afford me. My happiness is in godliness, in

God's house, in God's worship, and in seeing God's ways 'made known unto men, and his saving health among all nations.'

"The noonday prayer-meeting is held daily, opposite the side of this house, and as I do not go out evenings, I find that a means of grace. Give our love to all, and believe me, most affectionately,

"Your friend and pastor, B. C. CUTLER."

See his child-like confidence in all his Heavenly Father's dealings, in an extract from a note:

TO MRS. H——, NEW YORK.

"PHILADELPHIA, *January* 3.

"DEAR S—— —It is a fine winter day, but I am confined in the house by influenza. . . . . Though I feel poorly, I sit down to chat with you, to relieve the vacuum; for really I have too little spirit to write or read. But I can rejoice in the Lord, and rejoice that he reigns; and reigns for 'sparrows,' as well as for sages or saints. He has said, 'All things *shall* work together for good;' that is enough! Pray that I may have grace to glorify Him, anywhere and in every way. . . . . Love to Mr. H—— and Charlie.

"From your friend and pastor, B. C. CUTLER."

We now turn to some of his last precious thoughts, as gathered from his journal. With care, we transcribe every word, mingled with a feeling of sacred awe, for he was nearing the eternal world; and as we look at the written page and recognize his own hand, we almost hear a voice speaking in language not unlike that once addressed to Moses: "Put off thy shoes from off thy feet, for this is holy ground."

"*Philadelphia, Sunday, Jan.* 4, 1863.—I took a hoarse cold last week, and have been very miserable ever since. Had Dr. Morris yesterday and to-day. How I took the cold, I cannot tell; it has been very discouraging. But for all my *ills* and troubles, I have one sovereign remedy—looking up to God, as an infinite and gracious God looking down on me, and appointing all my trials, *little* as well as great. God is a *God* to me! He is all in all—ALL! my all is in him, and I come to him through Christ Jesus, his dear Son. 'All my fresh springs shall be in Thee.'—Ps. lvii. 7 (Psalter).

With indescribable solemnity and a trembling hand, we have thus lifted the veil for a moment, that reveals to other eyes the most sacred feelings of his soul, with the exception of a few lines, the *last* he recorded on earth. All his "springs" of joy had indeed been recognized as coming from the life-giving Fountain above, for more than half a century since his earliest youth, and most truly he might say:

> "My spirit, still hovering, half blest,
> 'Mid shadows so fleeting and dim,
> Ah! know'st thou thy Rock, and thy haven of rest,
> And thy pure spring of joy? Then to Him!
> Then to Him, fluttering spirit, to Him!"

Dr. Cutler's severe cough proved unusually obstinate, and finding himself growing weaker, he determined to retrace his steps homeward. He and Mrs. Cutler returned therefore, to the rectory at Brooklyn on the 8th of January.

Finding a letter from his early friend (one of the trio of intimate associates in former years), the Rev. Dr. Edson, awaiting him, he sent the following reply, the last note he penned to any clerical friend:

TO THE REV. T. EDSON, D. D., LOWELL, MASS.

"ST. ANN'S RECTORY, BROOKLYN, N. Y., *January* 9, 1863.

DEAR BROTHER—I returned last night after an absence of a month or so in Philadelphia. I found your letter and read it with sympathy. I have been, now am, ... a wounded soldier of Christ! I have not fought a battle for my Master in the pulpit for half a year! In fact, I am in the furnace; but he is with me, cooling the flames and easing the pains—leading me, indeed, in green pastures and beside still waters. Whether at sixty-five (nearly) I can expect my wounds to be healed, is another thing. Often do I think of B. C. C. P——; often gather courage and strength in making up for his loss, and always do I wonder why I am left!

"I had a fever in July which reduced me to a shadow, and left me with a cough, and with that I am battling now.

"Ten days ago I took a fresh cold, and my cough, which had fled, came back. My parish gave me the balance of the year to take rest; . . . . but I do not think I shall take it. I think of putting the small part of the candle that remains into a 'save-all,' and let my light shine until it burns out! . . . .

"As I grow old I am getting brimful of charity for men, and of compassion for their errors. *The main thing* now attracts or repels me—friendship or enmity to Christ!

"If any man have not the *Spirit* of Christ, no matter what else he has, he is none of his; and if any man have the Spirit of Christ, he is one of his; and if he is one of Christ's little ones or great ones, high ones or low ones, broad ones or narrow ones, he is my brother, or she is my sister and my mother, and I love him or her, and would come or go, and make my abode with him or her. Adieu! A Happy New Year may you all have, for Christ's sake!

"Affectionately, yours, B. C. CUTLER."

Is this not a spirit akin to heaven? and was he not catching the influence of that atmosphere of *love* which, beams down from the Divine Source, and is reflected from the face of every angel and saint above—of that perfect love which inspires every note which swells from the harps and voices of the innumerable host of the redeemed?

On the 10th of January his cough had considerably increased, and at midnight became so severe he was obliged to leave his bed, and sit up till morning, Mrs. Cutler and sister being with him all the time.

"*Brooklyn, Jan.* 11, 1863. *Sunday.*"—He writes: "To-day, I am better, but weak. But I am what and where? He who made me and owns me has placed me here!"

These are the *last* words of his journal. He had, indeed, come home, but it was—*to die!* to pass from under the shadow of his church, where he had so long testified of Jesus, into his blissful presence above! Neither the untiring devotion of the nearest and dearest friends, nor the unceasing kindness of an affectionate flock, could detain him here below. His strength temporarily revived in a few days, and thus were elicited, in a note to a parishioner, some grateful thoughts:

TO MISS M—— C——.

"*January* 14, 1863.

"I am not well enough, my dear friend, to reply to your note, so overflowing with kindness and generosity. But I lose no time in saying, that in the depth of my trial, the hope and belief that my life and labors have not been in vain, does afford some consolation.

"The 'communion of saints' affords more. I love all who love our Lord Jesus Christ in sincerity, and to feel that I am loved of them, is indeed a rich treat. If those who are living have this affection for so unworthy a brother, those made perfect in heaven may have more, and to be loved by so large a circle is most truly delightful; and yet, my heart and mind rest on the love of GOD! The former love, I know; the latter *passeth knowledge.* He who loves me thus lays on the rod day by day, and heals the wounds as fast as they are made. 'All my fresh springs are in thee,' oh, my God!

"Affectionately and gratefully, your pastor, B. C. CUTLER."

He was now drawing near the end of his earthly cares and trials. He was able to drive out occasionally, when the cold was not too severe, but soon found even this produced great weariness. His cough prostrated him to an alarming degree, and he could scarcely leave his room. Days of weariness and nights of exhausting pain were now allotted to him. His nervous system seemed strung to its utmost tension, and the irritation of mind and body which his cough produced would not allow him long to rest, nor could he give his attention to any subject for any length of time. But his heart was fixed on God, and he knew "no other will but his." His intervals of comparative ease were employed in reading short passages of Scripture and religious tracts, or in perusing some favorite hymns. At times he would repeat or listen to them. Either excessive pain or extreme weakness, however, he was enduring all the time.

"Suffering is the *work* now sent:
Nothing can I do but lie
Suffering as the hours go by;
All my powers to this are bent.
Suffering is my *gain*: I bow
To my Heavenly Father's will,
And receive it hush'd and still;
Suffering is my *worship* now!"

He rallied a little on the 20th of January, and on the following day he wrote the following note to a friend (then absent in Europe), in acknowledgment of a letter of affectionate sympathy. They are the *last* sacred words his pen ever traced. How touching is the thought! Those fingers were so soon to be employed in tuning his golden harp to sing, with the multitude of the heavenly host, "the song of Moses and the Lamb!"

TO G. D. M——, ESQ.

"St. Ann's Rectory, Brooklyn, N. Y., *January* 21, 1863.

"Very Dear Friend—I thank you very much for your letter, dated Naples, December 30, which I this day received. You will be sorry to hear that I am in a very sick and perilous condition. Hours of this day I could not have signed my name to this note, such has been my distress! I should be in bed, but I cannot stay in bed. I have a most dreadful cough. I had a spasmodic cough that sent me southward to Philadelphia. But I took cold there and had to come home, and am very much worse since my return.

"Some one else will probably finish this note, and tell you how much I thank you for your Christmas present, ... and how much I love and value you and yours.

"Our dear Jesus guard and save us all! Amen, and Amen!

"Unalterably yours, B. C. Cutler.

"P. S.—*January* 22, 1863.— . . . I rose at 5 A. M., to cough. Pray for me! Love to all. Not a sparrow falls to the ground without your Heavenly Father, and even the hairs of your head, etc., etc.

"Yours, affectionately, B. C. Cutler.

"O Lord, in thee do I put my trust!"

All hope of prolonging a life so holy and precious was

now fast fading away from the minds of his nearest kindred. The fondest affection could not bear to see him suffering, and yet longed to detain him, hoping for a favorable change. The struggle was intense, but it ere long gave way to the agonizing conviction that he would soon be parted from all earthly ties.

His paroxysms of suffering now became intense. So severe was his cough that he was apprehensive of suffocation, and was compelled to be silent for hours together, thus affording little opportunity for conversation even with his nearest friends.

On the 24th of January, he took a short drive in his carriage, but the effort he made to repress his spasmodic cough soon weakened him, and he came home exhausted to such a degree that he could scarcely enter the house, and some time elapsed before he was able to reach his room. His physician coming in at this moment, expressed surprise at his extreme prostration, and advised the immediate use of further tonics and stimulants.

After that day he was unable to leave his bed again. It was only occasionally, in the intervals between his cough, that he could see any of his friends. His friend, Rev. S. H. Tyng, D. D., was privileged to see him on Friday, the 30th of January; it was an interesting interview to both of them, and after minute conversation and prayer, and many expressions of tender encouragement on the part of Dr. Cutler, they bade a final farewell to each other. Dr. Tyng thus refers to this visit, and to the expressions of his early friend, who was now on the verge of the eternal world:

"He was sitting, propped up in his bed, cheerful and contented, calmly, humbly waiting for his Lord; in his outward appearance painfully altered since I had seen him last. Our conversation was familiar and free. He spoke without difficulty, though with evident fatigue. Much that he said was personal and deeply interesting to myself. Among other more general expressions, were these affecting words: 'My dear brother, I am ready to take the hand of the poorest beggar that ever went into the kingdom of God, and enter there with him.'

"'They ask me if I have new views of heaven or heavenly things. Heaven is Christ, and Christ is heaven. I shall be with Christ; that is what I think of.'"*

His thoughts now seemed day by day to be concentrated on eternal things, and especially on the happiness of being in the very presence of the Saviour above. He had long seen him (to use the apostle's expression) "through a glass darkly," now, his chief desire was to see him "face to face." He had an inward assurance he should soon be there, and behold that Jesus, whom having not seen, he had here so ardently loved and so faithfully served.

"Beyond the smiling and the weeping,
I shall be soon.
Beyond the waking and the sleeping,
Beyond the sowing and the reaping,
I shall be soon.
Love, rest and home,
Sweet hope!
Lord, tarry not, but come!"

Though at times in much physical suffering, he often said, when inquiries were made about his condition, "*the undercurrents are all peace;*" and it was evident to his family, that while the poor body was daily sinking in the struggle with disease, his soul was stayed on God.

He could bear no excitement, and it was impossible for him to see the many dear clerical friends in Brooklyn and New York, who often called, and who would have rejoiced to have a moment's interview had his situation allowed; and he preferred to be alone, as it seemed, in close commun-

* See "Son of Consolation," p. 85.

ion with his God. The beloved partner of all his joys and sorrows for forty years, could not be with him as much as she desired. There was an inability on his part to speak, combined, perhaps, with a fear that the prospect of sundering so strong a tie to earth might momentarily disturb his composure.

On the 1st of February, Mrs. Cutler informed him that she had sent a telegram to their nephew, the Rev. Dr. Bancroft, of Montreal, urging him to come at once to Brooklyn; to which his only reply was, "I expected it"—pleased, evidently, with the idea of once more seeing this relative.

On Tuesday morning, February 3d, Dr. Bancroft entered the room, and was greeted with the same affectionate welcome which he had so often received before from his beloved uncle. "We were here all night together," said he (referring to his wife and her sister). "How happy to live together and die together, trusting in God."

At his request, his nephew read a portion of the sixteenth chapter of St. John, from the Testament which lay before him opened at that place, and then offered prayer. As if to fix his mind permanently on some precious portion of heavenly manna, to sustain him in his passage over Jordan, Dr. Cutler also desired his nephew to read the twenty-third Psalm.

Each day of that week Dr. Bancroft read to him portions of Scripture, and at the bedside of the suffering saint, offered up earnest and fervent prayer. God was arranging every thing kindly for his dying servant. He was at home, with his loved ones near him, under the shadow of the dear parish church, and as he entered the dark valley he enjoyed what he desired to have—the presence of an abiding Saviour, who placed beneath him "THE EVERLASTING ARMS," and buoyed up his soul, making him strong in spirit, when the body was in weakness and pain.

How often had Dr. Cutler repeated the saying of the

Rev. John Newton, "Tell me not how a man died, tell me how he LIVED!" The same sentiment was strong within him now, and in reference to dying testimony he said, "*I have said my say;*" intimating, by quaint and forcible language, that he had nothing to add, and nothing to change; and, like the late Mr. Simeon, of England, he shrank from any unnecessary declarations or any parade of religious feelings at such a time, abhorring from his very soul what has been styled "a death-bed scene."

He deemed a sinner's place to be in humble adoration at the Saviour's feet. If it pleased God that his lamp should shine out brightly at the last, it were well, for he would be glorified in his strength. If it pleased him that the light should sink and go out in its socket, that were well, too; for he would be glorified in his weakness.

It was of small moment to him what might be the *manner* of his departure, when he knew that "PRECIOUS in the sight of the Lord is the death of his saints;" and in death, as in life, he trusted all to God.

On Saturday, the 7th of February, he desired an interview with his assistant (Rev. L. H. Mills), who was residing at the rectory, seeing him but seldom, as he himself was so closely occupied with the accumulated burdens of parish duty. As he approached the bed, he perceived that he asked for prayer, and he immediately knelt down and prayed. Dr. Cutler, then taking his hand in one of his and stretching out his other arm toward heaven with an open hand, looking upward with strong and earnest gaze, said, "Eye hath not seen, nor ear heard; neither have entered into the heart of man the things which God hath prepared for them that love him! I know whom I have believed. I know that my Redeemer liveth! I love the Saviour! I love his people! I love all that belongs to him!" He could say no more, and after a silent pressure of the hand, his friend withdrew. He was now

> "Nearing the bound of life,
> Where we lay our burdens down;
> Nearer leaving his cross,
> Nearer wearing his crown!"

On Sunday, the 8th of February, he requested his nephew (Dr. Bancroft) to read that appropriate prayer in the service of the church for "the Visitation of the Sick," where the souls of the departing are commended into the hands of God, and after he had concluded, said to him, "the peace, the peace," referring to the final blessing, which was then pronounced.

During all the preceding week, prayers were offered in various churches for one who was so universally revered and beloved. In St. Ann's, there was a meeting for prayer held each day at 4 P. M. On the afternoon of Monday, February 9th, many of his friends were gathered together, as usual, in prayer for him; Dr. Shelton, of Newtown, L. I., who was present, had made a touching reference to their long friendship. Dr. Bancroft was also present at the meeting, and as they were kneeling side by side, the latter was sent for, as Dr. Cutler seemed to be near his end, and had desired to see him. On entering his room, he beckoned to him to pray; and after the prayer was finished, rising in bed with great energy, he raised his hands and his eyes toward heaven, and exclaimed, "Come, Lord Jesus, come quickly! I *do* want to go to Jesus!"

Strong was his desire to depart. His course was almost finished, his warfare nearly ended, and the soul longed for entire emancipation from its earthly bondage. Friends were bowed in speechless sorrow in the adjoining rooms; eyes were heavy with weeping, and hearts were well-nigh breaking; he himself, with quiet assurance, eagerly awaiting the moment of dismissal from the worn body. Utterance nearly failed, but he seemed to say, by every look and motion,

"Let me go, I may not tarry,
Wrestling thus with doubts and fears;
Angels wait my soul to carry,
Where my risen Lord appears!"

Could we have withdrawn the veil, we might have seen the angels and seraphs waiting on the other side of the river of Death. As they drew near, at the bidding of the King upon the throne, imagination could almost hear their notes of welcome, in reply to his earnest entreaties to go hence:

"O Valiant-for-the-Truth,
Hail! from thy battle-field;
A Christian warrior from thy youth,
Who never knew to yield;
The conquering armor here lay down,
For the white robe, the palm, the crown!"

At 10 o'clock the same evening, with great composure, he gently said (after prayer): "Lord Jesus, receive my spirit!"

The night rolled by and the early dawn of Tuesday (February 10th) found him still here. Soon, however, about 7 A. M., he summoned Dr. Bancroft and Mr. Mills to his room. Speedily they came, and in a moment, with earnest beckonings, he drew them to his bedside, and said, "Lift me up, lift me right up!" and as they raised him up and supported him, he quietly bowed his head, gently breathing. They thought him asleep, but his head bent forward more and more, and in the arms of his first and of his last assistant he ceased to breathe, and they knew it was the sleep that "knows no waking!"

His soul was with Jesus; but the tabernacle of the body was before us, and there still lingered a smile upon the countenance, which told us how fully his wishes were realized; for he had said many years before, "My ambition is to smile, while laying my head on a dying pillow."

It may be that the angels in heaven ceased their song, and rested on their harps awhile, as another soul entered the courts above, and heard with wonder his story of Jesus' love through life's pilgrimage. Many, many glorified ones came forth to greet him, saying, "*You* brought me first to Jesus;" and overcome with the blissful sense, he cast himself and his crown still lower at the feet of that Saviour, exclaiming, "THOU ART WORTHY!"

Then, while we wept on earth, the heavenly choir retuned their harps and sang REDEEMING LOVE!

"Brother, thou art gone before us,
Where thy saintly soul has flown;
Tears are wiped away for ever,
And all sorrow is unknown;
By the burden of the body
Never more to be opprest,
Where the wicked cease from troubling,
And the weary are at rest!"

On the announcement of Dr. Cutler's demise, wide-spread expressions of public grief testified to the worth of this eminent man of God.

The religious press proclaimed the depth of sorrow which pervaded the minds of all classes in the community, and the secular press was equally emphatic in its utterance. Various societies gave expression to their sense of his loss by published resolutions.

Christian ministers of every name mourned for a brother indeed, and the clergy of his own church of every shade of opinion, united in heart-felt tributes to his memory.

Obituaries, interesting in detail, swelled the volume of testimony to his rare excellence and great worth.

Official communications and private letters expatiated upon his transcendently sweet and attractive Christian character, and his useful labors.

So great and universal was the mourning in the parish of St. Ann's, that it seemed as if "there was not a house where there was not one dead!" The vestry paid a grateful tribute of sympathy, embodied in their resolutions.

The tide flowed in upon the bereaved household from all parts of the land, and even from other countries, exhibiting in a most touching manner, how much real affection and tender sympathy still entwined itself around our fallen humanity.

The views of many were well expressed in a note from a former assistant minister of St. Ann's to one of the vestry of the same church:

"A leader has fallen in the ranks of the Christian host who has fought a good fight, whose cheerful presence, truthful words, and earnest appeals have for so many years enlisted and animated the soldiers of the cross. . . . . His praise is in all the churches, and his memory will be widely and deeply cherished. Long years has he worn the Christian armor and battled with faithfulness and zeal. He has gone to receive his crown. Let us not murmur at the providence of God, whose ways, though past finding out, are yet goodness and truth. . . . .

"In sympathy with his stricken family and a sorrowing people, I remain,

"Very truly, yours, G. L. Platt."

His bereaved widow felt her loss to be truly irreparable. Nature almost sank under the blow, but grace sustained her, and she still lives to testify—and feels it her privilege so to do—that Jesus is all-sufficient for life's heaviest calamity, for the heart's deepest woe.

The numerous and various letters of condolence received in the time of unutterable anguish, were a source of exquisite soothing. We instance the following, recognizing immediately the strong and forcible language of the honored Bishop of the Diocese of Pennsylvania :

"MY DEAR MRS. CUTLER—Amid the shock of your sore bereavement, and the crowd of condolences which press upon you, you will not miss mine. But I cannot refrain from saying how fondly for thirty-seven years I have loved your husband ; how much I have enjoyed his radiant temperament and conversation, and how profoundly I have always been impressed with his thorough honesty and fervent piety. Little did I think when I last saw him in Philadelphia, a few weeks ago, that he was so near the spirit-world. It was better for him to depart and to be with Christ ; but how vast the breach, how saddening the thought, that we all, but especially you, must henceforth wend your weary journey without the cheering influence of his presence and his prayers.

"The friends of our youth fall around us on every side, and we seem left alone, straying in generations that have now to take our place and do our work.

"Enough, if as pilgrims, we are preparing to lay aside our staff and scrip, and enter on our rest.

"May the good God be very gracious unto you! May he lift up the light of his countenance upon you, and give you PEACE! Ever affectionately yours,

"ALONZO POTTER.

"PHILADELPHIA, *February* 23, 1863."

The funeral of Dr. Cutler was attended at St. Ann's Church, Brooklyn, on Friday, February 13th, and was an affecting ceremony. A large meeting of the clergy was held in the chapel at 12 o'clock, at which the Rev. Dr. Muhlenberg presided. Appropriate resolutions were offered by the Rev. Dr. Canfield (rector of Christ Church, Brooklyn), which were adopted, after remarks from the Rev. Drs.

Johnson and Vinton, and the Rev. Messrs. Shelton and Moore, of the Episcopal Church, and also from Rev. Drs. Cox and Spear, of the Presbyterian communion.

At the appointed hour, (1 o'clock) the clergy formed in procession, with the Bishop of the diocese at their head, and repaired to the parsonage adjoining the church and received the remains, which were borne from the house by the following clergymen, acting as pall-bearers:

REV. DR. SHELTON,	REV. DR. TYNG,
REV. DR. MUHLENBERG,	REV. DR. CANFIELD,
REV. DR. DYER,	REV. DR. F. VINTON,
REV. DR. JONES,	REV. DR. TAYLOR.

At the entrance of the church the remains were met by the officiating clergy, the Rev. Messrs. Littlejohn, Morgan, Flagg, Johnson and Paddock.

So intense was the desire on the part of the public to pay the last tribute of respect to his memory, that the galleries were filled long before the appointed hour; and as soon as the coffin was carried into the church, the spacious building was filled to overflowing.

The church was appropriately draped in mourning.

The body having been placed in front of the chancel, the anthem, "I know that my Redeemer liveth," was sung, after which the Psalter, commencing, "Lord let me know mine end," was solemnly chanted by the choir. Dr. Littlejohn read the lesson from 1 Cor. xv., which was followed by the singing of the 191st hymn:

"Vital spark of heavenly flame,
Quit, oh, quit this mortal frame!"

The revered Bishop of the Diocese of New York, the Rt. Rev. H. Potter, D. D., laboring under deep emotion, then delivered a memorial address, which was a fitting and beautiful tribute to the character of the deceased.

After the remaining services were concluded, an opportunity was offered to the weeping multitude of parishioners and friends who thronged the edifice, to look upon his face for the last time. The body was then taken to Greenwood Cemetery, followed by a long train of carriages. At the grave, the Rev. Dr. Canfield conducted a short service, committing " dust to dust " in " a sure hope of a joyful resurrection."

As we turned away from the spot, the sun had just sunk beneath the hills, but there lingered a clear and golden light encircling the horizon, cheering our hearts with the hope of a brighter day. For our brother, we had the assurance that he had entered in where there was no night, and where he realized the fullness of the promise, " THY SUN SHALL NO MORE GO DOWN, NEITHER SHALL THY MOON WITHDRAW ITSELF ; FOR THE LORD SHALL BE THINE EVERLASTING LIGHT, AND THY GOD THY GLORY !"

How life-like is the following sketch by the Rt. Rev. the Bishop of the Diocese of Massachusetts:

"BOSTON, *January* 9, 1868.

"MY DEAR MR. GRAY:

"You have asked me for some reminiscences of my old and dear friend, Dr. Cutler, and I gladly put on paper my recollections of him; although I am quite sure that I can furnish nothing that will not have been communicated to you by others, who were brought into frequent intercourse with him during his long and faithful ministry.

"I first met Dr. Cutler, more than forty years ago, at the house of his brother-in-law, the late Mr. Samuel Ward, in New York; and I remember being attracted by the singular purity and simplicity of his countenance, and the sweetness and refinement of his manner. I afterwards saw him again in Boston, during a visit which I made to that city in the summer of 1825. But my intimate intercourse with him only began several years after, when, at the suggestion of Mr. Ward, he was appointed minister of a free church in Vandewater Street, New York, under the auspices of what was then known as the Protestant Episcopal City Mission. After a brief but active course of labor in this field, he became the rector of St. Ann's, Brooklyn; and from that time until my removal from New York I was often brought into contact with him. And I am sure that no man could have lived in intercourse with him, without feeling his faith strengthened in *the reality of religion*. In calling up those days to memory, as well as in recollecting my occasional interviews since my removal to Massachusetts, I have been strongly impressed with the remembrance of one thought which suggested itself to me whenever I saw him: 'Here is a person evidently born again from above, led by the Spirit, and taught of God.' In fact, who that knew Dr. Cutler did not feel the perfect certainty, that religion with him was not something put on, but was the new nature of the man—the atmosphere in which he lived—the spring of all his thoughts, and all his words, and all his deeds?

"During my residence in New York, Dr. Cutler was often called upon, and never declined, to deliver addresses at our missionary meetings in two or three of the churches of that city. And what he said on these occasions was always impressive, because it was always *real;* and evidently came from the heart of a man who desired to extend the healing remedy of the gospel, because he himself had tasted the value of the Great Physician.

"Dr. Cutler being, like myself, in the habit of daily exercise on horseback, we used for a long time to ride together on the morning of every Saturday. And I also remember a journey of two days we made in this way along the banks of the Hudson, for the purpose of participating in some services in Peekskill Church. I recollect that during this latter excursion, as well as during other rides, the fervor of his cheerful, grateful, and abounding spirit of praise would often break forth from him suddenly, in a way that, to a stranger, might seem like eccentricity, but which in him was the mere utterance of a remarkably heavenly mind. He would sometimes stop, and begin to pray, while sitting in the saddle; or he would sing a hymn as we travelled along the road side by side. And yet so naturally and easily was all this done, and so obviously did it flow from a deep fountain of love, that the thought of display or cant, in connection with these acts of his, never could have suggested itself for one moment to the mind.

"My dear old friend always exhibited, in his daily course,

a beautiful combination of the gentleman, and the faithful ambassador of Heaven. He had the ease and self-possession to be expected from a man who had been accustomed to the intercourse of polished life; and yet he never allowed himself, from a false notion of the claims of courtesy, to sink the minister of salvation in the *mere* gentleman. Delicate in constitution, and liable to severe assaults of illness, he was kept thereby in a near view of the eternal world; and this gave him a constant sense of the importance of leading others to consider the infinite worth of the soul. He was, therefore, anxious to lose no opportunity of letting fall a word in season, which, with the Divine blessing, might bear fruit unto eternal life. This habit of his I have often witnessed, not without being humbled by it, and, I trust, with benefit to me in other respects as I marked his shining example. In truth, my departed friend was one of the last men to whom one would have turned, as an illustration of Mr. Cecil's striking remark on that kind of intercourse of a clergyman with his hearers, which seems to say to them, On the Sunday I am ready to do *my* business, and in the week you may do *yours*.'

"Dr. Cutler, born in our beloved and Scriptural Church, was a devoted and glowing lover of its polity and ritual. But he chiefly loved it because its services are so full of Christ; and because its Liturgy and Offices so effectually hand down the saving truth of the gospel from generation to generation. And this attachment, founded on his loyalty and gratitude to the bleeding Lamb of God, led him to love all, of every name, who love our Lord Jesus Christ in sincerity; and also to lend his aid to those great institutions, which, embracing all the followers of Emmanuel, and yet without compromising our allegiance to our own Church, have for their object the diffusion of Christ's saving health among all nations. And in this respect he was in harmony with the spirit of our Church, and was one of its true representatives. And thus that admiration, on the part of all Christian people, which formed no portion of his motives of action, he yet secured during his honored life; and now that he is gone, he is embalmed in their grateful and abiding recollection.

"I have nothing to add, but my prayer that the volume which you are preparing to my revered friend's memory may be accompanied by the Holy Spirit's blessing.

"Believe me to be faithfully yours,

"MANTON EASTBURN."

CHAPTER XVII.

CONCLUSION.

TRAITS OF CHARACTER, ETC., ETC.—HIS VIEWS ON PREACHING—PASTORAL WORK—CONNECTION WITH PUBLIC SOCIETIES, ETC., ETC.

THIS volume should not be closed without further allusion to several points which have only been touched upon in the progress of the work. It would be difficult to give an adequate analysis of Dr. Cutler's character, and superfluous, perhaps, since in many important particulars this has already been done, by the rector of St. George's Church, New York, in the impressive sermon delivered by him, in St. Ann's Church, Brooklyn (at the request of the vestry), on the second Sunday after Dr. Cutler's decease. The discourse was afterward embodied in a little work, entitled " The Son of Consolation."

It was an elaborate tribute to the memory of his early friend; and in assisting our readers to form a just estimate of the man, and to glean for themselves those practical lessons which may be learned from his history, we shall merely suggest certain points which appear to be worthy of especial study.

We look back through Dr. Cutler's life, and trace the Infinite Wisdom and Love which marked out for him a path of early and continued suffering. This drew him nearer to Jesus in prayer, and from his sanctified trials flowed innumerable blessings to himself and to others.

1. He was in a remarkable sense *a man of prayer*.

Morning, noon, and night, he presented his petitions at

the throne of grace. No journey was undertaken, no plan devised, without seeking God's glory, and asking his direction. He was constant and regular in prayer, and allowed nothing to interfere with the discharge of this duty. Thus was the oil of Divine grace daily and steadily poured into his soul, and the light of his piety was kept brightly and unceasingly burning.

In daily family prayer, if clerical visitors happened to be present, he would request them in turn to offer distinct and separate prayers, and with such admirable tact was all this done, that no strange or abrupt transition from conversation to devotion was ever apparent. Few friends ever visited him, in his study, without his offering up prayer with them. As an illustration of this point, we give an incident which the present esteemed Assistant Bishop of the Diocese of Pennsylvania has related to us. Just before his consecration to the Episcopate, the Rev. Dr. Stevens (then rector of St. Andrew's, Philadelphia), being in New York, on business connected with the Foreign Committee, had occasion to call on Dr. Cutler. Being wearied, the latter offered him some simple refreshment, in his study, after which he said: "You are about to become a bishop, I am only an humble presbyter, and I may not perhaps talk so freely hereafter as now, but we are both poor sinners before God—let us kneel down in prayer together." After Dr. Stevens had finished, his friend and host offered up a fervent prayer that God would bless his servant in the exalted station to which he had been called, supporting him under all its burdens and responsibilities, and making him a blessing to many. This conversation and prayer left an indelible impression upon the mind of the Bishop elect. And through many a day of toil and hour of darkness the remembrance of this interview, will doubtless, like an oft-recurring sunbeam, cheer and refresh his spirit.

Absent friends were also requested (as we have seen) to

pray for Dr. Cutler and his people; and at an appointed hour, in different portions of the country, many friends were pleading for him at the Mercy-seat, while he was actually interceding in turn for them. However and whenever separated, the spirit of his heart was—

"Prayer shall a vast triangle form,
On whose wide base we still shall meet,
And whose high top surmounts each storm,
And joins us at our Saviour's feet."

In his private life, without any exaggerated language, he literally WALKED WITH GOD; the closeness of his walk was very unusual, even among the ministers of God; he went and told Jesus *every thing*, and thus, like a child, lived upon his guardian care. "Without ME ye can do *nothing*" was engraved on his heart, and communion with the invisible God was his very life. None but those who saw him, in all the phases of every-day life, can form a true idea of the symmetry of his Christian character and course. Continual prayer and intercession was the lattice or trellis, upon which all the graces of his Christian character were diligently trained and cherished, as they pointed upward, and thus the bloom and fragrance of spiritual life were everywhere apparent, investing his daily life with a sanctity and charm indescribably impressive and heavenly.

His study was a hallowed spot, where the prayer of faith received an abundant answer; there were sought, and there obtained, blessings for the souls of others. His ministry never would have exhibited the results that have come from it (and shall yet come, though he be dead), had it not been for the spirit of earnest devotion which pervaded and moulded his whole life.

2. He had *an abounding spirit of praise.*

If any man ever obeyed the apostolic injunction, it was he: "In every thing by prayer and supplication, WITH THANKSGIVING, let your requests be made known unto God."

Everywhere, in private and in public, this spirit manifested itself. If in prayer, the language of petition was often changed into that of adoring gratitude, and in this respect he followed the teachings of Scripture, and the example of eminent believers. "The true child of God (we quote the language of a recent work, entitled Professor Hart's "Golden Censer"), even when crying for deliverance, in some hour of sharp distress, finds it difficult to make his prayer *all* supplication, so natural is it to the grateful, loving heart of the believer, to rise from the language of entreaty to that of thanksgiving. Even in the Fifty-first Psalm, from the very depths of his penitent cries for pardon, David cannot forbear to 'sing aloud' of God's goodness. How frequently does St. Paul, in the very midst of close, compacted argument, burst out into some strain of rapt, sublime doxology! When faith sees with unclouded vision her risen Lord, it is impossible to withhold the warm ascription of praise ; and it is just where godly sorrow does its most perfect work, that of faith takes freshest and strongest hold of the promises. Hence, nothing is more natural than this transition from prayer to praise, from the low wail of penitence to the exultant loud-harping hallelujah."

Many will now remember how often our friend would commence "family prayers" with singing, almost exultantly, that unequalled hymn of Addison :

"When all thy mercies, O my God !
My rising soul surveys," etc., etc.

At feasts, among his friends, he often proposed to sing hymns ; and the brilliant assemblage gathered together at a banquet, on the occasion of a marriage of a relative at Newport, will not soon forget his asking the privilege of singing "grace" before sitting down. He then sounded the note of joyful gratitude, and united many a heart in the sentiment,

> "Praise God, from whom all blessings flow."

He was remarkably fond of good hymns. Sacred poetry of every kind proved often a solace to his heart. When sickness had slackened the cords of life; when mind and heart had become benumbed by his daily toil and care, the psalm or hymn, at a late hour, would restore his spirit; give renewed clearness to his mental vision, and lead his soul back to its place of *rest* in the presence of "things unseen and eternal."

And does not religious poetry, we ask, often lift the mind of the Christian above the dusty walks of ordinary life into a clearer atmosphere? Does not Cowper's "Task" contribute to this end? Have not the hymns of Addison and Doddridge, and the soul-stirring verses of Wesley, kindled the soul of many a wanderer, and shed light on his path to "the Celestial City?" May it not in truth be said that the "divine songs" of Dr. Watts have proved an abundant and universal blessing, and will not cease to be sung, till time shall be no more? "The Missionary Hymn" of Bishop Heber, too, is a resistless appeal, and it has everywhere thrilled the human heart. The converted Hindoo chants it, among the spicy groves of India; the African repeats it, by the rivers and plains of his country; while the Christian, in a land of light and liberty, catches up the strain, and pours forth the emotions of his heart in these glowing lines, as if the Seraphim had touched his tongue with a live coal from off the altar of God.

Of more modern hymns, Dr. Cutler took special delight in that well-known gem, by the Rev. H. F. Lyte, of the Church of England:

> "Abide with me; fast falls the eventide.
> The darkness thickens; Lord with me abide!

> When other helpers fail and comforts flee,
> Help of the helpless, oh, abide with me!"

3. He was *a spiritual and experimental Christian.*

True religion is the life of Jesus dwelling in the soul of the believer. But Christian experience varies, some of the children of God are more heavily afflicted, more frequently chastened, than others; have had more to do with providential dispensations; have had closer insight into their own hearts, and been permitted to learn more thoroughly their own native weakness and the fullness of grace that is in Christ, and, by such processes, have become more deeply spiritual than others. In this class we find the subject of this memoir. We may trace Christian experience, in some of its strongest colorings, in the recorded exercises of his soul, and in the deep interest he took in the religious welfare and advancement of others. His deep searchings of heart always marked his honesty of purpose; the lowly views he took of himself were accompanied with the fullest views of Christ, and from the lowest depths of self-humiliation he rose, cleaving with earnest and glowing faith more closely than ever to a Divine Saviour.

4. He was most emphatically *a man of benevolence*, in the original signification of the term.

He loved his race, and good will to his fellow-men was a special trait in his character. No selfish or narrow views bounded his sympathies, and the love he had for others flowed out spontaneously and unceasingly upon all around him. Apt, indeed, was that beautiful expression of opinion from the lips of a clergyman of another Communion, "*The breath of his benevolence saluted the world!*"

And wherever he went, or in whatever work he might be engaged, even in the most trivial affairs, he would seek to do good to his fellow-man. There was an impressibility about him, a magnetic charm, which all could feel who came under his influence. Instances might be given where men, through his kind instrumentality, have been taken literally from the streets, drunken and debauched, and made, with the blessing of God, respectable and useful members of society. The infidel has been reclaimed and brought to a saving knowledge of Christ through his persistent kindness. And to many a wayfaring man, and to many a sorrowful stranger, hath he given a temporary home, beneath his own roof. Thus he went about "doing good," following his Master, consecrating every power that he had to the glory of God and the highest good of man, never dwelling upon his own merits, or deeming himself in God's eyes any thing but an "unprofitable servant," and pressing forward toward the mark for the prize of his high calling of God in Christ Jesus.

> "Thy labors of unwearied love
> By thee forgot, are crowned above!"

5. He had great *moral courage*.

Others have spoken of his gentleness and amiability, but these characteristics did not constitute his whole character. From this level there rose up here and there strong and salient points, which, illumined by the Sun of Righteousness, cast a ray of light along his path, which encouraged many a Christian pilgrim who walked by his side. He was resolute in doing what he conceived to be right, no matter who opposed him. When asked to sanction any plan, which appeared favorable to the casual observer, but in which he detected leadings to evil, he firmly refused. Often did friends endeavor to persuade him to this or that course of action, but he was as inflexible as the earth on which he stood, and, like Scott's hero, he seemed to say:

> "Sooner shall this firm rock
> Spring from its base than I!"

He declined lending the aid of his name or influence, at

one time, to the erection of an "Academy of Music" in the city where he dwelt, fearing that under this specious name it would only become, in time, a *theatre*. Some thought him "righteous overmuch," but he braved all censure, whether direct or indirect, heeding the voice of man as little as he would the idle wind. In his various travels he never ceased to speak out boldly for his Master. In the early part of his ministry he was once travelling in Virginia, in a public vehicle accommodating several persons, and, of course, filled with individuals of various descriptions. For a long time the company were much annoyed by the great profanity of one of the passengers. Dr. Cutler rose and changed his seat, coming opposite to the person in question, and addressed him: "Sir, this is a public conveyance, and I have as much right to pray as you have to swear, and now, if you choose to profane God's name any more, I shall commence to pray, and as long as you swear, I shall pray, and we will see who will come off best." It is hardly needful to add that the company were troubled no further.

Dr. Cutler's *home* was a blessing to others, and *especially to the ministers of Christ.*

His house was always open to his brethren, and the prophet's chamber prepared at all times for a guest. Ministers of Christ from all parts of the country there often met, and found a genial welcome from the rector of St. Ann's, and from his kind help-meet.

Who that was privileged to gather with others around his board did not feel the pervading influence of his piety, as well as the deep interest his host took in his welfare?

Who ever left his house, after even a short interview, without feeling refreshed and strengthened in spirit?

What a blessed privilege his various assistant ministers enjoyed in dwelling with him, in seeing his example, and hearing his exhortations and prayers, can hardly be realized by others.

The poor and the suffering were often found there, and the tried believer loved to go, if it was only for a few hours, to enjoy the friendly visit, and to treasure up the words of encouragement and counsel he never failed to receive.

The rectory of St. Ann's was, indeed, like an oasis in the wilderness of a cold and ungodly world, to ministers and laymen, to relatives and parishioners, to all friends, old or young, rich or poor.

DR. CUTLER, AS A PREACHER AND PASTOR.

Dr. Cutler was eminently a *Christian* theologian, well read in the *books* of the various schools, but deeply taught by the *Spirit*—a truly evangelical divine, a thorough Episcopalian, and an ardent lover of the *Liturgy* of the Church, in which God had placed him from his birth, and trained him for its ministry. His intimate friends well remember with what enthusiasm, he would point to certain portions of the Prayer-Book, such as the "Te Deum" and the "Litany," and declare them to be the most suitable vehicles of expression for prayer and praise that could anywhere be found, and able to satisfy the wants of the most serious-minded Christians in every age.

He was properly ranked as a moderate or Low Churchman, yet was never a partizan. The hand of fellowship was freely extended to churchmen of every shade of opinion, and he looked far more deeply into the practice, than into the theory of his brethren.

The language of uncharitableness or bitterness was *never* heard at his table; nor did he ever indulge in those sweeping denunciations, which so often mar the conversation of many of radical opinions, and which never fail to inflict injury on the body of Christ.

He regarded Tractarianism as but incipient Romanism, and could not sympathize with those extreme views of the Sacraments, which he regarded as inconsistent with the word of God, and the true interpretation of the standards of the Protestant Episcopal Church. He often spoke of the wise and moderate statement of doctrine in the Thirty-nine Articles, and especially in the Seventeenth Article.

When asked whether he desired to be called a Calvinist or an Arminian, he would say, "Neither;" and in a rigid sense, he could not be exclusively identified with either party. The sermon of Faber, of the Church of England, on the points in dispute, seemed exactly to coincide with his views.

Both systems could be reconciled with certain statements of Scripture, and he felt it to be the duty of the Christian minister, while always magnifying the grace of God, to proclaim the truth as he found it in all its fullness, in the word of God.

One "Thus saith the Lord" was worth more to him than a thousand philosophical reasons. Like a little child, he received the mysteries of the kingdom, and God taught him, and unfolded their meaning, in a manner unknown to fierce disputants for human systems. However men looked at the truth, through the prism of earth's refracted colors; whether one dwelt more constantly on such a passage as this, "Without me ye can do nothing;" or another, on, "Ye will not come unto me that ye might have life," he felt that they would yet read and understand in the pure light of heaven, the fullness of that more comprehensive passage: "God so loved the world that he gave his only-begotten Son, that whosoever believeth in him should not perish, but have everlasting life."

As a *preacher*, Dr. Cutler was solemn and earnest. He loved to proclaim the gospel, as a message from God to perishing souls, and therefore seldom introduced any thing extraneous to the subject matter in hand. He knew no fear in declaring the truth, but with all boldness, and yet with ardent *love*, held up Jesus Christ as the only Saviour for guilty man.

In handling the doctrines of Scripture, he was more explicit than many, and excelled most men in originality of thought, and in striking utterance. He was always clear, simple, and discriminating in statement, and direct in appeal; and his discourses were generally of a searching and arousing nature; no one felt like playing the critic—they were too personal and solemn for this. In an age so full of ambitious sermonizing, when so much is put forth which savors of every thing but Christ, and when so many hide the Cross out of sight by the mists of philosophy, "falsely so-called," he was content to set forth "the Lord Jesus, and him crucified;" an uncompromising proclaimer of the pure gospel, always at his watch-tower on the walls of Zion; always forgetting himself, standing behind his message, intent on the one great object of preaching Christ; never thinking of "enticing words of man's wisdom;" never losing his direct aim in discursive or irrelevant currents of thought; while there was shed over all, an unction as from the Holy One, which told his hearers that the breath of the Holy Spirit had indeed passed over his own soul. Thus, and thus only, was he instrumental in the conversion of so many sinners to Christ, and in building up his people in the grace of God.

The tribute paid to the memory of his ministry by his Diocesan, the Rt. Rev. H. Potter, D. D., at the Convention of the Diocese of New York, in the autumn of 1863, was well deserved: "Amiable, gentle, and devoted, it was the winning grace and unction of Dr. Cutler's character that gave power and efficacy to his ministry. He was a remarkable instance of what is sometimes observed among men, and especially among Christian ministers, where it is seen that a certain sweetness of character, a certain spirit pervading and fashioning the whole man, within and without, is more than talent, more than learning, more than mere enterprise and activity, as a means of moving men for good.

Such a character is in itself talent of a superior kind. It is the product of fine, well-tempered, natural qualities, touched and kindled into heavenly beauty by the Spirit of grace. Let us be thankful, that such a character has been given to shed its light, and to leave its image along our path, and let us be studious to learn the lesson which it so impressively teaches."

Dr. Cutler knew and felt that he had the treasure of the gospel in an earthen vessel, and he was willing himself to be nothing, if the Saviour would only honor the word which he preached, as his ambassador; and God honored him, and gave him many souls, as seals of his ministry.

In connection with this topic, we make no apology for laying before our readers two letters of Dr. Cutler on preaching. The sentiments contained therein (quaintly expressed though they are), should not be lost upon the youthful ministers of Christ, and might well be written in letters of gold.

TO THE REV. F. M. MCALLISTER, SAN FRANCISCO.

"ST. ANN'S RECTORY, BROOKLYN, *November* 11, 1861.

"MY DEAR MARION— . . . . Should I live to see next June, it will complete forty years of my labors in the *pulpit*. Let me see what I can say that may be of use to you. First: *There is nothing that can compensate for the loss of personal piety.*

"Secondly: Hundreds of sermons are lost by not preaching CHRIST.

"There is great danger of flying off from the four or five great doctrines of the gospel, into a miscellaneous mode of preaching. Justification by faith, regeneration by the Holy Ghost, the atonement of Christ, the doctrine of the Trinity, and of the resurrection, are *the* topics.

"I would build a tower around a young converted preacher of these great stones, and make him study and preach them. His fidelity and his ingenuity should find out a way of engrafting all *practical truths* on evangelical discourses. But what are they? What a Pagan *could not*, and what a Jew *would not preach*, is just what a Christian evangelist should *harp upon!* and the less fashionable such preaching becomes, the more he should *stick to it.* Such preaching will ever be like THE SYBIL'S LEAVES—the less there remains of it in a community, the higher the price or value!

"Thirdly: No man can *build up a church* who does not know the meaning of the Latin word '*fovet*.' The bird that does not brood, or sit on its nest, does not hatch its young. The fisherman that does not carry home his fish is a poor one.

"If our Saviour made you any thing, he made you '*a fisher of men*.' He set you to *catch*, not to tickle men; to lift them entirely out of the element in which you find them, and *to put them in your basket*; not to let them *slip back* into the water. *Verbum sap.* . . .

"Your affectionate uncle, B. C. CUTLER."

TO THE SAME.

. . . . "You have only *one thing* to mind, *i. e.*, to give your mind up to, *the preaching of the gospel*, in public and in private, by precept and by example. No matter what others do, this is your work. 'PREACH THE WORD' constantly, in season and out of season. Say, in effect, as one of old did: 'Strike, but hear!' Gospel preaching is what is wanted in California, in New York, everywhere! You mind this, and the Holy Ghost will mind you, and make you a man of God, and a man of mark, whether you desire it or not. Don't trouble your head about any thing else; St. Paul said: 'None of these things move me.' Other things will take care of themselves. But the gospel trumpet must be sounded continually. Let others hope to compete and conquer by brick and mortar, by architecture and ornament, by taste and talent! I assure you that if you are a fervent and faithful preacher of Christ's Gospel, in season and out of season, *no man* who does not preach the gospel shall overcome, or overthrow, or overshadow you.

"I don't care what men say: I *know* all they do say, and can fancy what they have not said; but if you distinguish yourself by a zealous preaching of the gospel, on every occasion opening before you, you may have the whole, the entire work of *picking up the birds*, in preference to those who love to cook and eat, rather than kill the game.

"The conversion of sinful men—let this be your motto. Jesus Christ expects every MINISTER to do this. He will raise up men to do the *other* work of the Church. Any other course will secularize and spoil your fine spirit—by fine, I mean delicate sense of spiritual duty. God bless you, my son, and give you grace to take an old man's counsel! Psalm 1.

"Your affectionate uncle, B. C. CUTLER."

On the same topic he once addressed the following letter to a very dear friend, then at Winchester, Va.:

TO THE REV. J. F. S——.

"MY DEAR JOSEPH— . . . . I was glad to hear of your marriage, and of your pleasant settlement in Winchester. Now, dear friend, only preach Christ, and all will be well; think of HIM, talk of HIM; don't say the providence of God, and the wisdom of the Creator, and the goodness of the Deity. The Jews talked so, at least the Greeks did. Talk you about Christ, by whom all things were made, who is made of God, unto us wisdom. Just put the word *Christ* where you have been accustomed to put the word God, and describe the beauties of the spiritual creation in your sermons. Speak of the flowers of joy in Christ, the buds of hope, the golden beams of Jesus, the sun of righteousness. Preach about the omnipotence of the grace of Christ, of his care and concern, and the omniscience of his mind.

"Just sit down and say, as you review a sermon, 'What is there here which a Jew would not preach, and a Pagan could not?' Don't be following out the relations of cause and effect, dissecting the fitness of virtue, but run over the relations of the saint to the Saviour, and of the sinner to his Judge—Christ Jesus.

"Now, mark my words; those sermons which you now write which happen to be all about Christ—if they are composed with care, not to say with prayer—will be the sermons that you will, by and by, preach over and over to strange audiences;

"While your beautiful, your eloquent, your well-written, your scholastic discourses—those which get you credit with the BLIND—will be forgotten in the pile.

"Know nothing, dear J——, but Christ, and him crucified. Pray much to him in the desk—right to HIM—what is the great direction? 'Come *unto me!*' Go to him, then, dear brother, go to him! Say, in the beginning of your next sermon, I am preaching as a Christian, to Christians, of the Christian's God and Saviour! Believers were not called Christians for no purpose, but that they should *be* Christians. Take the text, 'Salvation will God appoint for walls and bulwarks,' and show that a Christian is enclosed and defended by Christ.

"Christ was once at a marriage—I hope he was at yours, but if not, pray that he may ever be with the married pair. Let him provide the *wine;* be sure if he is the provider, it will be *old* wine—as old as the days of Abraham; yea, even of Adam and the great promise. *Vale, Josephus secundus ubicunque, hic primus!*

"Yours, B. C. C."

With such views, one can readily see that Dr. Cutler's preaching was of that kind which, under God, brings sinners to the Saviour, and builds up believers strong in Christ Jesus. His last sermon (preached July 13, 1862) was from the text, "They shall cry unto the Lord because of the oppressors, and he shall send them a Saviour, and a great one, and he shall deliver them." Isaiah xix. 20.

As a *pastor*, Dr. Cutler was unsurpassed, and there are few men whose labors have been more highly owned and blessed of God.

He was wise and judicious and free from *self-seeking* to a remarkable extent, striving to say a word for the Master whom he served, wherever he went.

He was always a welcome visitant to the homes of the rich and of the poor, and the savor of his devoted spirit rested on every company in which he mingled. His ministry in St. Ann's was a blessed one, and the means, under God, of saving hundreds of souls. His record is on high.

Touching were the testimonies given after his decease. A parishioner in Europe wrote: "I cannot speak of him as I would. The event was unexpected, and the news fell upon us here with crushing weight. We are all mourners, for he was our spiritual father, and dearly loved pastor, and affectionate friend. . . . . He led us to Jesus one by one; he did more than all others to keep our feet in the narrow way. I owe to him more love and gratitude than to all other men; for he lifted up my heart, as I humbly trust, to the Saviour, to be more wholly his, to work for him, to consecrate my days to his service."

How appropriate and complete is the sketch of his ministry in the department of pastoral labor, given by the Rev. Dr. Tyng:

"As we survey this ministry in its long course of usefulness, now completed, we cannot withhold our testimony of its unusual excellence and beauty. With what simple faith in the truth and power of Jesus, with what delight in the conversion of souls to Christ, with what readiness to welcome all to this great Saviour of the lost, with what peculiar adaptation to cheer and comfort those who believe, has he moved and dwelt among the people to whom he was there sent. In his pastoral relations he was perfectly happy. The people always found him a loving, trusting pastor, and they esteemed him very highly in love for his works' sake. They who sought his counsel, in the eagerness of an awakened heart to find a Saviour, will never forget his generous smile, his tender voice, his simple teaching, his earnest practical prayers. To bring them to Christ was manifestly his single object, and to present Jesus clearly to them his earnest effort. They can look back with the most grateful acknowledgment in their testimony, 'We may have ten thousand instructors, but we cannot have many fathers.'

"As a father, he had no greater joy than to see his children walking in the truth. The sick, the sorrowing, can never forget his pleasant, gracious visits—the peculiar adaptation which the Holy Spirit had given him to cheer and comfort those who believe. The social elements of his character were remarkably developed and sanctified, and with a special tenderness toward the suffering.

"Like John, his head reposed in the bosom of his Lord, and, like John, he became changed into the same image, the messenger and the pattern of the Saviour's love to all who mourned."*

A beautiful tribute was also paid to Dr. Cutler's memory, (in which happy allusion is made to his pastoral intercourse) at the regular Wednesday evening lecture at St. Ann's, on the evening following his decease, by his endeared friend

* See "The Son of Consolation," p. 60.

and neighbor, the Rev. E. H. Canfield, D. D., the present rector of Christ Church, Brooklyn:

"Since we last met in these hallowed courts," said the preacher on this occasion, "there has been transferred from the scene of his earthly labors to his heavenly rest, one who, in a remarkable degree, was a follower and imitator of Christ. He was a burning and a shining light, who for nearly thirty years, in this city, has lived an almost unearthly life, going about doing good, comforting the weak, supporting the feeble-minded, relieving the distressed, and, both in his life and doctrine, witnessing, to small and great, for God and his truth. Such a praying Christian, such a living epistle of Christ, such spirituality of mind, such absolute and unreserved consecration to God, a man whose religion was so much his *life*, pervading all his feelings, and all his intercourse with his fellows, we very seldom find in this fallen world. . . . . . More than any other man whom I have ever known, his walk was like that of Enoch, his anointing like that of Aaron. . . . . . I do not remember that I ever met him in the street, in his own house, at my own residence, or in the committee-room, when he did not say something which plainly indicated that his conversation was in heaven. . . . . . He excelled as a pastor. Very few men have ever filled the sacred office who were more affectionate, tender, and sympathizing in this relation. His excellencies in this respect were rather natural gifts than attainments, and very few churches have been blessed with a pastor so faithful and devoted."

One of the public Journals said truly of him: "His was a thoroughly religious life; the ideal of a good pastor; holy, harmless, separate from sinners, as nearly like his Master as poor, fallen human nature often reaches; blending active usefulness with such unfeigned humility, gentleness, and Christian courtesy, that his example was a constant sermon, his presence a perpetual benediction."

In the Sunday-schools, Dr. Cutler was in his element, and great was the care he took in training up the young for the service of God. Every Sunday he was found watching over the interests of the lambs of the fold with unwearied vigilance, ever impressed with a sense of the great responsibility committed to his charge; and thus did he seek to obey the Divine injunction, and to look for the promised blessing, "Train up a child in the way he should go, and when he is old he will not depart from it."

Interesting incidents are scattered along his whole history in connection with his Sunday-schools, which we have not space to insert here. At each anniversary, when he could meet the assembled children of his flock, he addressed them with unusual fervor and delight. Not long before his death, in one of his letters from Philadelphia, he wrote home: "I think much and often of my own Sunday-school, and pray God that it may flourish, and be the savor of life unto life to multitudes of souls."

The influence of the Sunday-schools upon the spiritual growth of St. Ann's Church was marked and widely extended; with such coadjutors in the good work as Messrs. Peet, Congdon, Smith, and Bancroft, in earlier days, and the persevering, fruitful labors of Messrs. Morgan and Matthews, in later days, the growth and prosperity of the Sunday-schools of St. Ann's Church has been but seldom equalled; and now we are glad to state, that prosperity continues under the direction of the present faithful rector, aided as he is with a band of teachers and superintendents, all laboring with one heart and one mind. St. Ann's Church, with its noble Sunday-schools and widely-extended parochial agencies, is Dr. Cutler's monument now—"*si monumentum suum requiris, circumspice;*" in the city where he dwelt, he has left traces of his life and labors which will not soon be effaced.

His volume of sermons (published in 1857) received high

commendations from every quarter. A few smaller works of his have been printed from time to time. Fugitive pieces also often appeared from his pen, some of which have been printed in the form of pamphlets or tracts; but he had neither the health nor the time to devote himself to any great special work, other than to his sermons.

According to his own testimony, he had by nature a lively mind, prone to observation and reflection, and mere abstractions never had much power over him; as his feelings were enlisted, so his mind moved, feebly or strongly. Imagination and memory were more strongly developed with him than reason, while a controlling good-sense and a clear, practical judgment preserved the equipoise of his character.

He discriminated well in the selection of his reading, and digested well the works he perused. The old standard divines he never ceased to read, while he also kept his mind informed on the general literature of the day. The English Reviews—the "Edinburgh," the "North British," and the "London Christian Observer"—were his favorites. How penetrating and how frank he was, in writing these lines in his earlier days to his wife: "I have read five volumes of Gibbon (I would not advise you to read his third or fourth volumes); he has done me more harm than Newton and Scott can do me good, for a month of reading, although I see him all the time with his satanic sneer, and his skeptical smile. He dares not openly deny, and yet he darkly insinuates; he is too polished to stab you, and prefers the more genteel method of poison—poison in a golden cup, sweetened with nectar."

Over and above all other books, Dr. Cutler loved the Bible. On the fly-leaf of his pocket Bible (which he carried with him in all his journeys) was written this sentiment: "What the huntsman said of his *rifle*, that say I of my *Bible*: 'Wherever I go, my Bible goes; I never leave it behind; it is like a part of myself. There is no one who will take such care of it as I; and there's nothing will take such care of me as my Bible!' "

Dr. Cutler was also a *deep student of the word of God;* he was thus enabled to bring forth out of the treasure-house "things new and old," as a "scribe well instructed unto the kingdom of heaven." But while doing this, he did not fail to gather information on collateral topics, either of a literary or historical nature, from any source, and thus acquired a vast fund of information.

Possessing naturally an acute and versatile mind, he was enabled to turn all the knowledge he acquired to practical account for the good of others, and this, combined with his catholic spirit, made him so extensively useful in every department of labor to which he devoted himself.

He had an eminently *catholic spirit.* He found a brother and co-worker in every man who would labor with him to build up the Redeemer's kingdom. Here his character shined with peculiar beauty. He loved all who loved the Lord Jesus Christ. Much as he prized the Church of his birth, he never confined his sympathies within its borders.

He was a whole-hearted supporter of every institution of Christian benevolence, and cordially joined with his brethren of all denominations in the blessed work of giving the Word of Life to the destitute. No one could have heard the loving tribute in which Christians of other names united with those in our communion to do him honor, without feeling that Christian fellowship with *all* the children of God is indeed much to be desired.

He was a member of the American Church Missionary Society, the Evangelical Knowledge Society, the American Bible Society, the American Tract Society, the American Sunday-school Union, the American Educational Society, the American Seamen's Friend Society, the Colonization Society, the Board of Missions of the Protestant Episcopal Church, the American Board of Commissioners for Foreign

Missions, the Brooklyn Bible and City Tract Societies, etc., etc.

At his decease, a minute was put on the records of these Societies, expressive of their great sense of his loss.

The action of various public institutions in the Episcopal Church, at this time, expressed in their resolutions, and already printed in "The Son of Consolation," fully show in what high esteem he was held, and render further comment almost needless.

That of the Evangelical Knowledge Society was most complete and appreciative.

It is to this minute that a highly distinguished presbyter of our church (a former rector of Christ Church, Brooklyn) refers, in a note to us, dated

"PHILADELPHIA, *January* 1, 1864.

"REV. AND DEAR SIR— . . . . I regret to say that I have no letters from Dr. Cutler to furnish for the contemplated memoir of that good man. And if I were to write you what I think of him, I should but be saying over again what has been so well said already in various quarters. The last Annual Report of the Evangelical Knowledge Society contains a notice of Dr. Cutler, which, so far as a mere estimate or sketch of character is concerned, is very much what I should say. . . . . I spent eleven years by his side in Brooklyn, and those years were enough to fill me with love and admiration, such as every one felt for Dr. Cutler who knew him even less familiarly than I did. . . . . Dear Dr. Cutler! how few such Christians have we to lose! The Lord fill the Church with an ever-increasing number of such!

"Very truly yours, JOHN S. STONE."

The minute and resolution of the "Brooklyn City Mission and Tract Society" (of which he was the President) was also highly expressive, and equally so, was that of the "American Tract Society." No one in the Episcopal Church (save good Dr. Milnor, of sainted memory) has done more for this last-named institution.

The following letter from the Corresponding Secretary

of the Society bespeaks the preciousness of his memory in these relations:

"NEW YORK, *June* 13, 1864.

. . . . . "My intimacy with the Rev. Benjamin C. Cutler, D. D., was chiefly during the last ten years of his life, while he was a beloved member of the Publishing Committee of the American Tract Society. . . . . The fact of that Committee representing as many evangelical Christian denominations as there are members, and all the members being active pastors of prominent churches, and all their meetings being in delightful fraternal harmony, in the one work of making known 'Christ crucified' to a perishing world, seemed to give that Committee an unequalled charm, that stirred the warm and glowing heart of Dr. Cutler to its lowest depths. He often spoke of the happiness of meeting his dear brethren of the ministry, in the circle where their hearts and aims were so emphatically one, in the great object for which he lived.

"I have always thought that I perceived in Dr. Cutler, as in Dr. Milnor (his predecessor on that Committee), a heart-penetrating glow of love to *distinctive evangelical truth*, which characterizes those who in earlier life came near the shipwreck of the soul, by cherishing some form of religion or morality, in which they falsely trusted, till God opened their eyes to see the *fullness of Christ* as the sinner's only ground of hope.

"Plucked by the grace and spirit of God from the confines of destructive error, salvation by Christ became unspeakably dear to their hearts. Never did I see either of them so engrossed with pressing engagements, that the vital interests of the soul and of the kingdom of Christ were not first in the objects of their affections, and I believe Eternity will reveal this more clearly than it was ever seen in this present life. In every publication brought under review, in every plan of usefulness, in every topic of discussion, their hearts were true to this great theme as the needle to the pole!—a touchstone revealing the real, though perhaps not readily perceived, character and influence of what claimed their judgment and action.

"The whole-souled, unreserved frankness of Dr. Cutler, the cheerful, buoyant overflowing of his generous good-will, in intercourse with those beloved, was peculiar, and bound to him the hearts of multitudes.

"There was withal, an originality and a penetrating sagacity in his suggestions, which were often seen to be worthy of practical regard, and few at the close of such an interview could fail to feel the benefit.

"Frequently, in the intimacy of Christian friendship, topics of Christian experience, fidelity in duty to the souls of men, prayerfulness, and all that pertains to godly living and growth in grace, came up as the natural outgushing of his heart. Daily and almost hourly he was thus sowing 'precious seed,' kindling new desires to be faithful in all the relations of life, and awakening thankfulness to God, who had dealt with him so bountifully in spiritual gifts.

"There was beautiful emphasis in his reply (when near death) to an inquiry, whether he would leave any special message: '*I have said my say; I have no wish to change it.*' He *had* said it every day of his life, from the time of his conversion; he had said it on the right occasions, and in the right way; it was clear and emphatic, and he could not expect to better it as nature was dissolving!—as if he had said: 'Remember the words that I spake unto you, while I was yet present with you.' Dear, precious servant of Christ! Heaven has new attractions since thy departure! May we, like thee, be faithful unto death, and receive the gracious crown of eternal life!

WM. A. HALLOCK, *Secretary*."

How many there are who, in full accord with the above, can add their testimony, and, with thankfulness, remember his broad and catholic spirit, which, with unbroken and uninterrupted charity, was displayed in prayers, in labors, and fraternal recognition of the whole body of Christian believers.

In an interesting sermon, preached at St. Ann's soon after Dr. Cutler's decease, the Rev. L. H. Mills, the late assistant minister and now the devoted rector of St. Ann's, thus made allusion to him. We give the concluding paragraphs:

"Our whole Protestant Episcopal communion is bereaved. One who himself, whose very name, was a rallying-point around which the most earnest and devoted of her faithful ministry could gather, is no more! One foremost in the ranks of her most valiant warriors, one of the most devout in evangelical zeal, and one most sacredly loyal to her holy standards and her venerable offices, is gone! But, dear brethren, say 'Thy will, O God, be done!'

"Still wider and further has this affliction been felt.

The Church catholic has felt and testified her weighty grief. The Church universal, the blessed company of all faithful people, she has seen her standard-bearer fall! With what solemn grief, let the past and present testify; when the sorrow of Christians is so widely shared throughout a revering population, and a city mourns in union with a church bereaved. Great, great has been the loss to all who love our Lord, and who long for the advancement of his great kingdom. Yet, in view of all this, say 'Thy will, O God, be done!'

"Resignation is the solemn lesson for our stricken souls at this season. Be willing, therefore, that God's will may be done on earth as it is in heaven! As it is in heaven! There are no murmurs there. There are no doubts, no clouds, nor mists in that pure life; no shadows there cloud the face of our reconciled Father; all the innumerable, ever-varied forms of the bright multitudes that throng the golden streets of the New Jerusalem, bow in most adoring acquiescence to his holy will. . . . . . There are no revolts of the unsubdued will in heaven. There is no answering back of the insubordinated will there. 'Thy will be done!' This is the unceasing burden of an unending song, which rises in sweetest harmony from the variously graded ranks of those who throng the ethereal courts above.

"Let 'Thy will be done,' therefore, arise from all our hearts to-day. The deepest and holiest delight is ever enkindled, from the most humble resignation and submission. . . . . .

"But oh! this wonderful event! this sad affliction! to us so dark and so inscrutable!

"As the eye of Heavenly Wisdom looks down upon it, how blissfully is it transformed! We mourn for ourselves; but can we mourn for him that is gone? We did, in the infirmity of our inconsistent nature, even mourn and pray and intercede for him, as though in dying he were bereaved and deprived of his highest life. But oh! in the blest reality! as the dead in Christ behold it, as the angels behold, as the all-searching eye of God beholds it, what different conclusions are reached concerning his happiness, and the degree and character of his change.

"'How great the contrast,
In the way that earth and heaven the closing scene of death
Regard. On *earth*, a spectacle of tears!
Bedewed each cheek and swollen every eye;
In speechless agony each knee is bent
Round the saint's couch, importunate for life,
While still, life's pulses beat. In *heaven*, a prayer
Is uttered also for the dying one,
By mightier than mortal intercessor;
Emmanuel pleads; but his is not the prayer
For an extension of the transient breath.
He pleads for life *immortal as his own;*
While from below ascend the burdened sighs
Of weeping relatives, 't is thus he prays:
"Father, *I will!* thy dying sufferer I,
I have redeemed, be with me where I am,
To share the glory thou hast given me."
The prayer is heard! Omnipotence responds:
"Son, thou art ever with me, all I have
Is thine." To execute the embassy,
Eager, a glorious retinue attend.
"Go, angels, speed ye to the dying pillow
And waft the spirit into Abraham's bosom!" '*

"Such were the true scenes over which we now mourn. Oh, let us, dear fellow-Christians! with humble, chastened happiness, say, in the holy words of Christ's own prayer, 'Our Father, Thy will be done in earth as it is in heaven!'"

On the Sunday following Dr. Cutler's death, the Rev. Dr. Bancroft, of Montreal, preached at St. Ann's, Brooklyn, on "The unchangeableness of a Divine Saviour." A better subject could not have been chosen, and the people, in full sympathy with the preacher, manifested much emotion while

* "Wells of Baca."

highly appropriate allusions were made to the deceased. The Rev. Messrs. Mills, Sever and Gray also assisted in the services on the occasion.

It was an affecting circumstance, that on the very day of the funeral, a dear friend and parishioner was writing to him from Florence, Italy, in this strain :

. . . . . "I cannot believe that we are not to meet again here. I feel that the spring will bring relief to you, and I shall wait with deep anxiety of heart to learn of your condition ; but, my dear beloved pastor, if it is God's will that you should enter into rest before we arrive home, it will be to you a deliverance from much bodily suffering, from a weary mind and an anxious heart. It will be to you the beginning of that rest 'that remaineth for the people of God,' that joy that is to have no end, the meeting of those who have been saved, through Christ, by your faithfulness. We (if we are the children of Jesus) are the fruits of your kind and earnest labors, and we love you as our spiritual father and pleasant friend. You are very dear to our hearts, and I hope we may have the privilege of showing you love and affection for many years.

"Remember now, for your comfort, how long you have spoken for Jesus, the years of patient labor and devotion to his cause, and how many have accepted him through your teaching. May the Saviour make all your bed in your sickness ! . . . . .

"Ever affectionately yours, G. D. M——."

The above is only one among the many testimonies, to the unseen but blessed influences of his labors for Christ, which were brought to light after his decease.

Another came over the Atlantic from a gentleman in the south of England, who had been in Brooklyn, under Dr. Cutler's roof, but was now just on the eve of taking orders in the Church of England :

"Of our dear departed friend I can bear my testimony that when I was a stranger he took me in ; I was an hungered, and he gave me meat ; I was thirsty, and he gave me drink ; and will not the King say that, inasmuch as he did it unto me, who am the very least of his brethren, he did it unto him. Nor will his works end here, for will not every soul, who, through my ministry, is brought to the knowledge of the truth as it is in Jesus, only add an additional lustre to that glorious crown, which he, who was God's chief instrument in my own conversion, now wears?

"'Marvelous are thy works, Lord God Almighty; just and true are thy ways, thou King of saints!'

"He was called away as a shock of corn ripe for the harvest, from out of his country's trials and griefs, to that better city which hath foundations, whose maker and builder is God. . . . . .

"Ever, dear Mrs. C——, your faithful friend,

"J—— D——."

His words do indeed "follow him" yet, and he still lives among us, not in our hearts only, but in the undying influence of his holy life. Such is the power and "the *beauty of holiness*;" the light which shines through a good man's life outshines the sun in its meridian splendor.

In early youth he gave himself to the Lord and to the work of the ministry, and he made full *proof* of his ministry.

After twenty years' experience, in conversation with a friend, he used this language:

"I have enjoyed an uninterrupted peace of soul; in giving myself to God, I made a full surrender, keeping back nothing, and though it was a poor gift, it was all I had. I cannot speak of raptures and transports; I have no experience to tell, nor can I boldly boast assurance; but I know that my thoughts and affections have all been in one way, and that I do love the Lord and his people, the Saviour and his service." His friend remarked, "You are a happy man." He replied, "I *am* a happy man. I bless and praise the Lord for what he has permitted me to do. I have been twenty years in the ministry, and if he should call me to-day, or the next time I should enter the pulpit, this is done; and, although it has been poorly and imperfectly done, it has been done to the best of my ability, and in his service, and I will praise and thank him for the high privilege!"

Twenty years more of labor for his Master, and his work was done.

The lessons which his life impressively teaches are, that though the path of the child of God may be shrouded in darkness, yet He who sees the end from the beginning will cause a light to shine, and in that light, we may walk safely. Again, that we are to *go forward in duty*, leaving all results to God. We are to toil on a little while, and then go home; we are to gather encouragement from the faith and patience of those who have gone before; to take up and carry forward the work of the Lord, which dropped from their dying hands, until we, too, are summoned to rest from our labors and (through the sacrifice of Jesus) receive our reward.

The earthly remains of this dear servant of God now rest near Ocean Hill, in Greenwood Cemetery, Brooklyn, N. Y., over which the people of St. Ann's have erected a chaste and elegant monument of pure white Italian marble, bearing the following inscriptions:

On the front—

Sacred to the Memory

OF THE

REV. BENJAMIN CLARKE CUTLER, D. D.,

FOR THIRTY YEARS RECTOR OF ST. ANN'S CHURCH, BROOKLYN, N. Y.,

WHO DEPARTED THIS LIFE

FEBRUARY 10TH, 1863, AGED 65 YEARS.

On the right side—

This Monument

WAS ERECTED BY HIS PARISHIONERS,

IN

GRATEFUL REMEMBRANCE OF HIS UNTIRING DEVOTION TO THEIR WELFARE;

OF HIS PREACHING, DISTINGUISHED BY THE SIMPLICITY THAT IS

IN CHRIST, AND OF THE EXAMPLE HE HAS LEFT THEM

IN HIS CONSISTENT AND HOLY LIFE.

On the left side—

Acts xx. 25–27.

"AND NOW, BEHOLD, I KNOW THAT YE ALL, AMONG WHOM I HAVE GONE PREACHING THE KINGDOM OF GOD, SHALL SEE MY FACE NO MORE; WHEREFORE I TAKE YOU TO RECORD THIS DAY, THAT I AM PURE FROM THE BLOOD OF ALL MEN; FOR I HAVE NOT SHUNNED TO DECLARE UNTO YOU ALL THE COUNSEL OF GOD."

In St. Ann's Church, Brooklyn, N. Y., upon the chancel wall, there is placed a mural tablet (of rich, yet simple design), composed of the purest white marble, bearing this inscription:

REV. BENJAMIN CLARKE CUTLER, D. D.

Born in Roxbury, Mass., Feb. 6th, 1798.

Died in Brooklyn, N. Y., Feb. 10th, 1863.

RECTOR OF ST. ANN'S CHURCH THIRTY YEARS.

This Tablet has been erected by the Parishioners, in token of their love and of his devoted and successful labors.

"Hold fast the form of sound words, which thou hast heard of me, in faith and love which is in Christ Jesus."—2 Timothy, 1st ch. 13th v.

At St. Ann's Church, he was instrumental, under God, in building up a spiritual temple of living stones, upon which the Divine Architect has now placed the topmost stone, amid the shoutings of the angelic host, "Grace, grace unto it!"

May the mantle of his piety fall upon every successive pastor, and the power of the Holy Ghost be abundantly manifested in the future, as in the past, then shall not the glory depart, nor the doom of the Laodicean Church ever be written upon her walls.

The seals of Dr. Cutler's ministry from out of this church shall yet be gathered before the Lord, with those from other parts of the vineyard where he has labored, while he will be enabled (through the grace of God) triumphantly to exclaim, "Here, Lord, am I, and the children which thou hast given me!"

Through a long and honored course on earth, he exhibited what might be accomplished, (even amid physical weakness and pain) by entire consecration to the Lord's service. He endured hardness as a good soldier of Jesus Christ, endued with strength from on high, and richly refreshed by the consolations of the Holy Spirit; and his sun has gone down, at last, in perfect serenity and peace, the sure harbinger of a bright rising in that eternal kingdom where they that be wise "SHALL SHINE AS THE BRIGHTNESS OF THE FIRMAMENT; AND THEY THAT HAVE TURNED MANY TO RIGHTEOUSNESS, AS THE STARS FOR EVER AND EVER."

LAUS DEO!

APPENDIX.

A.

Page 103.

A Farewell Letter

TO THE PARISH OF CHRIST CHURCH, QUINCY, MASS., BY THE REV. B. C. CUTLER, ON HIS RESIGNATION OF SAID PARISH.

TO THE CONGREGATION OF CHRIST CHURCH, QUINCY:

MY DEAR FRIENDS—You have been informed that I have resigned the rectorship of this church, on account of my present infirm state of health. But if I judge rightly, you will hardly be willing that the connection which has subsisted between us should be broken, without bidding you *farewell.* I should be happy, if I could do this, by word of mouth; but it is denied me, and I must therefore put the few words I have to say upon paper.

I hoped to have stood up before you, once, at least, the last summer, and to have preached to you "the gospel of the blessed God," but my feelings were too strong, and my nerves too weak, for such an effort; and if I had attempted it, I should probably have said little for your edification.

I can with difficulty realize that I am to address you, as a pastor, for the last time. Alas! how fleeting the scenes of this life. Our intercourse seems like some solemn dream.

So it seems to *us*, but not so does it appear to God. He, doubtless, looks upon it as a reality; to him, its scenes are all separate and distinct. Every year of that intercourse, with all its instruction, and exhortation, stands charged against you, and against me, as either faithfully or unfaithfully delivered and received.

Of my imperfections in preaching, in visiting, and in every thing relating to you, I am aware; and I have not waited until this time, to make my confessions to God. But, perhaps, I ought to say, that, sensible as I am of my unworthiness in labors, I am not sensible of any intentions toward you but those of faithfulness and truth. I have endeavored to preach, as I thought you could bear it, the truth of God, as revealed in the Scriptures; and few, if any of you, I presume, could charge me in a future state with never having warned you of your danger. Who of you, my friends, can meet your pastor in the world of spirits and say: Wretched minister! you saw me living in sin, and going down to destruction, and never made known to me that Holy God, whom I was provoking? Wretched minister of Christ! you saw me denying the Son of God, and you never held him up in bleeding compassion, as able and willing to save my soul! Wretched man! you were placed over me, to set an example of deadness to the world, and you joined with me, in all its pleasures and pursuits! It may be, and I tremble while I think of it; it may be, if I had been more faithful in warning you, and more exemplary in living, some of you, who have long been halting between two opinions, would have decided in favor of God and your own salvation. God in mercy forgive me, for Christ's sake. But, my dear friends, consider whether my warnings, imperfect as they were, may not make you, without excuse; consider whether my poor ministry among you, may not be appealed to, in future, as increasing your condemnation.

What reply must I make, should such questions as these be

put to me?—Did you plainly warn that man to flee from the wrath to come? Did you repeatedly set before him the folly and danger of delay? Did you humbly and kindly advise him to come out of the world? Did you, in moments when his heart was softened by sickness, or affliction, drop words of invitation from me? O Lord God! he has had all this, thou knowest. I addressed him from the pulpit; and in his hours of sickness, I urged him by his mercies, to go to Christ —but I could not prevail. I have little doubt that both the pastor and the people, in looking by the light of Eternity upon this relation about expiring, will see cause of sorrow. I have sorrowed already. I have confessed my unworthiness, and unfaithfulness; I have asked forgiveness of God for the sake of Jesus Christ. I have blessed God again and again, that he did not cut me off, when I was so sick among you, but gave me time to examine my past life and ask forgiveness. Let me advise you to consider, seriously, whether you have been faithful on your part in hearing; to consider what account God may require of you, for the past instruction and persuasion which you have had; and also, for the sermons, the examples and the exertions of your present minister. May he be more successful than I have been. I shall rejoice in all his exertions; and though he may reap what another sowed, I pray that the time is at hand, when "he that soweth and he that reapeth" shall "rejoice together." Strengthen his hands, I pray you, my brethren, by affording him every assistance in your power, in the great work in which he is engaged—of promoting piety, good morals, and peace among men. Encourage his heart, by attending regularly on public worship and the preaching of the Word; and in your *families*, discover to him, as you have to me, a readiness to hear a word of exhortation, and to unite in prayer to God for blessings on your household. Now, I pray God that you and I, who have so often stood in the temple of God on earth, may stand together at God's right hand in his courts above. I commend you to God the Father, the Son. and the Holy Ghost, now and evermore. Amen.

To the Communicants of Christ Church:

Dearly Beloved in the Lord—Our separation will, I hope, be short; we are, I trust, and ever shall be, joined in spirit.

"Blest be the tie that binds
Our hearts in Christian love"

I look upon you as *relatives*, as members of the same family, who after a few more trials, neither distance of place nor death will separate. I have gathered most of you into the Church of the First-born, of which, although unworthy, I hope, I am myself a member. At the new birth of many of you, I have experienced the emotions of a father's heart, when he hears that unto him a child is born. Can I ever forget you? Can I ever give the place you hold in my heart to others? No; I have shed too many tears; I have experienced too many spiritual joys; I have taken too much sweet counsel with you, my beloved, *immortal* relatives, ever to forget you; above all, I am too much indebted to you for long-continued, ardent, effectual prayers, to which I attribute many of my blessings, ever to forget you. May I ask you to continue your prayers for me, and in return be assured of mine. I have made this allusion to my feelings, from a fear that you might suppose them to be easily changed. I believe they are sacred and lasting; yes, everlasting. I trust they are an earnest of our future inheritance, and whether I or you depart this life first, I anticipate with you a joyful meeting, a meeting of joy unspeakable and full of glory; and it may help to reconcile us to the sharpness of death, to think, when we shut our eyes upon the few friends weeping around us, that we shall open them the next moment upon a multitude of friends rejoicing with us, who, witnessing our last struggles, had been preparing cordials for our lips, the moment we had finished our cup of bitterness.

First. My beloved friends, be *earnest* in religion; make the salvation of your immortal souls, the great business of life. Read the Bible, pray to God, attend upon public worship, hear the preacher, and examine your hearts, as if every thing depended on these exercises. A wise man will leave no stone unturned to promote a great object. Think no means of grace too *small*, or too poor, or of too little importance for you to attend to it. I am convinced if we want to be safe and happy in religion, we must make it the all-absorbing object.

Second. Let us be *humble* in religion. If you and I are Christians, we are young Christians, weak Christians, and inexperienced Christians. Oh! how much have we yet to learn of Christ, of the work of his promised Spirit on the heart, of the great plan of redemption? How much have we to learn of "the deceits of the world, the flesh and the Devil!" I am afraid that my ministry, as it respects Christ and his cross, was but a poor one. I seem as yet to have learnt only the alphabet of that great mystery!" Let us then gird up the loins of our mind, and begin with new vigor the Christian life, as persons who, having learned the alphabet, have the whole language before them. Let us begin, as at the bottom of our class of Christians, and with a holy emulation strive to excel in virtue, that is, in the knowledge and love of Christ. The Lord cause us more and more to know and to love his Son!

Third. Let us be *charitable* in religion; if we are humble, we shall of course be charitable. I do not mean charitable in such a sense, that we care not what a man believes; but, that we make allowances for men, both as to what they believe and what they do. Let us not set up ourselves as being something, when we ought to be in our own estimation as nothing. In lowliness of mind, let each esteem others better than themselves. Philippians ii. 3. If we have experienced religion, let us not be hasty in deciding that others have *not;* but rather consider whether they, with our advantages, might not have experienced religion much better than we have.

To be charitable, in another sense, I need not write unto you; for you have ever been ready to bestow your alms for the relief of the bodies and souls of your fellow-men. I trust you are convinced of the truth of that saying, "He that hath pity upon the poor, lendeth unto the Lord;" and look! what he layeth out, it shall be paid him again; and no man ever served God for naught.

Fourth. Be devoted to reading and meditating on the Bible; there you will see *charity* described; there you will sit at the feet of patterns of piety, in contemplating whose excellencies you will be made humble; there you will find Christ your all in all; and as you look steadily unto Jesus, you will be transformed from your present defaced image of God, to an humble, but glorious image of him. Go to the Bible to learn your doctrines; hear your preacher, but hold fast your Bible. Common advantages in education; common sense, with earnest prayer to God, will ensure a right knowledge of the Holy Scriptures, and upon that knowledge, will greatly depend your salvation. Daily reading the works of some spiritual author, or approved commentator on the Bible, will also be of great service to you.

Fifth. Lastly, be steadfast and immovable. You are members of a pure and gospel church. Be not carried away by diverse and strange doctrines! You know now what you believe, and what, if they live, your children will probably believe, after you. For more than one hundred years this church has stood, the repository of "the truth as it is in Jesus;" and you have reason to believe, if *you* continue steadfast, if you support this church by your attendance, your example and your prayers, one hundred years more will roll by, and Christ will still be held up to your descendants, as their divine and almighty Saviour. Let nothing draw you away from the communion of a Church, whose moderation in doctrine, whose fervor in devotion, and whose order in ecclesiastical discipline, has been the admiration of the wise and good of many ages.

I have now only to commend to you, the minister whom you have called to take charge of the church. Beloved, be to him, as you have been to me, kind, attentive, and teachable. Remember him and his family in your daily prayers to God; remember him, in your intercourse, as the ambassador of God; every honor you pay him, you pay to his Master in heaven. Remember him, in providing for your households, as he is bound in Scripture to provide for his.

And now, farewell, dearly beloved in the Lord! Let the right hand of God be our place of meeting! When the trials and wanderings of life are over, may I not fail of reaching that place myself, and may I find no one of you absent. Let vice, and sin, and folly die in the grave of our conversion; and let us all rise to newness of life, by the power of the Holy Ghost, through Jesus Christ our Lord.

Thanks be to God, for his unspeakable gift!

Your friend and servant,

BENJAMIN CLARKE CUTLER.

LEESBURG, VA., *February* 3, 1831.

B.

Page 107.

Sketch of a Confirmation

AT ST. PAUL'S, ALEXANDRIA, VA., IN THE YEAR 1831, IN A LETTER TO MRS. WILLIAM JACKSON, BY THE REV. B. C. CUTLER, AND DESIGNED FOR THE ARTIST'S PENCIL.

I WOULD have the picture taken, just at the time when the Bishop had finished laying his hands on Bro. Mann's old African Christian—an old man. The first collection of young and beautiful flowers had risen from their knees and removed back a little, without breaking the circle ; then five or six young African women, with clean white turbans, being invited, came from a side aisle and kneeled down a little to the right of the front of the chancel, as I stood within the rails—an old black woman placed herself at the extreme right. Then came through the crowd, on the left, an aged black man, athletic in his form, and kneeled down ; his coat was much worn, there were large holes upon his shoulders, but his shirt was clean ; his head was bald, and his expression was one of indifference to every visible object around him. I touched your husband and said, "Look there! Is that a proper subject for confirmation?" Mr. Mann at that moment drew near, and the Bishop then laid his hands upon the head of this aged African. I said to myself, It is Lazarus, come to lay his head upon Abraham's bosom. There was the father of the faithful, the venerable Bishop (Moore), who is himself an inspiring object to every beholder, receiving this poor disciple to the peaceful bosom of the visible body of Christ, and if not *carrying* him, there were almost angelic forms *clustered around his beggar-like body.* Just at that moment, a friend was bringing forward a young lady, who had been kept back by the crowd, or her own fears.

The chancel was well furnished, if not filled, with ministers, and one or two were in the reading-desk.

The house was crowded, principally with female worshippers, thickly interspersed with children who had come to see their weekly school-fellows consecrated to God.

In front of the chancel, were a boy and girl in black, the son and daughter of the deceased and lamented Dr. Wilmer. The spirit of the father seemed to have brought his son, like Hannibal of old, at this youthful age, up to the altar of God to vow eternal enmity to sin. Oh may he fill his father's place in the army of Christ!

A mother, too, I saw, who was standing behind her daughter, thus early giving her up to God, and assuring the church that its youthful member would find in her parent religious encouragement and support. I looked up and saw the mystic dove almost dropping from above the pulpit on the hallowed scene. The brilliant light of the house, and the interest of the worshippers added a material lustre, but the belief that these were blood-bought souls, and heaven-born spirits, far eclipsed the other light. Here, " Barbarian, Scythian, bond and free," (Col. iii. 11.) were one in Christ.

The scene, so impressive, so holy and beautiful, made me exclaim: "There is a propriety in such a service itself, even if it had not been of apostolic authority!"*

* See "Memoirs of Rev. Wm. Jackson," by Mrs. Jackson, p. 150.

C.

Page 227.

Letter

FROM THE SUNDAY-SCHOOL GIRLS OF THE CHURCH OF ST. STEPHEN'S, COLEMAN STREET, LONDON, TO THE SUNDAY-SCHOOLS OF ST. ANN'S, BROOKLYN, N. Y.

July 8, 1843.

DEAR BROTHERS AND SISTERS IN CHRIST JESUS—During the visit of your beloved pastor to this land, we have been highly favored with his presence at our church and school, and were much pleased with the account he gave us of the progress of Christian religion in your Sunday-schools.

We received by him many pleasing and instructive lessons from you, for which we return our sincere thanks, and trust that we shall ever remember and live according to them; for how great will be our condemnation, if we neglect those blessed things we are taught. We think we are greatly blest in having such a pastor as the Rev. Josiah Pratt, for promoting our eternal welfare, and also encouraging us to go on with zeal in the missionary cause. Think, my dear fellow scholars, what a privilege it is for us to be born in a Christian land where the gospel is freely preached to all, with Sabbath-schools to attend, and so many dear teachers to instruct us in the way of salvation, and warn us to flee from the wrath to come. To our Superintendents, who are the Misses Pratt, we owe many thanks, and trust we shall ever be grateful for their kindness and instruction, and with the blessing of God, profit by them, and bring forth fruit, like good seed in a fruitful soil, knowing that we are not our own, but bought with a price. Oh, may we give our hearts to God in our youth!

> "Youth is the time, would we be blest
> With God's peculiar smile;
> The time the most approved and best,
> To learn his sovereign will."

God has said, "I love them that love me, and they that seek me early shall find me." We have every opportunity of doing so; let us embrace it, and walk in love, as Christ also has loved us, and given himself for us, an offering and a sacrifice to God.

Pray earnestly for the Holy Spirit of God to strengthen you; for "by grace are ye saved, through faith, and that not in yourselves—it is the gift of God."

Be obedient to your teachers, for in so doing you will please God. Pray for all nations round about you, and may your prayers with the prayers of England, be answered to the good of many souls.

The grace of our Lord Jesus Christ, and the love of God, and the communion of the Holy Ghost, be with you all, until your life's end. Amen.

Signed in behalf of the whole school, containing ninety girls,

MARTHA MILLER, EMMA NICHOLS,
ELIZABETH MILLER, MARY ANN KNAPP,
SARAH MILLER, ESTHER HUDSON,
SARAH HAM.

D.

ORIGINAL LINES BY THE REV. B. C. CUTLER, D. D.

Gazing on the Ocean.

I ASKED the Sea, when musing o'er
Its silent depths and boundless shore,
If on its waves, I could not find
Some lasting comfort for my mind;

Or, if with all its hidden store
Of jewels, pearls, and golden ore,
I could not purchase from above,
That *peace* for which I vainly rove.

The Ocean heard my useless cry,
And lifted up its voice on high,
"Not on my waves can peace be found,
Nor through my caverns traversed round;

"I rise and fall at His command,
Who holds me in his powerful hand;
And never, wilt thou comfort feel,
Until His word is, '*Peace, be still!*'"

B. C. C.

E.

Many have inquired what was the precise nature of the disease which terminated Dr. Cutler's life, and we therefore subjoin the following, under the signature of his medical adviser:

"The *post mortem* examination of the late Rev. B. C. Cutler, D. D., developed an immense abscess in the right lung; the lung was found adhering to the pleura by ossification, extending downward to the diaphragm. This caused the terrible spasmodic cough, which so distressed him the last few weeks of his life.

F. W. Ostrander, M. D.

Brooklyn, N. Y., *September* 3, 1864.

F.

"I Know that My Redeemer Liveth."

A REMINISCENCE OF THE REV. DR. B. C. CUTLER,

BY AUGUSTA BROWNE GARRETT.

It is marvelous what a sanctifying haze is thrown around an object, by its association with the sainted dead. Our inner world is thronged with sweet memories, inseparably linked with those gone hence. The above named sacred song, I shall never hear without a vivid remembrance of the benign countenance of that pastor beloved, the late Dr. Cutler, Rector of St. Ann's Church, Brooklyn.

In my mind, there are many hallowed associations connected with this song of songs. The tenderest of them, is with that of a young artist brother, who passionately loved its soul-elevating strains, and one of whose last requests was, to hear it, as he lay awaiting the coming of the "Redeemer" himself, to lead him through the dark valley; but the latest association is with that faithful and revered minister of God, the Rev. B. C. Cutler, D. D., with whom it was a favorite.

Some time previous to his demise, I had occasion to call at his house, and after a short conversation on literary topics, he arose from his chair, remarking that he would like to hear some music, and, opening the pianoforte, placed upon the desk, the Oratorio of the Messiah, and requested me to play and sing this most seraphic of compositions, "I know that my Redeemer liveth." When it was finished, he commented at some length, on its rare sweetness and expression of holy assurance, and told me that a few days previous, he had stood in the old church burial-ground on Fulton Street, where were, in the course of removal, the remains of hundreds, many of them his former parishioners, and that while he witnessed the mouldering fragments of humanity thrown up, he thought how utterly miserable we should be, if bereft of the surety of a resurrection to life eternal, and he could but dwell on those cheering words of hope, "I KNOW THAT MY REDEEMER LIVETH!"*

* "New York Observer," June 23, 1864.

www.ingramcontent.com/pod-product-compliance
Lightning Source LLC
LaVergne TN
LVHW021123110826
845150LV00005B/933

* 9 7 8 1 4 2 5 5 5 1 0 0 1 *